FORGED IN WAR

FORGED IN WAR

A MILITARY HISTORY OF RUSSIA FROM ITS BEGINNINGS TO TODAY

IN WAR

MARK GALEOTTI

OSPREY PUBLISHING
Bloomsbury Publishing Plc
Kemp House, Chawley Park, Cumnor Hill, Oxford OX2 9PH, UK
29 Earlsfort Terrace, Dublin 2, Ireland
1385 Broadway, 5th Floor, New York, NY 10018, USA
E-mail: info@ospreypublishing.com
www.ospreypublishing.com

OSPREY is a trademark of Osprey Publishing Ltd

First published in Great Britain in 2024

A catalogue record for this book is available from the British Library.

ISBN: HB 9781472862518; PB 9781472862501; eBook 9781472862495; ePDF 9781472862549;
XML 9781472862532; Audio 9781472862525

24 25 26 27 28   10 9 8 7 6 5 4 3 2 1

Plate section image credits are given in full in the List of Illustrations (pp. 7–10).
Maps by www.bounford.com
Index by Alan Rutter

Typeset by Deanta Global Publishing Services, Chennai, India
Printed and bound in Great Britain by CPI (Group) UK Ltd, Croydon, CR0 4YY

Osprey Publishing supports the Woodland Trust, the UK's leading woodland conservation charity.

To find out more about our authors and books visit www.ospreypublishing.com. Here you will find
extracts, author interviews, details of forthcoming events and the option to sign up for our newsletter.

Contents

List of Illustrations

Historical echoes are powerful in Russia. A Soviet poster from World
 War II exhorts the soldiers to 'Fight bravely, sons of Suvorov and
 Chapayev', under, from left to right, the shades of Alexander
 Nevsky from the 13th century, Alexander Suvorov from the
 18th century and Vasily Chapayev from the Russian Civil War.
 (Photo by: Photo12/Universal Images Group via Getty Images)
A re-enactment of typical longship river raiding at the time of the
 Varyagy. (Photo by Yulia Lilisentseva/Anadolu Agency/Getty
 Images)
Greek fire, shown in this 11th- or 12th-century manuscript, was the
 secret weapon of the Byzantines, feared by every Rus' raider.
 (Photo by Fine Art Images/Heritage Images/Getty Images)
The film *Alexander Nevsky* was hardly an exact historical
 representation, but this poster does convey a sense of the
 difference between the Russian warriors in their conical helmets
 and scale shirts, and the better-equipped Teutonic Knights.
 (Bettmann/Getty Images)
The Russians had cause to fear raids by the Polovtsians, as evoked
 in Viktor Vasnetsov's painting 'After the Battle'. (Photo by:
 Universal History Archive/Universal Images Group via Getty
 Images)
This engraving of the 1223 Battle of the Kalka River is of questionable
 historical accuracy, portraying the Mongols more like Turks, but
 does convey the chaos of the pivotal clash. (Photo by: PHAS/
 Universal Images Group via Getty Images)

A later illustration of a *basqaq* of the Golden Horde exacting tribute, accompanied by his bodyguard. (Photo by: Sovfoto/Universal Images Group via Getty Images)

A heroic representation of Dmitry Donskoi in Kolomna, where he mustered his forces for Kulikovo, in front of the walls of the town's kremlin. (Author's photo)

A contemporary representation of an early Strelets, with simple handgun over his left shoulder, and *berdysh* poleaxe on his right. (Photo by Fine Art Images/Heritage Images/Getty Images)

A fanciful representation of Kazan's surrender to Ivan in 1552 – the truth was that the defenders were largely massacred – but which captures the still-medieval look of so many of his soldiers well. (Photo by Fine Art Images/Heritage Images/Getty Images)

Fighting in the streets of Moscow between Russians and Poles in 1611. (Photo by Fine Art Images/Heritage Images/Getty Images)

A famous painting by Ilya Repin supposedly showing Zaporizhian Cossacks having fun composing a scathing and insulting reply to an ultimatum from the Turkish Sultan in 1676. (Photo by: Bildagentur-online/Universal Images Group via Getty Images)

A mural to Pozharsky and Minin in central Moscow. (Author's photo)

Yermak's Cossacks demonstrate the advantage in their firepower as they advance across Siberia in 1580. (Photo by Universal History Archive/Getty Images)

Greetings from the banks of the Lena River! An early 20th-century postcard from Yakutsk shows the classic wooden walls and towers of Russian stations across Siberia. (Photo by Heritage Art/ Heritage Images via Getty Images)

A contemporary representation of the 1714 Battle of Gangut, in which the Russian Navy won its first real engagement with Sweden. (Photo by Fine Art Images/Heritage Images via Getty Images)

The future Peter the Great training his 'play army'. (Photo by Fine Art Images/Heritage Images/Getty Images)

Catherine the Great was rarely treated kindly by European cartoonists, but nor was she considered irrelevant. Here, she and the monarchs of Prussia and Austria are dividing up Poland between them. (Photo by Hulton Archive/Getty Images)

The Battle of Poltava in 1709. (Photo by Fine Art Images/Heritage Images/Getty Images)

The Battle of Cahul, 1770, showing the Russians advancing on the Ottoman forces arrayed in the foreground. (Photo by Fine Art Images/Heritage Images/Getty Images)

Napoleon broods over his burning prize, as he rides into Moscow. (Photo by Fine Art Images/Heritage Images/Getty Images)

This view of the medieval towers that dot the Ingushetia countryside, with more mountains in the distance, helps convey the kind of terrain the Russians found themselves fighting in, as they extended imperial rule across the North Caucasus. (Photo by Alexander Manzyuk/Anadolu Agency via Getty Images)

However stylised, this picture of the Charge of the Light Brigade does convey the way their lines found themselves with guns to left, right and fore. (Photo by: Photo12/Universal Images Group via Getty Images)

Tsar Nicholas II blessing a regiment leaving for the Russo-Japanese War in 1904. It must have been a great comfort for them. (Photo by: Photo12/Universal Images Group via Getty Images)

Ships of the Black Sea Fleet getting under steam at Sevastopol. In the First World War, the Imperial Navy was able to dominate the Black Sea, but never leverage this for wider victory on land. (Photo by: Pictures From History/Universal Images Group via Getty Images)

Armoured trains like this one were a particular feature of the Russian military in the First World War and then the Civil War. (Photo by Fine Art Images/Heritage Images/Getty Images)

The Russian state soon started to run out of money in the First World War, and this poster advertises war bonds to support the troops. (Photo by: Pictures From History/Universal Images Group via Getty Images)

The famous Il-2 *Shturmovik* ground-attack aircraft over Berlin in 1945. (Photo by ullstein bild/ullstein bild via Getty Images)

Red Army soldiers supporting a T-34 advance during the Battle of Kursk, in July 1943. (Photo by: Sovfoto/Universal Images Group via Getty Images)

However little today's Russian government wants to admit it, assistance from the Western Allies was crucial. This is the HMS *Royal Sovereign*, a Revenge-class battleship, serving on loan in the Red Navy as the *Arkhangelsk*, before being returned to the Royal

Navy at the end of the war. (Photo by Keystone/Hulton Archive/ Getty Images).

A US Lockheed P-2 Neptune patrol plane overflies a Soviet freighter during the Cuban Missile Crisis in 1962. (Photo by Getty Images)

A Soviet tank during the suppression of the Prague Spring in 1968 is surrounded by angry Czechs. (AFP via Getty Images)

A Russian Mi-26 heavy-lift helicopter takes off from Grozny airport in 1995, with the carcass of a destroyed jet in the foreground. (ALEXANDER NEMENOV/AFP via Getty Images)

Russian peacekeepers in South Ossetia in 2008, on the eve of Tbilisi's attack – casualties to the contingent gave Moscow the excuse it was looking for to invade. (VANO SHLAMOV/AFP via Getty Images)

Local militia and Russian 'Little Green Men' stand guard outside a government building in Simferopol during the 2014 annexation. (Photo by Kyodo News Stills via Getty Images)

The cost of war: a Russian missile has just hit the Ukrainian city of Zaporizhia, in April 2022. (Photo by Vladyslav Kiyashchuk/ Suspilne Ukraine/JSC "UA:PBC"/Global Images Ukraine via Getty Images)

Mutineers and a tank from the Wagner mercenary army during their occupation of Rostov-on-Dun in June 2023. (Photo by STRINGER/AFP via Getty Images)

List of Maps

Author's Note

Translating out of Cyrillic always poses challenges. I have chosen to transliterate names as they are pronounced, and have also ignored the diacritical 'soft' and 'hard' signs found in the original. The only exceptions are names that have acquired common forms in English – for example, I use the spelling 'Gorbachev' rather than the phonetically correct 'Gorbachov', and 'Catherine the Great' rather than 'Yekaterina Velikaya'. I also accept local practice, so what used to be called Kiev is rendered as Kyiv after Ukrainian independence at the end of 1991, for instance. Finally, where words have become more widely used in English-language sources, I pluralize them with an -s, instead of the usual -y/-i of the original Russian.

Introduction

'War is such an unfair and evil thing that those who are fighting are trying to drown out the voice of conscience in themselves.'

'The is the paradox of the Russian. He wants peace, he wants peace so much he would burn the world to achieve it.'

'One part of me wants to live in comfort, spend quiet family evenings and work in the office, but when the thunder of guns begins outside the window (the front is 14km from my house), I understand that I am ready to drop everything and run there, to be in the centre of events. No, I'm not sick. My problem is that I was born Russian.'

Three quotes, from three very different Russians, yet all speaking to a central paradox of Russia, its identity, and its place in the world. The first is from the entry for 6 January 1853 in the diary of Leo Tolstoy, one of the country's greatest writers, whose sprawling epic *War and Peace* (1865) at once condemns war and at the same time unavoidably portrays a nation brought together by the threat of Napoleon's invasion in 1812. The second comes from a conversation I had in Moscow in 2013 with a recently retired Russian officer, a veteran of the Soviet war in Afghanistan (1979–88) and both of Russia's wars against the rebellious Chechens (1994–96 and 1999–2009), all ugly conflicts, which had together cost him an eye, a marriage and, judging by the amount he drank, most of his liver, yet who still managed to combine an idealistic notion about the importance of peace and the brotherhood of nations with a wealth of bloodcurdling tales of martial inhumanity. The third is from the online journal of Maxim Fomin from 10 September 2017, who by then had adopted the pen name Vladlen Tatarsky, a Ukrainian-born ethnic Russian who, after robbing a bank, went on to fight in a Russian-backed anti-government militia in Ukraine's Donbas region (2014–17), before becoming a high-profile pro-war 'military blogger' back in Russia. In 2023, he was killed by a bomb hidden inside a bust presented to him by what seems to have been a dupe of Ukrainian intelligence.

A pacifist; a career soldier; a military enthusiast. Yet together they embody a fundamental paradox that has been evident throughout my own experiences with Russia (the first time I visited was back in 1980) and, indeed, this country's rich, if often blood-soaked, history. Medieval church sermons on the divine grace of peace delivered to a military aristocracy for whom war was their profession. Seemingly sincere ruminations by tsarist officials who justified a series of imperial adventures, whether in Europe, the North Caucasus or Central Asia, in the name of civilization and mercy. Soviet propaganda proclaiming their commitment to a world without war set against the goose-stepping ranks of soldiers marching through Red Square. Vladimir Putin's own claims that his brutal invasion of Ukraine in 2022 was to save it from (mythical) Nazis.

Of course, hypocrisy is no Russian monopoly. Most countries' histories are full of those same contradictions, and that goes double for former empires. Yet on a purely personal level, Russia has always felt somewhat different. There is no question that Russians are deeply aware of the horrors and costs of war. Go to the Piskaryovskoye Cemetery in the north-east of St Petersburg, whose mass graves house the remains of some 420,000 civilians and 50,000 soldiers who fell in what was then Leningrad's 872-day siege during the Second World War, and you'll be reminded of the price paid in living memory – and that is only about half the toll of the siege, and one-eleventh of the total ethnic Russian casualties of the war as a whole. Yet this is also a nation where the military is everywhere, and without the ambiguity that dogs Western societies' attitudes towards their armed forces, where empty platitudes thanking soldiers for their service can often co-exist with a sense that they are somehow dangerous outsiders or an atavistic holdover from the past. In Russia, children climb over Second World War anti-tank guns – suitably rendered safe – in their school playgrounds, while teenagers wear *pilotka* side-caps during Victory Day, with a very un-teenager lack of irony. It is not just that the state invokes past martial glories, decorating the sides of buildings with murals that could just as easily be of Marshal Zhukov, one of the great commanders of the Second World War, or Alexander Nevsky, who beat back the invading Teutonic Knights in 1242. It is that ordinary Russians will still flock to see war films, encourage their children to join the paramilitary Young Army, or freely join the March of the Immortal Regiment, holding pictures of relatives who fought in what they call the Great Patriotic War. At the same time, the awareness of the true costs of war – that this is not some sterile computer game conflict – is keen and almost ubiquitous. For every gung-ho 'military commentator' enthusing over Russian military advances in Ukraine – in the safe confines of social media – you'll encounter a dozen people who will genuinely pledge the importance of peace. To quote another veteran of recent wars in 2016, 'Yes, Russians can do terrible things to protect their Motherland, but it's because we know the price of war that we understand the value of peace.'

LAND IN-BETWEEN

All states have been shaped by wars and conquest, but for few countries is this as true as for Russia. The stretch of land that would later be divided between European Russia, Ukraine, Moldova and Belarus was once a primal forest, scattered with small settlements divided among numerous tribal confederations. According to the 12th-century *Primary Chronicle* – a document of admittedly questionable historical accuracy:

> [T]hese Slavs came and settled on the Dnieper and called themselves People of the Clearings [*poliane*]; others called themselves People of the Trees [*drevliane*] because they settled in the forests; and different ones settled on the Dvina and called themselves People of the Polota [*polochane*], taking the name of the Polota River, which flows into the Dvina. And those Slavs who settled near Lake Ilmen called themselves by their own name – Slavs.[*]

The Vikings called it Gardariki, 'land of towers', but maybe it would have been more apt to call it 'land of rivers', which cut through the forest and represented crucial routes for warfare and trade. The Volga,

---

[*] This and later quotes from the *Russian Primary Chronicle (Povest Vremennykh Let)* are drawn from the online Russian-language texts at http://litopys.org.ua/index.html

the Dvina, the Dnieper, the Don, and all their tributaries, not only stitched the early Slavic tribes loosely together, but they attracted those Vikings – known to the Slavic tribes as *Varyagy* – who used them to pillage the villages along them for furs, honey and slaves, and to travel all the way to Miklagarth, 'Great City'. This was Constantinople, capital of the Eastern Roman Empire, and gateway to Serkland – Land of Silk – as the Vikings called the Arab lands.

This was, thus, very much a land defined as what it was in between, and from every direction came threats, stronger powers demanding fealty or tribute. North and east were the Vikings, who would conquer in the ninth century. It was this conquest that began the emergence of the very concept of something called the lands of the Rus'. South and east were the rolling steppes, which over the centuries would disgorge a procession of nomad horse empires, who would raid, settle, demand tribute and then often fall to another challenger from the east. The Bulgars and the Khazars, the Pechenegs and the Polovtsy, then the mighty Mongols, who would roll across the Rus' in the 13th century. The Mongol conquest would lock these lands away from Europe for 200 years, but by the time their grip loosened, it was already facing new threats from the west, whether crusading Orders determined to extinguish the heresy of their Orthodox Church or the rising Polish–Lithuanian Commonwealth and, in due course, the Swedes and the Danes, and the Turks to the south. Yet Muscovy itself was hardly simply on the defensive, expanding south, east and west.

However, Russia's location was also its tragedy: with no natural borders, and denied many of the natural resources and opportunities on which rivals' economies were built, from the agrarian revolution to warm-water ports, it was often pitched against the pre-eminent European or Asian military powers of the age, generally at a technological disadvantage. So war – its threat, and the need to be able to fight it – has driven the evolution of this state, from princes and tsars to commissars and presidents. When Tsar Alexander III reportedly asserted that 'Russia has just two allies: its army and its navy', he could just as easily have been saying it had two masters. To respond to this challenge, the Russian state has had to sit all the more heavily on the backs of its people, extorting the men and taxes its perceived security needs demanded. The result was often rebellion, whether flight – part of the reason for the steady expansion of the borders was, in effect, the state following the peasants who hoped virgin territory would offer them freedom – or violent risings. The result was the security state in all its murderous incarnations, whether Tsar Ivan the Terrible's black-robed *Oprichniki*, who massacred thousands when they sacked Novgorod in 1570 in response to rumoured defection to the Polish–Lithuanian Commonwealth, or the Bolshevik Cheka, or 'Extraordinary Commission', who launched the 'Red Terror' against real and assumed enemies during the 1917–22 Russian Civil War.

'THE CONTINUAL BEATINGS'

After all, this constant sense of vulnerability, of being trapped between the dangers of encroachment from without and rebellion from within, has shaped the mindsets of Russia's rulers. The greatest embodiment of this sense of constant vulnerability, one that could only be addressed through strength and aggression, was Soviet dictator Joseph Stalin, who memorably claimed:

> One feature of the history of old Russia was the continual beatings she suffered because of her backwardness. She was beaten by the Mongol khans. She was beaten by the Turkish beys. She was beaten by the Swedish feudal lords. She was beaten by the Polish and Lithuanian gentry. She was beaten by the British and French capitalists. She was beaten by the Japanese barons. All beat her because of her backwardness, military backwardness, cultural backwardness, political backwardness, industrial backwardness, agricultural backwardness. They beat her because to do so was profitable and could be done with impunity.[*]

He went on to say that 'we are fifty or a hundred years behind the advanced countries. We must make good this distance in ten years. Either we do it, or they will crush us.' Stalin said this in 1931, and ten years later, on 22 June 1941, Hitler launched Operation *Barbarossa*, the largest land offensive in history. It was the start of a struggle of almost inconceivable scale and brutality, as one totalitarianism fought a war to the death with another, yet the Soviet Union would survive and emerge as a superpower – even if one bled and traumatized. Nonetheless, its

[*] Joseph Stalin, 'The Tasks of Business Executives: Speech Delivered at the First All-Union Conference of Leading Personnel of Socialist Industry', 4 February 1931

survival was to a great degree thanks precisely to the degree to which Stalinism had been built around creating a warfighting state machine, from its economy to its capacity to mobilize and direct its people.

The Great Patriotic War remains central to their sense of themselves, and today's regime under Vladimir Putin seeks to wrap itself in its mantle, framing itself as locked in a similar existential struggle for sovereignty and survival. To Putin, his invasion of Ukraine was not an imperial adventure but a necessary act of self-defence, before Ukraine was turned into a political and military weapon against Russia by an implacably hostile West. We need not – should not – accept his skewed and self-justificatory logic, but we should recognize the degree to which, in his own way, he is just one more Russian leader who believes – as he himself admits he learned as a teenager running with gangs in a city that still bore the scars of war – that 'the streets of Leningrad taught me one thing: If a fight's inevitable, you must strike first.'*

Initially, I had the naïve notion that I could cover every war and battle Russia and Russians had fought in the past millennium and a half, but it quickly became clear what a foolish ambition that was. First of all, it would require not a book but a multi-volume set; second, it would quickly become simply a breathless list of context-free engagements and outcomes, like trying to novelize the football results; and third, because the wood would be comprehensively obscured by the volume of trees. Instead, the aim of this book is to combine a grand historical sweep of political, military, economic and social history across the centuries and the wars that punctuate it, with an introduction to some relatively little-known conflicts that help illustrate this tale, from the invasion of the Khanate of Kazan by Ivan the Terrible to the colonial wars in 19th-century Central Asia. In some cases, following a theme will mean some slight chronological hiccups, but I hope the reader will forgive that. Written as it is in the shadow of Vladimir Putin's murderous imperial war in Ukraine, a war that most Russians do not support, but accept, it becomes all the more important to understand the ways that war and military security have shaped not just Russia's past, but its own sense of its present – and the ways that there is real debate about its future.

*'Straight Outta Leningrad: Putin Says Streetfights Taught Him How to Tackle ISIS', *Newsweek*, 23 October 2015

PART ONE

The Forging of Russia

I

The Making of the Rus'

The Raid on Constantinople, 860

860   Askold and Dir's Raid on Constantinople
862? Arrival of Ryurik at Lake Ladoga
879   Death of Ryurik
882   Oleg takes Kiev and moves his capital there from Novgorod
907   The Raid on Constantinople that likely never was
911   Treaty signed between Kiev and Constantinople
912   Death of Oleg the Wise

Carved into the marble parapet of the upper gallery in Istanbul's Hagia Sophia, the Eastern Orthodox basilica that became a mosque, are the spiky Norse runes that read, 'Halfdan carved these runes' or, in effect, 'Halfdan was here.' It's a lasting sign of the presence of Viking mercenaries and traders in what was then the Eastern Roman capital of Constantinople – and of the continent-spanning raiding and trading routes that created Russia. What, after all, is in a name? The modern 'Russia' comes from the older term Rus', and that probably comes from the Finnish *ruotsi*, which, in turn, came from the archaic *roocci*, which has its roots in *rothr*, the Old Norse for a steering oar. The Rus' were the rowing folk, the Viking adventurers and conquerors who made their way in their oared longships not just to what are now Russia's shores, but down the rolling, broad rivers that could ultimately take them to that great prize of the ancient world,

Constantinople, the Great City. It was the Byzantines who, in their own Greek tongue, called these shaggy-maned travellers the 'Rossiya', from whence the modern Russian word for their own nation comes. The reason for this roundabout etymological exploration is precisely to demonstrate how the very notion of a Russian land and people is itself the product of conquest.

Of course, this is hardly unique to the Russians. England is derived from 'Englaland', land of the Angles, after the Germanic tribes that settled in Britain during the Early Middle Ages. Arguably, at least conquest is a better basis than whim. America owes its brand to Amerigo Vespucci, the Italian explorer who charted the Caribbean and South Atlantic, although in fairness he did not have the hubris to name a continent after himself. Instead, a cartographer named Martin Waldseemüller was looking for a name to give this landmass on a map he would go on to publish in 1507 and seems to have decided that this would be as good as any. Yet for Russia, what is especially interesting is the question of whether the very origins of their nation and indeed people came through conquest or assimilation.

A LAND FIT FOR CONQUEST

How Gardariki became a nation has become the subject of a founding myth that itself has been contested for political reasons over the centuries. The story goes that around 862, a Danish adventurer whom the Russians call Ryurik landed with his personal retinue on the shores of Lake Ladoga, far to the north-west. He came, it seems, not as an invader, but in answer to a plea. At this time, the territories that would become Northern European Russia were divided between a range of tribes, some Slav, others Finno-Ugric: the Krivichi and the Vyatichi, the Chud and the Merias, the Radimichi and the Veps, and many more besides. They were relatively small in number and scattered, but nonetheless skirmished and fought over crucial river crossings, supplies of furs, and other strategic resources. According to the *Primary Chronicle*, in due course they tired of their internecine conflicts. Failing to be able to agree on a leader from among them, they turned to the Varyagy, which is how they referred to the Vikings of Scandinavia. They had fought on and off against the Varyagy, who raided them for furs and slaves, but they also respected them as doughty warriors and canny war leaders, true to their word and, perhaps more to the point, outsiders unlikely to favour any one tribe over the others.

Out went the word: 'Our land is great and rich, but there is no order in it. Come reign over us.' And Ryurik heard it and came to take them up on their offer. First, he and his men built Aldeigjuborg, a fort on the banks of Lake Ladoga, and then an inland trading post by Lake Ilmen. This was built up into a stronghold that then became a city he called Holmgarth, and which would later be called the 'New Town', or Novgorod. The most northern of the great cities that would define the early Rus', wooden-walled Novgorod would be the most cosmopolitan of them all, a city first and foremost of merchants rather than warriors, with a thriving tradition of local governance – it would even be known as a republic – and even a limited and rough-and-ready kind of democracy reminiscent of the Scandinavian *thing*, or assembly of free men.

THE COMING OF THE VARYAGY

Unpicking fact from fiction, whether his name really was Ryurik, there was a Viking adventurer who did indeed arrive in north-western Russia in the early 860s along with his brothers (known in the *Primary Chronicle* by the distinctly un-Norse names of Sineus and Truvor) and enough warriors to start carving himself out a kingdom. Yet the *Novgorod First Chronicle*, which seems to predate even the *Primary Chronicle*, makes much of the way that, just a year or two earlier, the Varyagy had been unwelcome raiders, and the tribes 'rose against the Varangians and expelled them beyond the sea; and they began to rule themselves and set up cities.'* It seems a pretty quick turnaround from that to willing subordination to yesterday's reavers.

The answer seems to be that the Vikings were becoming an increasing presence all across Northern Europe. England may have begun to pay Danegeld, a tribute to stave off coastal raids, from the mid-860s. Around the same time, the Curonians of the Baltic coast were invaded by the Danes, and then the Swedes. It is hardly surprising that the tribes of what would become north-eastern Russia also faced increasingly fierce

---

*Novgorod First Chronicle (*Novgorodski Pervyi Litopis*), online in Russian at http://litopys.org.ua /novglet/novg.htm

and organized raids. First, the Vikings plundered. Then, they extorted tribute on pain of further raids, essentially protection racketeers in longships. Over time, this became a more structured and regular process, and may have evolved either to raiding rival tribes in return for payment, as the Varyagy were never averse to some mercenarying (and in the tenth century would also become famous as the elite Varangian Guard of the Byzantine emperors), or even joint operations. In his book *Power and Prosperity*, the American economist and political scientist Mancur Olson (ironically enough, of Norwegian origin) talked about the way so many governments emerge when 'roving bandits' with no stake in the local economy take over and become 'stationary bandits'. They still extort and exploit, but now have an interest in protecting their prey – their subjects – and even keeping them relatively happy.

This seems to be what happened here. However, a convincing case has been made that the real start of what we may think of as the earliest precursor to the Russian was a little way to the east, at a place called Gorodishche, in a defensible pocket where the Volkhov River flows into Lake Ilmen. Archaeological explorations suggest a fortified settlement that was prosperous thanks to trade and tribute, and this may have been the stronghold of a regional ruler whom the Byzantines called the *chaganus*, a Greek distortion of the title 'khagan', used by the Khazar Khanate to the east. The Byzantines knew of this figure because he dispatched an embassy to them in 838, and a year later some of these Rus' accompanied a Byzantine delegation to the court of Louis the Pious, King of the Franks and co-ruler of the Holy Roman Empire. Louis concluded that they were Swedes, but the description of their journey places their domain firmly in what is now Russia. Whoever the *chaganus* was – and we don't even have a record of his name – his main legacy seems to have been to establish the very beginnings of invader rule, although one cannot call it any kind of organized realm, and what little authority he had seems to have disappeared by the 860s. The presence of Gorodishche may well have decided Ryurik's decision to establish Holmgarth.

Able to build on these foundations, Ryurik founded his own principality in the north. Further south, though, two other Viking adventurers eager to turn raiding into rule would arguably prove every bit as important: Askold and Dir. Sometime in the 850s, they cut down to the south and took Kiev (later better known as Kyiv), a commercial

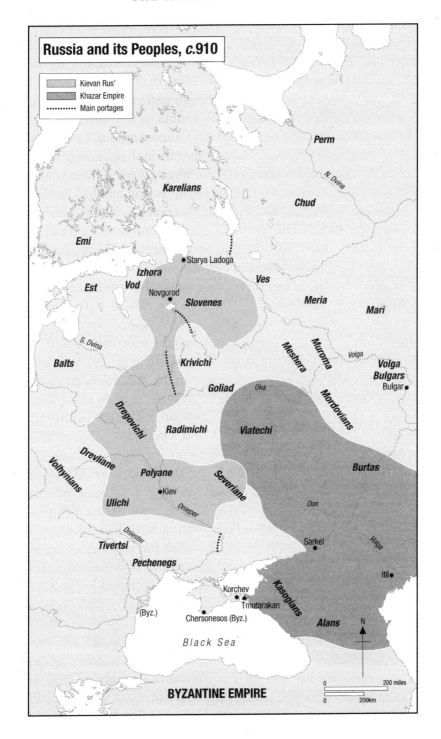

Russia and its Peoples, c.910

Kievan Rus'
Khazar Empire
········· Main portages

Perm

N. Dvina

Karelians

Chud

Emi

Starya Ladoga

Izhora

Ves

Est   Vod
Novgorod   Meria
Slovenes   Mari

S. Dvina

Balts   Volga   Volga
Krivichi   Bulgars
Meshera   Bulgar

Goliad   Oka   Muroma
Mordovians

Dregovichi   Radimichi   Viatechi

Drevliane

Volhynians   Polyane   Burtas
Kiev   Severiane

Ulichi   Don   Volga
Dnieper

Dniester   Sarkel

Tivertsi   Volga

Pechenegs   Itil

Korchev   Kasogians
Tmutarakan

(Byz.)
Chersonesos (Byz.)   Alans   N

Black Sea

BYZANTINE EMPIRE   0   200 miles
                                        0   200km

25

hub since at least the fifth century, lying on one of the key trade routes between Scandinavia and Constantinople and thus between Northern Europe and the Middle East. A capital of the Polyane ('plains' or 'clearing people'), it had been a tributary of the Khazar Khanate, but Askold, Dir and their men stormed the city and made it theirs.

It was Kiev rather than Novgorod that would emerge as the lynchpin of the new Rus' land (at least until it was sacked by the Mongols in 1240), so why such a focus on Ryurik and the legend that he had been invited? This was very much a later invention, meant at once to give special status to his bloodline, the Ryurikids – who would emerge as the dominant dynasty of the Rus' for the next seven centuries – and also to smooth over the tense social relationships between conquerors and conquered. Just as Normans and Saxons would mix to form a single English people after the conquest of 1066, so too Varyagy adventurers and the more numerous members of the local tribes would fuse into one people over time. Casting subjugation as invitation helped sweeten the pill, and would off and on be invoked and challenged over the following centuries as suited the political needs of the moment. Nonetheless, it is clear that these early years of the Rus', far from being a time of harmonious state-building, were shaped by war, treachery and plunder.

THE RAID ON CONSTANTINOPLE, 860

It is hard to overstate just how important Constantinople was to the region. It was rich, a hub for trade across Europe, the Middle East and Near Asia. It was powerful, not yet sapped by long wars with its Arab neighbours. It also wielded immense cultural authority: not for nothing the Rus' would later call it Tsargrad, 'Emperor City', and seek to build Kiev in its image. In short, for freebooting adventurers, it was a target as tough as it was irresistible. Did Askold and Dir have a raid on the Emperor City in mind when they took Kiev? It is impossible to know, but the attack that took place in 860 may well have been the culmination of a long struggle for trade routes. Back in the 830s, Byzantine engineers helped the Khazars build a limestone and brick fortress that became known as Šarkel ('White House' in the Khazar tongue) on the left bank of the lower Don River. Ever since the Tsimlyansk Reservoir was completed in 1952, Šarkel has been underwater, but excavations in the 1930s proved that this was both a thriving trading station along the so-called 'Khazarian Way' between the Baltic and Caspian Seas, and also a powerful stronghold. Along with its twin on the right bank, it controlled the crucial portage, a place where the Don and Volga Rivers were close enough that boats could be manhandled from one to the other.

But if they were taxing or blocking Rus' trade along the Khazarian Way, as some claim, why not attack the Khazars who commissioned and held the fort, rather than the Byzantines who just built it? It is difficult not to conclude that it was simply that Constantinople represented both a lucrative target, and one whose sacking would be worth a saga or two. Once Askold and Dir had taken Kiev, finding themselves in control of a key waystation on the river roads to the Emperor City, it appears to have been an irresistible temptation. In 860, they assembled a force in some 200 boats, typically made by excavating a single large tree trunk, making a boat light enough to be carried by two men in portage, shallow enough in draught to handle the sandbars and rapids of the river roads, yet able to be fitted out with sails, outrigger and planks fastened to the sides to raise the freeboard so that they could venture onto the open sea. It was a mix of fighting men: Varangians, the retinues of Slavic tribal chiefs, and levies from the villages. United in the dream of plunder, they caught Constantinople by surprise, 'like a thunderbolt from heaven', as Byzantine Patriarch Photius put it. The thought of a threat from these 'barbarians of the North' had been discounted. The real threat to the 'City' (as it was known by its own people, as if there was only one worthy of the name) would surely come from the east and the south. Emperor Michael III was away, campaigning with his army in Asia Minor. His navy – which otherwise could have fallen on the raiders as they crossed the Bosporus at twilight and unleashed their fearsome incendiary Greek Fire – was deployed in the Aegean and Mediterranean Seas. Constantinople still had a minimal garrison but was forced essentially to rely on its mighty walls. This meant that, at first, the raiders had a field day looting and burning the suburban settlements outside them.

To begin with, they ravaged the neighbourhood of Sycae, now known as Galata, to the east. The next day, they took to their boats and swept round the Sea of Marmara south of the City, where they fell upon the archipelago known as the Demonisoi, the 'Isles of the Demons' (now more kindly named the Princes' Islands). These were used to exile out-of-favour dignitaries, including former Patriarch Ignatius, who had been born Niketas, a son of Emperor Michael I. When his father was deposed, he had been castrated and forced into the clergy to make him ineligible for the throne: Byzantine politics were not for the faint-hearted. The former Empress Theodora had appointed him Patriarch of Constantinople in 847, but he proved to be as combative in his political life as he was prone to picking the wrong side. When Theodora was sidelined, he was forced to resign and sent into exile on the Demonisoi, where he had already founded three monasteries. He was forced to watch them plundered and many of his own supporters hacked apart by the raiders.

The Rus' were not versed in siegecraft, though, and at most a thousand raiders were not enough to storm the walls, let alone take a city that at the time housed more than a quarter of a million souls. Nor could the depleted forces inside the walls launch a credible assault on the attackers. A bad-tempered stalemate ensued, in which the Rus' tried to draw the defenders out by shows of defiance, such as all drawing their swords at once, and the Byzantines sniped at them from the battlements. Eventually, the Rus' withdrew, their boats stacked with plunder from the suburbs. They had been denied the glory of taking Constantinople, but could content themselves with their loot and the knowledge that they had demonstrated that they could defy even the Emperor City. The Byzantines would later conjure pious myths, claiming that the raiders had been driven away by the intervention of the Theotokos, the Virgin Mary, but in practice they would begin to take these barbarians of the North more seriously.

OLEG THE WISE

Askold and Dir were triumphant, but raiders and usurpers can never rest easy. In Novgorod, Ryurik had been consolidating power. He came accompanied by two of his brothers, who ruled as subordinate princes, but when they died, according to the chronicles, he became increasingly authoritarian and began appointing his cronies in charge of the settlements under his control: Polotsk, Rostov, Old Ladoga, Murom, Beloözero. None of this was easy: his Rus' followers were still relatively few in number, and for all the pretty myths of his having been invited in, they often had to maintain their rule by fire and steel.

For example, according to the *Primary Chronicle*, in 864, the locals in Novgorod, under one Vadim the Brave, rebelled, angered by the way the Rus' treated them virtually as slaves. They were violently supressed by the experienced Viking warriors, Vadim being killed and 'many other beatings' being dispensed to the other rioters.

Nonetheless, Ryurik not only managed to remain in power but created a crude political structure, knitted together by personal oaths of fealty and underpinned by the Vikings' awareness that they were a perilously small ruling elite surrounded by more numerous and often rebellious tribes, such that disunity could easily mean catastrophe. On his death in or around 879, his one-year-old son Igor (probably a later-Russified form of Ingvarr) could hardly succeed him, so Oleg, Ryurik's right-hand man, stepped in as regent. If this sounds a little like a coup, then it likely was one. Certainly, Oleg would demonstrate his ruthless aggressiveness soon after, turning his eyes to Kiev.

In 882, Oleg gathered an army of Varyagy and tribal warbands. They marched south, first taking Smolensk and then Lyubech. These two towns are essentially on a straight line from Novgorod to Kiev, but it seems that Askold and Dir were taken as unawares as the Byzantines had been in 860. Installing his own men in charge of these towns, Oleg continued south, down the mighty Dnieper River. As they neared Kiev, he kept most of them back, out of sight, and landed with a deceptively small force. Claiming to be a merchant from Novgorod with a cargo of jewellery and other trade items to be sold in Constantinople, he sent a messenger to Askold and Dir saying that he was ill but had an important matter to discuss with them, inviting them to his humble encampment. Trade down the Dnieper heading towards Constantinople was by then commonplace, as were side-deals and the peddling of information, so the co-rulers of Kiev appear to have taken Oleg at face value and gone to meet him with only a token guard.

It was a fatal mistake. According to the *Primary Chronicle*, when they boarded Oleg's boat, he is said to have told them, 'you are not princes and not from a princely family, but I am Oleg, a prince, and this is Igor, the Ryurikid prince', before having them killed. While it may seem unnecessary to deride his enemies' bloodlines before murdering them, there was actually good reason for this. Establishing some greater legitimacy was crucial to trying to build more stable structures of rule in what were, after all, still conquered territories where the Varyagy were a small minority, however militarily effective. Askold and Dir never seem to have pretended to have been more than adventurers, and those who lived by the main chance died by it, too. After all, a second reason behind this affirmation was to win over their men still in Kiev, and it seems to be the case that through negotiation, superior force and some judicious additional killings, Oleg had little trouble bringing Kiev under his control, interring the bodies of Askold and Dir outside the city walls, symbolically expelling and burying their influence, too.

He made this city, sitting astride the Dnieper routes to Constantinople, his new capital, and the story – one which for obvious reasons would subsequently prove contentious – is that he declared, 'Let this be the mother of Rus' cities.' Kiev would prove a demanding and acquisitive mother, though. Oleg, who gained the nickname 'the Wise', perhaps ought rather to be called 'the Energetic'. Novgorod became a tributary of Kiev, and for the rest of his reign, Oleg continued to expand the territories under his control. This should not be interpreted as building a kingdom so much as an extension of traditional Viking protection racketeering, forcing more tribes to pay tribute. First came the Drevlyans, the 'wood-folk', immediately west of Kyiv, subjugated in 883. Then, he turned to tribes that hitherto had been forced to pay off the Khazar Khanate: the Tivertsi to the south along the Dniester River, and the Severtsi and Radimichi to the north-east. For example, to the Radimichi, he was blunt, asking them, 'To whom do you give tribute?' When they replied the Khazars, he demanded, 'Don't give it to the Khazars, give it to me.'* In other words, he did not want just tribute, he wanted a monopoly of tribute, the initial basis of rule, and a direct challenge to the Khazars.

GODFATHER OF THE RUS'

By 890, his tribal conquests were more or less complete, and Oleg could claim a kind of authority across a broad swathe of territory, from the Black Sea all the way to the Baltic, anchored around Novgorod and Kiev, and held together by the river roads through the

*According to the *Russian Primary Chronicle*

dense forest. From time to time, Oleg might involve himself in local politics, but essentially, as long as towns and tribes paid their tribute in full and on time, and provided warbands when he needed them (not least with the promise of a share of the loot), then they largely could manage themselves. This was no kingdom but the loosest of confederations. Nonetheless, arguably it was Oleg the Wise who could be said to be the real godfather of Russia, rather than the much more widely feted Ryurik.

Still, however much he was eager to claim this right, Oleg was not a prince by blood. His legitimacy depended on his wits and his success, his ability to reward those who stuck by him and punish those who did not. The greatest fillip to his status would be some kind of understanding with Constantinople. According to Russian chronicles, in 907, Oleg launched his own raid on the City. The *Primary Chronicle* says that, leaving Igor in Kiev, he mustered a force of thousands, who landed to find the city gates again closed and the harbours blocked by chains. However, in an inventive and, sadly, highly implausible twist, Oleg had his boats fitted with wheels, so they rolled around the City, again ravaging the suburbs outside the walls. According to the legend, the frightened Byzantines – Greeks, as they were known by then – sued for peace, but treacherously set out poisoned food and drink. Oleg saw through their subterfuge and forced them to accept terms: a substantial payment in silver there and then, followed by further annual tribute and advantageous rights for Rus' merchants. Then Oleg hung his shield on the city gates of Constantinople as a sign of his victory and returned to Kiev in glory, his ship rigged with golden-woven sails the Greeks had had to sew for him.

It is a grand and stirring story, one which would undoubtedly fix Oleg's place in history – were it true. In fact, there are near enough no references to any such events in Byzantine chronicles, and the treaty granting their merchants special privileges and generally formalizing relations between Constantinople and Kiev seems to date to 911. There probably was no such raid: the details either seem too similar to the 860 raid or too fanciful (wheeled boats!). However, we do know that for years the Kievan Rus' had been launching smaller raids on Byzantine holdings and possessions. In one engagement, for example, a good part of a Rus' raiding fleet was burned with Greek Fire, the Byzantines' terrifying early flamethrowers.

Instead, the 911 treaty likely reflected the way that the Rus' posed an increasing threat to Byzantine interests, without being so dangerous as to warrant a full-blown campaign at a time when the City was still engaged with the Arabs. They were an annoyance to be bought off, not a conqueror to be appeased. Nonetheless, this was still quite an achievement for adventurers who had come to Gardariki less than a century earlier. Shortly thereafter, probably in 912, Oleg died, and Prince Igor, by now in his mid-30s, finally became Prince of Kiev. With this, the Ryurikid dynasty that would dominate Russia until the end of the 16th century began – but the irony is that it was Oleg the outsider who truly founded it. This marks the start of the era of the princes. Over the years, Varyagy and Slavs would intermarry, their languages and cultures blend, albeit with massive regional variations. Nonetheless, this would remain a divided land, still Gardariki in form if no longer name. The Prince of Kiev might be first among equals, but his writ only went as far as he could impose or negotiate it. There were new challenges emerging, though, above all the nomadic Pechenegs, but arguably the greatest threat would come from the very divisiveness of the Rus', for whom, according to the *Primary Chronicle*, all too often 'the devil stirred up strife among brothers.'

Want To Know More?

Simon Franklin and Jonathan Shepard's *The Emergence of Rus 750–1200* (Longman, 1996) is detailed, scholarly and as hard to penetrate as a Russian forest. Much the same is true of Pavel Dolukhanov's *The Early Slavs: Eastern Europe from the Initial Settlement to the Kievan Rus* (Routledge, 1996). *Vikings of the Steppe: Scandinavians, Rus', and the Turkic World* (Routledge, 2024) by Csete Katona does a good job of putting the early Russians in their wider context. The 2016 Russian film *Viking* is not exactly a historical source, but it is an entertaining enough window into a moderately accurate physical representation of the era.

2

The Wars of the Princes

The Harrowing of the Drevlians, 946

943   Igor's raid on Constantinople
946   Olga's harrowing of the Drevlians
972   Death of Svyatoslav
978   Vladimir the Great becomes Grand Prince of Kiev
988   Christianization of Kiev
1015   Vladimir's death triggers dynastic struggles
1054   Yaroslav's death triggers dynastic struggles
1097   Lyubech conference

Don't mess with a Rus' princess, nor take lightly the feelings of one's own retinue – or even one's vassals. The story of Olga, who avenged her husband Igor on the Drevlians, in many ways encapsulates some of the wider tensions in this emerging Rus' commonwealth. Olga wreaked havoc on the Drevlians thanks to her ruthless cunning and greater military might, but the whole feud was triggered by an incautious attempt by Igor to extort more tribute from the Drevlians than agreed. Feud, tribute and the struggles between Varyag cities and Slavic tribes were all defining aspects of the age of the princes, as the tenth through to the 12th centuries were marked by episodic struggles between the emerging principalities of the Rus' and with neighbouring peoples, from the nomadic Pechenegs to the Finnish Chud, as much as their subject tribes. In the process, a different kind of feudalism emerged, one anchored on shifting alliances of dynastic families attracting their own personal retinues, the *druzhina*s. While Kiev would emerge ever more clearly the dominant city, it would nonetheless never be the capital of a nation. The scattered villages, towns and handful of cities of the Rus' were at once isolated and connected. They were isolated by distance and the deep forests to the north, yet connected by flows of trade, power and migration. The result was a common culture which, with considerable local variation, blended a range of cultural influences: original Slavic, Varangian Viking, steppe horsepeople and, over time, more. This is evident still in the syncretic nature of the Russian language, which has never met a foreign tongue from which it did not want to borrow, and a pagan faith that blended Norse and Slavic pagan traditions.

THE HARROWING OF THE DREVLIANS, 946

These early politics were shaped by mutual ties of loyalty and obligation within themselves, as well as the delicate understandings and balances of power between dominant powers and their tributaries. The early Rus' princes had to maintain control over subject tribes, on whose tribute they depended, and yet who often outnumbered their overlords. This could be a dangerous process, as the notoriously rapacious Prince Igor of Kiev discovered in 945. His *druzhina* were dissatisfied because he had transferred the tribute from the Drevlians to one of his henchmen, Sveneld, and not them. 'The servants of Sveneld are adorned with weapons and fine raiment, but we are naked,' they complained. 'Go forth with us, oh Prince, after tribute, that both you and we may profit thereby.'[*] It did not work out quite so well when, as a result, he incautiously tried to extort a second tribute from the recalcitrant tribe. This was a breach of the Drevlians' understanding of their deal with Kiev. Ambushed by the Drevlians, his was not a neat end; according to the Byzantine chronicler Leo the Deacon, 'they had bent down two birch trees to the prince's feet and tied them to his legs; then they let the trees straighten, in this way tearing the prince's body apart.'[†]

---

[*] *Nikon Chronicle*, in *Polnoe Sobranie Russkikh Letopisei, vol. IX* (1862), pp. 26–27.
[†] This and subsequent quotes from the Russian-language version, *Lev Diakon. Istoriya* (1988), available online at http://oldru.narod.ru/biblio/ldiakon1.htm

These were, though, bloody times. She would be the first Russian ruler to be baptized a Christian, but that came later. At the time, Igor's wife Olga certainly did not turn the other cheek but instead embarked on a systematic campaign of revenge. The story is that, perhaps in the name of averting a feud, the Drevlians sent a delegation, saying, 'We have killed your husband, for your husband was like a wolf, robbing and plundering. But our princes are good, who cultivated the land of the Drevlians. Come (and marry) our prince, Mal.' Before they could even disembark from the boat in which they had reached Kiev, though, she had them seized, thrown into a pit and buried alive, as she sarcastically asked them, 'Is that honour good enough for you?' Then, perhaps pretending that the delegation had not arrived, Olga requested that a new one of the Drevlians' 'best men' be sent. This they duly did, and when the new arrivals were washing themselves in the bathhouse in preparation for being presented at court, she had the doors barred and the building burned down.

At this point, one might reasonably assume that the Drevlians would have smelled a rat. The story is that Olga and a small detachment of the Kiev *druzhina* then travelled to their lands to celebrate a funeral feast at her husband's graveside, as was the custom, and there they got the Drevlian elders drunk and had them killed. It is more likely that this was a raid, which may also have coincided with a visit to Igor's grave, because it was then followed by a full-blown punitive campaign that saw the Drevlian capital Iskorosten (now Korosten in north-central Ukraine) burnt and many of its inhabitants put to the sword. The Drevlians lost their status as an autonomous tribe and were brought directly under the rule of Kiev.

On one level, this was a petty, even if bloody, conflict, but the fundamental lesson is to remind us of the constant need for princes to satisfy their followers and the essentially exploitative and often ad hoc nature of tax collection. The Prince of Kiev may have expected tribute from other princes and tribes, but often needed to demonstrate the ability to enforce these expectations and agreements. By the same token, princes who failed to keep their *druzhina* happy could expect desertions and defections, while those who pressed their tributaries excessively would face rebellion. Squaring these circles demanded not just charisma, tact and a reputation for effective application of violence, but also either successful campaigns and the loot they generated or else more efficient management. Olga, who ruled for the next three years, until her son Svyatoslav's majority, clearly learned the lessons of Igor's greed, regularizing the system of tributes, known as *polyudiye*, such that it was less subject to the whims of princes. Many of her immediate successors were less far-sighted.

THE PRINCELY HOSTS

This tension between the new rulers and their enforcers was also evident in the early Rus' way of war. Princes and other potentates would maintain their *druzhina* (coming from the word *drug*, a friend or comrade), a personal retinue of warriors who were as much enforcers and cronies as soldiers. They were first and foremost fighting men, although they may well also farm, manage estates or even engage in some trade on the side, and they were largely armed in the Viking manner, with swords, spears and axes, clad in mail, and hefting round shields which could be used to form a shield wall in battle. Over time, the members of the *druzhina* would increasingly be drawn from the Rus' – although there remained a tradition of including foreigners that persists to the present day – and also landholders, either aristocrats or petty gentry. However, in the early days, they could be Rus' or anyone else willing to throw in their lot with the prince, from Finns to Turks, Greeks to Magyars.

After all, this reflected the adventurer, even freebooter origins of Rus' society, and was certainly not quite the European model of feudalism. First of all, this was based on the notion of a contract: a warrior swore his service to a prince as a free agent, and could as easily leave that service, albeit likely sacrificing whatever lands he may have been granted. Second, this was a personal relationship: the prince's role as leader of a warband was separate from his role as ruler of a particular city, and if he moved from one domain to another, he likely would bring most of his retinue with him, for example. Only by the middle of the 11th century, as the political system became more settled, were they considered tied to a city, and raised largely from its existing nobility. By the same token, a prince could never take his men for granted: it was dishonourable to the point of starting a feud to desert in battle or betray the contract, but wholly legitimate for them openly to leave his service if they felt they were not receiving the honour and riches they believed they deserved.

According to the Arab traveller and chronicler Ibn Fadlan, the Prince of Kiev in the early tenth century had in his castle, his kremlin, '400 men from among his champions', while archaeological study of a typical prince's stronghold suggested there was room for up to 250–300 warriors.* Over time, their numbers tended to increase, though, as princes became more settled, populations increased and with it the tax base. As a result, the *druzhina* was divided. The *Malaya Druzhina*, the 'Small *Druzhina*', was a standing force which could in some cases number in the hundreds and from which a prince would often select his court officials. They were typically supported by grants of land and villages, as well as a share of any loot from raiding neighbours. On the other hand, the *Mladshaya Druzhina*, the 'Younger *Druzhina*', was a more varied mix of aristocrats' children and commoners, many of whom worked in various roles in the prince's estate but would take up arms when needed.

Both forces increasingly would fight on horseback, and with that began to take on weapons and tactics of the nomads to the east. Warfare was primarily dominated by the raid rather than the siege or the stand-up battle. Mobility was more important than mass, especially for operations on the rolling steppe or against horsefolk such as the Khazars to the south-east and the Magyars, who had but recently migrated west to what is now Hungary. To this end, the princes would in due course come to engage auxiliary cavalry, especially mercenaries and outcasts from the steppe peoples. There seemed to be a steady succession of new challengers – nomad peoples who would displace their predecessors westwards or assimilate them, a process that ensured a constant supply of horsemen looking for new lands and masters. In particular, Turkic vassals who would settle in the Porosye region in what is now Ukraine became known as the *Chyornye Klobuki*, or 'Black Hoods'. Their fast-moving cavalry, especially horse archers, became a fixture of princely armies until the Mongol conquest in the 13th century, and the spiritual forebears of the later Cossacks.

However, the bulk of princely armies in all but the quickest of raids would be made up of levies from the towns and villages, commoners

*Richard Frye, *Ibn Fadlan's Journey to Russia: A Tenth-century Traveler from Baghdad to the Volga River* (Markus Wiener, 2009), p. 74

armed with spear, bow or axe. The town militias were typically better armed, not least as princes might have to equip them, but they also reflected the changing politics of the Rus'. The *veche* was a town council of sorts, an assembly where all free male citizens could make their views known. In practice, of course, the rich and the powerful, especially the merchant class, largely dominated them. A prince who wanted to be able to count on the militias had to be sure of the support of the *veche*, though. Indeed, in Novgorod, which was much more of a trading city, as well as one closely connected to the Baltic world, the *veche* ended up being more powerful than the prince, electing the *posadnik*, the mayor, and treating the prince more like their hired military commander than their liege, which is why it is often described as a republic, even as it retained a prince.

This was an era, then, when the needs of warfighting in numerous intra-princely conflicts and struggles with outsiders began to shape the very foundations of Rus' politics and society. Princes had to be competent generals as well as inspiring leaders, or at least effective politicians, able to secure the backing of the *veche*. Military power depended not just on the usual foundations of population size and tax base, but the capacity to command the personal loyalty of the *druzhina* and conclude deals with the *Chyornye Klobuki* and other auxiliaries. Until more settled principalities had formed, power had to be negotiated.

RUS' AND GREEKS

When Igor, son of Ryurik, had finally emerged from Oleg's shadow, after an enforced regency that lasted until he was 35, he was clearly intent on continuing on the same martial path. From around 915, the lands of the Rus' had faced a growing threat from the nomadic Pecheneg peoples, but nonetheless Constantinople remained the target of choice, offering both plunder and legitimacy. Twice, Igor launched raids on the City, in 941 and 943. The former was a clear defeat, thanks to Greek naval superiority. Liutprand of Cremona, an ambassador to the Byzantine court, claimed that Igor had gathered a thousand ships – which by chronicle convention really just means a large number – but the City had been forewarned by both the Bulgars and Greek agents. Besides, instead of striking directly at Constantinople, the Rus' had tarried to ravage and plunder ports and villages along the Black Sea coast of Asia Minor, allowing the Greeks to mass their fleet to meet them at sea, at the entrance to the Bosporus. The Greek triremes and dromons were larger than the Rus' raiders', but far fewer. However, they could rely on Greek Fire, which devastated the attackers – in the words of a Russian chronicler, 'It was as if the Greeks held heavenly lightning and, releasing it, burned us.' With his much-reduced forces, Igor launched a few more and largely unsuccessful raids on Byzantine holdings around the Black Sea, but then returned home to lick his wounds and learn his lessons.

As a result, in 943 (some chronicles say 944), Igor had mustered a new army from the Rus', dependent Slav tribes and Pecheneg mercenaries, and this time launched a two-pronged attack. His cavalry he led overland, while the bulk of the army moved by sea. Fearing the lasting damage that could be done to their defences by an assault which could not be countered by its navy, the City chose instead to buy Igor off. As his army prepared to cross the Danube, in what is now Romania, it was met by a Greek delegation offering rich tribute and even richer words of friendship. Igor accepted both: being treated as an equal by the Emperor of Constantinople was legitimacy, in many ways just as important a prize for the son of an adventurer as any amount of gold, silver, silks and spices. This also led to a new treaty, in 945. Kiev undertook to support Constantinople in war, and not only to waive any territorial claims to the Greek colony of Korsun on the Crimean Peninsula, but also to defend it against raids by the Bulgars, in return for limited Greek guarantees. More to the point, it represented a further acknowledgement that Kiev and the Rus' were now a serious power in the Black Sea and even the eastern Mediterranean.

From Constantinople's point of view, buying Igor off had made sense. It had too many dependencies and trading stations that were vulnerable to raids by the Rus', too much territory for its overstretched armies to control. It could hope to deliver a powerful blow against raiders with the good manners and bad sense to present themselves for a pitched battle, but could not afford to divert the forces for a devastating counter-strike. The irony is, this is exactly the strategic dilemma the Rus' faced in their wars with the horsepeople, and they would in due course turn to the Greeks for lessons in how to respond.

THE PECHENEG THREAT

After Igor's death at the hands of the Drevlians, he was succeeded by his son Svyatoslav. He was a warrior-prince, happy to let his mother Olga handle the humdrum affairs of state, and he died as he lived, sword in hand. He fought a war against the Greeks over Bulgaria, which he ultimately lost, and against the Khazars over the city of Šarkel that had so exercised Askold and Dir, which he won. Combative by nature, in 972, he met his end fighting the latest nomads coming from the steppe: the Pechenegs. His skull ended up as a gold-encrusted cup for one of their khans, Kurya. The Pechenegs, after all, were a rather more serious challenge. A confederation of Turkic tribes, they had been forced to migrate from their ancestral lands in Central Asia by pressure from even more powerful rivals. They moved westward, first settling between the Ural and Volga Rivers in the ninth century and raiding the more settled Khazars and hiring themselves out to the Byzantines. However, they were then forced into a new migration when the Khazar Khaganate and its allies, the Uzes, struck back. The Pechenegs continued to move westward, and by the tenth century had found new territories in the steppe lands along the Donets and Kuban Rivers and the Crimean Peninsula, in turn displacing the Magyars into what is now Hungary.

A semi-nomadic people, the Pechenegs had an economy still heavily based on raiding and hiring themselves out as mercenaries. They were now neighbours of the Rus', and from 915, the *Primary Chronicle* began noting Pecheneg raids, and thereafter lists a growing number of attacks and demands for tribute. This was nothing personal, and Pechenegs would also quite gladly fight for the Rus' when the opportunity arose and the price was right. Even just a year before Svyatoslav's death, for example, a contingent of Pecheneg horsemen had been serving alongside him during his Bulgarian campaign.

Ultimately, though, the Pechenegs posed the greatest threat yet to the Rus' in general, but Kiev in particular. Their raids were driving Slav settlers out of lands around the Dnieper they had been colonizing, but more to the point, they were beginning to deny that mighty river to Kiev. The semi-nomadic Pechenegs had taken the river valley as their summer grazing and hunting grounds, but to the Rus', the river was a crucial trade route. Almost 300 miles south-east of Kiev, the river goes through nine great cataracts, where its fast-flowing waters thunder over a series of granite ridges. Most of the year, these are impassable, so merchants and travellers had to drag their boats onto the bank and carry them overland. At these times, they were easy prey for the rapid and ruthless raids the Pechenegs favoured. Bit by bit, the Pechenegs were strangling the river road that gave Kiev so much of its wealth and importance, and which paid for the military might of its princes. Without that, even its capacity to exact tribute from the tribes and cities might be in doubt.

In keeping with the practice of the times, Svyatoslav had assigned each of his three sons their own realm. His eldest, Yaropolk, stayed in Kiev; his second son, Oleg, was granted the lands of the Drevlians; and the youngest, the illegitimate Vladimir, was sent north to be Prince of Novgorod. The practice of the time was, to put it bluntly, often a recipe for fratricidal violence. After Svyatoslav's death, Yaropolk turned against Oleg – or else Oleg turned against Yaropolk, as each chronicle has its own loyalty – and after the middle brother was dead, Kiev's forces turned on Novgorod. Vladimir fled but returned in 980 with an army of Varangian mercenaries and took Kiev and killed Yaropolk, thanks to a combination of clever strategy and treachery, suborning his brother's closest adviser. Svyatoslav had been a warrior, Yaropolk a schemer, and in Vladimir, Kiev now had a prince who was both.

VLADIMIR THE GREAT

Vladimir, who would become known as Vladimir I, Vladimir the Great or, to the Orthodox Church, as St Basil thanks to his decision to embrace Christianity, was a state-builder. He recognized the Pecheneg threat, and that as long as they had the advantage of strategic mobility, all the Rus' could do was defend to the best of their ability while their enemies chose when and where to fight. He needed a new style of war, one based on static positions able to provide advance warning of attacks and corral raiders into locations favourable to the defence, and on taking fuller advantage of the numerical and technological opportunities available to him. In other words, in his own way, he had to use the tactics the Greeks had used against the Rus'.

To this end – albeit as part of a wider strategy of consolidating not just the position of the Rus' but of Kiev as its first city – Vladimir turned to the Greeks. Most strikingly, he converted to Christianity and forced his lords and subjects to follow suit, at spearpoint if necessary. In 988, the great wooden idols of pagan deities that Vladimir had had built a few years earlier were toppled from their hilltop temple and Kiev's population baptized en masse in the Dnieper. There are the usual colourful legends as to why he decided on this dramatic move, but it represented shrewd politics. Growing numbers of his boyars, his aristocrats, had already been converting; a closer alliance with the City would only strengthen his status; and he wanted freer access to Greek military technology. Meanwhile, Byzantine Emperor Basil II was in a weak position, desperate for allies as he struggled with rivals at home. Vladimir was baptized at Chersonesos in Crimea – a fact that, 11 centuries later, would become part of Moscow's pretext to annex the peninsula – and married Anna, Basil's sister.

Vladimir's reign would be one of periodic warfare, as he conquered more tribes, such as the Slavic Vyatichi and the Balto-Lithuanian Yatvingians, and forced a peace on the Volga Bulgars. However, he was especially effective in holding back the Pechenegs, as will be discussed in more detail in chapter 5. This would be a long-term campaign. In 996, he lost his only battle against the Pechenegs, at Vasilyev, and the next year the nomads even briefly besieged Kiev. Nonetheless, he fortified his lands against them, using slave labour and Greek know-how, especially in producing unfired bricks with which to reinforce traditional wooden walls. Kiev was secured by the sweeping Snake Ramparts, more than 500 miles of earthworks topped by wooden defensive walls: a bastion was built at Pereyaslavl overlooking the Dnieper, and a chain of fortified harbours provided refuges for river traffic.

Vladimir was the Grand Prince of Kiev, but what did this mean in practice? For most of his 37 years in power, he was unchallenged, but in part that was because he knew not just how to rule, but when not to rule. Kiev was on the rise, but the writ of the Grand Prince was still limited by deep forests and poor communications. He appointed his sons and closest cronies as princes and governors of the cities of the Rus', and they moved from one position to another as need, circumstance and intrigue dictated. Given how Vladimir came to power, though, one could argue that he should not have put much faith in family ties, but realistically, what alternative did he have? As Vladimir aged, his sons began to jostle for power. His son Yaroslav the Wise, who had been granted the city of Rostov and then Novgorod, was the first to challenge his father, withholding tribute in 1014. Vladimir began to muster his armies but died before he could reimpose his control. This triggered a wider fratricidal melee. Kiev would be taken first by Svyatopolk, Prince of Turov, then Yaroslav. Increasingly, princes had to hire foreign mercenaries to supplement over-committed Rus' warriors: Svyatopolk turned to Poles from the west and Pechenegs from the east, while Yaroslav hired Varangians from the north. Yaroslav would win, but a precedent had been set: power went not to the legitimate but to the strongest. Those who could not take Kiev looked to other spoils. Briacheslav of Polotsk harboured designs on wealthy Novgorod, while Mstislav, Prince of Tmutarakan, a trading town on the Bosporus captured from the Khazars, made himself also Prince of Chernigov, when his own bid to take Kiev failed, and once he had fought off an expedition of Yaroslav's, he ruled his own domain as an effectively independent monarch.

THE PRINCELY WARS

Nonetheless, Yaroslav's reign, after its bloody beginning, proved successful. His raid on Constantinople in 1043, almost a rite of passage for a Grand Prince of Kiev, was a failure, but he was still able to secure a new treaty with the City. He pushed back Polish incursions and made conquests of his own along the Baltic coast, establishing the new fort of Yuriev in what is now Estonia. The Pechenegs were able to besiege Kiev in 1036, but Yaroslav broke them in battle with the assistance of forces from Novgorod, and this would be the last time they posed a serious threat to the Rus'. Pressed by other nomads from the east, the Cumans and the Tork, the bulk of the Pechenegs migrated further west to the Danube river valley, and after a crushing defeat at the hands of an alliance of Greeks and Cumans in the Battle of Levounion, 1091, they largely disappeared from history, becoming assimilated into other peoples.

Internecine wars gave way to peace and plenty, with trade flowing along the river roads, the cities growing, and Kiev beginning to rival even Constantinople in its splendour. None of the underlying challenges of the Rus' had been addressed, though. There was still no accepted system of succession, cities were treated as appanages, possessions to be gifted and traded, and while the Grand Prince of Kiev was accepted as the patriarch of the Ryurikid dynasty, in practice his power rested on his ability either to command the forces of other princes or to accept the costs and dangers of hiring foreign mercenaries. The Rus' lands were forever being washed back and forth between the forces of centralization and fragmentation, as a powerful Grand Prince began tightening his grip on the cities, only for them to break apart when circumstances allowed, especially as until the middle of the 12th century, a prince's lands would almost invariably be divided among his heirs on his death.

Thus, Yaroslav's death in 1054 prompted another violent power struggle (one of the contenders, who briefly held the throne of Kiev, was Vseslav Bryachislavich, who was immortalized in folklore as a werewolf) that was eventually resolved by the rise of another, longer-reigning Grand Prince, Vsevolod Yaroslavich, the first to style himself 'Prince of All Russia'. Despite a conference of princes in 1097 at Lyubech, meant to regularize succession, the next century and a half essentially followed a similar pattern – episodes of peace alternating with vicious struggles, more often among the Rus' than against foreign foes. Yet all the same, this was a time of growth. Kiev, for all that it was occasionally sacked, was always rebuilt, more splendidly than before, earning itself the soubriquet 'the Golden'. Novgorod opened new trade routes into Siberia to the east and the Baltic to the west, growing rich on trade in furs, silver and amber. The principality of Vladimir-Suzdal was in regular contention with the Volga Bulgars, but largely coming out on top, gaining loot and new lands.

Although new nomadic tribes emerged as a threat to the east – the Cumans and the Kipchaks, whom the Rus' lumped together as Polovtsians – they largely proved manageable, for all that they had been able to sack Kiev in 1096. Indeed, the Rus' learned many lessons from them, increasingly supplementing their heavier cavalry with horse archers and light raiders in the nomad style. Over time, the distinct identity of the tribes would diminish and a common Rus' culture become increasingly dominant. Furthermore, burgeoning trade saw the cities grow and with it the revenues to allow the *druzhinas* and militias alike to be larger and better equipped. However, the expansion of the Rus' lands would also, in due course, become a problem, as it brought them increasingly into collision not just with more powerful enemies in Northern Europe but also a new and more ruthless threat – wars driven not by hunger for land or loot, but the fanatical fires of crusade.

Want To Know More?

Fortunately, Simon Franklin and Jonathan Shepard's *The Emergence of Rus 750–1200* (Longman, 1996) can be supplemented with Janet Martin's excellent *Medieval Russia, 980–1584* (Cambridge University Press, 2007). *The Ruling Families of Rus: Clan, Family and Kingdom* (Reaktion, 2023) by Christian Raffensperger and Donald Ostrowski is a good, recent academic study. I cannot overlook some of the very accessible short illustrated studies from Osprey, such as David Nicolle's *Armies of Medieval Russia 750–1250* (Osprey, 1999) and Konstantin Nossov's *Medieval Russian Fortresses AD 862–1480* (Osprey, 2007). There is a Soviet-era film *Legenda o knyagine Olge* (1984), *The Legend of Princess Olga*, but in all conscience, I can't recommend it…

3

The Northern Crusades

Lake Peipus, 1242

Sergei Eisenstein's black-and-white film *Alexander Nevsky* (1938) is brilliant for its time, a representation of the defeat of the crusading knights of the Teutonic Order in 1242 that uses an army of extras, clever photography and a rousing score by Prokofiev to present an allegory for the USSR's position of the day, as war with Nazi Germany loomed. The Teutonic Knights, terrifying in their ruthlessness and discipline, are finally broken by the patriotism and spirit of the Rus', plunging to their deaths beneath the breaking ice of a frozen Lake Peipus. The unsubtle closing warning is that 'whomever comes to us with the sword, will die by the sword'. As cinematography, it is trail-blazing; as propaganda, it is superb; as history, it is distinctly dubious, not least as while there was a battle on a frozen lake (or more accurately, frozen swamps), there was in fact no mass descent into its icy depths.

Nonetheless, the film does convey just how shocking and, for a while, perilous the advent of crusaders from Europe would be to the Rus' of the north-west, especially Novgorod. They had fought many wars against Scandinavians and Lithuanians, but in the 13th century, these would be overshadowed by the arrival of the Order of the Sword and the Teutonic Knights. These fighting Orders were not only determined to wipe out Russian paganism and (as they saw it) schismatic Orthodox Christianity alike, but they had also monetized the Northern Crusades as a kind of chivalric package holiday industry, with knights from across Europe flocking to their Baltic strongholds and paying them for the opportunity to raid and war and feast.

The Baltic Sea was a cradle of trade and piracy as much as politics and conquest, with the Scandinavians leading the way. Over time, they would be challenged by Novgorodian and North German merchants, with ports such as Lübeck, Hamburg, Rostock, Gdańsk (Danzig) and Riga eventually forming the mercantile alliance known as the Hanseatic League. Although the Germans would come to dominate Baltic trade, the entrepreneurial Novgorodians were still significant players, and the neighbourhood the city set aside for foreigners was even known as the German Quarter. Novgorod was enriched by these connections not just economically, but also through political and cultural connections. German traders and colonists would push eastwards along the Baltic coastline, though, clustering in cities such as Riga, Reval (later Talinn) and Dorpat (Tartu). Faith, respective imperial designs over the scattered Baltic tribes, and economic competition would all ensure that conflict was inevitable.

THE NORTHERN CRUSADES

The most serious tensions were between the Catholic settlers, merchants and conquerors moving into the eastern Baltic coastal lands and the remaining pagan tribes there such as the Prussians, Livs and Estonians, as well as the powerful Grand Duchy of Lithuania (which remained predominantly pagan until the 14th century). At the Council of Clermont in 1095, Pope Urban II called for support for the Byzantines in their struggles against the Arabs, and an armed pilgrimage for the liberation of the Holy Land from the Muslims. This sparked centuries of periodic crusading zeal, driven by political calculation, economic opportunity, religious faith and personal ego. Kings, knights and knaves alike were promised spiritual salvation in return for martial commitment, and whole new crusading institutions – above all the military-religious Orders – emerged from this movement. The most famous of these crusades are, of course, those waged in the Holy Land, but there were also pagans in north-eastern Europe, in what are now Finland, Poland, Latvia, Lithuania, Estonia and Russia. Furthermore, there was land to be seized, labour to be forced, loot, glory and divine forgiveness to be won. By the mid-12th century, holy war had come to Northern Europe. There had long been conflicts between the pagan Finns, Balts and Slavs and their Christian Danish and Saxon neighbours, but now they were embittered and enlarged by a clear religious dimension, one that sanctioned the most brutal treatment of the pagans and also brought the Christians new allies, not least the chivalric (if often not very chivalrous) crusading Orders.

In 1147, St Bernard of Clairvaux, the fiery abbot who had also co-founded the Order of the Knights Templar, turned his fervour against the pagan Wends of north-eastern Germany, warning that 'we prohibit completely that a truce be made for any reason with these people either for money or tribute, until such time as, with the aid of God, either their religion or their nation shall be destroyed.' The result was a violent expedition that killed more than it converted, yet which arguably set the Northern Crusades in motion. The Swedes launched a crusade against the Finns in the 1150s, later joined by the Danes. Yet the main targets were the peoples of the Baltic coastline: the Old Prussians, Curonians, Latgalians, Lithuanians, Semigallians and others.

Crusading Orders arose: the Livonian Brothers of the Sword (1202) and the Order of Dobrzyń (1228), both of which would in due course be subsumed within the much larger Order of Brothers of the German House of Saint Mary in Jerusalem, better known as the Teutonic Knights. In 1230, Grand Master Hermann von Salza, in alliance with Duke Konrad I of Masovia, launched a crusade into the Prussian lands, kicking off 50 years of brutal conquest, forced Christianization and vicious guerrilla warfare. Nonetheless, the knights were successful, and the new lands formed the basis of their own autonomous state, the Ordensstaat. Over time, the Order pushed further east, even taking territory claimed by the Catholic King of Poland, and crusading became not just a religious duty but a lucrative business. In particular, they developed a novel model of what could be called 'crusade tourism', whereby knights eager for the intangible benefits of crusade – glory and a pardon for their sins – yet unwilling to accept the risk, expense and long journeys associated with an expedition to the Holy Land, could instead come to the Ordensstaat. There, for a generous fee, they could feast and joust in the Order's fortresses, until it was time for a *reyse*, a raid into pagan lands. After a few weeks on campaign, burning villages and battling unbelievers, they could return home, their souls duly cleansed, while the Order had the advantage of additional experienced fighters, who actually paid for the privilege of supporting its wars of expansion and conversion.

The Grand Duchy of Lithuania proved to be an enemy it could batter but never beat, but otherwise the Teutonic Order was also to extend its grip from Thorn (later Torun) in Poland through to Estonia to the east. This brought it to within 50 miles of the Rus' cities of Pskov and Polotsk, and while they were Christian lands, they were Orthodox, not Catholic. To the Teutonic Order, an institution founded on faith yet propelled by conquest, a schismatic was as good as a pagan.

PEREGRINUS EXPECTAVI

Novgorod was hardly the only principality with connections to the Baltic region, and given that it was largely interested in commerce rather than territorial expansion to the west, there were fewer of the kind of feuds and bad blood which often triggered violence. If anything, tribes in Latvia in particular became virtual clients. The principality of Polotsk, formed on the basis of the Slav Krivichi tribe, developed a close relationship with other tribes, such as the Yersik, Livs and Koknese, not least in the name of avoiding raids on its trade routes, while Pskov cultivated the Latgallian counties of Adzele and Tālava.

They were, as a result, hardly unaware of the steady eastwards advance of the crusaders, colonists and feudal lords right behind them, a territorial spread anchored on new forts and castles, garrisoned by knights and levies. Riga was founded in 1201 on the back of conquest and forced Christianization, a fortified bishopric and the home of the Order of the Brothers of the Sword. Reval was seized by Danish invaders in 1219, and later ceded to the Sword Brothers. Although Old Prussia was harder to crack, there too the crusaders would eventually win through, and the Teutonic Knights would build their great strongholds of Memel and Königsberg.

The first clashes were political and economic. Tālava renounced its links to Pskov in 1208, and Adzele would be conquered in subsequent military campaigns. In 1212, according to the *Livonian Chronicle of Henry*, after prolonged negotiations, the 'king' of Polotsk, 'perhaps by God's inspiration, freely gave the whole of Livonia to the bishop, so that eternal peace would be strengthened between them, both against the Lithuanians and against other pagans, and so a free path along the Dvina would always be open to merchants.' God's inspiration was probably helped by the fact that the clergyman in question was Albert von Buxhoeveden, the ruthless, zealous and indefatigable prince-bishop of the Sword Brothers, who had arrived to the parley at the head of an armed host. Polotsk abandoned any claims to disputed regions, along with tribute from the Livs and, more to the point, granted exemption from duties to German trade down the Dvina River that it controlled.

While the crusaders were happy to treat the Russians as fellow Christians when it was to their advantage, it soon became clear that they were not willing to end their mission there and then. In 1224, the Estonian town of Yuriev, a dependency of Novgorod, was conquered by the Sword Brothers, despite the 200-strong Novgorodian contingent supporting the defenders. It was renamed Dorpat, and made into the base of a new bishopric. By this time, the Rus' increasingly realized that the crusaders, whether Germans, Swedes or Danes, were coming for them. However, they bickered, while in 1229 Pope Gregory IX urged all good Catholics to unite to bring the true faith to the Rus'. He initiated a trade blockade (sanctions are nothing new for the Russians, it appears), and his representatives, and especially William of Modena, began working on pulling together a crusading alliance between Germans, Danes, Swedes and the Orders. In 1237, the Order of the Brothers of the Sword, which had just suffered a terrible defeat at the hands of the pagan Samogitians and Semigallians, was folded into the Teutonic Order. In 1238, Danish King Valdemar II and Hermann von Balk, Grand Master of the Teutonic Order, finally resolved long-standing disputes with the division of conquered Estonia. It was clear that the Rus' were next, but they were in no state to do anything but wait for the Catholics to initiate hostilities.

Meanwhile, troubles had flared up between Novgorod and the various Finnish tribes, whom they called the Yem. To a degree, this was less about Novgorod's own ambitions as those of its allies and subject tribes in the regions, such as the Izhorians, Korela and Votes. Nonetheless, these led to vicious raids back and forth, in which the Novgorodians often felt compelled to support their subjects. The first serious clash between Novgorod and the Finns had been in 1123, and thereafter further raids followed, especially when famine was gripping the tribes.

The Finns were both pagans and divided, which made them fair game also to the Swedes. The year 1150 saw the launch of what some call the First Swedish Crusade, taking advantage of the Finns' weakness after defeat the year before at the hands of the Rus'. The Swedes, after all, saw Novgorod as a serious potential rival and were happy to wrap geopolitics in the mantle of crusade. In 1171, Pope Alexander III – probably at their instigation – encouraged the Swedes to expand their control over the Finns by offering them protection from the Rus'. Swedish influence and Christianity slowly spread among the Finns, who continued to be squeezed between these two greater powers. A campaign of conquest launched by Grand Prince Yaroslav II of Vladimir in 1226 was arguably a Pyrrhic victory, as the Swedes took advantage of this to move into Finland, presenting themselves as the least-worst option. No wonder that, in 1240, Finns were part of the Swedish army that launched a raid down the Neva River into Novgorodian lands. Even allowing for the hyperbole of the *Novgorod First Chronicle*, which presented what was likely more of a raid in force as an epic struggle, the invaders were trounced when a force of Novgorodians supported by local Rus' from around Ladoga launched an amphibious surprise attack on their encampment at the mouth of the Izhora River. The chronicle claimed that they suffered terrible losses: 'And many of them fell; they filled two ships with the corpses of the best men, and sent them ahead of them to the sea, and for the rest they dug a hole and threw them in there without number.' Likely exaggeration aside, it was an early example of the successful generalship of the 20-year-old Prince Alexander Yaroslavich of Novgorod, who as a result became known as Alexander of the Neva: Alexander Nevsky.

THE RUSSIAN CAMPAIGN

Nevsky's real test would come two years later, when the Teutonic Knights launched a much more serious offensive, not a raid but a crusade intent on conquest, with Novgorod itself as their target. First, in 1237, they sent an embassy under Andreas von Felben, Landmeister or local commander of the Livonian Order, the Baltic branch of the Teutonic Knights. His ostensible mission was to explore the possibility of a joint expedition against the pagan Lithuanians and also to ascertain whether the Novgorodians were inclined to continue to help the remaining free Estonians in their resistance to the crusade. However, he was also there – like any good ambassador – to gather whatever actionable intelligence he could. When he heard about a new threat to the Rus' from the east, the invading Mongol army of Batu Khan, grandson of Genghis Khan and lord of the Golden Horde, which had crashed into the eastern frontiers of the Rus' in 1237, it was clear that this posed an opportunity for the Order, as Novgorod could not count on support from the other principalities.

This certainly seems to have prompted the Swedes to make their ill-fated attack in 1240. The Order, though, had been preparing for some time and was characteristically methodical. In particular, they had been cultivating Prince Yaroslav Vladimirovich, an ambitious claimant to Pskov. His father, Prince Vladimir Mstislavich, had ruled Pskov until 1222, technically as a dependency of Novgorod. Nonetheless, Vladimir had schemed to remove himself from Novgorod's control by leveraging Pskov's border position. In a particularly audacious move, he had married off his daughter to the brother of the bishop of Riga, and Yaroslav to a German Catholic. The Livonians had already been encroaching onto Pskov's territory, taking the fort at Otepää in southern Estonia in 1225, but when Vladimir Mstislavich died in 1227, the principality became the focus for a new political struggle between Novgorod, which hoped to bring it back under its control, and Yaroslav, who laid claim to its throne.

The boyars of Pskov favoured him, reasoning that he would not only keep Novgorod at bay, but his good relations with the Catholics might mitigate the Livonian threat. Yaroslav's accession did nothing to alleviate the pressure from Novgorod's Prince Yaroslav Vsevolodovich, but this only drove Pskov closer to the Catholics. Nonetheless, Novgorod and the powerful Vladimir-Suzdal dynasty, from whence came Yaroslav Vsevolodovich, would not be denied. In 1232, Yaroslav Vladimirovich was forced to flee to Otepää along with his supporters, begging sanctuary from his Catholic relatives. Pskov was placed under a Novgorodian governor, Prince Yuri Mstislavich, and its erstwhile prince was forced to become little more than a proxy for the Teutonic Knights.

In 1233, Yaroslav Vladimirovich tried to kick-start a return to Pskov with an assault on the border town of Izborsk, anticipating that it would welcome him. However, as his loyalists were leavened by Livonians, it closed its gates to him, and the pretender was captured when his troops were trapped between its walls and a relief force from Pskov. Yaroslav Vladimirovich was eventually ransomed in 1235, and forced to pledge Pskov to Hermann von Buxhoeveden, brother of Albert. From then, his remaining Pskov loyalists would find themselves fighting and dying in crusading campaigns in Lithuania, and his next campaign to regain power in his home city was a thinly disguised Livonian land grab.

In September 1240, notionally at the head of an army that was really a Livonian one in all but name, Yaroslav Vladimirovich finally took Izborsk and then invested Pskov. This fell after a week's siege; the chronicles suggest that this was because of treachery, that the Pskov *posadnik* (mayor) opened the gates, as Yaroslav Vladimirovich persuaded faint-hearts and his remaining supporters in the city to let his forces in. He was duly approved by the Pskov *veche* – which we may suppose convened at the point of Livonian swords – and he had regained the throne of Pskov, but as a vassal of the Bishopric of Dorpat.

This was, though, only seen as the first stage in a wider operation, with Novgorod as its ultimate target. In 1241, the Livonians built a castle at Koporye, close to the Baltic coast, as a supply station for their operations, and moved up the Luga River towards Novgorod, taking the town of Tesovo and waging economic war, intercepting Novgorodian merchants sailing down towards the Gulf of Finland and raiding villages which paid the city tribute. Novgorod prepared for war. Uniquely among Russian cities, power in this mercantile centre was vested largely not in its prince but in the *veche* and elected *posadnik*: princes were not so much rulers as military commanders, engaged by the *veche* when their services were needed. Alexander Nevsky's exploits against the Swedes had, ironically enough, made him too popular in the city for the merchant magnates' comfort, so they had dispensed with his services. Suddenly, they realized they needed a serious war leader, and a panicked delegation petitioned their former prince, Yaroslav Vsevolodovich, to come save them. By then, he had become Grand Prince of Vladimir and was disinclined to get involved. First, he proposed his 19-year-old son Andrei, but then Andrei's elder brother, Alexander, agreed to return to Novgorod. Was it pity, duty, a sense of the political opportunity this offered, or just a chance to rub the noses of the burghers who had sacked him a year earlier into how they now needed him? The chronicles don't say, but it may well have been a mix of all four.

THE BATTLE OF LAKE PEIPUS, 1242

So Alexander returned to Novgorod and, in characteristic style, moved onto the offensive. In late 1241, his forces took the Livonian supply base of Koporye, and in early 1242 they began to harry the Estonian territories of the Bishopric of Dorpat. This last was somewhat overambitious, and would begin to meet fiercer resistance from Chud – Estonian – tribal warbands and Livonian forces. At the beginning of April, the field commander behind them, Domash Tverdislavich, commander of the Novgorod militia, was ambushed during one such raid and killed. However, this element of the campaign may well have been intended simply to distract the Teutons, as in March, Alexander struck at Pskov. With the support of many within the city, who had grown disenchanted with Yaroslav Vladimirovich and his Livonian overlords, he was able quickly to retake it, overwhelming the small force of Teutonic Knights left as garrison without reinforcements.

Alexander then began advancing in support of the raiders, but when he received news of the approach of the main crusader army, he withdrew across the deep-frozen marches around Lake Peipus, north of Pskov, where the climactic battle took place. Although numbers are inevitably estimates, Alexander's forces outnumbered the crusaders by a margin of almost two-to-one. However, the bulk of his forces were militia from Novgorod, Suzdal and Pskov, or local Finno-Ugrian tribesmen. He had perhaps a thousand seasoned fighting men from the various *druzhinas*, as well as several hundred Turkic horse archers, mercenaries drawn from the nomad tribes. Against them was a force of around a thousand Chud warriors, an equal number of seasoned Danish and German knights and soldiers, and a hundred elite Teutonic Knights.

The two armies met on the morning of 5 April 1242. At first, the crusaders marched north across the lake in the hope of flanking Nevsky's forces, but the Russians proved more mobile, and formed up at the narrowest crossing point across the lake, overlooked by the promontory known as Raven's Rock. True to form, the crusaders moved into the attack, relying on the sheer weight of a wedge of chivalric cavalry to carry the day. The Teutonic Knights under von Felben formed the vanguard, supported by Danish knights to their left and German knights under Prince-Bishop Hermann von Buxhoeveden on their right. The Chud warriors – who, arguably, had much more experience of fighting in such conditions – were left with the rest of the infantry as a reserve to the rear.

Against them, Alexander broke with tradition and put only around a third of his force in the centre of his battleline, largely seasoned *druzhina* infantry from Novgorod, with stronger forces to the wings, especially to the right, where he concentrated cavalry and horse archers, including Suzdalian forces under his brother Andrei. Predictably, the crusader charge smashed through the screen of horse archers in front of the main Rus' line and into that central force, 'like a wild boar', in the words of the *Novgorod Primary Chronicle*. However, the Novgorodian infantry were able to put up enough resistance to blunt the charge. Instead of being able to break the Russians and cut them down as they fled, the crusaders were embroiled in hard close-quarters fighting. This meant that Alexander could swing his flanking forces round to engage the knights. The scrum on the ice was as bitter as it was exhausting, and although the knights tried to withdraw in good order and re-form with their infantry, the arrival of Russian cavalry on their flank, as well as the unfamiliar experience of clouds of arrows fired by horse archers, turned this into a rout.

The Livonian Order's own *Livonian Rhymed Chronicle* makes passing references to some knights, while being pursued, venturing onto thin ice and falling through it, but the cinematic image of an army disappearing beneath the frigid waters is wholly mythical. As it was, the defeat was serious enough. Hundreds of Chuds died when the crusader army broke, and the same is true for the German and Danish knights and levies. The Teutonic Order's records suggest fully 70 brother-knights died and six were taken prisoner, although this likely includes the 20 or so who fell or were taken at Pskov. Even so, 56 out of 100 or even 150 was a catastrophic loss, reflecting their place in the van. The *Livonian Rhymed Chronicle*, written almost a century later, tried to save the Order's face with the hyperbolic claim that 'the Russians had so many troops that there were easily sixty men for every one German knight', but even so, it had suffered a blow from which it would take a generation to recover."

The crusade against Novgorod was over. The Order would conclude a treaty with the city, ceding all territories it had taken in this campaign, and there were continued further clashes, but the real threat from the West would in due course become a Christianized Lithuania. The Teutonic Knights' expansion to the east was ended, and the border between Western Catholicism and Eastern Orthodoxy was essentially drawn. This had also demonstrated the diverging styles of war between East and West. The armies of feudal Europe would for centuries be dominated by the knight, a highly trained and heavily armoured representative of a military aristocracy, suited by temperament and tactics alike to the smashing blow of the charge. Their infantry were, with some conspicuous exceptions, largely unskilled levies, there to support the knights and mop up in their wake. However, the armies of the Rus', while acquiring some of the military art and technologies of Europe, were also deeply influenced by their constant struggles with the horse nomads of the East. It was not simply that Alexander fielded mercenary horse archers from their number. It was also that the armies of the Rus', accustomed to operating across large distances, lacking the tax base of their Western counterparts, and needing to be able to counter the highly mobile nomads, relied more on lighter cavalry and heavier infantry. The cavalry could, some of the time, meet the nomads in the field on equal terms, while blocks of armoured infantry, bristling with spears, could limit their room for manoeuvre.

This time, they had proven up to the challenge of fighting off an enemy from beyond the border, but while Nevsky was winning in the north-west, the Rus' were losing against another foe that would prove vastly more dangerous, and that would impose its will upon them for the next two centuries: the Mongols. At the start of Eisenstein's film, Alexander Nevsky is approached by an emissary of the Mongol Golden Horde, who offers him a high position because of his fame and martial prowess. In the film, he refuses. In reality, while Nevsky may have vanquished the Swedes and the Finns, the Germans and the Danes, he would be forced to bend the knee to the Great Khan.

Livonian Rhymed Chronicle, quoted in David Nicolle, *Lake Peipus 1242* (Osprey, 1996), p. 75

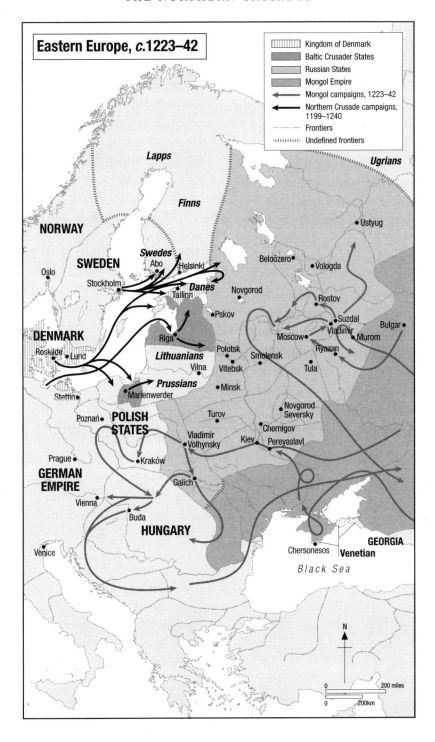

Eastern Europe, *c.*1223–42

Kingdom of Denmark
Baltic Crusader States
Russian States
Mongol Empire
Mongol campaigns, 1223–42
Northern Crusade campaigns, 1199–1240
Frontiers
Undefined frontiers

Lapps

Ugrians

Finns

NORWAY

Swedes
Abo
Helsinki
Beloôzero
Vologda
Ustyug

SWEDEN

Oslo

Stockholm
Danes
Tallinn
Novgorod
Rostov

Pskov
Suzdal
Bulgar

Moscow
Vladimir
Murom

DENMARK
Riga
Polotsk
Smolensk
Ryazan

Roskilde
Lund
Lithuanians
Vilna
Vitebsk
Tula

Stettin
Prussians
Marienwerder
Minsk

Poznań
POLISH
STATES
Turov
Novgorod
Seversky

Prague
Vladimir
Volhynsky
Kiev
Chernigov
Pereyaslavl

GERMAN
EMPIRE
Kraków
Galich

Vienna

Buda
HUNGARY

GEORGIA

Venice
Chersonesos
Venetian

Black Sea

N

0   200 miles
0   200km

Want To Know More?

The best work on the Baltic Crusade is Erich Christensen's *The Northern Crusades, 2nd edition* (Penguin, 1997), although William Urban's *The Teutonic Knights: A Military History* (Greenhill, 2002) is also a must-read. My own *Teutonic Knight vs Lithuanian Warrior: The Lithuanian Crusade 1283–1435* (Osprey, 2023) digs into aspects of the earlier struggle, while David Nicolle's *Lake Peipus 1242* (Osprey, 1996) is an excellent exegesis of the battle itself. A rather different kind of source is the board wargame *Nevsky: Teutons and Rus in Collision 1240–1242* (GMT, 2020), a lovingly and sometimes painfully detailed exploration of feudal warfare at the time.

4

The Steppe Threat

Suten River, 1103

The VDNKh, the Exhibition of Achievements of the National Economy, is a kind of Soviet and now Russian patriotic theme park and trade centre. Once, it had pavilions for each of the constituent republics of the USSR, from Armenia to Uzbekistan, as well as others devoted to everything from radio-electronic engineering to the space programme. The Soviet Union may be gone, but Vera Mukhina's 25-metre-high stainless-steel statue, *Worker and Collective Farm Woman*, still towers near the entrance, his hammer and her sickle in perpetual, proletarian synchronicity, and a representation of Lenin still stands before the main pavilion. Neglected and shabby in the 1990s and 2000s, it has been thoroughly refurbished, but increasingly with a Putin-era nationalist twist. It acquired eventually a 'Donbas' exhibition after the start of the undeclared war in south-eastern Ukraine in 2014 that included luridly lit recreations of schools allegedly shelled by Kyiv's forces, but most striking is the *Rossiya – moya istoriya*, or 'Russia – My History' pavilion. This offers a superficial but also engaging account of the emergence of the nation, as suits Putin's narrative. It not only presents the country as facing constant threats, from east, west, north and south, but also hammers home the line that in the face of such challenges, Russians should set aside their differences and unite behind a strong leader (a cynic might suggest that Putin is proposing himself). Why? Because a disunited Russia is a weak Russia, and a weak Russia is – as Stalin himself so vividly put it – prey.

This point was made most starkly in the section of the exhibition devoted to the early Rus' and the challenge they faced from horse nomads from the East up to and including the Mongols (also called Tatars). Across a vividly coloured video map showing the various principalities of Russia was slapped the single word *Razdroblennost'* – Fragmentation. Just in case the message was not clear enough, as arrows showing the steppefolk incursions started to stab into the Russian lands, in the corner appeared in blocky type the words 'Undefended Against Foreign Attacks'.

This is, of course, history mobilized with more glitz than subtlety for political ends. After all, time and again, the Rus' had faced the onslaughts from the steppes, but time and again, they had found ways to fight, assimilate, divert or destroy them. Nonetheless, it is true that disunity left them especially vulnerable, and the irony is that the ultimate expression of that vulnerability – the devastating Mongol conquest that left Kiev a wasteland strewn with bones, Novgorod neutered, and most of the Rus' paying tribute to their new masters for two centuries – would also arguably be the greatest force unifying the new Russian nation, albeit it under Moscow, the rising collaborationist power. For 200 years, the Russians would be under progressively weakening Mongol control, exposed to new ways of rule and war. As Nevsky demonstrated, in many ways, the Russian way of war would be shaped by the collision between Western notions of chivalric heavy cavalry and fast-moving nomad tactics – and so too would the very foundations of its rule. Yet at the same time, for them to be able to deliver game-changing defeats to the nomads, such as the 1103 Battle of Suten River, where troops from a dozen different cities, flanked by horsefolk auxiliaries, began to break the power of the fearsome Polovtsian, they needed somehow to combat the fragmentation that was their perennial problem.

THE WAVES FROM THE EAST

The lands of the Rus' were doomed by geography to bear the brunt of successive waves of nomadic and semi-settled peoples from the steppes that sweep from Mongolia to Hungary, raiding, migrating or invading – these activities were often hard to distinguish from each other. It is easy to think of these incursions simply as disruptions, as wild men from beyond the pale of civilization shattered the sober endeavours of Europeans slowly building the modern world. While the conflicts that ensued were often bloody, though, they were as much engines of progress as anything else. Not only did they bring new ideas and technologies, from the stirrup to gunpowder, but according to archaeologist Warwick Ball in his wide-ranging *The Eurasian Steppe*, they even drove the early emergence of what would eventually become the nation-state. He argues that 'the incipient idea of a nation-state might have been stronger with the nomadic groups from the steppe, who were bound more closely by tribal loyalties' than peoples rooted in the soil, who might be divided by language, faith and culture, even while suffering under the same overlords. People who move need a better sense of self to keep their communities alive than people who have lived on the same patch of muddy earth for generations. Thus, the successive steppe invasions, culminating in Mongol conquest, provided both practical and philosophical reasons for an end to that fateful *razdroblennost'*.

In the ninth century, the Judeo-Turkish Khazar Khanate of the Black Sea steppe had been the main rival of the Rus' for control over the Volga River trade routes until Svyatoslav of Kiev sacked their capital Atil in 968. The Pechenegs then came to dominate a wide swathe of the south-east European steppe and the Crimean Peninsula, and their raids began to pose a serious threat to the north–south river trade with Constantinople, and thus represented an economic and political challenge above all to Kiev, which the Pechenegs besieged in 968. The result was a series of wars and counter-raids, but even compared with the fragmented principalities of the Rus', the Pechenegs were divided between and within their tribes, and do not seem to have adopted anything that could even generously be described as a strategy towards their enemies.

On the other hand, the princes of Kiev, understanding the threat they posed, would prove more methodical in their eventual response.

They would devote what were, for the time, considerable resources into building fortifications precisely to prevent the Pechenegs from exploiting their greatest advantage: their strategic mobility. It was not just that Kiev was rebuilt to withstand future nomad attacks; lines of walls, studded with watchtowers, such as the aforementioned Snake Ramparts, stretched across the lands south of the city to create a more secure heartland. Meanwhile, once again the pressures were building up behind the Pechenegs. Other steppe peoples – above all the Oghuz Turks and the Cumans – would attack them from the east. After defeats at the hands of Vladimir I and Yaroslav I, by the mid-tenth century, the Pechenegs had all but disappeared from history; many pushed further into Europe and assimilated into the local populations of Bulgaria and Romania, their name disappearing all but forgotten (until revived in 2001 for a new Russian machine gun).

THE POLOVTSIANS

The Cumans or Kipchaks, known as the Polovtsians to the Russians, were an even more formidable threat. Like their predecessors, this Turkic people comprised a federation of autonomous tribes under their own khans, rather than a single, unitary state, but they demonstrated particular skill and discipline in battle, and came to dominate the steppe from the Danube to the Irtysh River, far beyond the Ural Mountains. They settled in the lands north of the Black Sea and along the Volga, yet their authority also stretched to Crimea – where their language essentially became the peninsula's lingua franca – and all the way eastwards as far as the mighty Khwarezmian Empire of Central Asia. Inevitably, their expansion to the west brought them in contact with the Rus', but from the first this would be a complex relationship shaped by war but also involving much diplomacy and even mutual cultural and political interpenetration.

In 1055, the first Polovtsians reached Pereyaslavl, south-east of Kiev, a city ironically founded to mark a great victory over the Pechenegs. Prince Vsevolod was able to negotiate peace with his Polovtsian counterpart, Khan Bolush, but in part this was simply because they were outriders, not strong enough to take on a fortified city. That would soon change. In 1061, the Polovtsians attacked and sacked Pereyaslavl, the first in a series of raids in force that would also see the principalities of Chernigov and Novgorod-Siversk regularly ravaged, and whole villages enslaved. Initially, the Russians were at a loss, as the tactics they had developed against the Pechenegs proved rather less effective: the Polovtsians were, to be sure, also horse nomads, but their skill and their numbers were greater than those who had come before. At the Battle of the Alta River in 1068, the combined armies of Kiev, Chernigov and Pereyaslavl were so convincingly beaten by Khan Sharukan the Old that Grand Prince Izyaslav I of Kiev and Prince Vsevolod of Pereyaslavl fled back to Kiev and refused to engage with the invaders again, even as they raided the very outskirts of the city. The *veche* convened in its market square, both princes were roundly berated, and demands were made that if they and their *druzhinas* were not going to fight, they should at least arm those Kievans willing to defend the city. When they refused, an angry mob forced Izyaslav to flee to Poland and freed the rival prince Vseslav of Polotsk, whom he had had imprisoned for trying to usurp him, and declared him prince.

Vseslav proved no more willing to take the field against the Polovtsians, so it was just as well for Kiev that their attacks on villages around his city prompted Prince Svyatoslav of Chernigov to raise a new army and convincingly defeat the raiders at the Battle of the River Snov later that year. Although outnumbered by the Polovtsians, the Russians were able to pin them against the river, such that a charge by their heavier cavalry was able to scatter the raiders and cut many down in the rout.

From this point on, the Polovtsians were a constant threat along the eastern and southern borders of the Rus', but also increasingly a factor in the internecine conflicts between principalities. Sometimes, they were backing one rival against another; at others, they became more directly connected with dynastic politics, such as when Grand Prince Svyatopolk of Kiev, after seeing another joint army smashed by the Polovtsians, this time in a one-two punch at the Battles of the Stugna River and Zhelyany, both in 1093, next year made peace with Khan Tugorkan by marrying his daughter. What was interesting was that she was then baptized a Christian, taking the name Yelena. In other words, although the Polovtsians were proving not only more militarily capable than the Pechenegs and other nomad invaders but also more politically engaged, they were not dominant but negotiating with the Rus' as equals.

Nonetheless, the Rus' adapted. They built more ramparts to inhibit their enemies' mobility. They even more actively recruited their own horse nomads. Known as the *Chyorniye Klobuki*, or 'Black Hoods', they were drawn from the losing factions of various other nomad peoples and formed a loose, multi-ethnic community which – like the later Cossacks – traded military service for land and privileges. Some were Pechenegs; most came from smaller tribes such as the Torks, which had been caught between them and the Polovtsians, but they shared an understanding of the steppe rider ways of the new enemies the Rus' were facing and a similar mobility and flexibility. Largely recruited by successive princes of Kiev, over time they would become assimilated, but at a crucial moment for Russia they would provide a sizeable force of troops who could fight the steppe nomad way and also provide useful extra muscle during the internal wars and spats between princes. That said, in a time when there was no clear overall nation-state nor clear chains of succession or sources of legitimacy, their loyalties were as negotiable as anyone else's. According to the *Kievan Chronicle*, for example, four chieftains of the Berendei (part of the Tork), who had been supporting Prince Izyaslav Davydovich, reached out to his rival, Mstislav Izyaslavich, in 1159, saying, 'we are both good and bad for you, O Prince. If you will be as devoted to us as your father used to be, and will give to each of us a better town, then we will abandon Izyaslav.' Mstislav duly met their price, and they switched sides.

THE BATTLE OF SUTEN RIVER, 1103

Over time, the Polovtsian threat began to force the fractious Russian princes into closer cooperation. The 1097 Council of Lyubech had ended one era of particularly fierce princely strife, assigning family dynasties specific lands to end the constant rotation and competition for the most lucrative. In effect, it brought something a little more like Western European feudalism to Russia. It hardly signalled an end to internal struggles, but not only encouraged the rise of consolidated centres of power – notably Kiev, Vladimir-Suzdal and Galich-Volyn (Galicia-Volhynia) – but was also convened in part because of an awareness of the Polovtsian threat. A disunited Russia was indeed a vulnerable Russia. According to the *Primary Chronicle*, 'they said to one another, "Why do we ruin the land of Rus' by our continued strife against one another? The Polovtsians harass our country in diverse ways, and rejoice that war is waged among us. Let us rather hereafter be united in spirit and watch over the land of Rus'.'" Pious words, but they reflected a growing awareness of the need for a common front, which culminated in the Council of Dolob at the start of 1103. Grand Prince Svyatopolk Izyaslavich of Kiev and Prince Vladimir Monomakh of Pereyaslavl agreed to lead a common campaign against the Polovtsians that saw them win a substantial victory later that year.

This was a campaign that drew not just on the Russians' understanding of the cycles of the nomadic lifestyle, but also their newfound unity. The Russian army was drawn from the forces of a dozen cities, including not just Kiev and Pereyaslavl and also allies and tributaries such as Chernigov and Polotsk. They moved into the steppe in the early spring, when the horses of both sides had not yet regained their strength after the long winter. The Russians were able to draw on their settled agrarian base, but the Polovtsians' mounts were especially hard-hit, as in the Dnieper region, deep snow in winter was the norm, making migration then to the pasturelands around the Sea of Azov impossible. This strategy was both unusual and controversial, the brainchild of Vladimir Monomakh, and many within Svyatopolk's and even his own *druzhina* objected. They were, after all, also feudal gentry who derived income from their lands, and thus their concerns seem to have been about the impact of drafting *smerds* – peasants – during the planting seasons. 'We will destroy the *smerds* and their arable land,' they complained, but Monomakh won the argument, replying that 'I find it amazing that you feel sorry for the horses you use to plough. Don't you think that while the peasant is ploughing, the Polovtsian will shoot him with an arrow and take his horse, and then when he reaches the village, take his wife and his children, and all his property?'*

Unlike the Polovtsians, the Russian force included substantial contingents of infantry, who were transported along the Dnieper on boats so as to keep up with the cavalry. They travelled as far as Khortitsa, the largest island on the Dnieper, where the infantry disembarked and the army marched eastwards into the steppe for four days before engaging with the Polovtsians on the banks of the Suten River (now called the Molochnaya). The Polovtsians were at once overconfident and

---

*Quoted in Ergun Cagatay & Dogan Kuban (eds), *The Turkic Speaking Peoples: 2,000 Years of Art and Culture from Inner Asia to the Balkans* (Prestel, 2006), p. 206

under-prepared. One wily old campaigner, Khan Urusoba, apparently appreciating this, counselled caution, advising his fellow khans to seek some kind of a deal, as 'We have done a lot of evil on earth to them.' His younger peers shouted him down, jeering that 'although you are afraid of Russia, we are not; once we have beaten them, we will go to their land and take their cities, and who will deliver them from us?'* One of the loudest voices for war came from Khan Altunopa, who was rewarded with command of the Polovtsian advance guard, considered a position of particular honour.

He eagerly closed with the Russians as soon as they were spotted, planning to use the traditional nomad tactic of the feigned retreat, hoping to draw out the enemy cavalry into a trap, separating them from their footmen. However, it was again clear that the Russians had learned some of the hard-won lessons of previous wars. A mix of Russian cavalry and *Chyorniye Klobuki* which had been deployed in advance of the main force engaged and destroyed Altunopa's contingent, denying the main Polovtsian army some of its best horsemen and also the battlefield intelligence they could have provided. This meant that the Russians retained the initiative. While the Polovtsian force was apparently numerous – 'like a forest', in the words of the chronicles – their horses were noticeably tired, so they were unable to rely on their customary advantage of speed and mobility. Besides, Monomakh also made use of a new tactic (for the Russians, at least), of fielding dense blocks of well-armoured infantry, bristling with spears, both to blunt the nomads' attacks and also to channel them into closer spaces where they could be peppered with arrows and then, once exhausted, charged by fresh Russian cavalry.

It was a decisive Russian victory: the Polovtsians broke, were harried in the rout, and lost their baggage train and many of their best troops and leaders, including fully 20 khans, among them both the foolhardy Altunopa and the cautious Urusoba. Svyatopolk's men captured Khan Beldyuz, especially notorious for raiding Russian lands, and although he offered a huge ransom, he was handed over to Monomakh, whose territories had particularly suffered. Chastising him for breaking past treaties, he had the Polovtsian killed there and then, 'cut into pieces, as a

*This and the following quotes are from the *Russian Primary Chronicle*

warning to those who decide to disturb the peace in the future'. Perhaps more satisfying yet to the soldiers was the loot from the nomads' camp, and whole herds of cattle and horses and flocks of sheep were driven back into the lands of the Rus', even novelties such as camels.

Thus began an eight-year on-and-off campaign that culminated in a scouring of Polovtsian tribes along the Seversky Donets River and the equally decisive Battle of the Salnitsa River in 1111, where some 30,000 Russians under Monomakh, Svyatoslav and Prince Davyd of Chernigov beat 45,000 Polovtsians. Again, the Russians were triumphant not least because they were united – Monomakh in particular made a point of bringing a sizeable contingent of priests along with the army, who sang hymns on the march and gave the campaign something of the status of a crusade. Beyond that, they also won several of the 'wars' behind the actual clash of arms: of intelligence, logistics and strategy. One of Monomakh's trusted subordinates, the voivode (governor) Dmitry Ivorovich of Vladimir, had managed to reconnoitre the Polovtsian territories in 1110 and collected crucial advance warning not just that the tribes were gathering for a concerted counter-offensive, but where they would be gathering. Thus, Monomakh resolved to strike early, in late February, when snows and thaw-saturated muddy conditions would hamper the movements of the horsemen. Instead, he relied heavily on boats to transport cavalry and infantry alike, or even sleds where the ground was still frozen, bringing them to the battle quickly and fresh. Again, he built his strategy around his infantry, for too long looked down on by the aristocratic *druzhina* cavalry. When the Polovtsians attacked, they were forced to come relatively close in order for their archery to take a proper toll on the armoured and shielded infantry, especially as a sudden and heavy rainstorm soon began to dampen their bowstrings and obscure their lines of sight. The battlefield along the banks of the Seversky Donets was slippery with mud and slush, though, and they were unable to withdraw or re-form when attacked by Russian cavalry. Although the monkish chroniclers attributed the victory to divine favour of a rather bloody sort – hosts of Polovtsians were apparently 'invisibly killed by an angel that many people saw, and heads flew to the ground, invisibly chopped off' – in fact, it was down to tough fighting, good generalship and, above all, a strategy that reflected Russian strengths and nomad weaknesses.

FRAGMENTED AGAIN

While the Polovtsian threat did not wholly disappear, it was essentially broken. Indeed, now that the Russians were demonstrating the capacity to stage campaigns deep into the steppe, many migrated into the Caucasus region, where a number took service with King David IV of Georgia, also known as David the Builder, and helped him unite his country and drive out the Seljuk Turks. Russia's gain was thus also Georgia's. Monomakh's authority among the Rus' was at its peak, and two years later he would become Grand Prince of Kiev. The irony was, though, that as the Polovtsian threat waned, the temptation for princes to fall out and feud inevitably grew, creating new opportunities for the nomad raiders. Indeed, after Monomakh's death in 1125, the consequent dynastic struggles tempted princes into engaging rather than fighting the Polovtsians. In particular, Vladimir-Suzdal tried to use them as an equalizer against the often-stronger forces of Galicia-Volhynia. Meanwhile, the cunning and ruthless Prince Vsevolod Olgovich, who had participated in the 1111 campaign, nonetheless regularly called on Polovtsians in his ambitious efforts to rise from control of Novgorod-Siversk to Chernigov and finally to Kiev in 1139.

Conversely, in 1151, when Prince Vladimir of Chernigov fell amid a battle for dominion over Kiev between Yuri Dolgoruky ('Yuri of the Long Arm') and Izyaslav Mstislavich, his widow fled to the Polovtsians. She married Khan Bashkord, a former ally of Vsevolod Olgovich's, who would go on to support Prince Izyaslav Davydovich with an army said to number 20,000 horsemen in his successful seizure of Kiev. All such alliances were temporary and transactional, though: if your enemy allied with one Polovtsian tribe, there was no reason why you could not ally with another, and today's allies could as easily be tomorrow's enemies. Grand Prince Svyatoslav Vsevolodovich, who had taken the Kievan throne with the help of his own Polovtsian allies, Khans Konchak and Kobyak, nonetheless was a key force behind a combined expedition down the Dnieper in 1184 mounted by Kievan troops and their Black Hood auxiliaries, along with the forces of the Pereyaslavl, Volyn, Turov and Galician principalities.

The consequent Russian victory at the Battle of the Oryol River was the last substantive engagement against the Polovtsians, even if there were still smaller raids and the temptation for hard-pressed princes to offer one khan or another pay and loot in return for service continued. The epic poem *The Tale of Igor's Campaign* recounts an unsuccessful expedition by Prince Igor Svyatoslavich of Novgorod-Siversk against them in 1185, when 'from early morning to eve, and from eve to dawn, tempered arrows fly, sabres resound against helmets, steel lances crack,' until 'the black sod under hooves was sown with bones, and irrigated with gore.'* In many ways, though, its real message was a renewed call for the Russian princes not to return to their bickering ways now that the immediate threat was waning. It fell on deaf ears. After all, the Polovtsians were beaten, with some even embracing Christianity and settling, marrying into the Russian aristocracy. Others continued to drift south, towards the Black Sea and the Caucasus regions. The real threat, one that would drive the Polovtsians conclusively away from the Eurasian steppe and pose the kind of existential challenge to the Rus' that none of the previous horse empires had, was just emerging, far to the east.

Want To Know More?

Warwick Ball's *The Eurasian Steppe* (Edinburgh University Press, 2021) has a refreshingly broad scope, as indeed does *Nomads as Agents of Cultural Change: The Mongols and Their Eurasian Predecessors* (University of Hawaii, 2017), edited by Reuven Amitai and Michal Biran. *Mounted Archers of the Steppe 600 BC–AD 1300* (Osprey, 2004) is a short summary of the various horsefolk. For the Russian perspective, the early chapters of Janet Martin's *Medieval Russia, 980–1584* (Cambridge University Press, 2007) are helpful. The Pechenegs become a recurring enemy in season 2 of the not rigidly historical TV series *Vikings: Valhalla*, by the way.

---

*Vladimir Nabokov (transl.), *The Song of Igor's Campaign* (Ardis, 2003), p. 45

5

The Storm from the East

Kalka River, 1223

1223   Battle of Kalka River
1235   Grand Kurultai approves renewed push to the west
1236   Mongol invasion of Russia
1240   Fall and sack of Kiev
1241   Battle of Mohi
1242   Death of Ögedei
1259   Fragmentation of the Mongol Empire

Part of modern Russia's claim to 'great power' status as a birthright is its belief that it earned it by repeatedly saving civilization. Napoleon and Hitler both found their nemesis in the East, the narrative goes, their dreams of empire broken on the anvil of Russian will and might. Most recently, a history textbook co-written by the former culture minister has even claimed that Moscow saved the day by its invasion of Ukraine in 2022, arguing in impressively circular logic that had it been allowed to join NATO (the North Atlantic Treaty Organization), then Russia would have had to declare war on the whole alliance, and 'this could have been the end of civilization. [We] could not let it happen.'* Second only to this surreal claim is the belief that the Rus' protected

*'Uchebnik Medinskogo: istoriya ili vzvolnovannaya agitka?' *DW*, 9 August 2023

Europe from being conquered by the Mongols in the 13th century. By their resistance, the Rus' so weakened the Mongols that they were unable to advance further. It is an appealing way to spin two centuries of vassalage as heroic self-sacrifice. It is, of course, entirely wrong.

'TERRIBLE STRANGERS'

Born sometime around 1160, Temujin was the oldest child of Yesugei, a chieftain of the Mongol Borjigin clan. He was just eight when his father died and his family was cast from the tribe. Nonetheless, by force of will, ruthless tactics and personal physical prowess, he would not only survive but come to unite the Mongols under his rule, a process confirmed at a *kurultai*, or gathering of the tribes, in 1206. Then he took on the title by which he was to become infamous: Genghis Khan.

Convinced of his and his people's manifest destiny – a mandate to extend their rule to all the lands under the gaze of the Blue Sky, lord of their shamanic pantheon – he embarked on perhaps the most ambitious and successful campaign of conquest the world had ever seen. First, he turned his attentions to China, forcing the Western Xia to pay tribute and seizing the northern half of the Great Jin Empire. Then he turned towards Central Asia. The Khanate of Qara Khitai fell in 1218, and the Khwarezmian Empire followed. With each conquest, the Mongols gained new armies, and an increasingly formidable reputation. Disciplined, hardy and capable of covering ground faster even than most nomad armies, they were soon reaching well past the Ural Mountains. The remaining Polovtsians, increasingly settled and intertwined with the Rus', found a dangerous enemy pressing on their eastern borders before they had even gathered any real sense of who they might be. In winter 1222, Khan Koten turned up at the court of his son-in-law, Prince Mstislav the Bold of Galich, with the warning that 'terrible strangers have taken our country, and tomorrow they will take yours if you do not come and help us.'*

As new accounts came of a Mongol army on the banks of the Dniester River, in April 1223, Mstislav marched to meet them,

*Quoted in S. L. Tikhvinskii (ed), *Tataro-Mongoly v Azii i Evrope* (Nauka, 1977), p. 188

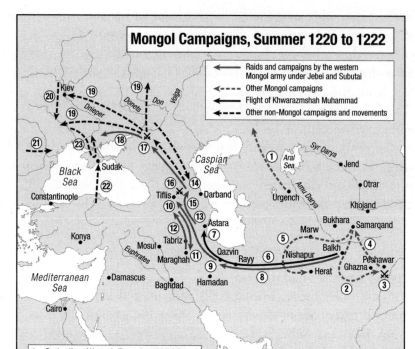

Mongol Campaigns, Summer 1220 to 1222

←—— Raids and campaigns by the western Mongol army under Jebei and Subutai

◄- - - - Other Mongol campaigns

◄—— Flight of Khwarazmshah Muhammad

◄- - - - Other non-Mongol campaigns and movements

1. Destruction of Urgench (December 1220) followed by a campaign to the north of the Caspian Sea by a Mongol army under Jochi, against the Qangli Turks (eastern Kipchaqs or 'Wild' Polovtsians).
2. Genghis Khan pursues Jalal al-Din, son of the Khwarazmshah Muhammad; destroys Balkh (spring 1221) and Ghazna (spring 1222).
3. Genghis Khan defeats Jalal al-Din near the river Indus (25 November 1221).
4. Genghis Khan returns to Transoxania.
5. Campaign by a Mongol force under Tolui, 1221–22; destroys Marw (February 1221) and Nishapur (April 1221).
6. Flight of Khwarazmshah Muhammad.
7. Death of Khwarazmshah Muhammad on a small island in the Caspian Sea near Astara.
8. Western Mongol army under Jebei and Subutai pursues the Khwarazmshah Muhammad.
9. Western Mongol army destroys Qazvin (early 1221).
10. Western Mongol army devastates the Kingdom of Georgia (February 1221).
11. Western Mongol army captures Maraghah and Hamadan (February–March 1221).
12. Western Mongol army raids Georgia for the second time (October 1221).
13. Western Mongol army winters on the steppes of Azerbeijan near the Kür (Araxes) river; Subutai received orders from Genghis Khan to cross the Caucasus Mountains after the snows melt and to attack the Polovtsian Khanate ('Civilized' Polovtsians or western Kipchaqs) in conjunction with a planned assault by a Mongol army under Jochi, then to return to Central Asia via the north of the Caspian Sea.

14. Polovtsian army assembles on the Terek river lowlands and is joined by Alan, Iasian and Kosogian forces.
15. Western Mongol army crosses the Caucasus Mountains but is trapped in the narrow Daryalsk ravine by combined Polovtsian, Alan, etc. forces.
16. Mongols convince Polovtsians to break their alliance with the Caucasian peoples; Mongols then attack and defeat Alans, Iasians and Kosogians.
17. Western Mongol army invades the Polovtsian Khanate and defeats the Polovtsian army near the river Don.
18. Western Mongol army spends winter (1222–23) in the steppes north of the Crimean peninsula.
19. Surviving Polovtsian leaders flee to various Russian princes in search of support (late 1222); Khan Koten goes to Galicia; the main Polovtsian army retreats west of the river Dnieper while steppe lands east of the Dnieper fall under Mongol control.
20. Prince Mstislav Mstislavich takes control of the Principality of Galicia (1221).
21. Catholic Church sends Dominican missionaries to the court of the Polovtsian Khan Koten (1221).
22. Seljuk Sultan of Rum (Anatolia) imposes his suzerainty on the nominally Genoese trading outpost of Sudak (1221).
23. The defenders of Sudak, probably with Seljuk assistance, repulse a combined Russian-Polovtsian attempt to take control of the town (1221–22).

confident that with an army of some 10,000 of his own troops, and half as many Polovtsians in support (contemporary forces claim figures ten times this size, but later historians and archaeologists have cut the chronicles down to size), he could handle yet one new nomad threat from the east. As far as he was concerned, 'So long as I am in Kiev, on this side of the Yaik, the Pontic Sea, and the Danube, the Tatar sabre cannot be brandished.' Besides, he was backed by the other two most-powerful Rus' princes, confusingly enough all sharing the same name: Mstislav the Daring of Galicia and Mstislav Svyatoslavich of Chernigov. It wouldn't be the first time Russians underestimated the Mongols.

THE ROAD TO KALKA RIVER

The invading forces had divided along two main axes of attack. Jochi, the eldest of Genghis Khan's sons, had led an army south, around the Aral and Caspian Seas, where he was engaged with the Kingdom of Georgia. Jebei and Subutai, two of the khan's greatest generals, led a push against the Polovtsians. The latter had paused on the eastern side of the Dnieper River, anticipating the arrival of reinforcements from Jochi, but as he had fallen ill, these were not forthcoming. However, their scouts soon noted the mustering of the Rus' army. First, Jebei tried diplomacy, sending envoys to Mstislav to argue that they had no cause to fight:

> We have not touched your land, neither your cities, nor your villages... Be at peace with us; if [the Polovtsians] run to you, drive them away and take away their property; We heard that they did a lot of harm to you, as well; We beat them for this too.[*]

He had, after all, been able previously to divide the Polovtsians from their allies the Alans, but this time it failed to work. Mstislav had the envoys killed and moved on, joining his forces with those of Galicia and also those of Volhynia, under Prince Daniil Romanovich. Another delegation met Mstislav and effectively declared war, but

[*]From the *Russian Primary Chronicle*

with his army now being reinforced by Galician infantry who had been transported by boat down the Dnieper, he saw little reason for concern. After all, the Mongols were retreating, clearly realizing their weakness.

Through the latter half of May, the Rus' and their Polovtsian allies clashed with the Mongol rearguard, winning victory after victory. However, this force was there as bait, no more than a thousand men, and most of them drawn from younger and less-skilled fighters. It was hardly surprising that they were not able to hold back the attackers, but the engagements were carefully watched by Subutai and Jebei to get the measure of their enemies. What was quickly clear was that while the Polovtsians were able horse archers – though not the equal of the Mongols – and many of the Rus' doughty fighters, there was no real coordination between the forces. Each principality had raised its own mix of *druzhina* and militia. The former were relatively heavily armoured and experienced, typically cavalry, but the bulk of the army were levies, often unarmoured and unskilled, armed with axes and spears. Above all, each feudal contingent was fiercely independent, with no overall commander beyond the fragile consensus of the council of princes – while Subutai, in the 20 campaigns he fought in his life, would be reckoned to have conquered more territory than any other commander in history.

The Mongols were engaged in one of their favoured stratagems: the feigned retreat. Like so many of the steppe peoples, the Mongols relied heavily on speed, flexibility and manoeuvrability. Their operational art rested on the use of multiple, fast-moving columns which could outflank enemy armies, cutting supply lines and laying waste to crops and settlements alike, as much to demoralize the enemy as reduce their capacity to replenish troops and food. This depended on careful advance reconnaissance, using outriders and spies to gather intelligence but also to spread rumours intended to wrong-foot or divide the enemy. Many argue that the Russian penchant for *maskirovka*, strategic deception and camouflage, has its roots in Mongol practice. Certainly, they were often caught off guard by practices like sending a diversionary force dragging branches behind it to kick up enough dust to look like a whole army, or lighting multiple campfires to give the impression of much greater numbers.

CARNAGE ON THE KALKA, 1223

For nine days, they led their enemies in a chase of their choosing, allowing the Rus' and Polovtsians to become overconfident but also more dispersed, as slower elements fell behind and more zealous princes – Mstislav the Bold and the Polovtsians in particular – drove their forces ahead of the rest. Subutai and Jebei finally reached what they felt the best place to stand and fight, on the banks of the Kalka River. On the last day of May, the Rus' would first get a taste of what it truly meant to fight a Mongol army.

Theirs was a style of war similar to those of the other steppe people, but more ruthless, ordered and coordinated. In battle, they sought to disorganize the enemy, breaking up their formations and ruining their plans by rapid attacks often equally rapidly disengaged. These would be preceded by hails of arrows from their infamous composite bows, which had a range of more than 1,500 feet, and once the enemy were sufficiently discomposed, their flanks enveloped and their commanders killed or blindsided, heavy cavalry would be unleashed for the killing blow. Perhaps most crucial, though, was their highly evolved command and communication, which prevented this fluid style of war from devolving into a chaotic scrum. The soldiers were divided into squads of tens, hundreds, thousands and the *tumen*, 10,000 men. Commanders, ideally occupying higher ground for a better view, would rely not simply on dispatch riders to bear their orders, but also on flags, trumpets and drums, signalling lamps and even smoke signals.

By contrast, the fractious Rus' princes could not agree a common plan of attack, so the Polovtsians, eager to drive the Mongols from their lands, and the headstrong Prince Daniil and his Volhynians took matters into their own hands and moved against the Mongol army, which numbered perhaps 20,000 troops. Mstislav Svyatoslavich of Chernigov followed shortly thereafter, but the Kievans hung back. This meant that the attackers were already strung out and crossing the river when the Mongols struck. Demonstrating the tactical flexibility for which he was known, the one-eyed Subutai – arguably Genghis Khan's most able general – opted to unleash his heavy cavalry from the first, against the Polovtsian horse archers. They were quickly swept from the battlefield, allowing the Mongols the freedom to engage with the Russians at will. Each Rus' contingent was feathered with arrows and broken by charges in turn, which meant that the ones behind were disrupted by fleeing remnants of the previous units, even before the Mongols turned on them. The Rus' army collapsed, different princes leading their own forces in different directions.

Prince Mstislav of Kiev, from his vantage furthest from the fighting on the other side of the Kalka, had the time and presence of mind to form the wagons of the army's supply train into a makeshift fort. Over the next three days, they would slowly try to edge their way westward, under a steady hail of arrows, but it was clear there was no escape, and their water would soon be running out. At this point, Subutai offered terms, saying that if they surrendered, the princes and leaders would be ransomed, and no blood would be spilled. A desperate Mstislav agreed, but he would quickly realize that not only did the Mongols regard terror as a useful weapon of war, but they also would not forgive the murder of their envoys. The soldiers were either killed or enslaved, but Mstislav and the other noble prisoners were bound and laid beneath a platform of wooden planks, atop which Subutai and Jebei held a victory feast. They died, slowly crushed to death – but, technically, no blood was spilled.

Mstislav the Bold had managed to escape the Mongols with a small force of survivors, but this was – quite literally for his Kievan counterpart – a crushing defeat for the Rus'. As the *Novgorod Chronicle* puts it,

> for our sins, there came an unknown tribe, whom no one exactly knows, who are, nor whence they came out, nor what their language is, nor what race they are, nor what their faith it, but they call them Tatars... and [only] every tenth [Russian warrior] returned to his home.*

At first, the Rus' braced themselves for a new onslaught, but as none came, they began to feel confident, and told themselves that they really hadn't been defeated so comprehensively, or that their courage in battle had deterred the Mongols, also known as Tatars, from further incursion. If only.

*Neville Forbes et al (eds), *The Chronicle of Novgorod 1016–1471* (1914), pp. 64–66

THE MONGOL CONQUEST

Both this force and Jochi's armies, formidable that they were, had been no more than exploratory probes, nothing to the main Mongol forces. This was something of a sideline to major campaigns against the Kipchaks along the Volga River, who were putting up stubborn resistance. Besides, after Kalka, that Mongol army had suffered an unusual and unexpected defeat at the hands of the Volga Bulgars when they turned north. Then, the Mongol advance would be delayed by Genghis Khan's death in 1227, but after two years of wrangling, his third son and heir Ögedei would be elected to succeed him at a great *kurultai*, or gathering of the chieftains, and the march of empire would resume. The focus was still in the East, with wars against the Southern Song dynasty in China, and campaigns in Korea and Tibet. However, the Jochids, successors of Jochi, were ardent advocates of another push to the west. Before his death, Genghis Khan had split his empire into semi-autonomous khanates, one for each of his four surviving sons during his lifetime. The *ulus*, or dominion, granted to Jochi and then his sons had been the western end of the empire, from the Ural Mountains 'as far as the hooves of Mongol horses had trod'. They had to rely largely on subject peoples, which is why this Golden Horde became increasingly Turkic and Muslim over time, but they had had little success expanding their territories. These Jochids had supported Ögedei's claim to the throne, and at a *kurultai* in 1235 they called in their favour and persuaded him to launch a new campaign to the west under Batu, the deceased Jochi's second son and favoured successor.

The next year, then, the Rus' faced a full onslaught, as Batu led a force of perhaps 150,000 men westwards. The last remnant of the Polovtsians were mopped up on the way, and the Mongols had their revenge on the Volga Bulgars, taking and sacking their cities in turn, as the predominantly cavalry army was accompanied by a siege train with engineers recruited from China and Persia. In 1237, Batu sent envoys to Prince Yuri II of Vladimir-Suzdal, offering them a chance to surrender, but although they were this time allowed to return home, bearing gifts and honeyed words, he clearly had no intention of bending the knee to those he privately described as 'evil bloodsuckers', and so it would be war.

Batu's army first took the eastern city of Ryazan in 1237, after just three days of siege, and sacked it with the performative viciousness that had become the force's trademark – as much as anything else, to deter future resistance. The *Primary Chronicle* recounts that 'there was none left to groan and cry' after the attackers had done their bloody work. The army then moved north-west to Kolomna and Moscow – both of which were burnt to the ground – before swinging north-east to Vladimir. In February 1238, after another three-day siege, Vladimir fell and was also put to the torch. From there, Batu's forces split into several columns: one moved north-east to Kostroma; another north to take Rostov and Yaroslav, before engaging with and destroying an army led by Prince Yuri at the Battle of the Sit River (March 1238); and a third went west, taking Tver and heading towards Novgorod.

All told, some 14 cities across north-eastern Russia would fall to Batu. Many fell with – for the Rus' – horrifying ease, their walls battered by the Mongols' trebuchet catapults, their defenders swept away by their seasoned and disciplined fighters. The fortified town of Kozelsk became famous for the seven weeks into May that it held out under the boy-prince Vasily, but to a degree this was by then because the invading army was getting tired and, more to the point, rains and melting ice created conditions unpropitious for a cavalry army. Even so, the city did fall, and while those of its defenders who were not killed were enslaved, Batu was still so infuriated by Kozelsk's defiance that he forbade any mention of its name in his presence thereafter. Conversely, although there are some claims that the army heading towards Novgorod became bogged down in the dense woods on the way, the truth of the matter is that the canny mercantile elites of the Republic were quick to realize that this was not a force they could fight and negotiated a quick surrender, something that would ensure that city prospered over the coming years of the 'Mongol Yoke'.

Without a single ruler with whom to negotiate surrender, though, the conquest would have to be piecemeal. In 1238 Batu turned to Crimea in the south, and then the next year resumed his conquests of Russia. This time, he struck from the south-east, taking Chernigov and Pereyaslavl, and by November 1240 he had invested Kiev. The year before, the seizure of Chernigov had prompted Grand Duke

Mikhail to flee to Hungary, and in a triumph of opportunism over sense, first Prince Rostislav of Smolensk had seized the city and then he was promptly ousted by Daniil of Galicia-Volhynia. Daniil did, at least, have the wit also to be in Hungary when the Mongol advance guard under Batu's cousin Möngke reached the greatest city of the Rus', but when Möngke offered the city terms, Daniil's lieutenant, Voivode Dmitry, had the envoys killed. The lessons of Kalka clearly had not been learned.

While Batu led a force to shatter the Black Hood cavalry who were coming to reinforce Kiev, Möngke began the siege. Their catapults battered its walls, finally breaking through on 6 December. The Kievans were no match for the forces that swarmed into the city, and a last, defiant defence was staged around the Church of the Tithes. So great was the weight of terrified cityfolk who had crowded into the church in the hope of finding sanctuary that its balcony collapsed. The battle was bloody, but the aftermath even more so. Not only did Kiev have to be razed as an example to remaining Rus' cities, but the murder of the emissaries had to be avenged. Before the invasion, the city was home to some 50,000 souls; after, only a couple of thousand were picking through its smoking and rubbled ruins. Not all the rest were killed – some were enslaved, and there were also refugees fanning out across southern Russia – but enough that Vatican diplomat Giovanni da Pian del Carpini seems to have written (for there is some debate about the authenticity of this text), following his passage through these lands in 1246, that he 'came across countless human skulls and bones from the dead scattered over the field', and that Kiev had been 'reduced to almost nothing'.[*]

THE GOLDEN HORDE

It seemed nothing could stop the Mongols in their drive to 'reach the ultimate sea' and bring all the known lands under their rule. From

---

[*]Giovanni DiPlano Carpini, *The Story of the Mongols Whom We Call the Tartars* (Branden, 1996), p. 68. This detail only appears in the second redaction or version of his account. However, it is likely only to be an embellishment; even in the first version, he writes that the Mongols 'put the inhabitants to death.'

Kiev, Batu continued westward, conquering Galicia and Volhynia and then moving on into Hungary, routing the Hungarian army at the Battle of Mohi (11 April 1241), and taking Pest shortly thereafter. Even as they seemed unstoppable, though, the Mongols were wavering. Despite depending on his tactical acumen, Batu – an indifferent and impetuous commander by some accounts – was becoming resentful of Subutai, and more and more of his captains were becoming unhappy with his leadership. Meanwhile, losses were mounting, and the further west they pushed, the fewer the chances for reinforcement. Nor were the conditions so suited to the Mongols' style of manoeuvre war: the more densely populated European countries meant more sieges, and a spell of warm, wet weather was also swelling rivers and turning plains into mud, hardly conducive to rapid mounted operations. It may have been a blessing for the beleaguered and increasingly short-tempered Batu that news arrived in 1242 that Ögedei had managed, through considerable personal effort and dedication, to drink himself to death. He would have to return to distant Karakorum for another *kurultai*, and his armies duly withdrew.

They paused their westward wars of conquest, but that does not mean they abandoned what they had taken. A north-western portion of the lands of the Rus', encompassing Polotsk, Minsk, Turov and Grodno, remained outside their control, but the rest was now under what became known as the 'Mongol Yoke', and for two centuries the Rus' would, while not truly cut off from the rest of Europe, also be exposed to new ways of war and governance. In 1259, the unified Mongol Empire would in effect break apart into a number of autonomous khanates. One, which would come to be known as the Golden Horde, would encompass the Rus' lands through to the Ural Mountains to the east and the Caucasus and Black Sea to the south. It, in turn, would comprise an array of subject principalities, cities, tribes and regions, granted considerable latitude of their own, as long as they accepted the dominion of the khan. What this meant, as Kiev painfully rebuilt and Novgorod paid for its survival with plentiful silver, was that a new power would arise among the principalities: Moscow.

Want To Know More?

Peter Jackson's *From Genghis Khan to Tamerlane: The Reawakening of Mongol Asia* (Yale University Press, 2023) is densely written and sourced, but is a first-rate scholarly account of the rise of the Mongols. *The Horde: How the Mongols Changed the World* (Belknap, 2021) by Marie Favereau lacks Jackson's punctiliousness but is rather shorter and a little more digestible. David Nicolle and Viacheslav Shpakovsky's *Kalka River 1223* (Osprey, 2001) is a comprehensive study of the battle and the respective armies. *The Story of the Mongols, Whom We Call the Tatars* (Branden, 1996) is a translation of da Pian del Carpini's account of his 13th-century travels all the way to Karakorum. The Russian film *Furious* (2017), also sometimes found as *Legend of Kolovrat*, is rather Marvel-meets-medieval but is nonetheless an evocative action tale set around the Mongol siege of Ryazan.

6

Throwing off the Yoke

Kulikovo, 1380

1325	Ivan I Kalita becomes lord of Moscow
1359–81	Great Troubles beset the Golden Horde
1362	Battle of the Blue Waters
1380	Battle of Kulikovo
1382	Tokhtamysh sacks Moscow
1471	Battle of Shelon River
1480	Great Stand on the Ugra River

While researching an earlier book on the recent wars in Chechnya, I was struck by a particularly florid passage in a military broadcast, extolling one fallen soldier:

> After more than 25 hours on duty, he was finally stood down, enjoying a plate of dumplings with his fellow soldiers, when cunning terrorists killed the guard with their knives and attacked the camp. He did not hesitate, but rushed forward like a bull, catching the intruders off guard and pushing them back long enough for the rest of the squad to arm themselves and repel the attack. In the process, though, he was severely wounded, and though a doctor was soon in attendance, this Russian hero died there on the field, sword and shield for his fellows.[*]

[*] *Sluzhu Rossii*, Zvezda-TV, 12 January 2014

It may not have won marks for style or understatement, but what struck me was the density of words which actually had their origins in the Mongol tongue. The rather dated word for sentry or guard, *karaul*, is from the Mongol *kharuul*; *byk*, bull, derives from *bukh*; to push, *tolkat'*, is from *tulkhekh*; a doctor, *vrach*, comes from *bariach*; while *myech*, sword, is from the more generic Mongol word for weapon, *mes*. As for the traditional Russian folk heroes, the *bogatyrs*, their name descends from the Mongol term *baatar* for a hero – which is written *bağatur*, with a silent g. For that matter, the boiled, meat-filled dumplings Russians call *pelmeni* also came from their eastern overlords.

THE YOKE

This is a valuable reminder that empires leave their marks. After the conquest, there followed some two centuries that would later be known as the time when Russia, the lands of the Rus', laboured under the 'Mongol Yoke'. At the time, though, no one used the term 'yoke'. Why would they? The Mongols were warriors, not administrators. They were content to roam and settle in the broad pastures of the Pontic and Caspian Steppe, close enough always to be able to discipline unruly vassals, yet free from the confines of the city and the humdrum realities of managing subject peoples. As a result, although they collected tribute from the Russians, and they expected and demanded deference and obedience on pain of renewed violence, their hand rested lightly on their subjects. They were not interested in imposing their ways, values or faith; they were not road-builders like the Romans, or evangelists like the Spanish Conquistadores. Their goal was conquest, and once they were victorious, they were happy to rule through local princes, as long as they knew their place.

This was thus a time in which Russia was to a degree cut off from the technological and philosophical evolution of Europe – from spinning wheels to humanism – but conversely exposed to new influences from the East. The Mongols may have been regarded by those they fought as bestial hordes, 'wild beasts out of the desert [brought] to eat the flesh of the strong', in the words of the *Novgorod Chronicle*, but they brought with them ideas they in turn had plundered from China, from the Abbasid Caliphate of the Middle East, from the Khwarezmian

Empire of Persia, whether gunpowder or the postal roads, ornate Asiatic decorative styles or plov, a rice and lamb pilaff from Central Asia.

Indeed, so too was the dominance of Moscow. Kiev had been razed and Novgorod humbled. The ruined and burnt cities soon recovered, but the centre of political gravity would shift and a new city would rise to dominance. First as the Golden Horde's most ruthless and capable agents, then as the self-promoted champions of Russian independence, through the Battle of Kulikovo in 1380 to the Great Stand on the Ugra River 100 years later, the princes of Moscow would 'gather the Russian lands' into their grasp. From this would finally come a single Russian state, even if the very legitimacy of Muscovy was built on highly mythologized tales of martial glory. Nonetheless, out of this process would emerge a distinctive style of war, ever more directly influenced by Mongol ways, yet still not divorced from its western roots.

PRINCELY SPATS

At the end of 2023, at a time when Vladimir Putin's government was trying to redefine itself as at once part of the European cultural mainstream yet also beyond it, the hawkish international relations scholar Sergei Karaganov noted in an interview that 'I never tire of reminding you that Alexander Nevsky travelled for a year and a half, first through Central Asia, and then through Southern Siberia on the way to Karakorum, the capital of the Mongol Empire. In fact, he was the first Siberian Russian.'* Of course, what Karaganov paints as some expression of Russian orientation towards the East was actually a reflection of subordination – and ambition.

The death of Yuri II Vsevolodovich at the Battle of the Sit River in 1238 had left the powerful (and lucrative) position of Grand Prince of Vladimir vacant. Grand Prince Yuri's younger brother, Yaroslav II Vsevolodovich, was the obvious successor and perfectly willing to pay fealty to the Golden Horde for the opportunity. As discussed in chapter 3, Yaroslav and his sons, Andrei and Alexander (Nevsky), had in 1242 supported Novgorod against the Teutonic Order and that, along with his role as – now that Kiev was sacked – foremost prince of the

*'Kuda techet reka – 2024', *Rossiiskaya Gazeta*, 27 December 2023

Russians, ensured that he was the first to be summoned to Karakorum, to pass between two fires, to purify him of evil spirits, and prostate himself before the Great Khan. It was a long and arduous journey, but he arrived in time to witness the accession of the new Great Khan, Güyük, eldest son of Ögedei, in August 1246. He was duly confirmed in his position and granted the all-important *yarlyk*, or patent to that effect. However, almost immediately afterwards, he died in mysterious circumstances followed an invitation to dine with Töregene, Güyük's mother and, for the five years previous, a canny and ruthless regent in his name. Pian del Carpini certainly had no doubts, recording that after being 'given food and drink from her own hand', Yaroslav 'immediately fell ill and died seven days later, and his whole body miraculously turned blue.'* Theories abound – especially as Prince Mikhail of Chernigov had only just been killed for refusing to prostrate himself to the Great Khan – but Andrei and Alexander did not hesitate to travel to Karakorum in turn, Andrei being confirmed as Grand Prince of Vladimir and Alexander as Prince of Kiev. However, when Güyük died in 1251, his successor Möngke again demanded his Russian princes pledge their obedience, although fortunately for them they only had to travel to the new capital of the Golden Horde at Sarai, close to where the Volga flows into the Caspian Sea, less than half as far away.

Even so, Andrei refused, but Alexander complied, and while his elder brother was exiled to Sweden, Nevsky became Grand Prince of Vladimir. This was an honour, but also a burden, as he was expected in effect to be Sarai's chief enforcer among the Russian principalities. When, in 1259, Mongol census-takers and tax collectors came to Novgorod, for example, popular protests against what the *Novgorod Chronicle* called 'accursed, raw-eating Tartars' forced them first to demand protection from the governor and then from Alexander. He was forced to lead an army of Russian and Mongol troops to the same city he had served and defended, to impose Sarai's order, even cutting the noses off some local officials in punishment.

This would be the model for the next century. The principalities would retain their own identities, then, and princes much of their

*Giovanni DiPlano Carpini, *The Story of the Mongols Whom We Call the Tartars* (Branden, 1996), p. 111

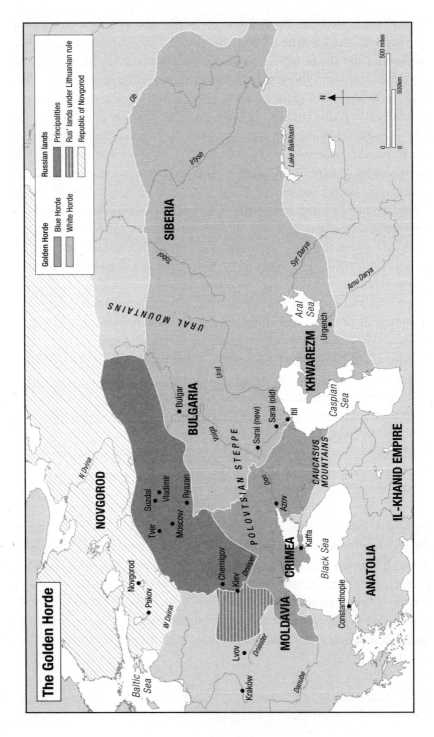

The Golden Horde

Golden Horde
- Blue Horde
- White Horde

Russian lands
- Principalities
- Rus' lands under Lithuanian rule
- Republic of Novgorod

autonomy, as long as they deferred to the khans and their *basqaqs* (governors), paid a tithe of their wealth in tribute, and obeyed when additional demands were put on them, from providing soldiers for war to hosting travelling delegations in the extravagant manner they expected. The principalities survived, even though many weakened themselves by the custom of appanage, so that lands were left not just to the oldest son, but in holdings to every son, such that families' lands would continually fragment, only sometimes recohering by conquest, marriage or alliance. Others retained the old principle of lateral succession, whereby the throne and its lands passed whole from brother to brother and thereafter to the eldest son of the eldest brother who had ruled.

THE RISE OF MOSCOW

There was still ample scope for conflict. The Mongols did nothing to protect their Russian vassals from raids and incursions from the west, whether by Poles and Lithuanians, Swedes or Germans, and would mount their own expeditions of reprisal when a city failed in its obligations. Of course, often these were exploited or even encouraged by rival Russian princes, who would do their best to use the Golden Horde as a weapon against their foes. None were more adept at this than the Ryurikids of Nevsky's line. They became rich and powerful as the Mongols' most capable agents, largely managing to keep the *yarlyk* of Grand Prince of Vladimir-Suzdal within the family, and steadily adding to their dynastic lands.

None more so than Ivan I, who came to power in 1325, and who became known as Ivan *Kalita*, or 'Ivan Moneybags', for his wealth. This he used as a weapon, bringing territories under Moscow's control through strategic marriages and buying the debts of impoverished princes. What could not be bought was taken, though. In 1326, for example, Prince Alexander of Tver was granted the *yarlyk* for Vladimir, a clear reversal for Ivan, but a year later, a popular revolt broke out against the brutal behaviour of a Mongol potentate, who had ensconced himself in the city. The resulting massacre of Mongols and their allies demanded an equally violent reprisal from Sarai. Ivan seized the opportunity, mustering an army which, along with a sizeable Mongol force, retook the city and forced Alexander to flee. Ivan was rewarded with the duchies of Novgorod and Kostroma, but above all, Tver was humbled and would never again challenge Moscow.

Crucially, the Ryurikid dynasty practised primogeniture, steadily building on the family holdings rather than constantly fragmenting it. This also encouraged investment in those holdings, notably Moscow itself. As it acquired new walls, fortresses and monasteries, its prestige grew such that, in 1325, Metropolitan Pyotr formally moved his seat from Vladimir to Moscow: it was now the capital of the Russian faith. So Moscow rose, and as it rose it acquired new rivalries. After Tver came Suzdal, then Novgorod, from which it took the strategic and lucrative town of Torzhok, controlling its routes into the central Russian lands. Military, political, economic and even spiritual power were all intertwined.

DONSKOI'S GAMBLE

This was a model that could not be sustained forever. In the mid-14th century, the Black Death would kill perhaps a quarter of the Russian population, which in turn meant a scarcity of labour on the land and thus tribute and tax. More to the point, the Golden Horde would begin to decline, the ruthless vigour which had seen its leaders and soldiers cross a continent on horseback softened by the comforts of tribute and luxury. In the period known as the Great Troubles, between 1359 and 1381, they experienced a series of internecine struggles between contenders for power, with coup, plot and counter-coup elevating and then eliminating a series of short-lived khans. This also, incidentally, worked very much in Moscow's favour, as whenever there was no clear ruler of the Horde, it would simply keep the tribute it had collected.

One by-product of this turmoil was the loss of Kiev, as rivals came to see that the once-fearsome Tatars were disunited, distracted and in decline: the Golden Horde was increasingly divided between the Blue Horde to the west, which held Sarai, and the White to the east. At the Battle of the Blue Waters in 1362, Algirdas, Grand Duke of Lithuania – at the time one of the great military powers of north-eastern Europe – broke a Golden Horde army and conquered the principality of Kiev. The putative 'mother of Russian cities' had been in dispute between the Tatars and the Lithuanians since the 1320s and was likely paying tribute to both, but this decisively separated it from the rest of the Rus' until the grandly named Treaty of Perpetual Peace in 1686 saw it passed from the Polish–Lithuanian Commonwealth to the Russian tsars. This was a blow to the sitting ruler in Sarai, Emir Mamai. A cunning political operator, he was nonetheless not a Genghisid – a descendant of Genghis Khan – and thus had to rule largely through puppet khans.

Increasingly under pressure from his rivals and sensing that Moscow was perhaps getting too powerful to be a comfortable underling, he fell back on the old staples of divide and rule. What he seems to have failed to realize was that Moscow was also beginning to question its deal with the Golden Horde. It had benefitted from being weak when the Horde was strong (as it preferred to elevate less-dangerous vassals) and then strong when the Horde was weak (as it became more useful, even necessary), but times were changing. The more the Tatars fought between themselves, the less useful they were as patrons, especially given that the Silk Road, that great network of trade routes across Eurasia, was becoming less viable and valuable as wars raged along and across its length. The more Sarai demanded, the more enemies Moscow was making among the principalities of Russia – just at the very time the Tatars could offer less support.

Prince Dmitry of Moscow was able and ambitious, and while he certainly did not start out dreaming of challenging Sarai, Mamai ironically drove him to it. He began making unrealistic demands for tribute, because he needed the silver to pay off allies and supporters alike as he was facing a rising challenge from Tokhtamysh, Khan of the White Horde, a general rather than a schemer, and a Genghisid, to boot. In 1375, when Dmitry balked, Mamai granted the *yarlyk* of Grand Duke of Vladimir to his bitterest rival, Prince Mikhail of Tver. He failed to appreciate the degree to which he was backing Dmitry into a corner. Unwilling to lose face and power, Dmitry mustered his forces, besieged Vladimir and forced Mikhail to cede the city to him. In doing so, Dmitry, whether he appreciated it at the time or not, was crossing his own Rubicon: directly taking Vladimir, and with it the status as first among Russia's princes, rather than petitioning Sarai for it on bended knee.

Mamai needed two things in his struggle against Tokhtamysh: ever more silver, and a chance to demonstrate that he, too, was a successful war leader. In 1380, he demanded even greater tribute while, anticipating that Dmitry would be unable or unwilling to gather it, he began assembling an army for an expedition into Russia. Dmitry had not set out to be a rebel, but given that it was clear Mamai wanted to take by force what he was demanding by decree, the prince realized he had no real choice. If he was going to turn against his former overlord, though, he was going to need cunning, allies and, not least, luck.

THE BATTLE OF KULIKOVO, 1380

Luckily for Dmitry, he had all three and was able to win an unexpected and against-the-odds victory that both consolidated Moscow's dominance over the Russian principalities and would allow it to rewrite its reputation. The arch-collaborators, the Ryurikids of Moscow, would reinvent themselves as the great patriots of Russia. Mamai assembled an army of some 50,000 men, reflecting the reach of the Golden Horde. The epic tale the *Zadonshchina* recounts how 'Grey wolves ran howling from the mouths of the Don and Dnieper... ready to rush into the Russian land. But these were not grey wolves but vicious Tatars, who wanted to fight their way through all the lands of the Rus'.'* While the bulk were indeed Tatar horsemen, a mix of archers and heavier lancers, they by no means represented the totality of Mamai's force. He had also raised Armenian foot and horse and medium cavalry from the subject Adyghe tribes of the North Caucasus, and even hired a thousand Genoese mercenary crossbowmen and infantry, from their trading station at Kaffa (the present-day Feodosia), on the Crimean coast. Furthermore, he had struck a deal with Grand Duke Jogaila of Lithuania, who was leading a 5,000-strong force to join him, as was Prince Oleg of Ryazan with 1,000 of his men. It was not that Oleg had any love for Mamai, but Ryazan was well to the south-east of the Russian lands, too close to Sarai to permit any defiance or equivocation.

Against him, Dmitry could gather no more than 30,000 soldiers. About half came either from Moscow or its subject cities, the rest from elsewhere across Russia. Nonetheless, such was the jealousy of Moscow and suspicion of Dmitry that there were noticeable absences, including Novgorod and even Suzdal, all the more striking as its prince, Dmitry

---

*Quotes from the *Zadonshchina* come from 'Prostrannaya redaktsiya "Zadonshchniny" po spisku Gosudarstvennogo Istoricheskogo Muzeya', in B. A. Rybakov & V. A. Kuchkin (eds), *Pamiatniki Kulikovskogo tsikla* (Institut Rossiiskoi Istorii, 1998), pp. 124–33

Konstantinovich, was Dmitry of Moscow's father-in-law. The heart of his force was *druzhina* cavalry, in many ways closer to Mongol warriors than Western European knights. After all, while heavy plate armour and visored helmets had reached Russia, these aristocratic horsemen preferred to stay more mobile, wearing mail and carrying composite bows derived directly from the Mongols'. Their way of war continued to emphasize speed and agility over the sledgehammer blow of the knightly charge.

Both generals had their reasons for closing quickly to battle. Dmitry wanted to pre-empt the arrival of the Lithuanian and Ryazan contingents, while Mamai was afraid that, if Dmitry could stave off a decisive engagement long enough for winter to halt campaigning, he would be denied the quick victory he needed. After all, he needed to be back in Sarai – with all the glory and silver he planned to accrue – to see off Tokhtamysh. The Russian army mustered at Kolomna, south-east of Moscow, then continued south until the two armies met at Kulikovo Field ('Snipes' Field') in a horseshoe bend on the Don River, 185 miles south of Moscow. Mamai was already encamped in open pasture as he awaited his reinforcements, while Dmitry paused on the other bank, out of sight. Just as the sun rose, while still shrouded in early morning mist, the Russians took to the field. Dmitry wanted to array his forces so as to minimize the Tatar forces' ability to take advantage of their superior numbers and manoeuvrability, by occupying a bottleneck between thick woods on one side and the steep banks of the Nepriadva River on the other. He also detached a substantial force of heavy cavalry under two of his most loyal commanders as the so-called Ambush Regiment, and hid them in the Wood of Green Oaks on his left flank. It was a risk, as it deprived his front line of seasoned troops, but Dmitry knew he needed an ace in the hole.

He also knew that he would be a particular target, so in an act of ruthless subterfuge, he exchanged armour with Mikhail Brenok, a young Muscovite aristocrat, who would play his role at the front of the army. It was a wise move, as Mamai, confident of victory and fully aware that the Russians knew the usual array of Tatar stratagems, opted not for any subtlety but instead for a grinding melee. It was a brutal, bloody fight as 'men fell like hay under the scythe, and blood flowed like water in streams', but after three hours of hard fighting, Tatar numbers were beginning to prevail as they began to push back the Russians' left flank, starting to pivot them in a bid to pin them against the Nepriadva.

As the main Tatar heavy cavalry force crashed into the Russians, Brenok fell, and for a moment, Russian morale wavered until the real Dmitry revealed himself. Still, the Russians continued to be pushed back, even as they took a bloody toll on the Mongols for every step. By around 2pm, their left flank was disintegrating and the Tatars were preparing to roll round into the Russians' rear.

However, Dmitry still had his last card, and this was the perfect moment to play it. By all accounts, the aristocratic cavalry of the Ambush Regiment three times already had very nearly ignored their orders and joined the fray, but Voivode Dmitry Mikhailovich Bobrok-Volinsky had managed to restrain them: 'Wait a little, violent sons of Russia, the time will come when you'll feel better, because you'll have someone to play with!' At last the order came and, still fresh and eager to redeem the Grand Price's faith in them, they thundered from the wood and plunged into the wearied and unsuspected Tatar flank 'like fierce wolves amongst a flock of sheep', in the words of *The Tale of the Rout of Mamai.**

The Tatar flank was turned and Mamai's army wavered, then broke. He managed to flee, albeit by leaving his Genoese guards to be massacred, buying him time, but his army was shattered. Jogaila turned back for home, and the canny Oleg of Ryazan, who had dawdled precisely in the hope of being too late to battle, got away with a formal submission to Dmitry. The Grand Prince had lost perhaps a third of his army, and according to the *Zadonshchina*, 'the corpses of Christians lay like stacks of haystacks, near the banks of the Great Don, and the Don river flowed with blood for three days.' On the other hand, the Russians captured the Tatar camp and baggage train, not only enriching the survivors but also ensuring that, even if he could have found the troops, Mamai lacked the logistical wherewithal for another expedition that year. Perhaps most importantly, Dmitry – who acquired the epithet *Donskoi*, 'of the Don' – won for himself the reputation as the Russian champion able to defeat the irresistible Golden Horde. (Mamai also won a certain kind of immortality: in Russian, there is still the phrase

*Quotes from *The Tale of the Rout of Mamai* come from *Skazanie o Mamaevom poboishche, variant Udol'skogo*, in B. A. Rybakov & V. A. Kuchkin (eds), *Pamiatniki Kulikovskogo tsikla* (Institut Rossiiskoi Istorii, 1998), pp. 134–222

kak Mamai proshyol, 'as if Mamai had come through', to mean that everything is now in an utter mess.)

THE GREAT STAND ON THE UGRA RIVER

Of course, the fiction that this meant the end of Sarai's grip on Russia was just that. Mamai's was a spent force; after being defeated by Tokhtamysh on the Kalka River next year, he fled for his power base of Crimea, where he met his end at the hands of the Genoese, whose men's lives he had so casually sacrificed. As undisputed Khan of the Golden Horde, Tokhtamysh demanded formal submission and tribute from Dmitry Donskoi, who was eager to avoid a confrontation. He offered the former but not the latter, but this was not enough, and so in 1382, Tokhtamysh mustered an army of maybe 90,000 men and marched on Moscow, which Dmitry judiciously fled. After a three-day siege and a duplicitous offer of mercy, Tokhtamysh took the city when its defenders unwisely opened the gates. Oleg of Ryazan, forever in the middle, had tried to ingratiate himself with the khan by identifying fords along the Oka River south of Moscow, but that did not save his unlucky city from being sacked as the Tatars returned to Sarai – and then later again at Donskoi's hands as punishment for his betrayal.

Having made his point, though, Tokhtamysh was willing to compromise with the Russians – and even Moscow – both because he could not afford constant conflicts and as he was more interested in restoring the Golden Horde's authority to the south and east. Expeditions into Azerbaijan, Khwarezmid Persia and Central Asia brought him into conflict with his erstwhile patron, Timur, better known as Tamerlane, founder of the Timurid Empire across Persia, Afghanistan and Central Asia. Timur would break Tokhtamysh at the Battle of the Terek River in 1395, sacking Sarai and delivering the Golden Horde a blow from which it would never recover. Indeed, within 50 years it would be disintegrating into a number of smaller khanates.

The Tatars' loss was Russia's gain. The princes remained notionally vassals, but the degree to which this meant anything diminished over time. This gave Moscow scope to continue the 'gathering of the Russian lands' under its rule, and a century on, Grand Prince Ivan III was able to complete the task begun by his great-grandfather, Dmitry Donskoi. This was in part a question of asserting Moscow's control over the rest of the Russian principalities not under Polish-Lithuanian control. In particular, Novgorod was finally humbled. It had hoped to be able to turn to those same Polish-Lithuanians, in defiance of an earlier treaty with Moscow that granted the Great Prince a veto on any such agreements, but Ivan struck first, and victory over a larger but disorganized Novgorodian army at the Battle of Shelon River in 1471 was arguably the beginning of the end of the city-state's independence. Seven years later, Ivan returned, ostensibly in response to 'the rebellious spirit of its people' (in the words of the *Novgorod Chronicle*), but in practice because he finally felt able to close his fist fully on this rich trading city. After a month's siege, it surrendered, had most of its huge territorial holdings in northern Russia seized and, as a symbol of its subordination, saw the great bell that was used to summon the *veche* – the public assembly that, in republican Novgorod, was meant to be the final source of authority – taken down.

What was left was finally to resolve relations with the Great Horde, the successor khanate based at Sarai. The Russians had already stopped paying tribute in the 1470s, but in 1480, Akhmat Khan decided to attack Moscow in the hope of reasserting control, perhaps scenting an opportunity in rivalries at Ivan's court and his alliance with Casimir IV of the Polish–Lithuanian Commonwealth. Akhmat's sizeable army met the Russians along the Ugra River, south-west of Moscow. What followed proved unexpectedly anticlimactic. For almost four days, Akhmat's forces manoeuvred along the Ugra and made sporadic efforts to cross it, which were met by hails of Russian arrows and the fire from some early arquebuses. The river was wide and fast-moving, but even so, a determined assault would have stood a good chance of making a bridgehead. For a month, the two armies then watched each other warily across the Ugra through October. Fearing that the river would freeze when winter arrived, allowing the invaders to advance, Ivan began preparing fall-back positions to shield Moscow – when Akhmat unexpectedly withdrew. The arrival of Russian reinforcements, combined with Casimir's failure to follow through with his promised support as he was dealing with a rebellion at home and raids by the Crimean Tatars (at Ivan's urging), seem to have dispirited Akhmat, whose forces were in any case running low on fodder and far from resupply. The fact that, as he withdrew, he raided a succession of towns under Lithuanian control certainly suggests a degree of pique towards his notional ally.

No longer would there be even the fiction of Tatar dominion over the Russians. In the next few years, the Great Horde would be destroyed and a familiar pattern would re-emerge as Russia again faced regular raids from the successor khanates, especially those of Kazan and Crimea, even though these were settled states rather than nomadic peoples. Likewise, both the emerging state of Muscovy and the Lithuanians would ally with khanates for momentary gain rather than have to regard them as existential threats. The tectonic plates of geopolitics across Eurasia were shifting, and the Russians were freed from rule from the East. Instead, the threats they faced and the opportunities they saw were increasingly to be found to the west. The Russians had never been wholly isolated from Europe during the 'Mongol Yoke', as travellers, traders and diplomats still passed back and forth, and although they did imbibe some of the unyieldingly brutal ways of the Horde, the authoritarianism that emerged arguably owed as much to the imperial habits of Constantinople. Either way, Ivan III, who would be known as Ivan the Great, had not only finally thrown off the 'Yoke' but also closed Moscow's grip on those principalities not under Polish-Lithuanian control. It was Muscovy's time, and it was time for Russia to return to Europe.

Want To Know More?

Peter Jackson's *From Genghis Khan to Tamerlane: The Reawakening of Mongol Asia* (Yale University Press, 2023) and Marie Favereau's *The Horde: How the Mongols Changed the World* (Belknap, 2021) are both still relevant. Charles Halperin's *Russia and the Golden Horde: The Mongol Impact on Medieval Russian History* (John Wiley, 1985) and Donald Ostrowski's *Muscovy and the Mongols: Cross-cultural Influences on the Steppe Frontier* (Cambridge University Press, 1998) are scholarly classics on the effect of Mongol rule. My own *Kulikovo 1380: The Battle that Made Russia* (Osprey, 2019) is a short study of that fateful battle, and there is a decent little tabletop boardgame, *Kulikovo 1380: The Golden Horde* (ATO, 2006).

PART TWO

Forging an Empire

7

Ivan's Musketeers

Kazan, 1552

1533	Ivan IV crowned Grand Prince (at age of three)
1547	Ivan IV crowned tsar
	First Kazan campaign
1550	Second Kazan campaign
	Streltsy formed
1551–53	Conquest of Kazan Khanate
	Conquest of Astrakhan Khanate
1564	Formation of *Oprichnina*

It is a regular frustration that all too often, when out to illustrate a story about the Kremlin, picture editors will, instead of the high-walled red-brick fortress on one side of Red Square, slap in a picture of the Cathedral of the Intercession of the Most Holy Theotokos on the Moat, better known as St Basil's Cathedral. This is perhaps understandable considering how this asymmetrical confection of nine multi-coloured onion domes sitting astride the south of the square is instantly recognizable, a distinctive combination of traditional Russian and Byzantine styles. What is perhaps less understandable is that this fairytale structure was built at the orders of Tsar Ivan IV, the sinister autocrat better known as Ivan the Terrible, and was meant to commemorate the capture of Kazan and Astrakhan. Then again, Ivan himself was a paradox. His epithet, *Grozny*, is generally translated as 'Terrible' but really conveys a sense of a force beyond the normal, dread or awesome in its capacities, regardless of whether they are put to good use or bad. That sums up his reign well, for the deeply troubled and often homicidally paranoid Ivan was at once the architect of the foundations of the modern Russian state, and very nearly also the man who destroyed them all.

In part, this apparent contradiction was a reflection of the times in which he was living. Ivan IV was the first monarch to be crowned tsar – emperor, rooted in the Roman 'Caesar' – but the term began to be used during the reign of his grandfather, Ivan III, and in many ways he was a direct inheritor of Ivan the Great's work. It was not just that Ivan III had 'gathered the Russian lands' and finally shrugged off Tatar rule. He also elevated Moscow's claim to be the 'Third Rome' after Constantinople's fall to the Ottoman Empire in 1453, and from this not just religious authority but also a style of autocratic rule that became increasingly imperial, even visible in the appropriation of the Byzantines' double-headed eagle. Moscow under Ivan the Great grew as an imperial capital, with the fortified Kremlin complex at its heart rebuilt larger than ever, with high, red-brick walls designed by Italian architects at the cutting edge of Renaissance military construction. His realm, generally called Muscovy, was still prey to raids and incursions from the descendants of the Golden Horde, the Khanates of Kazan and Astrakhan and the Nogai Horde, but was to a greater degree looking west. Of course, the Rus' had never lost their connections with Europe, not least thanks to their back-and-forth border struggles with the Poles and Lithuanians, but now they were becoming active players in the continent's wider politics.

With contact came economic, social and military change. The first Russian use of primitive firearms dated back to the 14th century, with both crude bombards and the small, simple cannon known as the *tyufak*, which fired *drob*, a hail of stones and metal offcuts, used (with little success) in the defence of Moscow against Tokhtamysh in 1382. Only in 1475 was the first cannon foundry established, though, as these guns became more reliable, accurate and effective. The Pushechny Dvor, or Cannon Yard, inside the Kremlin complex would become the centre of Russian gun-making, not least thanks to the hiring of foreign specialists.

The changing character of European warfare was not simply a matter of technology. The old model of ad hoc armies of aristocratic cavalry backed by local levies, with battlefield commands distributed on the basis of social rank rather than ability and experience, was becoming anachronistic. In 1447, King Charles VII established his *compagnies d'ordonnance*, local standing forces that could be mustered as the core of a French army in war. They were, to be blunt, often no more than thuggish bands of brigands, but they showed the way that war was headed. In the mid-15th century King Matthias Corvinus of Hungary assembled the *Fekete Sereg*, or Black Army, of mercenaries that allowed him to take Vienna and even beat the Ottoman Empire in 1479. Tellingly, a quarter of the Black Army was armed with an arquebus, a clumsy matchlock musket.

Even when established, standing armies would remain relatively small elements of national armies. The aristocracy feared handing the sovereign so much independent power instead of forcing him to rely on them (a key reason why England lacked one until the 17th century). They also cost money, and demanded constant funding rather than the kind of emergency wartime taxes and levies that had been the norm. In other words, as Ivan the Terrible would seem to realize, they demanded a more complex and professional apparatus of state.

IVAN THE STATE-BUILDER

Ivan the Great's son, Vasily III (r. 1505–33), consolidated his reign, but died in 1533 when his son and heir, also Ivan, was just three. There followed over a decade of brutal political infighting, as boyar families battled for the right to rule as his regent, during which his mother seems to have been poisoned. The young Ivan became a neglected and brutalized figurehead (by his own account, he often had to scavenge for scraps to eat). Yet he learnt the hard arts of Moscow court politics well. At the age of just 13, he had a prince who got on his wrong side arrested and beaten to death, and although he needed the boyars to manage the country for him, he would never trust them. In 1547, he was crowned Ivan IV, Tsar of All the Russias, and a new and dangerous era for Russia – and its neighbours – would begin.

Ivan's life would be shaped by a constant, never-to-be-satisfied quest for security. At times this would take extreme form, such as his decision in 1564 in effect to establish his own realm-within-a-realm, known as the *Oprichnina* ('Separation'). However, he was dealing with very real challenges. The boyar families were unruly and self-interested, and in the years of his regency, their infighting had diminished Moscow's authority over the country. The *namestniki*, local governors, all too often became virtual local tyrants. Poor governance bred banditry and revolt. Even the Church, still a bulwark of the monarchy, was divided and corrupt. Officials relied on the practice of *kormleniye*: 'feeding', extorting payments from whomever they could, whenever they could. In his desire to secure himself, Ivan took momentous steps towards the creation of a royal government answerable only to the tsar, and many of modern Russia's institutions date their history back to these years. The Ambassadors' Office, for example, was the forerunner of today's Ministry of Foreign Affairs, while the Ministry of Internal Affairs is a descendant of his Banditry Office. Overall, the boyars and the *namestniki* were reined in (at least for a while), *kormleniye* was banned (though never truly disappeared) and, against the entitled (in every sense) aristocracy, Ivan set a new elite of career civil servants and service gentry.

Ultimately, states are machines to raise and spend taxes, and the more they want to do, the more revenue they have to collect. In earlier times, this was often an indirect process: instead of paying salaries, the state granted people lands or privileges off which they could live, in return for service. Ivan the Great's humbling of Novgorod had given him the opportunity to begin to challenge the boyars. He seized the city's massive territorial holdings, and parcelled much of them out as small estates. These holdings went to a new class of petty gentry, the *pomeshchiki*, in return for a commitment to military service directly to the state. This system, known as *pomestye*, would not only allow Ivan to field a larger army, but it would increasingly challenge the old feudal hierarchies. As well as a new class, it created an incentive for the tsars to conquer new territory, but also seize boyar lands, for the opportunity of creating more *pomeshchiki* from their followers and cronies. This was a system custom-made for a ruler eager for conquest, ruthless in his methods and deeply mistrustful of the boyars – a man, in short, like Ivan *Grozny*.

TARGET KAZAN

There was little doubt as to the first target the newly crowned tsar would pick, intended both to defang a potential threat and open up new lands with which he could buy followers. As a child, Ivan IV had witnessed not just the regular raids from the Kazan Khanate but their near-successful attempts to take the fortress-city of Murom in both

1537 and 1540. He was already facing continued threats from the Lithuanians, Swedes and Poles to the north-west and did not want to risk fighting on two fronts. In the year of his coronation, 1547, Ivan launched an ill-fated winter expedition. It was usual in such campaigns to treat the frozen rivers as virtual thoroughfares, but when his army stopped at the island of Robotka on the wide Volga on 3 February, they discovered the next morning that, in the words of the *Nikon Chronicle*, 'by some act of God, it grew warm and a thaw came, and all the ice was covered with water, and many cannons and guns fell into the water ... And many people drowned.'* Ivan returned to Nizhny Novgorod, while what was left of his army soldiered on, even as the thaw turned roads into muddy tracks and made fords impassable. Unsurprisingly, by the time it reached Kazan, the army was in no fit state to storm its fortified walls and headed home after seven days of desultory siege.

Ivan was displeased, to say the least, but learned the lessons. He would need more able commanders than the high-born amateurs who had led this expedition; he would need proper preparation as much in intelligence as logistics; and he would need better troops, more suited to modern gunpowder war. Ivan realized that he could not count on winning a war with the Khanate of Kazan in a single bold move. In 1549, the wily Khan Safa Girey died, leaving his two-year-old son Utameshgaray as notional khan and his mother Soyembika as regent. Ivan saw this as an opportunity and in 1550, ignoring offers of negotiation, led an army to Kazan, besieging it in February. Again, an early thaw – which hindered reinforcement and resupply – forced him to withdraw, but not only was Kazan's hinterland ravaged, but an island at the confluence where the Sviyaga River flowed into the Volga was identified as a good location for a fortified advance base for future operations. The question was how to build it, and quickly, and the answer came from the Russians' traditional skill in woodcrafting. The fortress of Sviyazhsk was perhaps the world's first prefabricated fortress, built in sections upstream, then floated down the river and assembled in just four weeks. Like modern flatpack furniture, each section was numbered and accompanied by a plan showing how it fit together; unlike so much modern flatpack furniture, it worked.

Polnoe sobranie russkikh letopisei, vol. IX (RAN: 1862), online edition

Meanwhile, and perhaps in response to the Russians' evident preparations, a peace faction came to power in Kazan. They installed Shah Ali, who had been a favourite of Vasily III, turned Utameshgaray and his mother over to the Russians, and released 60,000 Russian slaves. For a moment, it looked as though war might be averted, but as word spread that Shah Ali was going to hand power over to a Muscovite governor – it is unclear whether this was true or not – he was toppled in a rebellion and replaced by the more bellicose Yadegar Mokhammad, a direct descendant of Genghis Khan. Shah Ali headed straight to Moscow to join the army Ivan was assembling.

KAZAN, 1552

One of Ivan's dilemmas had been the danger that, if he stripped Muscovy of its defences, it might be raided by the Nogai and the Crimeans. In 1551, though, a deal had been struck with the Nogai, securing their neutrality. In June 1552 – after two abortive winter campaigns, he was not going to rely on the deep freeze again – Ivan assembled his army. The *Kazan Chronicle* puts the Russian army at 150,000 men and the defenders at 60,000, but as usual this must be an overstatement. Muscovy could not field this many men at once, and Kazan physically could not have held this many defenders. Instead, the armies were probably closer to 70,000 and 30,000, respectively, but while the Russians may not have fielded the 150 heavy guns also claimed, it is clear that the forgemasters of the Pushechny Dvor had been working overtime and the army included an unusually large siege train. In 1547, the artillery had been made a separate service, and even if they lacked the aristocratic pedigree of the *pomeshchiki* or the political clout of the later *Streltsy*, the gunners were already something of a separate caste, versed in mathematics and often working in the Pushechny Dvor to understand their lethal instruments better. Of course, this was still a motley force. Its core was still the *pomeshchik* cavalry, supported by footmen: infantry, archers, musketeers. Shah Ali was there for the kill, along with a handful of his followers who had also been driven from Kazan. There were Tatar allies under Khan Shigaley, Mordovian and Circassian warriors, and even foreign mercenaries including Italians, Poles and Germans.

In what proved a piece of perverse luck, just as Ivan was ready, word arrived that the Crimeans had launched a raid on the southern borders.

This massive army was able neatly to send them fleeing home and could march on Kazan confident that the way was clear. On 15 August, they crossed the Volga on specially made barges, another sign of the unusually careful preparations that had been made for the attack. Kazan forces tried to prevent the crossing but were broken in a three-hour battle that left the Russians in full control of the beachhead.

On 23 August, Ivan's forces encircled Kazan. The tsar offered terms promising the people of the city their lives, their property and the right to continue practising their Muslim faith, in return for complete subordination. Unsurprisingly, Yadegar Mokhammad refused, not least as he was still hoping for assistance from the Nogai, not knowing of their deal with Moscow. Instead, the defenders made a sortie, hoping to deliver a decisive blow before they had had the chance properly to establish their siege lines. It was a tough battle; one chronicle recounted that 'it was impossible for anyone to make themselves heard over the exchange of fire and the thunder of the cannon, the shouts and screams and battle cries of the people, the clash of arms.' Nonetheless, the Tatars were pushed back into the city and the Russians quickly established a tight noose around Kazan, digging trenches and gun pits under the supervision of Italian siege engineers, while an English specialist by the name of Butler assisted Muscovite Ivan Vyrodkov in mining operations, the excavation of tunnels to undermine the city's walls.

Gun positions covered and battered each of Kazan's main gates, and a wooden tower, some 13 metres high and fitted with ten lighter guns, was then erected and rolled closer, so it could fire over the battlements and into the city itself. This was a month into the siege, and it provoked another desperate sortie by the defenders. The fighting was fierce, but the Tatars were pushed back into the city, and they even lost control of the Arsk Gate on the south-eastern walls. There were calls from Ivan's generals for a general assault, but Ivan was hesitant. Bad weather had delayed the arrival of food and gunpowder, and he did not want to leave anything to chance. The Russians kept the Arsk Gate but resumed efforts to breach the rest of the walls by cannonade, fire and mine. More gun positions were dug; the city's ditch moat was filled in with earth and timber, and spanned by bridges. Then, the new supplies of gunpowder arrived.

It was enough. The decision was made to launch the final assault on 2 October. The defenders were hungry, tired and increasingly subject to disease, but the attackers were also feeling the strain. Nonetheless, the first stage of the assault went as planned: the walls were overwhelmed and the remaining Tatar soldiers pushed back to the environs of the Khan's Palace, a fortified complex in the north of the city. At this point, the attackers' momentum wavered as many began looting the city. This allowed the defenders time to regroup and launch a counterattack, and for a moment the Muscovite forces were on the edge of panic. It took forceful measures, including the summary execution of a number of looters, to restore discipline, and momentum swung back to Ivan. The last and conclusive fight took place at the mosque of the Khan's Palace. The paved square around it was soon slick with blood as the final remnants of Yadegar Mokhammad's forces were slaughtered. By the end of the day, the city was Ivan's.

THE STRELTSY

The seizure of Kazan demonstrated how far Muscovy's forces had come. Of course, command was still often in the hands of headstrong boyars, overseeing motley collections of auxiliaries, mercenaries and levies. However, this was not a medieval army, nor one dominated by the horse-nomad influence. It was increasingly looking west for inspiration, technology and technique, and willing to hire the specialists it needed. Instead of defensive actions against raiders, it could now launch major offensive operations against well-prepared and fortified foes, with the logistical tail to allow it to maintain lengthy and high-intensity sieges.

While the *pomeshchiki* provided the tsar cavalry independent of the boyars, Ivan still needed a solid corps of infantry, something Moscow's princes had always lacked. This would lead to the creation of Ivan's own standing army, the *Streltsy*. This translates as 'the Shooters', but is best rendered as 'Musketeers'. After all, they supplemented the traditional Russian crescent-bladed poleaxe, the *berdysh*, with a growing number of arquebuses (for which the *berdysh* also doubled as a handy prop). The first began to be recruited in 1550, and in 1555 Ivan founded what became the Streletskaya Prikaz, or Musketeers' Office, specifically devoted to recruiting, training and maintaining this force. Unlike the aristocratic cavalry, they were raised largely from free commoners: farmers, urban labourers and craftsmen. It was important that they had some trade, because unlike the *pomeshchiki*, they were not granted estates, so much as paid a minimal salary of four rubles a year, but allowed to go about their normal business when not on duty or in the field. Furthermore, they were granted a bread dole and tax concessions and encouraged to settle in Moscow's expanding suburbs, notably Zamoskvorechie ('Across the Moskva River'). This was because, when not at war, they also became guards for the Kremlin and even patrolmen on the capital's streets, serving for one week in four. They swore an oath to the tsar and received additional perks, such as the extra rouble paid for serving in the tsar's personal guard on feast days, and a share of plunder when on campaign.

Eventually, the *Streltsy*, like most Praetorian Guards, became more of a threat to the throne than a protector. Over time, membership would effectively become a hereditary right, and as changing military realities demanded reform, they would resist. They continued, for example, to deploy in the once-innovative but increasingly anachronistic *gulyay-gorod* (walking city), a rolling fortress of sorts made of wooden screens on wheeled frames that would be pulled together to form defensive positions. They were hardly early modern tanks, but against the steppe nomads, they provided useful mobile protection. Once Muscovy was up against enemies with infantry able to lap round them, and cannon to blow them apart, their value diminished dramatically, but to the very end, the *Streltsy* continued to use them. In 1662, some joined the Copper Coin Riots triggered by a financial crisis, and then, in 1682, they revolted in support of their favoured candidate for the regency following the death of Tsar Fyodor III. A horrified nine-year-old prince who would become Tsar Peter the Great watched the lynching of his own supporters, such as Artamon Matveyev, possibly the man who sparked Peter's lifelong fascination with the sea. No wonder that, after they rose against him again in 1698, he would dissolve the *Streltsy* as a fighting force.

NEW ENEMIES, NEW WARS

For now, though, they represented an important stage in the evolution of the Russian military, a core of versatile infantry, around which a larger army still mainly drawn from levies and mercenaries could be assembled. Either way, the tsar now had his own forces, reducing his dependence on the nobility, and a solid incentive to expand Muscovy's borders to increase the tax base and provide more *pomestye* land. But where? Pacifying the Kazan Khanate would take another couple of years of fighting bandits and guerrillas in its hinterland. Nonetheless, Kazan would become a Russian bastion in the south, from which a campaign to annex the Astrakhan Khanate would be launched in 1556. Yadegar Mokhammad was captured and taken to Moscow, where he would later convert to Christianity, as would Utameshgaray, while Soyembika married Shah Ali. This was, after all, a time of cultural interpenetration and political pragmatism, but also one in which the character of Muscovy was changing. As its territory expanded, the tsar would increasingly not simply be the monarch of an Orthodox Christian realm but also ruling over new faiths, new cultures – and facing new enemies.

Muscovy's expansion southwards brought it into contact and competition with the expanding Ottoman Empire, a rivalry that would endure for centuries, beginning with a Turkish attack on recently captured Astrakhan in 1569. This was beaten back, but Muscovy's southern flank was by no means secure, and in 1571, reinforced by Ottoman Janissaries and regarding itself as next on Ivan's shopping list, the Crimean Khanate launched an invasion that made it all the way to Moscow: they failed to take the city, but much of it was consumed in a terrible fire. (Thanks to Ottoman protection, this last khanate would survive until Russian annexation in 1783.)

Meanwhile, rivalries over trade and Baltic Sea access would embroil Russia in the Livonian War of 1558–83 which, name notwithstanding, was less one war than a messy series of campaigns against a revolving cast drawn from Denmark, Lithuania, Poland and Sweden. There would be no real winner, nor real peace at the end, yet Muscovy would end up viewed not so much as some distant backwater – a 'rude and barbarous kingdom', in the words of English travellers – but an increasingly serious European power. Indeed, for this very reason, England became interested in Russia as both a trading partner (the English Muscovy Company was an early arrival in 1555) and also a potential ally. England's 'Virgin Queen', Elizabeth I, was able politely to refuse Ivan IV's proposal of marriage, but the prospect of allying her sea power with Muscovy's land army must have been an interesting one. In any case, it was to come to nothing, not least because Ivan was about to all but tear apart the country he had been building.

Want To Know More?

The best biographies of this deeply troubled man, both called *Ivan the Terrible*, are Andrei Pavlov and Maureen Perrie's (Pearson, 2003) and Isabella de Madariaga's (Yale University Press, 2006). Robert Crummey's *The Formation of Muscovy 1304–1613* (Longman, 1987) is dense, but detailed, while *Armies of Ivan the Terrible: Russian Troops 1505–1700* (Osprey, 2006) by David Nicolle and Viacheslav Shpakovsky is a compact and nicely illustrated study. Eisenstein's classic film *Ivan the Terrible* (1944), largely shot in black and white, is distinctly clumsy to modern eyes, but *Ivan Vasilievich Changes His Profession* (1973), also known as *Ivan Vasilievich: Back to the Future*, is a rather different beast, a time-travelling Soviet slapstick comedy.

8

Times of Terror and Troubles

Moscow, 1611

1558–83	Livonian War
1565–72	*Oprichnina*
1584	Death of Ivan the Terrible
1590–95	War with Sweden
1598–1613	Time of Troubles
1605	Death of Boris Godunov
1605–18	'Dmitriads'
1611	People's Militias free Moscow
1613	Coronation of Mikhail I Romanov
1618	Truce of Deulino

In 2021, looking for new ways to challenge Western influences among Russia's youth, and also to hammer home its message that Russia was forever under threat, the Kremlin turned to the world of video games. The state-run Institute for the Development of the Internet stumped up about half the cash for a game explicitly intended to try to wean gamers off imported foreign titles. Launched in 2024, it was called *Smuta*, or *Time of Troubles*, referring to a period that ran roughly from 1598 to 1613. It had foreign invasions, imposter-tsars, hunger, disease, anarchy and civil war: how could it possibly be dull? Alas, it turned out to be a sumptuous recreation of early 17th-century Russia, from the wooden churches to the deep, snow-covered forests, but a singularly bad game, repetitive in story and clunky in its code. Who would have thought that a bureaucratic state committee wouldn't have the magic computer game touch?

Nonetheless, it is telling that the Institute chose this era for its first foray into patriotic video games: not a time of victory but one of Russia's darkest hours. For Putin, after all, a fundamental lesson from history is that to be weak, to be divided, is to be under threat, and that there is nothing more weakening than the absence of a strong ruler. Even before his death, Ivan the Terrible was destroying the very institutions of his state, but after, Russia would descend into a period of violence and vulnerability that still casts its shadow to this day.

THE *OPRICHNINA*

The Estonian city of Narva stands as an object lesson to the changing borders and allegiances of Central Europe. Now at the front line of a new Cold War, facing the Russian city of Ivangorod just over the Narva River, it is still considered a potential security risk given the number of Russian-speaking Estonians living there. First the Danes conquered it, building Hermann Castle there, before the city was sold to the Livonian Order by King Valdemar IV in 1346. Sigismund II Augustus, ruler of the Polish–Lithuanian Commonwealth, feared Russian expansion into the region, as the Livonian Order declined, and hoped to leverage it into becoming a dependency. In response, in 1558, Ivan IV invaded, quickly seizing Narva and other Estonian cities, where his men were welcomed as liberators. In 1560, his forces won such a convincing victory over the Livonians at the Battle of Ērģeme that the Order was dissolved. Ivan seemed at the peak of his powers: Kazan and Astrakhan had fallen, and the Ottomans for the moment had been rebuffed. He now had new ports and fortresses along the Baltic, and his diplomats were even at court in London. Yet he was about to begin a dark and bloody slide into violence and madness that would ultimately open Russia to invasion and civil strife.

In 1560, Ivan's beloved first wife Anastasia Romanovna died, and he suspected poison and enemies within, even as a degenerative and painful bone disease began to gnaw at his body. Soon thereafter, from 1562, the Livonian War would turn against Muscovy and then, in 1564, one of his closest advisers, Prince Andrei Kurbsky, defected to Lithuania. Ivan's incipient paranoia and mistrust of the nobility suddenly took hold. First, he took himself and his trusted henchmen to the fortified town of Aleksandrova Sloboda. There, he issued an intemperate decree, in effect abdicating, and blaming the boyars for their 'treasonous deeds'. Although many would likely have loved to see him gone, with his heir Prince Ivan being only eight years old, and fearing an outcry from the nation, the boyars had no option but to beg him to reconsider. He allowed himself to be persuaded to return, but only if allowed to rule however he saw fit, ignoring the boyars' ancient rights and privileges. Even so, in 1565 he divided the country into the *Oprichnina* ('the Exception'), which became his personal realm, while the rest of the country, known as the *Zemshchina* ('the Land'), was to be managed – in his name – by the Boyar Council.

There followed a time of chaos and violence. Ivan established a personal army, the *Oprichniki*, who were at once his enforcers and his guards. Wearing black monastic robes and bearing a broom and a dog's head – for they were the tsar's hounds, who would sweep away his foes – they are sometimes described as the first Russian secret police, but there was nothing secret about them. They raided the *Zemshchina*, sometimes at Ivan's behest in pursuit of some imaginary enemy or other, but increasingly just for loot and the hell of it. The result was a growing series of interconnected crises: peasants fled from the vicinity of the *Oprichnina*, food grew short, trade was strangled. When the Crimeans burnt down half of Moscow in 1572, the danger to the country as a whole became obvious. Ivan, who had already begun to realize that the *Oprichniki* were getting out of control, abolished them and returned to Moscow. Nonetheless, he would remain aloof, erratic, paranoid and vindictive. He saw plots on every side and dealt with them murderously, and while in 1576 a successful expedition into Danish-held parts of Livonia forced them near enough out of the war, in 1577 Ivan's local proxy Prince Magnus of Holstein turned against him (more betrayal!), and the Swedes and Polish-Lithuanians united against Muscovy. Narva would fall to Swedish mercenaries in 1581 – the same year Ivan accidentally killed his heir, Prince Ivan, in a fit of rage.

By the time Ivan died in 1584, of a stroke suffered in the middle of a game of chess, the country was already on the edge of chaos. The nobility was divided between rival families, and between the old holdouts and Ivan's favourites. Peasants had fled conscription and the *Oprichniki*, leaving fields untilled and crops unharvested. Hunger bred banditry, and banditry further destabilized the economy. Ivan IV's remaining heir, Prince Fyodor, was well meaning but naïve, more interested in church ritual than ruling (his soubriquet was Fyodor the Bellringer), making him little more than a figurehead for his brother-in-law, the ruthless and ambitious former *Oprichnik* Boris Godunov.

TIME OF TROUBLES

Godunov was undeniably able but had no real claim to the throne. His part-Tatar blood and *Oprichnik* past left him open to the taunts, sneers and plots of the established boyar clans. Godunov responded by purging the rival Belsky family, then the Shuiskies and the Nagoi. Arguably, few would truly mourn them, but Ivan also had a three-year-old son, Dmitry Ivanovich. Technically he could not succeed to the throne because he was the issue of the tsar's seventh and final marriage, and the Church only recognized his first three as legitimate. Nonetheless, he and his mother were essentially exiled to Uglich, and there Dmitri would die in 1591. The official judgement – that he had accidentally cut his own throat when he had an epileptic fit while shaving – understandably failed to convince. The people of Uglich rioted and were suppressed by force, and when his mother accused Godunov of being behind the death, she was forcibly dispatched to a nunnery in Beloözero. That death – assassination? – would, however, come to haunt Godunov and Russia fully three times in the near future.

Godunov was in many ways a clever and far-sighted regent. In 1590, he repelled a Tatar raid on Moscow, although an ill-fated war with Sweden in 1590–95 proved inconclusive. The 1595 Treaty of Tyavzino that ended it was also known in Russia, rather over-optimistically, as the Treaty of Eternal Peace with Sweden. He realized the need for modernization and for trade, and whereas Fyodor had sought to reverse his father's policy of deepening links with England, not least because successive ambassadors from London failed to treat him with the awestruck respect he demanded, Godunov offered them exemption from customs duties to encourage them. He also invested time and resources into building new towns and fortresses to secure the north-eastern and south-eastern borders, and pushed Moscow's rule further into Siberia.

In 1598, Fyodor would die, with no heir: the Ryurikid dynasty had reached its end. Ivan IV had created a consultative parliament of sorts, the *Zemsky Sobor*, or Assembly of the Land, and it elected Godunov tsar. He would die in 1605, though, having not really managed to establish the basis for a dynasty, nor done more than temporarily hold off the multiple crises looming over Muscovy. His 16-year-old son Fyodor would rule for little more than a month before being murdered. The scene was set for the *Smuta*, the so-called 'Time of Troubles', eight years of rebellion, war and feud, in which those crises, which had been smouldering under both Ivan and Godunov, blazed across the country.

The first was dynastic. Godunov's claim to the throne had been no better than many others', and with no legitimate ruling line, other boyar families could and would advance their own claims. In a time of faith, though, a sense that these all lacked divine favour helped explain the desperation for a legitimate monarch that led so many to accept the often transparently implausible claims of successive False Dmitries, pretenders who claimed that they were the real Dmitry Ivanovich, who had somehow not died after all. Nor was this just about who got to be tsar. Ivan the Great's reforms, especially as related to the military, and the tax base and bureaucracy needed to support them, had begun creating a centralized autocracy at odds with an aristocracy that enjoyed its autonomy. That an *Oprichnik* had become tsar was regarded as proof that 'new men' were on the rise. This was also a struggle between boyars and monarchical power.

As the hereditary boyars began to fear the challenge of the service gentry, they both faced a socio-economic crisis. Famine, banditry and labour dues had for years been forcing peasants to flee their lands. Landlords, desperate for labour, were even resorting to kidnapping their neighbours' serfs. In 1597, Godunov had tried to ban such transfers, but only with limited effect. Indeed, it was as if the very heavens were conspiring against him, as the early years of the 17th century were also unusually cold, likely the result of a massive eruption by the Huaynaputina volcano in Peru that cast a pall around the world. Harvests were hit, and as a result, between 1601 and 1603, famine swept Russia, killing some 2 million people – almost a third of the total population.

This also had very direct security consequences, as the military foundations of Muscovy were under threat. Its armies were still based on gentry cavalry, their service and equipment paid by revenues extracted from the peasants who farmed their lands. Yet as disease and peasant flight depopulated central Muscovy, it became harder and harder to support them. This was exacerbated by the growing size of the gentry class. New territories would be brought under the tsar in Siberia, but these were not immediately productive. Otherwise, there had been no major expansion of Muscovy since the conquest of the khanates in the 1570s. Indeed, the reigns of both Ivan and Godunov had seen Muscovy increasingly engaged with powerful nations to the south and west. Although there had been victories against the Kazan, Crimean and Sibir Khanates, these had not come cheap, and the state's treasury had been drained fighting inconclusive tussles with the Swedes (1554– 57, 1590–95), and outright defeat in the Livonian War (1558–83). Muscovy was not only weakened by its political and socio-economic crises; they could be and were exploited by these new enemies, above all Poland.

THE DMITRIADS

Although more generally known as the Polish–Muscovite Wars, the on-and-off conflict that raged from 1605 to 1618 is also known as the Dmitriads in Polish historiography, for the very reason that a series of 'False Dmitries' would prove so central to them. For the Poles, these were a series of attempts to humble or tame a dangerous neighbour; for many Russians, excited by the thought that maybe the Ryurikid dynasty had survived, and that somehow Dmitry had not died – or been killed – after all, they could represent a chance to recapture the old days of stability and relative plenty. 'Fake news' was already destabilizing governments in the 16th century.

Muscovy was too powerful for the Polish–Lithuanian Commonwealth to challenge alone and directly, but as it collapsed into anarchy and division, Sigismund III Vasa, the ambitious and aggressive King of Poland and Grand Duke of Lithuania, began to entertain thoughts of conquest, especially as discontented Muscovite boyars began making overtures of their own. After all, Poland's monarchy was defined and limited by the Golden Liberty, which granted considerable rights and freedoms to the *szlachta*, the nobility. They even elected the king. Ivan's *Oprichnina* and Godunov's purges, as well as the overall drive towards centralization of the state, left many Muscovite aristocrats frightened and unsettled. The prospect of Catholic Polish rule – as long as they retained their lands and grew their privileges – no longer seemed so unthinkable.

In 1603, the first 'False Dmitry' – likely a renegade monk called Grigory Otrepyev – appeared at the Polish court. Sigismund saw him as a potentially useful yet also deniable weapon against Godunov and indulged him with 4,000 zlotys, sufficient funds to hire a few hundred men, but above all placed no obstacles to his pitching his cause to more interested Polish magnates. The prospect of territorial expansion, enrichment and religious service together led a number to support him, and in 1605, he led an army of perhaps 4,000 men against Godunov. The tales of the pretender had already been undermining Godunov, even if in many cases it was more that it was a gift to cynical and disgruntled boyars looking for any excuse to question his authority, and a mixed bag of supporters, from 2,000 Cossack horsemen from the south (on whom more next chapter) to desperate peasants flocked to the False Dmitry's banner. They won an early victory at Novgorod-Siversk, taking Chernigov and Kursk, but were then savaged at Dobrynichy. The campaign could easily have turned into a rout, had Godunov not then died on 13 April 1605. Suddenly, the situation was changed as momentum swung to the invaders. Boyars began to defect in increasing numbers, as no one wanted to be the last to jump ship. Godunov's son and heir Fyodor II and his mother were imprisoned in their apartments and then strangled to death. On 20 June, Dmitry was welcomed into Moscow by the very boyars who had denounced him a few months earlier, crowned by the new patriarch he had just appointed – a Greek Cypriot – and joined by his wife, a Catholic Polish noblewoman.

Many ordinary Russians apparently welcomed what they believed was a resumption of the old line, but for the nobility this had always been an act of political expediency. The boyars were wary of Catholic and Polish influence, especially when they fully realized that the Golden Liberty actually set them on the same level as the lesser gentry. Once the

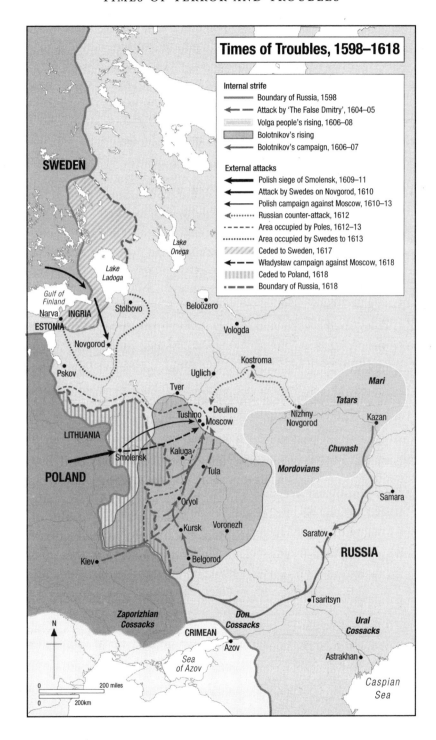

Times of Troubles, 1598–1618

Internal strife

- Boundary of Russia, 1598
- Attack by 'The False Dmitry', 1604–05
- Volga people's rising, 1606–08
- Bolotnikov's rising
- Bolotnikov's campaign, 1606–07

External attacks

- Polish siege of Smolensk, 1609–11
- Attack by Swedes on Novgorod, 1610
- Polish campaign against Moscow, 1610–13
- Russian counter-attack, 1612
- Area occupied by Poles, 1612–13
- Area occupied by Swedes to 1613
- Ceded to Sweden, 1617
- Władysław campaign against Moscow, 1618
- Ceded to Poland, 1618
- Boundary of Russia, 1618

SWEDEN

Lake Onega

Lake Ladoga

Gulf of Finland

Narva • INGRIA

Stolbovo •

Beloozero •

ESTONIA

Novgorod •

Vologda •

Pskov •

Kostroma •

Mari

Uglich •

Tver •

Tatars

• Deulino

Tushino •

Nizhny Novgorod •

Kazan •

LITHUANIA

Moscow •

Kaluga •

Chuvash

• Smolensk

POLAND

• Tula

Mordovians

Samara •

• Oryol

Saratov •

• Kursk

Voronezh •

RUSSIA

Kiev •

• Belgorod

• Tsaritsyn

N

Zaporizhian Cossacks

Don Cossacks

Ural Cossacks

CRIMEAN

Astrakhan •

Azov •

Sea of Azov

Caspian Sea

0   200 miles

0   200km

bulk of Commonwealth forces had withdrawn – leaving a few hundred thugs and mercenaries who quickly made themselves unpopular with the Muscovites by throwing their weight around – Prince Vasily Shuisky began organizing a conspiracy to unseat Dmitry. He wanted to impose Catholicism, his whisperers said, he was a homosexual, he was a Polish dupe (admittedly, that one was arguably true): within less than a year they had poisoned his reputation and prepared a coup.

They stormed the Kremlin on 17 May 1606, sweeping aside his bullyboys. Dmitry tried to flee but was shot, then cremated and, the story goes, his ashes were symbolically shot back towards Poland from a cannon. Prince Vasily was duly crowned as Tsar Vasily IV, but the story hardly ended there. He was no more legitimate than Dmitry and far less able than Godunov. From the first, he had problems asserting his rule over the country, and the next year a new 'False Dmitry' appeared. The success of the first meant that even more Polish magnates backed the second imposter, who quickly assembled a force of 7,500 men – a mix of Poles, mercenaries and Russians. By spring 1608, his forces were closing on Moscow, swollen by Russian peasants lured by the promise of the distribution of land confiscated from boyars who remained loyal to Vasily.

The second False Dmitry encamped at Tushino, a couple of hours' march from Moscow. Again, the pretender had the momentum. Cities, boyars, gentry and commoners alike hurriedly flocked to his side, while Vasily haemorrhaged forces such that one account spoke of 'Moscow's squares and barracks being equally empty.' Victory seemed assured, but this time Sigismund was not willing to leave things in the hands of outsourced agents. He mustered his own army and crossed the border in 1609, causing many of Dmitry's Polish supporters to abandon Tushino and march to join him as he invested Smolensk. Unfortunately for the pretender, at the same time Vasily's diplomatic overtures to Sweden bore fruit, and a joint army threatened his suddenly weakened position. He fled to Kostroma and, although the support of the Don Cossacks allowed him to remain a power in south-eastern Russia for a time, in December 1610 he would die at the hands of a Tatar princeling, Pyotr Urusov, whom he had once flogged, and whose passion for revenge Dmitry had underestimated.

The field was now Sigismund's. Heavily fortified Smolensk would hold out until June 1611, but after the famed Polish winged hussars

– so named for the wooden frames decked with eagle, falcon or vulture feathers fastened to their backs – routed a substantially larger Muscovite force in the Battle of Klushino (4 July 1610), the ever-flexible Russian elite realized which way the winds of war were blowing. Two weeks later, the so-called 'Seven Boyars' toppled Vasily and invited the 15-year-old Polish Prince Władysław to become tsar. His father vetoed this, on the grounds that he would have to convert to Orthodoxy, but instead for the moment graciously took upon himself the role of regent, installing a Commonwealth garrison in the Kremlin.

THE BATTLE OF MOSCOW, 1611

The story of the Time of Troubles is of armies – Swedish, Polish, rebel, loyalist – strong enough to take to the field and win battles, but never strong enough to maintain their grip on Moscow. So it was again, as the prospect of Catholic rule and the unruly behaviour of the Commonwealth garrison began to anger the people of Moscow. A series of incidents accumulated until a riot left 15 Muscovites dead. In January 1611, Patriarch Hermogenes issued a letter despairing 'how your Fatherland is being plundered, how they defile holy icons and churches, how innocent blood is being shed'.

This was enough to crystallize nationalist feelings in the country, the start of an initiative that would have echoes all the way into the 21st century. Prokopy Lyapunov, voivode of Ryazan, was inspired to organize the First People's Militia, a force characterized more by its enthusiasm than its experience. They were able to catch the Commonwealth forces by surprise and, as church bells rang across the city, were joined by thousands of Muscovites. The Russians were able to take much of the city, but the defenders were hard-bitten veterans, a mix of perhaps 5,000 Polish-Lithuanian troops and 2,000 German mercenaries. They retreated to the Kremlin and the fortified Kitay-Gorod neighbourhood, where they could hold off a ragtag militia largely lacking artillery or engineers. The attack wavered, not least as Polish agents managed to convince the Cossacks who were supporting it that Lyapunov planned to betray them. He was summoned to meet a council of Cossack leaders and promptly hacked to death.

The First People's Militia began to fall apart, as faction turned against faction. However, before the Commonwealth forces could make a concerted sally to retake the city, a Second People's Militia saved the day. In 1612, a merchant named Kuzma Minin and Prince Dmitry Pozharsky had assembled another force in Nizhny Novgorod, east of Moscow. Pozharsky was charismatic and dashing, a fitting commander, while Minin was an able organizer who, guided by Pozharsky's observations of the problem faced by First People's Militia, recruited siege engineers, not just soldiers. First, they blocked attempts to reinforce the Commonwealth defenders, forcing back a large cavalry relief force under Jan Karol Chodkiewicz in August 1612. After three days of inconclusive fighting, the battle was won when Pozharsky and Minin were joined by Cossacks who had been with the First People's Militia. The story is that it took a promise from the wealthy Trinity-Sergius Monastery to pay them to win them over. The garrison had since been depleted, and had ample powder and shot to continue to defend the Kremlin, but without Chodkiewicz's supplies, it also soon began to starve. Once they had eaten their horses, they turned to any dogs, cats, or even rats they could find. By the end of September, when they were resorting to chewing on their own leather belts, Pozharsky offered terms. Garrison commander Mikołaj Struś tried to hold out, but as desertions became an increasingly serious problem, he eventually bowed to the inevitable. At the end of October, again to the pealing of Moscow's bells, he surrendered.

At the time, Sigismund was mustering an army to put down this rebellion, but once he heard the news of the Kremlin's fall, he abandoned his plans for the moment, unwilling to test too far the patience of the *Sejm*, the assembly of the nobility. Even so, he would face a rebellion that would last until 1614. The Polish–Muscovite War was not yet over, though. In 1615–16 a force of rebel soldiers and bandits under the Polish nobleman and adventurer Alexander Józef Lisowski raided border regions, looting and burning as they went. More seriously, in 1617 Sigismund made one last bid to instal Władysław on the Russian throne. Ultimately, the Commonwealth again lacked the forces for a convincing push on Moscow, especially with no new imposters to attract Russian allies. In October, Moscow was invested, but the invaders lacked the supplies or supply lines for a long siege. When a desperate night assault on the city's walls failed, they withdrew.

A NEW START

The subsequent 1618 Truce of Deulino left the Commonwealth in possession of border territories, including Smolensk, but marked the end of Sigismund's ambitions in Russia, not least because 1613 had seen the coronation of a new tsar, Mikhail Romanov, and with him a new dynasty. The *Smuta* was coming to an end, and Russia was less vulnerable at last. Nonetheless, until Tsar Mikhail I Romanov's accession, perhaps 5 million Russians – up to half the total population – had fled or died as a result of famine, war and disease. Still, military lessons had been learned. Ivan the Terrible's reign had demonstrated an awareness that conquest demanded a shift from haphazard collections of feudal warbands to a standing army supplemented by the levy, with the capacity to field artillery and a range of military specialists. The Time of Troubles had shown that this was crucial for national defence, too. This was a new age, of gunpowder, growing urban populations and ever larger armies, too. Muscovy – increasingly known as Russia in the Romanov era – had to adapt, and that meant, above all, that the state had to be strengthened.

Nonetheless, even in an era of standing armies and professional generals, there was a role for the enthusiastic patriot. The militias that drove the Commonwealth forces out of Moscow were known as the *Opolchentsy*, and their increasingly mythologized story came to embody the notion that, in a time of crisis, every good Russian was expected to fight. Pozharsky and Minin were eventually immortalized by a statue in Red Square, right in front of St Basil's Cathedral. In some ways the notion of a 'Patriotic War' – a no-holds-barred, burn the ground and poison the wells defence of the Motherland, which really emerged in the fight against Napoleon – dates back to 1611. The *Opolchentsy* would also become useful archetypes in Russian propaganda. The term was revived in 2014 for the rebellious Russophone Ukrainians, Russian nationalist volunteers, mercenaries, thugs and Kremlin agents involved in the messy conflict – a toxic combination of rebellion and invasion – which erupted in the Donbas. Labelling them *Opolchentsy* was an obvious attempt to legitimize them in deep historical context.

These wars left a deep mistrust of Poland (richly reciprocated), and highlighted the growing importance of the Cossacks to the Muscovite state – and also their paradoxical role as rebels and loyalists, expressions of Russian power and godfathers of the independent Ukrainian nation, to which we will now turn.

Want To Know More?

Ian Grey's *Boris Godunov: The Tragic Tsar* (Hodder & Stoughton, 1973) is rather dated, but a very readable biography, to which Robert Crummey's *The Formation of Muscovy 1304–1613* (Longman, 1987) can provide the scholarly backdrop. There is something of a dearth of good standalone studies of the *Smuta*, but Chester Dunning's *Russia's First Civil War: The Time of Troubles and the Founding of the Romanov Dynasty* (Pennsylvania State University Press, 2001) is the most interesting. It may well be a blessing that the *Smuta* computer game is apparently not available except on the Russian VK Games platform, but there is a Russian tabletop wargame, *Smuta: The Time of Troubles 1605–1612* (Status Belli, 2010), which, I confess, I have never had the chance to play.

9

The Cossacks

Azov, 1637 and 1641

In his *And Quiet Flows the Don* (1932), Mikhail Sholokhov chronicles the life and fate of Cossacks living in the Don River valley through the First World War and then the Russian Civil War, when their community split between the 'Reds' supporting the 1917 Bolshevik Revolution and the 'Whites' opposed to it. Since the explosion of the undeclared war in Ukraine's Donbas region in 2014, a similar schism saw Cossack again fighting Cossack, as some backed the government in Kyiv and others the rebels and their Russian nationalist allies and instigators. In some ways, this was inevitable in a warrior culture that would prove as extravagantly enthusiastic in support of the tsar as in opposition.

Desperate to end the cycle of coup and invasion, in 1613 the *Zemsky Sobor* offered the crown to 16-year-old Mikhail Romanov, ushering in a dynastic line that would survive until 1917. With no particular enemies, his family exalted enough to be plausibly royal, but not so powerful as to raise fears among its peers, and watched over by his formidable father, Patriarch Filaret, the sense was not so much that he was the outstanding candidate as that, to be blunt, he would do. In fact he did more than just do, and his 32-year reign would see the conclusion of the wars with Sweden and Poland. While this entailed some territorial concessions to the west, it was more than offset by a massive expansion of Russian lands to the east. By the time of the accession of his son and successor Alexis, Russian explorers had even made their way to the Sea of Okhotsk and the Pacific Ocean.

The leader of that expedition, Ivan Moskvitin, was, needless to say, a Cossack. In many ways, after all, the story of the emergence of the Russian Empire – and its new iteration under Vladimir Putin – can be told as the story of the Cossacks, the semi-nomadic warrior-farmers of the southern steppes. Their fortified townships (*stanitsas*) swollen by the influx of deserters, refugees and outlaws, in due course they would become the elite light cavalry and enforcers of the monarch. They would also, though, become one of the forces and cultures behind the emerging Ukrainian identity, and thus the story of Russia's relationship with the Cossacks is at the heart of its complex one with its southwestern neighbour, too.

THE WILD FIELDS

The name Cossack emerged in the 13th century, likely derived ultimately from the Polovtsian word for free man. This is singularly appropriate, as the culture that they formed exalted freedom and a rough-and-ready kind of limited democracy. Although the origins of this society are unclear and disputed, their geographic roots were in the *Dikoye Polye*, the 'Wild Fields' of the Pontic Steppe, between the Ural and Danube Rivers, but above all in the lower reaches of the Dniester, Don and Dnieper. The lands were well suited to settled agriculture, but they were equally well suited to steppe nomad raids, which repeatedly foiled attempts to colonize and tame them. After the Khazars, they were claimed by the Kievan Rus', then the Mongols, briefly the Grand Duchy of Lithuania, then the Golden Horde and subsequently the Crimean Khanate. Claimed does not mean ruled, though, and to a large degree the Wild Fields remained relatively free.

Settlers had long tracked into the region, as much in flight as in hope. Remnants of broken steppe nomad tribes, serfs fleeing hunger or lordly persecution, bandits and deserters, optimists and adventurers, all sorts came to the Wild Fields, especially from the 13th century onwards. While some of the steppe ended up carved up by new nations, such as the Crimean Khanate and Moldavia, the central swathe of the Wild Fields remained largely lordless, with scattered settlements living a life of hunting and subsistence farming. Over time they grew, but however fertile the land, the settlers needed to be tough to cope with the regular threat of Nogai slave raids and similar human predators. To be a Cossack was as much to be a warrior as a hunter, farmer and horseman. Until around the 17th century, they accepted near enough anyone able and willing to contribute, and although eventually the Cossacks would be known for their Slavic and indeed Orthodox identity, before then, there were Turkish deserters, stray Bulgars, runaway slaves from Crimea, and every other human flotsam and jetsam of the regions in their number.

By the 1400s, there were numerous such communities, jealously protecting their independence from Poland, Lithuania, Muscovy and each other. Some might pledge loyalty to one of the neighbouring states, but this was typically a temporary and transactional matter. Over time, their numbers grew as more and more fled to this new frontier, building new connections between communities. In 1492, Crimean Khan Meñli I Giray complained to the Grand Duke of Lithuania that Cossacks had seized and looted a Crimean Tatar boat that had been sailing on the Dnieper. The Grand Duke replied that this had not been done by his men or on his orders, and instructed his local officials to investigate and provide restitution. The implication is that for all Lithuania's claims to these territories, outside the main cities, the Grand Duke's authority was severely limited.

By the mid-16th century, most (but by no means all) of these communities had cohered into two federations. The Zaporizhian Sich occupied the lands around the lower Dnieper (the root of Zaporizhia means 'below the rapids'), with Poland to the west and the Tatars to their south and east. Polish and Lithuanian merchants, missionaries and agents travelled among them, and they were often lumped into the 'Ruthenians', as East Slavs of what is now Ukraine were often known. By contrast, the Don Cossacks of the lower reaches of the Don, close to the Azov Sea, were sandwiched between the Nogai and Tatar tribes, with the Kazan Khanate between them and Muscovy. They looked towards the Rus', and as early as 1444, Cossack mercenaries were part of an army defending Pereslavl-Zalessky, for example. Later, foreshadowing the role they would play in the tsars' armies for centuries, a force under Ataman – chieftain – Susar Fyodorov joined Ivan the Terrible's armies besieging Kazan in 1552.

CROWN AND COSSACK

With the fall of Kazan in 1552, the Don Cossacks were on Muscovy's borders. Increasingly, they were engaged as mercenaries, as they began to develop a new relationship with the tsar, trading service for privileges. They were, of course, highly prized as scouts and light cavalry, in some ways as later counterparts to the earlier Black Hoods, and thanks to that, they remained self-governing. Nonetheless, their relationship with the tsars became increasingly important and in some ways could be considered another aspect of the emergence of a centralized military state; they received their first charter, from Ivan IV, in 1570, and founded their first capital, at Cherkassk.

The Cossacks would in due course swear oaths of loyalty to the tsar, and in return extracted distinctive privileges from the crown, including electing their own atamans, and felt that their special relationship with the tsar meant that they were more than vassals. The traditions of prickly Cossack independence would ensure that they were often not just the tsar's most enthusiastic protectors and enforcers – witness their use in suppressing riots and rising across the centuries – but also some of the most dangerous rebels against his rule, notably Stenka Razin in the late 17th century and Kondraty Bulavin and Yemelyan Pugachov in the 18th. In all three cases, to greater or lesser degrees, the rebellions had their deeper roots in Cossack resistance to efforts to curb their freedoms. Until the age of Catherine the Great, for example, serfdom was not practised in Cossack lands, so peasants continued to flee there, much to the chagrin of labour-hungry lords, and the crown. The ringleaders themselves combined military service, banditry and revolt in a distinctive Cossack way. Stenka (Stepan) Razin, for example, turned to banditry after a career as an official, and raised a substantial gang from Cossacks, deserters and other freebooters. In 1667, he infamously plundered the 'great water caravan', comprising the treasure barges of the rich merchant Vasily Shorin and Patriarch Ioasaf II, then took his fleet of 35 flat-bottomed river boats called *strugs* down the Volga, raiding along the way and trouncing a punitive expedition from Astrakhan. In 1668, they sailed out into the Caspian Sea and raided Persian shipping and coastal settlements along its western coast, and in 1669 even fought off a larger Persian force at the Battle of Pig Island. The Shah's men, eager to catch the raiders for performatively inventive justice, tried to trap them by chaining their ships together, but in practice only encumbered themselves, allowing the nimbler and better-armed Cossack barques to pick them off one at a time.

His coffers full of plunder, his fleet swollen by opportunistic volunteers, his legend going before him, Razin had become a power with which to be reckoned. Tsar Alexei was willing to pardon him his earlier antics, in return for peace, but although Razin at first seemed minded to accept these terms, once he was back in the Don, he seems to have been intoxicated by the opportunities. After all, the country had still not recovered from the 1654–67 Russo-Polish War, taxes were being hiked as a result, and the runaway serfs who had joined the Cossacks, known as the *golytba*, were landless and discontented, and saw a rebellion as an opportunity for loot and advancement. In 1670, Razin declared himself in revolt, although in a pattern repeated numerous times in Russia's tumultuous history, he claimed not to be opposed to the tsar (who was, after all, monarch by divine right) but the boyars, clerks, priests and governors who were misleading him and enriching themselves at the people's expense. It was an appealing message, especially when he was also offering to impose the Cossack socio-political system, in effect abolishing serfdom. Cossacks and serfs alike rose all along the Volga, as well as subject minorities such as Tatars and Mordovians.

Tsaritsyn fell, then Astrakhan, Saratov and Samara. The tsar dispatched a 60,000-strong army to suppress the rising, and in October 1670 Razin himself was injured when his army was defeated near Simbirsk. He was carried back to his base at Kagalnitsky in the Don region, where he planned to raise a new rebel army. However, the established Cossack leaders, fearing both the wrath of the tsar and also the unleashed passions of the *golytba*, turned against him, seizing Razin and delivering him to the tsar. In 1671, he was tortured, tried, and quartered and beheaded in Red Square, and his rebellion was suppressed with terrible ferocity, reflecting the fear such a social rising engendered among Russia's rulers.

THE ZAPORIZHIAN SICH

The Zaporizhian Cossacks, by contrast, largely looked south and west. From their *stanitsas* along the lower reaches of the Dnieper, they even raided in the Black Sea in the small boats they would sail down the river. As they began to reach a certain critical mass of numbers and ambition they became a more significant political actor than mere raiders, though. Dmytro Vyshnevetsky was both a symptom and driver of this process. Born into a rich and powerful family connected to the Lithuanian Gediminid dynasty, he first began by raising a Cossack force to fight the Crimean Tatars in 1550, building for himself a fort on the Small Khortytsya Island on the Dnieper. While naturally inclined towards the Lithuanians and by extension their Polish allies (this was shortly before the creation of the Commonwealth in 1569), he was hostile to Polish King Sigismund II Augustus and his policy of the aggressive promotion of Catholicism, and reportedly made overtures to the Crimeans. When this bore no fruit, he instead accepted an invitation from Muscovy to participate in joint expeditions against them. However, with the outbreak of the Livonian War in 1558, Tsar Ivan IV was distracted, and the raids on Crimea became a lower priority. Vyshnevetsky instead turned back to the Lithuanians, who were happy to engage his services. Eventually, in 1563, he would fall victim to his ambitions: induced into an ill-fated intervention into a civil war in Moldavia, to the west, he would end up captured, surrendered to the Turks, and tortured to death in Constantinople, hung on hooks inserted between his ribs.

Vyshnevetsky may have envisaged himself as the next ruler of Moldavia, but the irony is that by his willingness to act as an autonomous political actor and involve himself in the affairs of other nations – just like a monarch – he set a powerful example for the Zaporizhian Cossacks. Their word for a fortified encampment like Vyshnevetsky's was *sich*, and as more and more were built to protect the Wild Fields from marauders, the term became used more generally to define the Zaporizhian Cossack nation – metaphorically, a fortress against all threats.

Nonetheless, just as Muscovy and then Russia sought to turn potential poachers into gamekeepers, wooing the Don Cossacks into the service of the tsars, so too Poland would seek to domesticate the Zaporizhian Sich. In 1583, their lands were formally incorporated into the Kiev Voivodeship, within the so-called Lesser Poland Province. Nonetheless, within the Polish lands, the Sich became an increasingly coherent proto-state, governed by the *Sich Rada*, or Sich Council – which, tellingly, was also known as the Military Council. The Council elected a leader known as the *Kosh Otaman*, in what was a simple representative system that suited the essentially centrifugal nature of Cossack politics.

Just as with the Don Cossacks, the Sich would resent creeping attempts to tame them and strip them of their traditional rights. Rebellions were endemic, with the most serious being that raised in 1647 by Bohdan Khmelnytsky, a once-loyal soldier of the Commonwealth driven to revolt when the crown refused to support him against a rapacious Polish nobleman. However, the success of his rising was down not just to Khmelnytsky's undoubted charisma and ability, but precisely because he was articulating not just the grievances of the Zaporizhian Cossacks but also a stirring sense of nationhood. In 1648, the Rada elected him as their hetman, or overall leader and commander, and as more and more Cossacks flocked to his banner, he was able to impose a series of defeats on the Commonwealth forces dispatched to crush his rising. When he made a triumphant entry into Kiev on Christmas Day 1648, it was clear that this had become more than just a Cossack venture, but also offered something to other Ruthenians. When opening talks with a Polish delegation in February 1649, he called himself 'the sole autocrat of the Rus", highlighting the complexities of the evolving relationship between Muscovy and what would become called Ukraine. After early victories, Khmelnytsky's forces would suffer a catastrophic defeat at the Battle of Berestechko in 1651. Facing the threat of total defeat – and Polish reprisals – Khmelnytsky chose the lesser of two evils and would go on to sign the Treaty of Pereyaslav with Tsar Alexis in 1654. In return for Russia's protection, the Sich swore loyalty to the tsar. This sparked the Russo-Polish War of 1654–67. Despite some victories in battle, the Commonwealth was forced to concede thanks to an opportunistic Swedish invasion and internal unrest. The subsequent 1667 Treaty of Andrusovo saw the Russians finally regain

Smolensk, while the Commonwealth ceded the Ruthenian territories on the left (east) bank of the Dnieper, including Kiev. This became the new Zaporizhian Cossack state – but only at Moscow's sufferance, and in 1775 the Hetmanate was formally abolished and serfdom imposed on these lands after Hetman Ivan Mazepa had incautiously sided with the Swedes during the Great Northern War (1700–21), as will be discussed in chapter 12.

Medieval Kiev had been part of a sprawling Rus' culture that stretched to Novgorod in the north, and while Kiev itself had been conquered by the Mongols, from the 14th century it had been ruled by the Lithuanians, and much of this region had then been divided between Poland and Lithuania. The Ruthenians did not have anything like their own state, and were increasingly subject, especially in the west, to Polish and Catholic influences, as this land became known informally as Ukraine, meaning borderland, the limits of Polish rule in the east. No wonder that for many Ukrainians, Khmelnytsky's short-lived Hetmanate represents the first Ukrainian nation, and it would be memorialized and mythologized in the 19th century as Ukrainian nationalism began to emerge. In the schism between the Don and Zaporizhian Cossacks, one can see a metaphor for the wider sundering of the Rus'.

AZOV, 1637

The growing incorporation of the Cossacks into the Commonwealth and, even more strongly, Russia would be of considerable military value – and jeopardy. From Ivan the Terrible's creation of the *Streltsy* and expansion of the gentry cavalry, Muscovy had been moving towards a standing army of sorts, even though it was still essentially one that had to be mobilized seasonally. The Cossacks provided a new source of highly able light cavalry, and some mobile infantry and artillery units, too. They also came with their own interests and vendettas, which they expected the tsar to support, or at least indulge. This was most evident along Russia's southern border. Through the 15th century, the Cossacks and the Crimean Khanate had frequently been engaged in a low-level on-and-off conflict, staging raids against the other that were as often about revenge as liberating loot. The constant threat helped consolidate the martial nature of Cossack society but also a deep antagonism with their southern neighbour that was extended to the rising Ottoman Empire once the khanate had become its vassal in 1475. That said, the Cossacks were nothing if not practical, and from time to time were willing to strike deals with their Muslim enemies, at least in the early years.

One particular focus was the strategic Ottoman fortress of Azov. Scythians, Sarmatians, Polovtsians and Mongols had claimed what was once called Tanais; the Great Silk Road passed through it, Venetian and Genoese merchants established trading stations there, slaves and furs were exchanged there, and in 1475 the Ottoman Empire had claimed it and turned it into a military as well as mercantile stronghold. By its presence, controlling the mouth of the Don, it thus barred the Don Cossacks from raiding in the Sea of Azov and the connected Black Sea. More generally, it was seen as a challenge, as well as a lucrative target. In 1637, the Don Cossacks – supported by a smaller contingent of Zaporizhians – decided to take it, even though it was sheltered behind a moat and high walls, watched over by 11 towers and with a garrison of 4,000 of the Ottomans' elite Janissary infantry, provisioned with 200 cannon of various calibres and supplies for over a year's siege. At first, they appealed to Tsar Mikhail to bless and support their mission, sending an envoy to Moscow, Ataman Ivan Katorzhny, with the plea that 'we are dying of starvation, naked, barefoot and hungry', but they did not need food so much as ammunition and gunpowder. Having just ended a war with Poland, the tsar appears to have neither wanted to alienate the Cossacks nor face war with the Ottomans, and so he temporized, providing some ammunition but no artillery.

The Cossacks, though, were unwilling to be reined in. They seized the Ottoman ambassador on his way to Moscow to forestall talks, and announced a muster of the Host, the Cossack forces. In April, they launched their attack, under Ataman Mikhail Tatarinov. However, they failed to catch the defenders by surprise, and their initial assault was beaten back with heavy losses, raked by the fire of the well-trained and disciplined Janissaries along the walls. With only 90 cannon, the Cossacks' chances of breaching those walls seemed slender, and their morale wavered until Ataman Katorzhny arrived with the promised supplies from Moscow and also 1,500 extra men he had gathered on the way. What the defenders did not know was that Tatarinov had engaged the services of a German engineer with a particular specialism in sapping and mining fortifications. By 17 June, tunnels had been dug beneath part of the walls, which were stuffed with barrels of gunpowder. The next day, the mines were detonated, blowing a hole in the walls.

Half the Cossacks stormed the breach. Initially dazed by the blast, the Janissaries quickly reformed, responding with a storm of fire, as well as pouring molten tin on the attackers. However, at the same time the other half of the attacking force attacked the other side of the city, taking advantage of the way the Janissaries flocked to defend the breach. By the time they became fully aware of the threat, Cossacks were already within the walls. After hours of hard fighting, the surviving defenders were holed up in five towers. The next day, they surrendered, after an attempted relief by Ottoman forces outside Azov was intercepted and driven back by a flying column of Cossack horsemen. No prisoners were taken.

AZOV, 1641

After their victory, the Cossacks again sent to the tsar, begging his forgiveness for waylaying the ambassador and seizing Azov. Tsar Mikhail continued to sit on the fence, rebuking them for their actions and disassociating himself from the attack in his letters to Ottoman Sultan Murad IV, yet at the same time increasing the payments made to the Cossacks and promising more, while warning them, 'watch the Crimeans, tell the Nogai that, by their previous oath, they now come under your authority'. At the time, though, the Ottomans were at war with Safavid Persia and had no spare armies with which to retake Azov, so for a while the Cossacks were able to enjoy their new possession. Booty was shared out by shares, as was their tradition, and the Zaporizhians headed home. Meanwhile, Azov was declared a freeport and a Christian city. The Ottoman-Safavid War ended with the 1639 Treaty of Zuhab, but Murad died in 1640, and his successor, Ibrahim, was more dissolute than determined. The Crimean Khanate was deeply worried by the loss of Azov, especially out of fear that this was simply a deniable first step in a wider Russian push southwards.

It thus took until 1641 before a serious attempt to retake Azov was launched, by a sizeable Ottoman force supported by cavalry from Crimea: 90,000 men in total, with a large artillery train, including fully 129 siege guns, against perhaps 15,000 defenders. The city was battered day and night, with the Turks reportedly firing 700–1,000 shells every 24 hours. The walls were breached in a number of places, and by the end of the siege only three of the towers were still standing. Nonetheless, the Cossacks responded with almost suicidal courage, foiling repeated attempts to storm the walls. The battle continued underground, in a struggle of mine versus countermine. Some supplies and reinforcements from the Don Host made their way in, but by September, the end seemed to be in sight.

However, the attackers' morale was also running low, not least as they were surrounded by the constant miasma of rotting bodies. Disease was spreading through their ranks, and the tempo of their bombardment meant that their guns' barrels were wearing thin and their powder supplies running low. The Crimeans petitioned to be released from service as they could not forage in winter, and when that permission was slow in coming, took themselves off regardless.

Eventually, the Cossacks resolved on one last death-or-glory sortie, and on the night of 26 September 1641, stormed the enemy camp – only to find it deserted. That very same night, the Ottoman forces had themselves opted to withdraw. The Cossacks caught them by surprise in the retreat but were too few and too exhausted to turn it into a rout. It was at once a glorious stand and a Pyrrhic victory. It was the making of the Don Cossacks, fixing their reputation for determination and a bravery that went well beyond the bounds of common sense. It also consolidated their subordination to the tsar.

Ataman Petrov offered Azov to Tsar Mikhail, and he and his men were honoured, but a delegation from Moscow found that 'the city of Azov is broken and levelled to the ground, and there is nothing that can be done for the city at all soon.' Knowing that the Ottomans would return, the tsar ordered the city abandoned, and the last remaining defences destroyed before the Turks reclaimed it in 1642. The Cossacks were understandably disgruntled, and wrote to the tsar that 'in the siege, we gained much glory, not booty. Now we are hungry and weak from want, and have become so impoverished that by next spring we will not be able to equip ourselves... and not able to resist the combined strength of the Turk and the Tatar.' How far it was a genuine warning, and how far a negotiating tactic, is unclear, but Moscow responded with both payments and promises to defend the Cossacks in case of need. This would soon be tested when the Crimeans launched raids on border towns with Ottoman support in 1645, and Russian cavalry would fight side by side with the Cossacks.

Did Moscow play a double game, denying any connection to the Cossacks while cheering them on? Of course. But at the same time, the Cossacks managed, by demonstrating both military might and vulnerability before the Ottomans, to manoeuvre the tsar into offering them tax exemptions, freedoms and security guarantees, and all by ignoring his concerns and starting a war they wanted to fight. One of the lessons is the way that a Russia which consistently seeks military power over and above that it can reasonably afford, will rely on outsourced allies and proxies, from the Cossacks of the 17th century to the Wagner mercenaries of the 21st. In the process, the tail will regularly risk wagging the seemingly fearsome dog.

Want to Know More?

Most of the books about the Cossacks become intoxicated with their myth and deliver rattling good yarns more than judicious analysis, but Carol Stevens' *Russia's Wars of Emergence, 1460–1730* (Pearson, 2007) does a good job of putting them into their wider context. Though if rattling good yarns are what you're after and you don't mind that they are fictional, Harold Lamb's *Wolf of the Steppes* (Bison, 2006) may be what you're looking for. Albert Seaton's *The Cossacks* (Osprey, 1972) is a little dated but a short introduction that takes them all the way through to the Second World War, while Sergey Shemenkov's *Ukrainian Cossacks, Late 16th–Early 18th Century: Organisation, Clothing, Equipment, Armament* (Helion, 2024) is one for those after very granular detail.

10

The Conquest of Siberia

The Battle of Korcheyevskaya Cove, 1658

1581	Yermak's expedition to the Sibir Khanate
1639	Russians reach the Pacific
1650–52	Khabarov's expedition to Dauria
1650–89	Conflicts with China
1689	Treaty of Nerchinsk

Russia and the United States may frequently be geopolitically poles apart, but there are some ways in which they are similar, not least in the way their histories have been shaped by the scope to expand over what must have sometimes felt like infinite territories, subject to having to deal with often-inconvenient locals. (For that matter, the connection is sometimes even more direct: in the late 19th century, it was Russian migrants who did much to open up the American Great Plains to farming, drawing on the lessons of the steppes.) However, one crucial difference is that Russia had faced centuries of often-existential threat from the steppe. Its men and women had been dragged into slavery, sold in the teeming and miserable markets of Kaffa, Azov, Khiva and Bukhara. Its cities had been sacked and burned. Its colonists had been driven from their fields. Indeed, for two centuries, the Rus' had been ruled from the steppe after the Mongol conquest. No wonder that the trackless lands to the east were regarded as not just full of opportunity but also of danger. The conversion of the steppe nations directly on their borders only served to strengthen their conviction that the long-term security of Russia demanded the eventual taming of the lands to the east: not just the open steppe but also the deep forests rich in timber and 'soft gold' or furs.

There were settled polities such as the Kazan Khanate, there was the loose imperial confederation that was the Sibir Khanate, there were nomadic tribes such as the Kazakhs and the Nogai, there were semi-nomadic societies such as the Kumyks. They traded with the Russians, not least selling horses at the *Ordobazarnaya Stanitsa*, which translates roughly as the 'Travelling Bazaar of the Horde', but at the same time, for many, raiding and slave-taking were crucial elements of their economies and social structures. The emerging Russian state thus felt it was facing a constant threat, and while it was all very well to ransom its own people who were taken as slaves, far better to stop the practice in the first place. Generally speaking, though, these societies lacked the kind of authoritative ruler able to make any kind of a ban stick, even if they would be willing. When they were fending off the Polovtsians and the like, the Rus' could fortify their borders, but the larger the Muscovite and then Russian state became, the harder it was to secure its borders. The alternative was to find security by projecting that border outwards, by dealing with the inconvenient neighbours just over it. Then, of course, there would turn out to be a whole new collection of inconvenient neighbours and problematic relationships to manage. So, as the Russian state became more organized, and as gunpowder gave it a distinct military advantage, the temptation to reach further and further east became all the greater.

THE CONQUEST OF SIBERIA

The heralds of empire were largely Cossack adventurers, working for magnates or on the promise of some kind of indulgence from the crown. They were central to the expansion of Russia to the Volga and the growing confrontation with the Ottoman Empire to the south. However, they were particularly important in spearheading the push into Siberia from the 16th century, which at this time was essentially being outsourced to adventurers and magnates. The Siberian Khanate, another of the descendants of the Golden Horde, had long been in decline, torn by rivalries between two dynastic families and between original animists and Muslim converts. The vastly wealthy Stroganov family, exploiting their position within Ivan the Terrible's *Oprichnina*, had been the first systematically to exploit the new opportunities to the east, securing the tsar's permission to raise a private army to do so in return for a steady tribute of rare furs such as mink and sable. Stroganov trading stations in Siberia were often virtual armed camps, because relations with the khan or locals frequently became acrimonious.

Realizing that their businesses were at risk if they had constantly to fend off attacks, in 1581 the Stroganovs bankrolled an expedition by Yermak Timofeyevich intended to clear neighbouring regions of potentially hostile forces. An ataman of the Don Cossacks and a notorious bandit, he nonetheless was deemed to have the kind of charisma and zeal a mission into Siberia demanded. He set off down the Kama River with some 500 Cossacks and a few hundred German and Lithuanian mercenaries on 80 *strug*s, which could be rowed or rigged for sail, as conditions warranted. Invading the lands of the Voguls, a vassal tribe of the Siberian Khanate, Yermak was deliberately looking for trouble. Transferring by portage to other rivers as their route demanded, they first found that trouble at the Tatar settlement of Yepanchin (now called Turinsk), east of the Urals. In what was a recurring theme of the campaign, Tatar bows proved no match for Cossack arquebuses and cannon. Yermak's men burnt and plundered their way along the rivers of southern Siberia until Khan Kuchum mustered his forces to confront them at the confluence of the Tobol and Irtysh Rivers. He had assembled an army perhaps 15,000 strong, including mercenaries and troops from the subject Ostyak and Vogul tribes. However, many of his best troops were too far away to join the fight, and the Ostyaks and Voguls abandoned him at the height of the battle. The Cossacks formed a square, blasting Kuchum's men with concentrated firepower. Although they were finally able to close with the square, they were unable to break the Cossack ranks, and when their general, Mametkul, was wounded, they withdrew in disarray.

Kuchum fled, abandoning his capital, Isker. The field was Yermak's: he had lost just over a hundred men, against up to 2,000 of his enemies, the Sibir Khanate was effectively dead, and he had opened the gates of Siberia to Russian exploitation and expansion. Further expeditions saw Ostyak princes swearing allegiance to the tsar, and although Yermak would be killed in 1585, shortly thereafter another Cossack force would

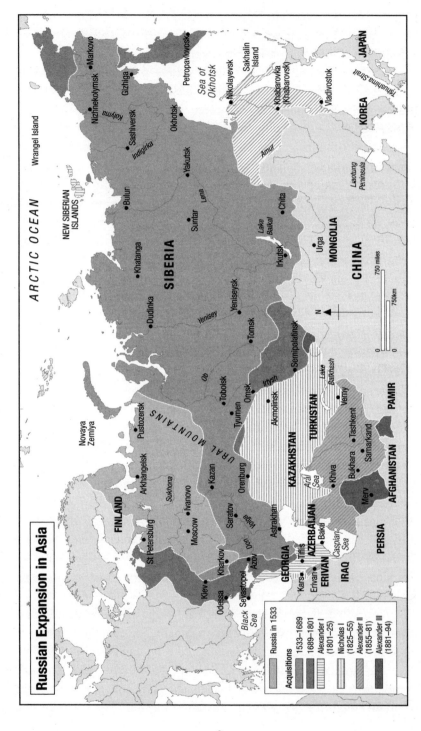

Russian Expansion in Asia

Acquisitions
- Russia in 1533
- 1533–1689
- 1689–1801
- Alexander I (1801–25)
- Nicholas I (1825–55)
- Alexander II (1855–81)
- Alexander III (1881–94)

found the first Russian fortified town in Siberia, Obskoy, at the mouth of the Irtysh River. More and more tribes and territories submitted to the crown, and Siberia was open for Russian business, exploitation and administration, as soldiers, governors and tax collectors followed in the wake of the Cossacks and their merchant masters, as well as the tide of fugitives, carpet-baggers, prospectors, trappers and explorers, eager to take advantage of this new frontier.

MEETING 'PRINCE BOGDOI'

In due course, the Cossacks penetrated into lands claimed by China, sparking a series of small-scale conflicts that nonetheless would begin to define their respective spheres of interest and set the scene for subsequent border disputes. The fall of the Sibir Khanate had opened the door to further expansion and exploration, and in 1639, the explorer Ivan Moskvitin reached the Pacific shores at Okhotsk. Much of the land east of the Yenisei River was scarcely fit for agriculture, with the exception of Dauria, a territory south of the Stanovoy Range and north of the Amur River. The Daur people were notionally Chinese subjects, but in practice most of the time they were left largely to their own devices.

However, in 1643, Pyotr Golovin, governor of the Lena Razryad (a *razryad* was a military administrative region), north of the Stanovoy Range, heard tales about the wealth of Dauria. He dispatched 133 Cossacks under one Vasily Poyarkov, on a brutal mission of reconnaissance and plunder, which drove many of the Daurs to flee to the right bank of the Amur River, seeking protection from the Chinese. Next was the better-known Yerofei Khabarov, who scouted out a better route to the Upper Amur; he persuaded Golovin's successor, Dmitry Frantsbekov, to support another expedition. In 1650–52, he took over the Daur fort of Albazin, and followed Poyarkov's rapacious example. The Daurs called the Cossacks *luocha*, a term derived from flesh-eating demons in Buddhist mythology, and their behaviour certainly merited it, as villages were burnt and people tortured or killed for loot, reprisal or sport: 'With God's help, we cut them all down, head by head,' Khabarov reported. He then built a stockaded fort at Achansk, further down the Amur, and held it against an attack by a large force of Manchu and Korean soldiers, before returning northwards.

The Russians truly did not understand that they were now encountering not simply more, as they saw them, backward tribes, but another empire. Frantsbekov had given Khabarov letters from Tsar Alexis demanding that the Daurian Prince Lavkai of Albazin and one 'Prince Bogdoi' submit or be conquered. After all, when the Daurs had been asked to whom they paid tribute, they replied, 'the Bogdoi Khan'. The assumption was that 'Bogdoi' was simply another petty local chieftain. It was, however, just one more of the many titles of the Emperor of China. This was not going to end well.

The next Cossack to lead his men south was Onufry Stepanov. In 1653, he had been charged with taking over Dauria with 320 men, but so depopulated was it now that they had problems finding food and timber, so he struck south down the Amur to find – and loot – what they needed, albeit not without a fight. However, the Manchu Chinese authorities were beginning to react to this new threat. They deported the local population in these more southern regions, to deny the invaders sources of food and labour, and sent the able general Šarhūda to Ningguta (now called Ning'an), their northernmost garrison, to take command of combined Chinese and Korean forces.

His first engagement did not go so well. In April 1654, Stepanov was leading a force of some 400 men in 39 boats down the Songhua River, when they were engaged by 160 boats carrying almost a thousand men. However, the larger Russian boats gave them an advantage of height and protection, and in the exchange of fire that followed, Russian flintlock muskets proved their superiority to Chinese matchlocks, too. The Chinese forces broke, and it was only an ambush by Korean musketeers on a hill overlooking the river that prevented a Russian pursuit. This was a Russian victory on points, but Stepanov withdrew and fortified an old position at Kamora, rightly anticipating that this was not the end of it. In February 1655, a large force possibly 10,000 strong besieged Kamora, but was ultimately forced to withdraw when its supplies ran out. Stepanov realized that he was facing a much more numerous and powerful enemy than anticipated and appealed to be allowed to withdraw back to the safety of Yakutsk and the Lena Razryad. Instead, he received the thanks of the tsar and orders that he and his men 'conduct themselves bravely' – but not enough food and, more crucially, not enough gunpowder and shot. Unsurprisingly, desertion became a growing problem.

THE BATTLE OF KORCHEYEVSKAYA COVE, 1658

In 1657, the Russians established the Daurian Voivodeship and dispatched the notoriously exacting Afanasy Pashkov to be its new governor, charged with building a fort on the Amur and preparing for colonists. This venture, in effect annexing a Chinese territory, however much in the boondocks, he was meant to accomplish with a force of just 600 soldiers. Having wintered in the Transbaikal, in 1658 he set out to Dauria, heading down the Amur, as Stepanov began to sail up the river so that the two contingents could unite. Fatefully, Stepanov divided his forces, sending almost half on ahead under his second in command, Klim Ivanov, to scout the way.

What the Russians did not appreciate was that Šarhūda had been studying the reports of the various engagements, not least with an eye to matching the Russians' river fleet. He started building larger river boats able to carry more troops and also mount cannon, with fully 40 of them built by 1658, along with another 12 transports. He also gathered a substantial force of perhaps a thousand troops with 50 light cannon. With such a force, he was ready to take the fight to the 'devils'. On the morning of 30 June, his flotilla left the Songhua River for the Amur. Six miles along they encountered Stepanov's attenuated force, anchored in the middle of the river apparently awaiting a fair wind. Faced with a much larger force, they fled, but the Chinese split into three distinct detachments and pursued, slowly overtaking the heavier Russian boats. As an artillery duel ensued, it was clear that the Russians were heavily outmatched, and so Stepanov had his boats take up a defensive line at the mouth of the Korcheyevskaya Cove.

Šarhūda led his flotilla in closer and there followed a vicious exchange of musket and cannon fire. The Chinese had the advantage in heavier artillery, but the Cossacks were well armed with quicker-firing flintlock *fuzeya* muskets. They were running low in ammunition, though, and soon the superior Chinese numbers began to tell. Some Cossacks fled ashore; others tried to shelter from the hail of incoming fire in their boats' holds, allowing the Chinese to close and board. They had hoped to capture both the boats and the accumulated tribute on board, but when the defenders rallied, Šarhūda's men resorted to firing arrows, setting seven of the remaining 11 boats alight.

The remaining Cossacks again tried to flee ashore, under heavy fire. That night, some managed stealthily to recapture one of their boats, which had been anchored in the cove under guard, and escape up the Amur. Another 65 or so were able to slip away through the forest. However, Stepanov and 270 of his men were dead. A few days later, Ivanov's force, on the return, would spot the sizeable Chinese flotilla and the wreckage of Stepanov's boats. They would also be joined by some of the survivors, who had been hiding on the banks. Realizing that they were outnumbered and outgunned, they turned and headed back up the Amur, and Šarhūda let them go, presumably because they already had too great a lead.

In August, Ivanov met Pashkov's expedition heading south and reported on the ignominious end of Stepanov's force. The voivode bowed to the inevitable, especially as by this time the identity of 'Prince Bogdoi' had become clear. Pashkov abandoned any thought of a fort on the Amur itself and instead set up his capital at Nerchinsk, rather further west and north than originally planned. After the brutal siege of the Cossack fort at Albazin – at which 600 defenders died, but so too did perhaps 1,500 Chinese soldiers, largely from hunger and disease – both nations were willing to make a deal. The subsequent 1689 Treaty of Nerchinsk, the first between Russia and China, saw the latter abandon any claims to the territories south of the Stanovoy Range but also opened up lucrative new trade opportunities. Russia would eventually annex the Amur basin in 1858, but for now it was at bay.

PUBLIC-PRIVATE EMPIRE

The battle that the Chinese name Hutong and the Russians Korcheyevskaya Cove was a relatively small skirmish that scarcely gets a reference in many histories. Nonetheless, it demonstrates some of the complexities of the Far Eastern frontier, first of all, the Cossacks' role as the outriders of the Russian Empire. From the 16th century onwards, they would be at the forefront of every attempted and successful instance of imperial expansion. It was not just because of their hardiness and adventurous spirit but also their status as both in and out of the state apparatus. At a time of growing centralization and attempts to bring political and economic power more tightly into the grip of the tsar, there was also value in forces closely enough tied to the tsar to be loyal, yet independent enough that their actions could as easily be denied as endorsed. In the process, a custom emerged that has lasted all the way to the 21st century, as witnessed by the role of so many such 'hybrid warriors' – including Cossacks – in the 2014 'Russian Spring', Moscow's half-hearted and half-admitted early meddling in Ukraine's Donbas region.

Another complexity is found in the drivers of that expansion. It is often tempting – especially in light of developments under Putin – to characterize the Russian state in its various incarnations as inherently expansionistic. However, this is not down to some imperialist DNA so much as the circumstances in which it found itself, with no natural borders and facing neighbours that were often either aggressive threats or destabilizing by their very vulnerability. Just as the conquest of Azov in 1637 was driven not by the tsar but by Cossack ambitions, so too it was the Stroganovs and Frantsbekovs who expanded the empire, leaving the state scrambling after them. The dominant principle for much of this time was empire on the cheap. In his *The Expansion of England* (1883), the 19th-century British historian Sir John Seeley famously (if perhaps controversially) remarked that 'we seem, as it were, to have conquered and peopled half the world in a fit of absence of mind.' If this is true, tsarist Russia became a land empire spanning two continents often because it was willy-nilly presented with territories by all kinds of opportunists and adventurers.

In the process, just as Muscovy would find itself facing powerful new rivals as it pushed south towards the Ottomans and west into the spheres of interest of Poland and Sweden, so too its eastern expansion would bring it fatefully into contact with China. The Chinese Empire was less technologically advanced than that of the Russians (although their experiments with composite iron and bronze cannon from the 17th century in many ways gave them a temporary advantage), but larger, with a population of 185 million in 1680 to Russia's under 10 million. At the time it was also in one of its more organized and efficient phases. Dauria had not been a priority for it but nor, for that matter, was it for distant Moscow. Successive tsars had been happy to encourage expansion eastwards, but really only as long as it was largely a case of extorting *yasak* – tribute – from a succession of tribes through what would now be called a public-private partnership. This involved minimal expenditure from the state, brought in much-needed revenue, provided a safety valve for the ambitions of noble magnates and murderous adventurers alike, and also offered a mechanism to deal with smaller-scale local instability on the borders. When they encountered strong resistance, the kind that would demand serious commitment from Moscow, they stopped.

Besides, expansion to the east was always the least important for tsarist Russia, even if it would later transpire that it brought access to gold, diamonds, oil and so many of the other raw materials for industrialization. The threats and opportunities to the south obviously mattered, especially in the heyday of its struggle against the Ottoman Empire. However, by the 18th century, the tsars and their nobility were increasingly determined to be considered Europeans, and it was to the west they would look for their darkest threats and most glittering opportunities, even before Peter the Great opened his famous 'window on the West'.

Want To Know More?

Too little has been written about this fascinating period and process, but Michael Khodarkovsky's *Russia's Steppe Frontier: The Making of a Colonial Empire, 1500–1800* (Indiana University Press, 2002) is still the seminal analysis. W. Bruce Lincoln's *The Conquest of a Continent: Siberia and the Russians* (Random House, 1994) is a beautifully written account of Russia's relationship with Siberia, from the Mongol conquest to the Soviet era, while Janet Hartley's *Siberia – A History of the People* (Yale University Press, 2018) focuses on the human-scale experience. Erika Monahan's *The Merchants of Siberia: Trade in Early Modern Eurasia* (Cornell, 2016) is more scholarly, but does a great job of evoking a time when trade drove empire, not the other way round. Of course, it's also essential to remember the histories of the conquered, not just the conquerors, and Anna Reid's *The Shaman's Coat: A Native History of Siberia* (Phoenix, 2003) does this admirably.

PART THREE

A European Power

11

Peter and His Navy

Grengam, 1720

1654–67	Russo-Polish War
1656–58	Russo-Swedish War
1676	Death of Alexis; Fyodor III becomes tsar
1682	Abolition of *mestnichestvo* system
	Death of Fyodor III
	Moscow Rising
	Co-coronation of Ivan and Peter
1689	Sofia unsuccessfully tries to unseat Peter
1696	Ivan's death: Peter becomes sole tsar
1697–98	Grand Embassy to Europe
1700–21	Great Northern War
1720	Battle of Grengam

As a 16-year-old, Peter had come across the shell of the English sailing boat *St Nicholas*, bought by his grandfather and since neglected. He had had it repaired by the Dutchman Karsten Brandt, and – encouraged by another Dutchman, his tutor Franz Timmerman – thus began his lifelong obsession with ships and the sea. From this would come the Russian Navy, and the proliferation of loanwords from Dutch for everything related to shipping, such as *matros* and *verf* (seaman and shipyard, from *matroos* and *werf*). It was a passion that never made Russia more than a limited and local maritime power, but would not stop it from trying, coming closest only during the height of the Cold War, when Admiral Sergei Gorshkov, Soviet Naval Commander-in-Chief 1956–85, would claim – with more enthusiasm than accuracy – that 'the flag of the Soviet navy now proudly flies over the oceans of the world. Sooner or later, the US will have to understand that it no longer has mastery of the seas.'

After Tsar Mikhail Romanov came Alexei, often more generally known as Alexis, then his brother Fyodor III. Disfigured and disabled from birth, Fyodor left no heir when he died in 1682. Next in line was his younger brother, the 15-year-old Ivan, yet he was scarcely much healthier and regarded in court as incapable of rule. The boyars, terrified of another Time of Troubles, generally seemed eager to see the crown pass instead to Pyotr, Ivan's ten-year-old half-brother by Fyodor's second wife. Ivan's older sister Sofia had other ideas, and stirred up discontent among the Moscow *Streltsy*, spreading rumours that Pyotr's mother's family, the Naryshkins, had poisoned Fyodor and strangled Ivan. Whether or not they truly believed this, the *Streltsy*, like so many Praetorian Guards through the ages, had become complacent, corrupt and suspicious of those they feared might supplant them. They stormed the Kremlin, looting and lynching officials and boyars they suspected were part of the Naryshkin plot, and forcing a compromise whereby Ivan and Pyotr be crowned as *dvoyetsarstvenniki*, double tsars – with the scheming Sofia as regent.

The brothers got along well enough, as Ivan never had much interest in governing, but when Pyotr was 17 and looking to shake off the regency, Sofia tried the same tactic. While the rumours that the Naryshkins were about to kill Ivan were enough to bring mobs onto Moscow's streets, though, this time the *Streltsy* were largely unwilling to rebel. Sofia was sent to a monastery, Pyotr was in power (although he would formally remain just co-tsar until Ivan's death in 1696), and the new monarch – who would become known as Peter the Great – had also been taught a lesson about the dangers of depending on the *Streltsy* that would see him in due course disband them. He himself, after all, had spent much of his time as a teenager at the royal estate of Preobrazhenskoye, building his so-called 'play army', which ended up being anything but – two companies strong, with their own artillery and cavalry, trained and equipped in the West European manner.

FOLLOWING THE FOREIGNERS

Peter's rise to power was, after all, accompanied by a determined effort to learn the Western arts and technologies of war. The 17th century saw Romanov Russia increasingly competing with Poland and Sweden for dominance in north-central Europe, notably in the Russo-Polish War of 1654–67 and Russo-Swedish War of 1656–58. As a result, Russia had to evolve to be able to field mass armies, build and use modern artillery and learn the latest siegecraft, forcing a further evolution of the state.

Tsar Alexis had resented the growing influence of foreigners, and in particular their disturbingly new ideas. Perhaps this should not surprise, given that he also oversaw a return to what were regarded as original rites and liturgies within the Russian Orthodox Church, even at the cost of triggering a schism. Foreigners in Moscow were confined to the so-called 'German Quarter' (as the term for German, *Nemets*, was used for all non-Russians), and in 1675 he banned Western clothes and styles from his court, apparently fearing that it was just one step from hooped skirts and men's hose to the spread of dangerous foreign notions. Nonetheless, it was impossible to avoid the connection between modernization and military power. Gunpowder had bought Russia's Siberian empire, but in an age of European conflict, with Russia engaged in periodic struggles above all with Sweden and Poland for dominance in north-eastern Europe, Moscow could not pretend not to need to stay abreast.

Indeed, Alexis recognized this when he made a Roman Catholic Scottish mercenary, Patrick Gordon, one of the tutors for his rambunctious son Pyotr, who would also owe much of his education in military matters to the Swiss mercenary Franz Le Fort. His ailing and bookish successor, Fyodor III, recognized the need for more systemic change, and even if his own interests were more theological than practical, they laid the groundwork for later military reform. Ideas could not simply be copied from the rest of Europe; they needed to be generated at home, and applied by people who understood them. Artillery, for example, would prove something of a social leveller, in that its correct use required an understanding of mathematics for everything from the angles of fire to the correct quantities of propellant. As a result, even when the officer corps of the infantry and cavalry remained the preserve of the aristocracy, across Europe, the artillery offered opportunities to smart scions of the middle class and petty gentry (including in due course one Napoleon Bonaparte). Fyodor established the Slavic-Greek-Latin Academy, Russia's first institution of higher learning, and while it was especially concerned with theology and the humanities, in due course it would herald the rise of other, more practical colleges.

However, a crucial step was his abolition of the *mestnichestvo* ('place order') system in 1682. Since the 15th century, this had dominated Russian military and civil service appointments, defining a complex hierarchy of inherited status which ensured that the boyars monopolized the most important positions, regardless of their qualities or qualification. Tsars had been able to enforce exceptions for particular favourites, but overall this represented a formidable obstacle to any kind of meritocracy. Even after he had been instrumental in driving the Poles from Moscow in 1612, for example, Prince Dmitry Pozharsky's subsequent military career was repeatedly constrained by *mestnichestvo*, meaning that he could never be put in charge of an operation. Liberating Moscow clearly took second place to being from the right family.

THE PETRINE WAR MACHINE

Peter was a literally larger-than-life figure, physically towering over his peers. He was also energetic and ambitious, a deeply pragmatic man less concerned with the whys of life than the hows, eager to acquire new skills, engaging with the world with his hands rather than through books. He enrolled in his own 'play army' as a mere bombardier, drilling with the other men, his face blackened by gunpowder smoke and his lungs heaving as he touched off the priming charge with a burning slowmatch to fire a cannon.

He inherited a complex and problematic international context. Under Sofia's regency, Kiev had been returned to Moscow's rule under the 1686 Eternal Peace Treaty with Poland (if only its title made it so), while the 1689 Treaty of Nerchinsk had forestalled a potential war with China. However, her consort, Prince Vasily Golitsyn, proved an able diplomat but an unlucky general. He led two disastrous campaigns against the Crimean Khanate in 1687 and 1689. In both cases, the

Russian armies were defeated not by Tatar military might as much as scorched earth tactics that highlighted Moscow's failure to come to terms with the need to approach logistics with the same enthusiasm and attention as tactics and weaponry. Peter, in many ways a craftsman at heart, would demonstrate that he was much more willing to engage with the substructures of military power, both because of the threats to Russia, and also because he was obsessed with warfare. This would cost: by 1705, Russia's military was devouring more than two-thirds of the central budget. One can question whether Peter was a modernizer in any philosophical terms – he was still an undoubted autocrat who, when given the chance to watch British parliamentarianism in action, concluded that 'English freedom is not appropriate' for Russians, and by implication that the implicit constraints on the English monarch did not suit him – but he certainly realized that he needed completely to revamp the Russian state in order to build the war machine he wanted and Russia needed.

The basis of the state's finances was the institution of serfdom, which provided tax, labour and soldiery. For years there had been resentment at this virtual land slavery, but Peter doubled down, making it even more draconian and inflexible. To stop them from fleeing, serfs were required to carry passports even to leave their home district, and anyone who hid or sheltered a runaway faced serious fines. Meanwhile, conscription into the army was expanded and supplemented by the forced labour that would see thousands press-ganged into working on major construction projects, not least Peter's new capital, St Petersburg. Moscow had too many bad memories for Peter and was insufficiently grand and modern, so he would bring in Italian, German and French architects to design him a new seat of government in the latest European style – but built in the most medieval of ways, 30,000 peasants dying through accident or overwork as they crafted him his 'window on the West'.

The harder the peasants could be worked, the more productive the countryside – at least in theory. That was necessary because the state had a desperate, voracious need for money that also led to a swathe of new taxes. Beards, beehives and bathing – all were subject to new dues. Yet everyone had their place in Peter's militarized regime. If the abolition of *mestnichestvo* meant that status and heredity determined your position in the state, the introduction of the Table of Ranks in

1722 turned this round, essentially making aristocrats into civil servants. To rise up through the 14 ranks, they would need to serve, and do so ably. This was not in any way a perfect meritocracy, as wealth, family and patronage still mattered, but it established a crucial principle: that service to the state was the basis of privilege. With it came another corollary: officials who rose to a certain rank became members of the aristocracy. A captain in a Guards regiment, for instance, was in the seventh rank, equivalent to a court counsellor. In a manner of speaking, even the boyars now became serfs of the state. As did the priests: in effect, the Russian Orthodox Church was nationalized, its huge lands squeezed for more revenues.

So the money kept rolling in. Much of this, as described in the next chapter, would go on building his armies and fighting the Great Northern War. However, there was also enough – Peter would ensure there was enough – for the tsar's particular passion: finally building a Russian navy. This was, after all, the man who mused that it was 'happier to be an admiral in England than a tsar in Russia'.

THE GRAND EMBASSY

Russia had had a navy of mean and meagre sort before, and for a time it had seemed that fate was determined to keep it that way. The *Frederik*, a three-master commissioned by Tsar Mikhail, had been built by shipwrights from Holstein, at Balakhna on the Volga River. Setting off on its maiden voyage in 1636, it sailed down the Volga and then into the Caspian Sea, where it was caught in a violent storm and ran aground. It never sailed again. In 1656, a flotilla of Russian oar-powered boats managed to board and seize a six-gun Swedish galley at the Battle of Kotlin Island, which Russian accounts rather over-generously describe as modern Russia's first victory at sea. During the 1656–58 Russo-Swedish War, the Russians captured the Swedish fortress at Kokenhusen (Koknese in Latvia) and began using it to build ships, but when it was returned to the Swedes as part of the 1661 Treaty of Kardis, all the hulls still being built were destroyed. The man behind this venture, the boyar Afanasy Ordin-Nashchokin, went on to engage Dutch shipwrights to build another three-master, the *Oryol* ('Eagle'), at Dedinovo, on the Oka River. This was launched in

1669 and by all accounts was captured and burned by Stenka Razin's rebellious Cossacks the next year.

After all, Russia had always been essentially a land power, without the capacity or need for any substantive maritime presence. However, with St Petersburg offering a new port on the Baltic, and the expansion of Russian control along the Black Sea coast, there was greater opportunity. Furthermore, as Russia's economy grew, and with it connections to distant markets, control of shipping routes, or at least the capacity to protect them, would become all the more important. Arguably, though, such strategic considerations took second place to simple enthusiasm. Peter wanted a navy and he would have one. In 1693, a new shipyard was founded near Arkhangelsk on the frozen northern coast. There another collection of Dutch shipwrights would build first the yacht *St Peter* and then a merchant ship, the *St Paul*. More shipyards would follow, at Preobrazhensky and Voronezh, and by the time of the 1695–96 Azov campaigns, the next rematch over this strategic fortress, Russia was able to deploy a flotilla to block Ottoman reinforcements. With two ships-of-the-line, four fire ships and 23 galleys, it was hardly a formidable force, but it was able to fight off the Turkish ships that tried to break the siege during the second, 1696 campaign, such that Azov was taken. (Until it had to be handed back to the Turks in 1711.)

This was a success, but only partial. The fortress had been taken, and with it access to the Sea of Azov. However, while this small flotilla had been able to interdict Turkish reinforcements, it was nowhere near strong enough to force passage through the Kerch Straits and out into the Black Sea, which would be the real strategic objective. That would require a much greater force, and so on 20 October 1696 – the date now regarded as the official birthday of the Russian Navy – the Boyar Duma voted to authorize the construction of a 52-ship fleet.

This would become a focus of Peter's reign, and such was his personal curiosity (and impatience with many of the more bureaucratic and ceremonial chores of being emperor) that in 1697, he personally led the Grand Embassy, which ended up being an 18-month tour of Swedish Livonia, the Netherlands, England, the German states and Austria. The ostensible goal was to gain allies against the Ottomans, and in this the

Embassy delivered few results. The Nine Years War (1688–97) that had pitted France against the Grand Alliance of England, Spain, the Holy Roman Empire and the Dutch had left the respective powers exhausted, unwilling to enter into further commitments.

However, for Peter – travelling undercover in the pretty-transparent guise of seaman 'Peter Mikhailov' – this was also an opportunity not just to find new places in which to carouse (in London, he so misused the house he rented that he caused more than £305 in damage, a fortune at the time, leaving every chair broken or used for firewood, and 300 window panes broken) but also to learn about the latest in shipbuilding and naval warfare. Two mock sea battles were staged in the Solent for him, and in England and especially Holland, he hired experts to help build him a fleet and train his own Russian shipwrights. He also engaged the services of the Norwegian-Dutch officer Cornelius Cruys, in due course the first commander of Russia's Baltic Fleet.

THE BALTIC FLEET

Given the importance of the Azov campaign in making the case for a navy, it is perhaps ironic that Peter's fledgling fleet would initially operate in the Baltic. The needs of the Great Northern War (1700–21), discussed in more detail in the following chapter, would take precedence over the long-running struggle with the Ottomans. The beginnings of the Baltic Fleet were in the oared galleys that began being built in a number of smaller shipyards from 1702, but it was clear that Russia would need sailing ships, including heavily gunned ships-of-the-line, if it were to be able to interdict enemy shipping routes and take the war to the Swedes and the Danes. The first such ship, the 28-gun frigate *Shdandart* ('Standard') was launched in 1703, and the next year the Admiralty Shipyards were opened in St Petersburg, providing new capabilities to build the larger, modern vessels Russia needed.

At the start of the Great Northern War, in 1700, Russia had only three armed sailing ships, and they were all in the White Sea Flotilla, in the waters off the Arctic coast. While in theory they could have been sailed into the Baltic conflict zone, in practice it would have been impossible, not least as the largest, the frigate *Svyatoye Prorochestvo*

('Holy Prophecy'), having been bought from the Dutch in 1693, had been converted into a merchant ship, and would need to be re-armed. Meanwhile, the Swedes could boast the fourth most-powerful navy in the world (after England, France and Holland). They also faced the Royal Danish Navy, but it could only boast 29 ships-of-the-line to Sweden's 38. Inevitably, then, from the Russians' perspective the early stages of the war would be fought on land, with amphibious landings only when the Swedes were not in a position to scour their galleys and troop transports from the waters.

It is a mark of just how quickly Petrine Russia could mobilize its resources, though, that by the end of the war, it had over a hundred modern sailing ships, including 25 ships-of-the-line mounting 50–90 guns. By comparison, while the Royal Navy fielded fully 79, Sweden and Denmark only had 22 and 25, respectively. Every bit as important, it had begun building the necessary culture, educational structures and technical capacity. Officers were nobility, but they needed to know their craft, and were thus required to attain a degree of professionalism still alien to many of their army counterparts. They were trained at the School of Mathematical and Navigational Sciences, founded in Moscow in 1701, and from 1715 also the Naval Guard Academy in St Petersburg. Especially in the early years, many of their tutors, as well as their commanders were foreigners, not just Cruys but also figures such as Thomas Gordon (no relation to Patrick, but another of the Scots who were such a fixture of 18th-century Russia), the Danish-German Peter von Sivers, and the Montenegrin Matija Zmajević, all of whom rose to be admirals. Indeed, many young naval officers also ended up studying abroad, and this helps explain why the navy also became regarded with some suspicion by the more hidebound Russian army as a haven for cosmopolitans, radicals and dangerous modernists of every stripe.

THE BATTLE OF GRENGAM, 1720

To a large degree, the role of the Baltic Fleet during the Great Northern War was either to try to foil Swedish landings, or in support of Russian ones. In 1703, for example, the Russians had taken the Swedish fortress of Nyenskans at the mouth of the Neva River. A modern fort of pentagonal design, built to ensure its guns had overlapping fields of fire in every direction, it nonetheless could not resist an army of 20,000 men with just 600 defenders. That allowed Peter not only to start building St Petersburg but also Kronshlot, a fort on the island of Kotlin, near the mouth of the Neva, which would in due course become the Kronstadt naval base. This became the focus of regular engagements, as the Swedes sought to prevent the Russians dominating the eastern Gulf of Finland. This led to periodic combined sea and land operations, in which the Swedes had the initiative but ultimately failed to strike with sufficient forces or determination ever to break the Russian defences. Only in the latter stages of the war did the Russians have the kind of naval strength such that open sea engagements were possible, although even then these tended to be small scale and almost incidental. The Battle of Grengam in 1720 (the Battle of Ledsund for the Swedes) was the last naval engagement of the war and in many ways illustrative of the different approaches of nations that seek to rule the waves, and those who are content rather with denying their enemy that victory.

Sweden had been getting the worst of the war but was refusing Russian terms, and was heartened by its alliance with Great Britain in 1719 and the arrival in the Baltic of a British naval squadron, albeit under orders not to initiate hostilities. The British were also able to broker peace between Sweden and Prussia and Denmark, though, depriving Russia of its allies. Uncertain at first what the British squadron intended, Peter was initially cautious, but once it became clear that this was an essentially demonstrative deployment, he returned to the offensive in 1720, deploying the Baltic Fleet and a substantial force of soldiers under General Mikhail Golitsyn to ravage the Swedish coast. Heading back towards the Åland Islands, Russian scouts spotted a Swedish squadron. As the winds were not conducive to an attack, the Russians diverted to the waters around the island of Granhamn – Grengam to the Russians – which were notoriously dense with skerries, small rocky islets, which would deny the Swedes proper scope to manoeuvre.

With one ship-of-the-line, the 56-gun *Pommern*, four frigates and a number of smaller boats, in total mounting 156 guns, Admiral Carl Georg Siöblad's squadron would seem to have had the advantage over the Russian fleet, which comprised no large sailing ships, albeit fully 61 galleys and 29 boats, under the Montenegrin Admiral Matija Zmajević.

In the high seas, that would certainly have been the case, and under the initial, punishing Swedish bombardment, the Russians withdrew, but they did so to draw the Swedes into the shallow, rocky coastal waters where their pursuers were at a disadvantage. The nimbler and shallower-hulled Russian galleys closed to ranges at which their smaller but numerous guns were effective, and were able to board and capture all four enemy frigates, before Siöblad beat a retreat.

The Swedes talked this up as a victory against daunting odds, which forced the Russians to withdraw from Åland, unable to launch further offensives before the war ended with the 1721 Treaty of Nystad. In practice, though, this was a Russian victory that demonstrated the degree to which it was now a Baltic naval power – but more to contest the waves than rule them. In other words, then, as now, Russia remained a land power, with its navy essentially intended to support its army, such as in landing operations, or to deny neighbouring seas to the enemy. It is, after all, a lot easier to deny than to dominate.

Such an insurgent mindset may explain why, in 1719, there was not more resistance when Peter listened to the illiterate carpenter Yefim Nikonov, when he pitched a vessel that would 'lie quietly under the waves, then destroy warships, at least ten or twenty, with a projectile'. The notion of the submarine was not entirely novel: Leonardo da Vinci had doodled his version, and Dutch engineer Cornelius Drebbel had demonstrated the world's first operational submarine in and under the Thames in 1620 but had failed to win the support of the Admiralty. However, Peter was enthused and, for a nation that was still an insurgent naval power facing fleets that were often larger or more advanced, such a secret advantage seemed doubly appealing. Nikonov was appointed as his 'master of stealthy vessels' and set to work.

Over the period 1724–27, three prototypes – essentially large, leather-wrapped wooden barrels propelled by oars – were tested, each time ending in a mishap. Peter's death in 1725 deprived Nikonov of his patron, and with the third failure he lost his exalted title and was sent as an ordinary carpenter to the shipyard in Astrakhan. This was a failure, but an intriguing historical 'what if?' moment. Eventually, the Russians would become infamous for their stealthy hunter-killer submarines in the later 20th century, but as Nikonov ultimately failed to give them a head start, they would instead have to win their new status as a Baltic power on land.

Want To Know More?

Peter the Great, by Lindsey Hughes (Yale University Press, 2002) is still considered the benchmark biography of this extraordinary man. There is a striking lack of good studies of the Great Northern War, although Robert Frost's *The Northern Wars: War, State and Society in Northeastern Europe, 1558–1721* (Routledge, 2015) is a useful overview. There is even less worth noting about the early Russian Navy, although Evgenii Anisimov's *The Reforms of Peter the Great: Progress Through Violence in Russia* (Routledge, 2015) provides an interesting and opinionated, if sometimes slightly heavy-handed, perspective on his modernization as a whole. Although riddled with errors and anachronisms, the *History of the Russian Fleet During the Reign of Peter the Great by a Contemporary Englishman*, published in 1724, edited by Vice Admiral Cyprian A. G. Bridge (Leopold Classic reprint, 2015) is an interesting artifact of its time.

12

The Great Northern War

Poltava, 1709

1610–17	Ingrian War with Sweden
1631	Introduction of New Order Regiments
1632–34	Smolensk War
1654–67	Russo-Polish War
1656–58	Russo-Swedish War
1696	Ivan's death: Peter becomes sole tsar
1698	Streltsy mutiny
1700–22	Great Northern War
1708	Mazepa's rebellion
1709	Battle of Poltava
1710–11	Russo-Ottoman War

In June 2022, Vladimir Putin, a man whose passion for history is only equalled by his inability truly to understand it, was speaking on the 350th anniversary of Peter the Great's birth and felt compelled to draw parallels with his war in Ukraine:

Almost nothing has changed. It can be surprising when you start to understand this. Peter waged the Great Northern War for 21 years with Sweden and apparently annexed some territories. He didn't annex anything, he reclaimed them!... It appears that it is our lot to reclaim and strengthen [Russia's sovereignty].*

Indeed, Putin regularly compares himself with Peter, and reportedly Foreign Minister Sergei Lavrov believes that, in practice, 'he has three advisers – Ivan the Terrible, Peter I and Catherine the Great'.† In part, this is inevitable for an autocrat who clearly holds to the view that great men (and women) shape their times, not the impersonal forces of economy, technology, geography, demography and society. It also speaks to the inner yearnings of a man clearly obsessed with his historical legacy, not least given that Peter did, on the face of it, challenge a dominant and seemingly more powerful alliance to the West and master it, forcing Russia into the ranks of the great European powers. The desire to follow in his footsteps is clear; his actual success, as will be discussed later, rather less so.

BEAR VERSUS LION

Through the 16th and 17th century, Sweden had become the dominant force in the Baltic and Northern Europe, gaining territories from not just Denmark, Norway and the German states but also Russia. In the chaos of the Time of Troubles, when the Polish-backed Second False Dmitry was enthroned in Moscow, the city of Novgorod had appealed to Sweden's King Charles IX to instal one of his sons as their ruler. When the Poles were expelled and Tsar Mikhail Romanov had been crowned, though, the Swedes had no intention of ceding this strategic city. Indeed, there was even thought of extending their Russian holdings, but the ensuing war proved inconclusive. The Swedes failed to take Tikhvin, north-east of Novgorod, in 1613, and the Russians then failed to retake Novgorod in their counter-offensive. Gdov on Lake Peipus fell to the Swedes, but the more important Pskov did not. The Swedes were too few (and often too unmotivated), while Mikhail was still too wary of Polish intervention and stripping Moscow of its defenders to commit fully to the war. Eventually, the 1617 Treaty of Stolbovo resolved this

---

"Putin zayavil, chto Petr I v gody Severnoi voiny u Shvetsii nichego net ottorgal, "on vozvrash-chal"', *TASS*, 9 June 2022
†'How Putin blundered into Ukraine – then doubled down', *Financial Times*, 23 February 2023

ill-tempered tussle. Moscow regained Novgorod, but at the cost of losing the province of Ingria along the south-eastern shore of the Gulf of Finland and thus its access to the Baltic Sea.

This was a serious blow, not just to Russian prestige but Russian trade, which now had to head for the White Sea port of Arkhangelsk, which is ice-bound through the winter. Nonetheless, there was nothing, at the time, that Moscow could do. It was not just that its own position was too precarious, facing both Poles and an Ottoman-Crimean alliance; it was also that Sweden was the pre-eminent military power of its age. Its forces tended to the small size, but were professional, well trained and well equipped. In the earlier years, like most European armies, the Swedes relied on mercenaries and conscripts, but from the 1640s their armies were raised from citizen-soldiers, volunteers granted small plots of land in return for regular training. As a result, they could be mustered quickly and were already well prepared, able to undertake long, hard marches and conduct themselves well on the battlefield, famously able to fire volleys from their muskets more quickly than most of their enemies. Meanwhile, a competent and (relatively) honest administration ensured there was enough money to pay and supply them.

By the end of the 17th century, though, there were signs that the Swedish lion's days of dominance may be in decline. Its military model had been, like those of most European powers, something of a pyramid scheme: the costs of expansion were expected to be met by the plunder, tax and tribute it would gain. Wars were getting more expensive, though, and easy pickings harder to find. Sweden was a rich mercantile nation but still a relatively small one: in 1650, it had a population of perhaps 1.25 million, compared with England's 5.5 million and France's 20 million. This would not just put limits on the tax base; it would also mean that the costs of war in human terms would tell all the more. Sweden did not just rely on qualitative advantages of training, generalship and technology because it could, but because it needed to.

Russia had taken decades to recover since the Time of Troubles, but its population was perhaps ten times' Sweden's. Much of this was impoverished, however: what it needed was a more efficient state apparatus to squeeze a greater amount of tax out of these masses, and then for these resources to build a modern military. And Peter was resolved to do just that.

NEW MODEL ARMY

Even before Peter, the Russian military had begun to experience piecemeal reform. So-called 'New Order Regiments' began to be raised in the 1630s, a mix of conscripts and volunteers, but paid by the central government and commanded and trained by European mercenaries. The first two were formed in 1631, then eight more during the 1632–34 Smolensk War, fought in an unsuccessful attempt to retake that city from the Polish–Lithuanian Commonwealth. Disbanded afterwards, they were reformed during the 1654–67 Russo-Polish War, after which they remained within the army's order of battle. They were classed as heavy cavalry *Reiters*; pistoleers, or mounted infantry dragoons; Hussars in the Polish style; and the lower-prestige *Soldaty*, infantry musketeers and pikemen. There was still a strong class element, with the gentry often becoming *Reiters*, and *Soldaty* conscripted from state serfs. Nonetheless, they represented the start of a European-style force.

Peter's childhood 'toy army' was informed by the lessons he learned from tutors and was very much closer in style to the 'New Order Regiments' that by then accounted for about half the Russian army. In 1691, they became the Preobrazhensky and Semyonovsky Regiments of the regular military, and Peter continued to drive them hard. In 1693, he marched them all the way to Arkhangelsk, and in 1694 they were part of a 30,000-man realistic training exercise at Kozhukhovo outside Moscow in which real ammunition was used, and there were real human casualties. Prince Boris Kurakin, Peter's brother-in-law, was impressed: 'hardly any of the European rulers could organise "military training" better than this.'

One of the obstacles to comprehensive military reform, though, was the *Streltsy*. Once an innovation and a step towards modernity, they had over time become an increasingly hereditary and wilful force. They could still fight fiercely, but they lacked the discipline necessary in an age when battle was decided by the ability to manoeuvre with precision and volley fire at speed. More dangerously, they resented and sought to prevent the raising of the 'New Order Regiments'. Feeling themselves under threat and out of time, the *Streltsy* often joined the rebellions endemic to the time, and Peter himself, as a ten-year-old, had been a terrified spectator to the mutiny of the *Streltsy* in 1682, when his uncle had been murdered before his eyes. He never forgot that, and never forgave, but there were some 55,000 *Streltsy*, including more than 22,000 in Moscow alone, and he could not easily turn on them – he would need an excuse.

He would get it in 1698, when he was on his Grand Embassy. He had left Russia in the hands of his faithful 'Prince-Caesar', Fyodor Romodanovsky. Disgruntled *Streltsy* who felt their service at Azov had been discounted found common cause with the former regent and schemer Sofia, and in June more than 2,000 of them marched on Moscow, planning on installing Sofia again as regent and punishing the Petrine loyalists and foreign advisers they blamed for their woes. General Patrick Gordon led four infantry and a cavalry regiment against them and quickly suppressed the mutiny, even before Peter had managed to return to Russia, but although this was a relatively isolated case, he would use it to break the *Streltsy* for once and for all.

Under savage tortures, suspects would obligingly and inevitably incriminate other *Streltsy*, who would in turn do the same once they faced the whips, red-hot irons and thumbscrews of the interrogators. In an orgy of public vengeance, over a thousand were executed, and in 1689 the force was formally disbanded, although some regiments would later instead be assimilated into the new regular army. Peter had made a savage point about the inadvisability of rebellion, but he had also cleared the way for the creation of his new army. In 1698, the army was expanded, with a new model of conscription that saw one peasant taken under arms from every 20 households every year, serving for life. New programmes to train junior officers were launched, with even more foreign mercenaries engaged to train and lead the new regiments. At last, Peter was building the army he wanted.

THE GREAT NORTHERN WAR

It almost came too late. In 1699, the secret Treaty of Preobrazhenskoye was signed between Peter, Frederick IV of Denmark–Norway and Augustus II the Strong, Elector of Saxony but also King of Poland and Grand Duke of Lithuania. Sweden was then ruled by the 17-year-old Charles XII, and the three monarchs believed they spied the opportunity to break the regional hegemon and partition its territories between them. They would discover that the lion still had more than a little fight left in it.

In 1700, the three allies launched respective attacks on the Swedish possessions of Holstein-Gottorp (Denmark), Livonia (Saxony), and later Ingria (Russia). Charles XII proved able and decisive, though. The Danes were blocked at Travendal, and then forced out of the war when Charles threatened Copenhagen. The Saxons failed to take Riga. Then the Russians suffered a humiliating defeat at Narva. Peter had raised fully 31 new regiments for the war, bringing his army to 200,000, but his efforts to reform the officer corps left many positions unfilled or occupied by inexperienced and under-trained young noblemen. They, in turn, had not the skill or time to drill their units into proper campaign condition. In any case, simply equipping them all properly had been impossible. Russia still did not mass produce muskets, for example, and could not import enough in time.

Peter invested the fortress of Narva in October 1700 with 37,000 men and 195 guns, although the siege did not go well: poor weather made resupply of gunpowder difficult (and its quality was also often poor), and many of the guns the Russians were using were too lightweight to have much of an impact on the city's thick walls. Prince Alexander of Imereti, the overall commander of the Russian artillery, was a crony of Peter's and a loyalist, but only 26, with no more than a few months of theoretical exposure to the arts of gunnery in The Hague. It was a classic example of Peter's challenge at the time: his old tutors Le Fort and Gordon had both died, he did not trust many of the old guard, or believe they understood modern war, and the younger men still had not had the chance to learn.

Speaking of younger men, Charles responded aggressively, gathering and leading a relief force of 10,500 men, which turned out to be sufficiently small that the Russian generals assumed it must only be the vanguard of a larger force, inclining them to caution, so that they stayed inside their siege lines. With Narva's walls to their backs and the Swedes in front of them, they had neither the initiative nor much room to manoeuvre, and in the early afternoon, the Swedes attacked under cover of a snowstorm. Exhausted after a long, hard march, they nonetheless stormed the trenches and walls of the Russian lines and after fierce fighting managed to break through their centre. This allowed them to roll up the separated flanks, and the inexperienced Russian forces quickly broke: a pontoon bridge over the Narva River even collapsed, so great was the scrum trying to escape over it.

The Preobrazhensky and Semyonovsky Regiments salvaged some credit for the Russians, forming a square and resisting, but the bulk of those Russian forces which did not flee surrendered. Charles had defeated an entrenched force three times the size of his own, and suffered fewer than 700 dead, one-tenth his enemies' butcher's bill. It was a humiliating defeat for Russia, but Peter was phlegmatic: 'What surprise is it for such an old, trained and practiced army to find victory over such inexperienced ones?'

The next few years would see the anti-Swedish coalition and its fortunes ebb and flow. Denmark–Norway had been knocked out of the war early, and a Swedish counter-offensive against Augustus would see Warsaw fall and him temporarily forced from his throne in 1706. For a while, Russia was alone, and attempts to come to terms with Charles were ignored. He recognized that they represented the most serious long-term threat to Swedish hegemony, and was determined to deliver a devastating blow while he could. In the process, though, even the young prodigy would overreach, while Peter was able to use the time and the experience of war finally to build the military machine he wanted – and get to use it at Poltava in Ukraine, in 1709.

POLTAVA, 1709

In 1706, a Russian army narrowly escaped being trapped by Charles at Grodno in what is now Belarus. Unable to intercept it, the 'Lion of the North' instead finally closed his grip on Saxony and saw the Commonwealth leave the war. Then, all that was left was to deal with Russia. Through to 1708, inconclusive Swedish attacks often ground to a halt due to a lack of provisions, the Russians practising the scorched earth tactics with which they often greeted invaders. That year, though, there erupted another of the periodic Cossack rebellions, led by Ivan Mazepa, Hetman of the Zaporizhian Host.

Born in the Kiev Voivodeship in the Polish–Lithuanian Commonwealth, Mazepa served the Commonwealth, travelling across Europe and learning Italian and German. On his father's death, he inherited his position in the Zaporizhian Host which, since the 1654

Treaty of Pereyaslav had owed fealty to the tsar. Ironically enough for someone who would become a Ukrainian nationalist icon, in 1687, he managed to oust the existing hetman by accusing him of conspiring to break with Moscow, and was elected as his successor. He became rich and powerful – he was considered one of Europe's largest landowners – but he became increasingly concerned that Peter's reforms represented a threat. Centralization could mean less autonomy for the Cossacks, and they were increasingly being expected to provide forces for wars far from home, stripping their defences against the Tatars and the Poles. It was bad enough that the story was spreading that Peter intended to replace him with his venal favourite, Alexander Menshikov. When the tsar also refused to commit troops to defend the Cossack lands from a Polish attack – in breach of the Pereyaslav Treaty – Mazepa raised the banner of rebellion and joined the other side.

This was especially significant because Charles's plans to march on Moscow were being hampered not just by the general supply problem – especially after a relief army lost most of its 4,500 supply wagons at the Battle of Lesnaya (October 1708) – but also by unusually harsh weather, culminating in the Great Frost of 1708–09, the coldest winter in Europe for 500 years. Mazepa offered his lands to Charles for his forces to winter, and so the Swedes headed south. In spring 1709, Charles resumed his campaign, investing Poltava in April, a strategic fortress city east of Kiev. A crucial military depot, taking Poltava would not only regain momentum for the Swedes, but provide much-needed food and ammunition.

One of Charles's strengths had always been the speed with which he could move his armies. Indeed, the Danes and Saxons had suffered from their tendency to let themselves be bogged down in sieges, just as the Russians had at Narva. This time, though, he was the one caught when Peter led a relief army some 80,000 strong against his 37,000 men. Poltava's defences had not looked so formidable – Field Marshal Rehnskiöld, Charles's ruthless and capable right-hand man, even wondered, 'Are the Russians really so reckless they will try to defend themselves?' – and the Swedes had perhaps hoped for a quick victory. Their troops were tired, however, and their guns largely lighter ones, and the city held out until Peter's force neared, at the end of June.

The Russians made camp near the village of Yakovtsy, some 5km from Poltava. Peter had learned caution in the past nine years of war, and he built not just a fortification to his rear, but a series of earthworks along his front, with forests to either side. He had also brought with him a formidable artillery train with over a hundred guns, including modern cannon and mortars. After one last attempt to storm Poltava, Charles decided with characteristic boldness to give battle, and to rely on the Swedish discipline and élan in the attack that had served them so well in the past. His plan was for the Swedish infantry to move out in the early morning under cover of darkness, to bypass the redoubts with the advantage of surprise, while a force of cavalry would sweep round from the north to support an attack on the fortification and cut off any line of retreat. This was based on the assumption that, as in the past, the Russians would be slow to respond and essentially reactive, on the defence, and that the Swedes could close quickly enough that their enemies' artillery advantage would be essentially nullified.

Once, this might well have worked, but Charles was fighting a different Russian army, seasoned in battle. For that matter, after nine years of war and a hard winter foraging, his was not his old army, either. It took longer than expected for the Swedish columns to form, and the Russians were alerted and began battering them with their cannon. The Swedes attacked in the early light of dawn. Two unfinished redoubts fell quickly, but instead of getting tied up assaulting the others, the advance line moved on. However, the redoubts split the line, and the Swedes were then attacked by a large force of Russian dragoons, which delayed the attack further.

Eventually, the dragoons were withdrawn, and although some headstrong Swedish cavalry wanted to pursue, Rehnskiöld recalled them, fearing a ruse – and that without cavalry support, his infantry would be vulnerable. By five in the morning, the Swedes had reached the fortified camp, and although they had taken losses from Peter's cannon and the garrisons of the redoubts (they were still unaware that one of their columns, under General Roos, had become isolated and was eventually forced to surrender, depriving them of almost a third of their infantry), they were in confident mood. All that was left, surely, was one last push, and fragile Russian morale would crack?

The Swedes paused to regroup into a line of battle. Once their intention was clear, Peter did the same with his substantially larger forces, moving out of the camp. They ended up in two lines, much more tightly arrayed than the enemy's. The Swedes had not anticipated that the Russians could redeploy in formation so quickly or neatly, however, let alone stand ready for the charge. Indeed, Rehnskiöld was sufficiently surprised by the reports he received that he went and looked for himself. Still, the Swedes had beaten the odds enough times that they did not hesitate and advanced. They ran through a storm of cannon fire, exchanged a volley of musketry with the Russians, and crashed into their line with sword and bayonet. Under the impact, the Russian line began slowly to fall back. The Novgorod Regiment on the left flank began to fall apart, opening a dangerous gap for the Swedes to exploit, until Peter himself led the last of the reinforcements to steady the line. On the right flank, though, his Guard regiments quickly put their enemies to flight, and slowly but surely, the Swedish line began to be enveloped by the more numerous defenders. The Swedish line lost cohesion, and so too did many of the component regiments. A disorderly retreat became a rout.

Charles XII himself was spirited to safely, along with Mazepa, by his cavalry escort, and withdrew with the rearguard and whatever forces had managed to escape the defeat: no more than 1,500 men. The Russians lost 1,500 men, the Swedes perhaps 6,000–7,000, with another 3,000 captured – including Field Marshal Rehnskiöld and Count Carl Piper, the Marshal of the Realm, who, ironically, had counselled Charles unsuccessfully against taking his war to Peter. The captured Swedish commanders were welcomed by Peter, who drank to them, calling them his 'military tutors'. Piper ruefully acknowledged that 'he had taught his teachers well.'

ALL OVER BAR THE SHOOTING

And so he had. The Russians won at Poltava thanks to almost a decade of relentless effort to accomplish Peter's designs and learn the lessons of Narva. The regiments trained hard, until switching and holding formations – from the square to repel cavalry, to the line that could maximize the musket volley – became second nature. The callow young officers of 1700 learnt the ways of war or died in battle. The Baltic Fleet graduated from oared galleys to ships-of-the-line. The war was not yet over. Charles would flee to Ottoman-controlled Moldavia and would spend years there in exile, even while ruling his nation from afar.

Historical echoes are powerful in Russia. A Soviet poster from World War II exhorts the soldiers to 'Fight bravely, sons of Suvorov and Chapayev', under, from left to right, the shades of Alexander Nevsky from the 13th century, Alexander Suvorov from the 18th century and Vasily Chapayev from the Russian Civil War. (Getty Images)

A re-enactment of typical longship river raiding at the time of the Varyagy. (Getty Images)

ALEXANDER NEVSKY Directed by Sergei Eisenstein
Produced by Mosfilm, Moscow, U.S.S.R.
Distributed by Amkino Corp.   printed in U.S.A.

Above Greek fire, shown in this 11th- or 12th-century manuscript, was the secret weapon of the Byzantines, feared by every Rus' raider. (Getty Images)

Left The film *Alexander Nevsky* was hardly an exact historical representation, but this poster does convey a sense of the difference between the Russian warriors in their conical helmets and scale shirts, and the better-equipped Teutonic Knights. (Getty Images)

The Russians had cause to fear raids by the Polovtsians, as evoked in Viktor Vasnetsov's painting 'After the Battle'. (Getty Images)

This engraving of the 1223 Battle of the Kalka River is of questionable historical accuracy, portraying the Mongols more like Turks, but does convey the chaos of the pivotal clash. (Getty Images)

A later illustration of a *basqaq* of the Golden Horde exacting tribute, accompanied by his bodyguard. (Getty Images)

A heroic representation of Dmitry Donskoi in Kolomna, where he mustered his forces for Kulikovo, in front of the walls of the town's kremlin. (Author's photo)

A contemporary representation of an early Strelets, with simple handgun over his left shoulder, and *berdysh* poleaxe on his right. (Getty Images)

A fanciful representation of Kazan's surrender to Ivan in 1552 – the truth was that the defenders were largely massacred – but which captures the still-medieval look of so many of his soldiers well. (Getty Images)

Fighting in the streets of Moscow between Russians and Poles in 1611. (Getty Images)

A famous painting by Ilya Repin supposedly showing Zaporizhian Cossacks having fun composing a scathing and insulting reply to an ultimatum from the Turkish Sultan in 1676. (Getty Images)

A mural to Pozharsky and Minin in central Moscow. (Author's photo)

Yermak's Cossacks demonstrate the advantage in their firepower as they advance across Siberia in 1580. (Getty Images)

Greetings from the banks of the Lena River! An early 20th-century postcard from Yakutsk shows the classic wooden walls and towers of Russian stations across Siberia. (Getty Images)

A contemporary representation of the 1714 Battle of Gangut, in which the Russian Navy won its first real engagement with Sweden. (Getty Images)

The future Peter the Great training his 'play army'. (Getty Images)

Catherine the Great was rarely treated kindly by European cartoonists, but nor was she considered irrelevant. Here, she and the monarchs of Prussia and Austria are dividing up Poland between them. (Getty Images)

The Battle of Poltava in 1709. (Getty Images)

The Battle of Cahul, 1770, showing the Russians advancing on the Ottoman forces arrayed in the foreground. (Getty Images)

Top Napoleon broods over his burning prize, as he rides into Moscow. (Getty Images)

Centre This view of the medieval towers that dot the Ingushetia countryside, with more mountains in the distance, helps convey the kind of terrain the Russians found themselves fighting in, as they extended imperial rule across the North Caucasus. (Getty Images)

Bottom However stylised, this picture of the Charge of the Light Brigade does convey the way their lines found themselves with guns to left, right and fore. (Getty Images)

Above Tsar Nicholas II blessing a regiment leaving for the Russo-Japanese War in 1904. It must have been a great comfort for them.
(Getty Images)

Centre Ships of the Black Sea Fleet getting under steam at Sevastopol. In the First World War, the Imperial Navy was able to dominate the Black Sea, but never leverage this for wider victory on land.
(Getty Images)

Bottom Armoured trains like this one were a particular feature of the Russian military in the First World War and then the Civil War. (Getty Images)

The Russian state soon started to run out of money in the First World War, and this poster advertises war bonds to support the troops. (Getty Images)

Top The famous Il-2 *Shturmovik* ground-attack aircraft over Berlin in 1945. (Getty Images)

Centre Red Army soldiers supporting a T-34 advance during the Battle of Kursk, in July 1943. (Getty Images)

Below However little today's Russian government wants to admit it, assistance from the Western Allies was crucial. This is the HMS *Royal Sovereign*, a Revenge-class battleship, serving on loan in the Red Navy as the *Arkhangelsk*, before being returned to the Royal Navy at the end of the war. (Getty Images)

A US Lockheed P-2 Neptune patrol plane overflies a Soviet freighter during the Cuban Missile Crisis in 1962. (Getty Images)

A Soviet tank during the suppression of the Prague Spring in 1968 is surrounded by angry Czechs. (Getty Images)

A Russian Mi-26 heavy-lift helicopter takes off from Grozny airport in 1995, with the carcass of a destroyed jet in the foreground. (Getty Images)

Russian peacekeepers in South Ossetia in 2008, on the eve of Tbilisi's attack – casualties to the contingent gave Moscow the excuse it was looking for to invade. (Getty Images)

Above Local militia and Russian 'Little Green Men' stand guard outside a government building in Simferopol during the 2014 annexation. (Getty Images)

Left The cost of war: a Russian missile has just hit the Ukrainian city of Zaporizhia, in April 2022. (Getty Images)

Mutineers and a tank from the Wagner mercenary army during their occupation of Rostov-on-Dun in June 2023. (Getty Images)

Through the Sultan's mother, he even managed to persuade the Ottomans to launch an opportunistic invasion that forced the distracted and ill-prepared Russians to sign the 1711 Treaty of the Pruth, which saw Azov again returned to their control. To Charles's chagrin, though, Sultan Ahmed III was not willing for a full-scale war with Russia, but the treaty did also grant him safe passage back to Sweden. Even so, there was relatively little even he could do.

Russia's victory at Poltava breathed new life into the anti-Swedish alliance. Denmark and Saxony rejoined, and Augustus was returned to the Polish throne, largely thanks to the Russians. As discussed in the previous chapter, Russia built a navy able to challenge the Swedes in the Baltic, and in 1710 they would take Riga and Tallinn, bringing Livonia and Estonia under their control. That year, sensing the way the wind was blowing, Hanover joined the alliance, followed by Brandenburg-Prussia in 1713 and Britain in 1715. The Russians pushed into Finland, while Charles launched new campaigns against Denmark–Norway. He died in battle, probably from a stray grapeshot, at the siege of Fredriksten in November 1718. Under his sister, Ulrika Eleonora, Sweden continued to fight, but with diminishing hope and chances. Indeed, already the alliance was beginning to fall apart as its members squabbled over their prospective spoils, making their own respective peaces with Sweden. Britain, true to its eternal policy of preventing any one European nation from becoming too powerful, even sided with them temporarily. The final peace was the 1721 Treaty of Nystad with Russia, granting it Ingria, Estonia, Livonia and Southeast Finland, while the Swedes regained the rest of Finland.

It was a significant expansion of Russian territories that not only spelled the end of Sweden's imperial age, but above all marked the triumphant entry of Russia into European politics as a true great power. This was built not on trade, culture or alliances, but raw military power, something that would be reaffirmed in the 1722–23 Russo-Persian War. Once, Russian forces had been unable to maintain operations against Crimea; now they could strike over the Terek River to the south and impose a partition of Transcaucasia, taking the western and southern coasts of the Caspian Sea for themselves and ensuring that the Ottomans could not take advantage of the declining power of Persia. It was what Peter the Great had been working towards all these years. No wonder Putin hoped, in vain, to wrap himself in his mantle.

Want To Know More?

Peter Englund's *The Battle That Shook Europe: Poltava and the Birth of the Russian Empire* (IB Tauris, 2002) is the classic study of the battle, an excellent read as well as a good study, while for the debacle at Narva, Michael Fredholm Von Essen's *Peter the Great's Disastrous Defeat: The Swedish Victory at Narva, 1700* (Helion, 2024) is a comprehensive account. The prolific Angus Konstam's *Peter the Great's Army*, volumes *(1): Infantry* and *(2): Cavalry* (Osprey, both 1993), as well as his *Poltava 1709: Russia comes of age* (Osprey, 1994) are clear and accessible works. *Russia's Wars of Emergence 1460–1730* (Pearson, 2007) obviously covers a wider span but is especially good on Poltava and how it reshaped Russian military thinking. The 1987 TV mini-series *Peter the Great* has a distractingly intrusive soundtrack but was shot on location in Russia, so gives a good sense of the backdrop.

13

A European Power at Last

Kunersdorf, 1759

1725	Catherine I's coup
1733–35	War of the Polish Succession
1735–39	Russo-Turkish War
1740–48	War of the Austrian Succession
1741–43	Russo-Swedish War
1741	Elizabeth's coup
1756–63	Seven Years War (Russia joins in 1757)
1762	Catherine II's coup

Consider the city of St Petersburg. Undoubtedly a beautiful and baroque new capital for an empire that considered itself on the rise. Yet while Peter's 'window on the West' had been built as a new, European city, it was now the capital of what was, in so many ways still a medieval country. Most of the population were serfs, with no incentive but the whip to work harder or to improve the productivity of land not their own. Which was the real Russia?

There was no question that Peter the Great had transformed European notions of Russia as both a state and a warfighting power. Following its victory over Sweden, Russia became the main power in Central and Northern Europe. As with Ivan the Terrible's victories, it presented the country with a difficult legacy, because this triumph meant Russia was inevitably entangled in the messily complex European politics of the times, doomed to involvement in an array of 18th-century struggles, such as wars of Polish and Austrian Succession and the Seven Years War. For more than a century, Russia would emerge successful from almost every conflict in which it became embroiled, but in many ways this was the product of circumstance, mass and luck, and hid growing international challenges.

It also meant that the country was trying to keep up with an image that flattered it. To be sure, Peter had demonstrated that Russia could take on the major northern land power of the age (although it had not tangled with French land or British sea power), but it had done so in part by outlasting and exhausting relatively small Sweden, and with its forces only partly modernized. They were substantively improved on the army Peter had inherited – let alone the essentially non-existent navy – but, much like St Petersburg, one could argue that Russia was only cosplaying modernity. It could buy or hire the best from Europe – just as St Petersburg was built by Italian and French architects – but could it emulate them?

THE HALF-MODERN ARMY

When Peter died, the Russian army comprised 130,000 men, to which could be added perhaps up to 100,000 Cossacks able to be mobilized in time of need. In Europe, only France could match these numbers. However, the cost of maintaining this as a peacetime force was ruinous – adding in the sums spent on fortifications and the navy, it was devouring two-thirds of the state's budget, and demanded levels of taxation that risked further revolts. Even so, it was still a crude military machine, largely manned by peasant conscripts paid a pittance, officered by younger sons of the nobility who had few career alternatives. The main expense was feeding and housing them, and even this was done on a shoestring. In a practice that even re-emerged briefly in the 1990s, soldiers were often in effect forced to fend for themselves, whether making their own uniforms, raising their own food, or being hired out as labour. Even as late as 1899, General Mikhail Dragomirov, commander of the Kiev military district, bemoaned that 'in July, enlisted personnel fan out in hay-mowing, in forests, along railway lines, in towns for building; they sew clothing... they become unaccustomed with discipline and lose their military bearing.' In many ways, horses – whether cavalry mounts or drays – and their fodder were a great deal more of a burden on the budget, and something that could not as easily be skimped.

After all, European warfare was increasingly becoming the preserve of professionals. Not just tacticians, siege engineers, artillerymen and the other battlefield gods of war, but the inventors behind even such small innovations as the cylindrical iron ramrods that helped the Prussians shave a few seconds off the time it took to reload a musket, and, perhaps most crucially, the quartermasters and farriers responsible for logistics. The larger the army, the more food it needed. The more rapid the fire, the more gunpowder and ammunition consumed. This was an age in which the most effective armies came to realize the limitations of trying to forage on the march and instead established centralized magazines stuffed with supplies of every kind.

In this context, as in the past, Russia would be found wanting. There certainly were signs not just of tactical but technical innovation. The engineer Andrei Nartov, for example, invented a novel machine for drilling out cannon barrels, and even experimented with a quick-firing mortar, with 44 small copper 3-pounder guns on a rotating mount. This ingenious 'machine-mortar' was ahead of its time: it was impossible to build a mount sturdy enough not to shake itself to pieces when firing a full salvo. More practically, Count Pyotr Shuvalov, General of Artillery from 1756, saw renewed attempts to catch up with and even overtake Western Europe. His so-called 'secret gun', the 95mm M1753 howitzer with an oval muzzle specifically for firing canister shot, tin cartridges which would burst on firing and blast out a cloud of lead balls, proved an unsuccessful experiment. However, his patronage did allow a team of gunners to invent an innovative cross between a howitzer and a cannon that had a better range than the former and the rate of fire of the latter. Technically the M1757, this became generally known as the *Yedinorog*, or unicorn, after the heraldic detailing on the barrel, which hardly accidentally also reprised the Shuvalov family arms. Various calibres and model of these guns remained in service for the next century, and were also adopted by the Austrian and the Poles.

Yet it is also telling that while Shuvalov was able to reorganize the artillery more efficiently, forming specialized brigades and founding the United Artillery and Engineering Noble School in 1758 to train officers, as well as divide the country into military districts to make conscription more effective, his attempts to establish a network of military grain reserve stores ultimately came to nothing. The logistical tail continued to fail to wag the front-line dog.

YET ANOTHER RUSSO-TURKISH WAR

A recurring leitmotif of Russia's 18th century was its inability to isolate itself from the instability of the geopolitics of Europe, broadly defined. Thus it would find itself sucked into new conflicts in Europe, as well as very familiar old ones. For example, the Crimean Tatars continued to raid the Cossack Hetmanate, sheltering under the Turks' protection, while the Ottomans continued to look for opportunities in the Caucasus, and Russia continued to hanker after unfettered access to the Black Sea. In 1735, as part of a treaty with Persia, Russia abandoned Derbent and the Caspian regions. However, the Sunni Muslims of coastal Dagestan, fearing rule by Shia Persia, began withdrawing into the mountains, and the Ottomans declared themselves the protectors of all the Muslims of the Caucasus. Their ambition was to bring the North Caucasus under the control of their proxies, and Crimean forces promptly began moving into the region, in a clear challenge to Persia and breach of Turkish treaty obligations with Russia.

Rather than try to play hide and seek with the Crimeans in the valleys of the North Caucasus, in autumn 1735, 30,000 men from the Russian Army of the Dnieper marched for Crimea. They fell foul not of enemy action but an unexpectedly early winter and a consequent lack of water and fodder for the horses. The Russians were forced to withdraw before reaching the peninsula, having lost 9,000 men and, arguably even more importantly, almost as many horses. In spring 1736, a new offensive was launched, this time under the German-born Field Marshal Burkhard Minikh (Münnich), a two-pronged operation striking at both Azov and Crimea. Azov was soon taken by the Army of the Don, while the main thrust into Crimea quickly took the strategic fortress of Perekop, guarding the entrance onto the peninsula, and pushed into the interior. With wells poisoned and fields burned before them, the Russians were unable properly to forage, so they diverted westwards to take the port of Kezlev (now Yevpatoria) and its warehouses. Leaving it burning, Minikh then continued to Bakhchisarai, the khan's capital. This was plundered and razed. However, these were plague years. That and a renewed lack of supplies forced the Russians to withdraw, punitively ravaging as they went. Of all the losses Minikh's army suffered, only one in ten were from battle, the rest coming from hunger and disease.

This established a recurring pattern: the Russians could smash into Crimea and burn Tatar towns and cities. However, each time they ended up forced to withdraw, low on food and, above all, decimated by disease. Whatever the battlefield prowess of commanders such as Minikh, they were time and again let down by the administration of the army. Endemic corruption and inefficiency ensured that the Russians, while unable to be beaten, could never win. Indeed, as Turkey entered the war directly, Minikh was forced to divide his attention. In summer 1737, he led a large force to take the Turkish fortress of Ochakov on the Black Sea coast, to forestall it being used as a base to prevent his armies from entering or leaving Crimea. Often impatient in the siege, Minikh tried several times to storm the triple-walled fortress with little success, until heavy Russian artillery fire eventually set off the Turks' main powder magazine. The simultaneous explosion of 500 barrels of gunpowder flattened the centre of the town in one blast, killing thousands and forcing the shell-shocked defenders to surrender. Nonetheless, the Russian army was losing men faster than it could be reinforced, faced the constant threat of plague, and could not deliver a fatal blow to the Crimean Tatars while having to watch its flanks for the Turks. In 1737, Austria had joined on the Russian side, seeing an opportunity to strike a blow against its old enemy, the Ottoman Empire. It proved a serious miscalculation, as they would lose a series of battles, eventually even losing Belgrade in 1739, forcing them into hurried peace talks. With Austria out of the fight, even though their forces were making headway against the Turks in what is now Moldova and eastern Ukraine, the Russian leadership decided that it was time for a deal. After all, the Ottomans had allied with Poland and Sweden, and the fear was that a heavy deployment of forces in the south would leave the north-west vulnerable. The consequent 1739 Treaty of Niš left Russia in control of Azov (albeit barred from fortifying it), but at the price of abandoning its claims to Crimea and Moldavia and hopes of having a fleet in the Black Sea.

SUCCESSIVE WARS OF SUCCESSION

No one was left content, and the fundamental question of which empire – Russia, Habsburg or Ottoman – was dominant in south-east Europe had not been resolved, just as new struggles for dominance in Northern and Central Europe were emerging. The death of Augustus II in 1733 raised a particular challenge for the Polish–Lithuanian Commonwealth and its odd form of aristocratic democracy, whereby the succession was determined by a vote within the *szlachta*, the nobility, and thus increasingly subject not just to factionalism at home but influence and interference from abroad. Thanks to French intrigue, Stanisław I Leszczyński, the man whom the Swedes had previously imposed on Warsaw, was elected. Russia, though, backed Augustus's son, Frederick Augustus III of Saxony. The result was a civil war which dragged in other European powers. With the Bourbon dynasties of France and Spain backing Stanisław, and Russia and the Habsburgs of Austria upholding Frederick Augustus's claim, other nations quickly lined up: Sardinia and (predictably) Sweden in the former's camp, Prussia and (equally predictably) Saxony in the latter's. A Russian army under Field Marshal Peter Lacy – another Irishman – quickly occupied Poland itself, but the war then spread across all of Europe. France seized the Duchy of Lorraine then moved further into the Holy Roman Empire, reaching Mainz in the Rhineland before the emperor could properly muster his forces and begin pushing them back. Spain gave the Austrians a bloody nose in southern Italy, retaking the territories it had lost earlier in the War of the Spanish Succession. With Russian forces solidly holding Poland itself, though, and divisions beginning to emerge between Paris and Madrid, a ceasefire was agreed in 1735. The eventual 1738 Peace of Vienna saw Augustus III officially recognized as King of Poland. The days of Polish regional dominance and, indeed, the Commonwealth, were numbered, and in the Third Partition of Poland of 1795, it would no longer exist as an independent nation.

Perhaps the Habsburgs should have avoided tempting fate, because two years after the Peace of Vienna, the death of Austrian Emperor Charles VI led to an equally expansive continental spat over the right of his daughter, Maria Theresa, to succeed him, and not just to rule over Austria but as Holy Roman Emperor, with dominion over the rising German states of Prussia, Saxony and Bavaria. Britain, the Dutch Republic and Hanover supported her. Collectively known as the Pragmatic Allies (after the 1713 Pragmatic Sanction, Charles's attempt to clear his daughter's path to the throne), they favoured the existing continental status quo. France, Prussia and Bavaria, by contrast, were not backing a rival candidate as much as using her alleged lack of legitimacy to excuse attempts to wrest territory from the Habsburgs. The Prussians marched into Silesia, the Spanish tried and failed to roll up northern Italy, while France moved into the Austrian Netherlands. Meanwhile, Britain capitalized on its naval power to bombard enemy ports and blockade their shipping.

Again, other powers were sucked into the conflict for their own reasons, and in 1741, Russia joined the Pragmatic Allies, although it never actually ended up engaging in hostilities. In 1748, an army of 36,000 men under Prince Vasily Repnin set out from Livonia through Bohemia and Bavaria to the Rhine. However, while they were still on the march, the Anglo-Dutch forces lost Maastricht, their last remaining redoubt in Flanders. The resulting Treaty of Aix-la-Chapelle truly pleased no one. Again, it brought peace, but without settling any of the underlying tensions in Europe. Indeed, it led to the next phase of the so-called 'stately quadrille', the perennial shifting of alliances in Europe, with Austria (which resented being forced to give up Silesia and parts of Bavaria and Milan) aligning itself with France, the Prussians (a rising power, which London began to woo) turning to Britain, and the Dutch opting for neutrality. Three-quarters of a million were dead – and the scene was set for the even bloodier Seven Years War.

KUNERSDORF, 1759

What some argue was the first global war was triggered when Britain tried to expand into French-held territories in North America in 1756. London had hoped to keep the conflict confined to the other side of the Atlantic, but France, aware of the relative power of the Royal Navy, had no intention of playing games by British rules, and launched an attack on the island of Minorca in the Mediterranean. Once the war had begun to spread, Prussia anticipated that Austria would seize the opportunity for a rematch, now that it was allied with France, so it pre-emptively took Saxony. Austria and most of the German states of the Holy Roman Empire declared war in response in January 1757, as did Sweden, which had its eyes on regaining Pomerania. Spain was treaty bound to support France. As for Russia, it feared Prussian inroads into the Polish–Lithuanian Commonwealth – better a divided and declining neighbour than a vigorous and ambitious one – and just as importantly, Empress Elizabeth, one of Peter the Great's daughters who ruled from 1761 to 1762, harboured a deep personal dislike of Prussia's King Frederick II.

Frederick would become known as 'the Great' with reason, as he was a capable and decisive military leader who was also leading perhaps the best army in Europe, and one that would moreover be backed not so much with British troops but with that other key instrument of British power: money. An annual subsidy of £670,000, equivalent to around £20 million today, helped hire and feed soldiers and buy quite a bit of gunpowder and shot. The Prussian army could march fast and shoot fast, and Frederick took advantage of this to win early successes against the Austrians and the French. However, mass does tend to tell over time. By 1758, he was facing too many threats, and even though he was victorious in battle more often than not, he could not count on being able to reconstitute his forces for the next threat. Soon, he was fighting to keep his enemies away from Berlin rather than looking able to mount a serious offensive.

The following year, a Russian army under Prince Pyotr Saltykov joined with a smaller Austrian force commanded by Baron Ernst von Laudon – who had served in the Russian army and offered his services to Frederick before being hired by Austria – and made a renewed drive towards the Prussian heartlands. A Prussian army under Frederick himself marched to meet them at Kunersdorf in Silesia (now Kunowice in western Poland). He had some 48,000 men, facing 41,000 Russians, including 8,000 Cossack and other irregular cavalry, and 18,500 Austrians, so the odds were not that badly against him, especially as Saltykov and Laudon did not get on especially well. However, his soldiers were tired, and years of war had culled Prussia's best officers and men: 'I would fear nothing, if I still had ten battalions of the quality of 1757,' wrote Frederick.

He was known for his mastery of the oblique order, concentrating forces on one flank and rolling that up, while the rest of his forces pinned the remainder of the enemy army. Taking advantage of the Prussians' superior discipline and drill, Frederick believed – and had proven – that this way, 'an army of 30,000 could beat an army of 100,000.' The problem was precisely that, by now, his enemies were aware of this. Saltykov, not a general known for his tactical brilliance, nonetheless arrayed his forces precisely to meet such an attack, concentrating his best troops at the centre of his line, and building an especially dense array of field fortifications on his flanks, including abatis – pre-modern tank traps, dense lines of branches and sharpened tree trunks emplaced to slow an advance. One Austrian officer observed that 'like any peasants, at least Russian troops know how to grub in the earth', a tellingly snobbish but not wholly inaccurate statement; if the Prussians could march and shoot fast, then the Russians demonstrated, as they would many times in the future, that they could dig fast.

Frederick had pushed his army hard to the Oder River north of the Russian force, so that while a smaller force under Lieutenant General Finck attracted their attention to the south, his main force could fall on them from the north. Perhaps most importantly, Frederick was operating on partial and inaccurate information. From nearby heights, he could see troops on three hillocks – the Judenberge, Mühlberge and Walkberge – but not the size of the main body of the allied army, which was concealed behind them, nor the three large ponds that would end up limiting his men's room for manoeuvre. Most crucially, he could not tell that, while Saltykov had certainly begun by focusing his defensive work to the south, his scouts had alerted him to the Prussians' advance and his men had already come about, so that Frederick would be attacking their front, not their rear.

Frederick, true to his aggressive style, opened the battle with a bombardment by his artillery, which was better placed on commanding heights to dominate its Russian counterparts, followed by an advance on their less-well-fortified left flank. The Russian batteries were quickly taken, and the troops on that flank retreated, leaving the Prussians in control of the Mühlberge. So far, this was a classic oblique attack, and Frederick became confident of victory. Although some of his generals, aware of just how spent the army was after a forced march and day's hard fighting in the summer heat, counselled caution, he signalled a renewed attack.

However, the bulk of the Russo-Austrian forces had not yet been engaged, and instead of breaking, as Frederick had anticipated, they repelled a subsequent series of infantry attacks, as Saltykov steadily fed reserves into the line. Unwilling to abandon the field, Frederick gambled on a cavalry charge, and this too failed; he himself had a horse shot from under him. The stalemate was finally broken when fresh reserves were unleashed: some Austrian infantry who had arrived late to the battle, and some Russian cavalry. Facing this new onslaught, the Prussian army uncharacteristically broke, men who had been the dour terror of the war throwing down their muskets and fleeing for their lives. Saltykov unleashed his Chuguyev Cossack Regiment, lancers on nimble little ponies who harried the routing troops mercilessly, and might even have captured Frederick if not for the bravery of a last handful of Prussian cavalry.

It was a crushing defeat for the Prussians, who lost over a third of the precious troops who had marched to Kunersdorf. It had also been a bloody victory for the Russians and Austrians, whose casualties were about a quarter of their total force. Arguably, though, it was more true to say that Frederick had lost the battle, rather than that Saltykov had won it. He had allowed himself to fight on a battlefield of his enemies' choosing, failed properly to assess their strength, and been goaded into futile attacks, blinded by his contempt for his enemies (especially the Austrians). Yet one cannot take away the fact that, despite suffering terrible losses, the Russians had held their ground against the fearsome Prussians and might yet have marched all the way to Berlin, had Saltykov had the verve of a, well, Frederick the Great.

As it was, after shaking off a period of understandable depression, Frederick was able to reconstitute an army of sorts from stragglers, reserves and the force he had left behind to protect Berlin. A combination of attenuated supply lines and irresolute leadership meant that the Russians only played a limited role in the next year, so Frederick was able to concentrate on the Austrians. In any case, the death in 1762 of Empress Elizabeth and the succession of her nephew Peter III was about to change everything. Thanks to the intricate interconnections between the royal dynasties of Europe, Elizabeth's heir presumptive, Peter, was not only a grandson of Peter the Great but also a great-grandson of Charles XI of Sweden. More to the point, he was born in Germany, could scarcely even speak Russian and on his coronation, a tsarina who feared and disliked Frederick was succeeded by a tsar who idolized him. He immediately signed a treaty with Russia and switched sides, forcing Vienna to start the talks that led to the 1763 Treaty of Hubertusburg between Austria, Prussia and Saxony. Five days later, the Treaty of Paris between France, Spain and Great Britain saw London acquire French and Spanish colonies, to its considerable satisfaction.

COUPS AND CATHERINES

In fact, the belligerent Peter planned a new war against Denmark, but before he could unleash it, just six months into his reign, he was unceremoniously toppled in a coup by his wife, Princess Sophia Augusta Frederica von Anhalt-Zerbst, who would become rather better known as Catherine the Great. These had become something of an 18th-century tradition in Russia, especially as, like the *Streltsy* before them, the elite Guard regiments would gain an appetite for kingmaking – or, more usually, empressmaking. Peter I, never one to let tradition stand in his way, had abandoned the principle of primogeniture: an emperor could choose his own successor. What was perhaps intended to strengthen the crown only weakened it, though, as it left the legitimacy of any succession down to the word of the deceased monarch – or the successor's muscle. His bookish eldest son Alexis despised his boisterous and belligerent father and reportedly had said, 'I won't launch any ships; I shall maintain troops only for defence, and won't make war on anyone.' He even briefly fled to Austria, and on his return under Peter's safe conduct, was instead seized and, interrogated under torture, suspected of treason. After 40 strokes of that distinctive and vicious Russian whip, the knout, he died. Peter had declared his second wife, Catherine, to be tsarina, empress, in her own right. Of common birth, and lacking a strong personal power base, she likely could not have succeeded him when he died in 1725, had she not been adopted as a figurehead by Prince Alexander Menshikov and a cabal of other 'new men', former favourites of Peter's who feared the old boyar elite would otherwise seek to re-establish their power. They had the Guard regiments on side, though, and were able to install Catherine I as empress, even if they were pulling the strings.

After Catherine, Peter's only male-line grandson, also named Peter, became underage emperor, dying three years later, having neither ruled in his own right nor fathered an heir. The Supreme Privy Council – which had replaced the Boyar Duma – opted next for Anna, younger daughter of Peter's original co-tsar, Ivan V, thinking she would be more biddable. They were wrong. Anna refused to be a figurehead, purged the Council and packed it with her cronies. In 1740, close to death, she made her two-month-old grandnephew Ivan her heir, apparently as a way to secure a future for her German lover, Ernst Biron, as his regent.

However, Russia was destined to have another empress. Elizabeth, Peter I's energetic, intelligent and, it turned out, ruthless second daughter, had assiduously courted the Preobrazhensky Life Guards Regiment, originally one of her father's 'toy army' units. In 1741, they staged a coup in her name, and she would reign until her death in 1762.

It was not a lesson lost on the wife of the obnoxious and small-minded Peter III, whom Elizabeth had taken under her wing. Sophie learned Russian, was baptized as Yekaterina – Catherine – into the Russian Church, and charmed and cultivated the Izmailovsky and Semyonovsky Regiments, who backed her coup. Peter III had, they felt, humiliated Russia by his fawning courtship of Frederick; Catherine promised them a new age of glory for the country – and she meant to deliver.

Want To Know More?

Franz Szabo's *The Seven Years War in Europe: 1756–1763* (Routledge, 2007) is a useful counter to an orthodoxy that is sometimes too kind to Frederick. *Empire and Military Revolution in Eastern Europe: Russia's Turkish Wars in the Eighteenth Century*, by Brian Davies (Bloomsbury, 2013), is much broader than its title implies, and is recommended. One must, of course, also mention Angus Konstam's *Russian Army of the Seven Years War (1)* and *(2)* (both Osprey, 1996) and Daniel Marston's *The Seven Years' War* (Osprey, 2001). For the wargamers, *Prussia's Glory II* (GMT, 2006) is a perfectly decent simulation that covers four pivotal battles (although Kunersdorf hardly counts as glorious from Prussia's point of view).

14

Tsarina versus Tsargrad

Cahul, 1770

1762	Catherine the Great comes to power
1768–74	Russo-Turkish War
1773–75	Pugachev rebellion
1787–92	Russo-Turkish War
1788–90	Russo-Swedish War
1792	Russo-Polish War
1794	Polish Uprising
1796	Third Russo-Persian War
1796	Death of Catherine; Paul I becomes tsar

Empress Catherine II, known with good reason as Catherine the Great, had many lovers and dalliances, but her enduring favourite was Prince Grigory Potemkin. An endearing and enduring myth – though myth it seems to be – is that he arranged fake villages and crowds of seemingly happy and prosperous peasants along the route of her river journey to inspect her new Crimean possessions in 1787. After all, while he had successfully conquered the peninsula, his efforts to encourage colonization to the region had fallen short. Rather than admit failure, he put on a show. It likely never happened, but 'Potemkin village' has entered the lexicon for an artful façade to hide unpalatable realities. Arguably, though, later 18th-century Russia itself was a Potemkin empire.

After all, while Catherine is often hailed as a modernizer, and to a degree she was, as much as anything else, she was a mistress of spin, convincing a credulous Europe that Russia had evolved, almost overnight, from medieval periphery to glittering European great power. Of course, it was actually a little of both. Away from the salons and balls of the be-wigged aristocracy, most Russians still laboured in conditions that had barely changed for centuries. Even by the end of the century, 96 per cent of Russians lived on the land, and half of those were serfs, virtual land slaves, tied to the land they worked. According to the Fifth Imperial Census carried out in 1795–96, some 57 per cent of the total male population were serfs, for example, on land owned by private landlords, the Church or the state, and while this proportion was steadily declining, the circumstances of the free peasantry were scarcely much better. Indeed, even much early industry and trade was conducted by state serfs: the government and the crown between them owned more than 3.3 million of them. The basis of the Industrial Revolution that was spreading from Britain to Europe and North America – and which would also revolutionize warfare – had been the earlier Agrarian Revolution, which had generated surpluses able to feed growing urban populations, stimulate trade and fuel investment. Between 1700 and 1750, for example, agricultural productivity in Britain would increase by half, and by 1850 was two and a half times that of 1700. In Russia, by contrast, a combination of heavy soils, harsh climate, a lack of investment capital and the perverse effects of serfdom meant that it did not increase across the 18th century. Any growth in production was simply accounted for by increases in territory and population. There was, of course, some industrial development, and also growing domestic and international trade, not least thanks to the acquisition of Baltic ports. Yet this was not an economy able to keep up with the demands of the time, from the frequent wars to the profligate habits of the monarchs. (Catherine's Brilliant Room in the Winter Palace was entirely devoted to housing her collection of jewellery.)

RIOT AND REVOLT

As a result, the state was forever seeking new ways to raise money, whether printing it, signing promissory notes for it, or squeezing more out of the countryside. (Indeed, by the early 19th century, revenue from vodka sales represented about a third of the total state income.) This would lead to frequent riots and revolts, and while most were essentially local, in 1773 Catherine had to face another of the major Cossack and peasant rebellions that were such a feature of Russian history, this time led by a Ural Cossack ataman, Yemelyan Pugachev.

In many ways, it was the same old story: a Cossack who had served in the military before falling foul of the authorities in circumstances that left him feeling hard done by. A man who combined charisma with a gift for tall tales (even while serving in the military, he had claimed that his sword was a gift from his 'godfather', Peter the Great), he stirred up dissatisfied serfs and Cossacks alike, claiming to be none other than Peter III and promising that perennial crowd-pleaser, an end to serfdom. He cannily played not just on the resentments of the serfs and peasants, but also minority communities such as the Bashkirs and Tatars, who were promised a return to their old ways of life.

Recruits flocked to his banner, and he scored a series of early and impressive victories against a large but unwieldy army that was also hamstrung by wilful disobedience on the part of badly paid and treated soldiers, who often had considerable sympathies for the 'False Peter'. In 1774, Pugachev stormed Kazan with 25,000 men, taking it briefly then leaving it in flames as he withdrew in the face of a relief column under General Johann von Michelsohnen. He would then go on to inflict another bloody defeat on the rebels at Tsaritsyn (later known as Stalingrad), and as his rebellion began to unravel, Pugachev tried to flee. His own Cossacks turned on him and angrily delivered him to the authorities: he was publicly decapitated and disembowelled in Moscow's Bolotnaya Square.

The significance of this, the most serious revolt under Catherine, was not only that the Cossacks lost even more of their special status, but that more garrisons were established all across the country. Catherine criticized the 'weak conduct of civil and military officials in various localities' in the face of the rebellion, but also recognized that they often simply lacked the authority and forces to act more firmly and quickly. There had, after all, only been 800 professional soldiers in Kazan facing Pugachev's hordes, and they ended up having to be supplemented by everyone from schoolchildren to firefighters. Besides, many of Russia's troops were already engaged in war with Turkey. Thus, Catherine was having to grapple with a dilemma which had long troubled Russia's rulers and which would become all the more intractable in the next century, as industrialization and urbanization finally began to reshape the country and create new political challenges: is the greater threat to the state that from without, or within?

THE SWEDISH FLANK

For now, though, the answer seemed to be the foreign enemy. The Ottoman Empire remained the primary regional rival to the south, not least with its alliance to the Crimean Khanate (which continued to raid Russia for slaves), but the ailing Polish–Lithuanian Commonwealth also offered Catherine further opportunities. All told, under her reign, the empire would absorb Lithuania, Courland and Belarus to the north-east, the North Caucasus, Novorossiya ('New Russia', or eastern Ukraine) and, with equal long-term implications, Crimea to the south-west: all told, some 200,000 square miles. Was this because she was an expansionist imperialist? Yes and no: like so many Russian leaders before and since, her view was that 'I have no way to defend my borders but to expand them.' The lack of natural frontiers, neighbours who were unruly raiders, hostile peers or decaying empires – all this generated and justified a sense that for Russia not to expand was to make itself vulnerable.

Neither the Swedes nor the Polish–Lithuanian Commonwealth, for example, seemed to have learned – as far as Catherine was concerned – that they were now in Russia's shadow. In 1741, before she had come to power, the Swedes had tried to take back territories lost in the Great Northern War in the so-called War of the Hats (the 'Hats' in question being a conservative political faction opposed by the 'Caps'). They seized on the assassination by Russian agents of a Swedish emissary to the Ottoman Empire to justify a war, but between their fleet being paralysed by an outbreak of disease and the army taking longer than expected to prepare, they lost the initiative and never really regained it, and in 1743 signed the Treaty of Åbo, ceding a further strip of Finland to Russia.

In 1788, though, they tried again. King Gustav III, thinking a tidy little victory would shore up his political position at home, and encouraged by Britain, the Dutch Republic and Prussia, all eager to see Russia taken down a notch, hit on an ambitious plan to force Catherine – who was a cousin – to make concessions by striking directly at St Petersburg. A feint would draw Russian troops from the capital to counter a seeming threat from Finland, with the real attack being a naval blockade of Kronstadt and an amphibious assault on St Petersburg. With Catherine distracted by an ongoing war with the Ottomans, anticipating open support from his Western backers and aware of the relative disrepair of much of the Russian Baltic Fleet, Gustav was confident.

Gustav's cunning plan soon began to fall apart, though, not least because of dissatisfaction among his own officers. The Russian fleet and army in the north-west were unprepared, but his hopes for a quick initial advance foundered on the first obstacle, the decrepit border fortress of Neyshlot (now Savonlinna in Finland). After a preliminary bombardment, Gustav demanded that its commander surrender and open the gates. The one-armed Major Kuzmin replied, 'I am without an arm, so cannot open the gates. Let His Majesty himself do it.' After continued shelling, the Swedes eventually retreated, even though Neyshlot's garrison numbered only around 200 men.

Indeed, the war was largely a dynamic stalemate, with numerous raids and local offensives and counter-offensives on land and sea, but all to little lasting effect. It was at sea that most of the action took place. By 1790, as another attempt to attack St Petersburg failed, Gustav was losing hope – and getting worried at the spiralling costs of the war, and the debts the government was incurring as a result. Fortunately for him, in July the Swedish fleet trounced the Russians at the Second Battle of Svensksund, the largest naval battle ever to be fought in the Baltic Sea, with some 500 ships involved. Catherine regarded this war as an irritating side-show, so Gustav was able to leverage his victory into peace talks, which led to the Treaty of Värälä, but even so, this essentially returned affairs to the pre-war status quo.

THE POLISH–LITHUANIAN FLANK

The point was precisely that both wars took place at a time when Russia's efforts were focused on the Ottomans, and a desire to ensure no distraction from unruly neighbours while focusing on the Turks also helped shape Catherine's policies towards the Polish–Lithuanian Commonwealth. In 1764, she had helped a former lover of hers to become King of Poland and Grand Duke of Lithuania. Stanisław II

August may have been grateful, but he was also a patriot and a reformer, whose efforts to modernize and stabilize his nation managed respectively to alienate conservatives at home, as well as Russia, Prussia and Austria, who had no desire to see a strong Commonwealth revived.

Russia had come to see it as a virtual protectorate, something codified in the 1768 Treaty of Perpetual Friendship. Poles in particular tended to think otherwise, and successive rebellions, generally directed against domestic enemies rather than Russia itself, led to a series of punitive partitions that ultimately saw the Commonwealth entirely occupied. The Bar Confederation (named for the fortress in which it was founded) was a cabal of magnates committed to opposing Russian influence and King Stanisław's reforms alike. The consequent civil war lasted longer than it might, as the Russians were distracted by another Cossack rebellion and then the outbreak of the 1768–74 Russo-Turkish War. Nonetheless, it was crushed by loyalists and Russian, Prussian and Austrian forces. The price was brutal: the First Partition. The Commonwealth lost almost a third of its territory and its population to its three neighbours, accelerating its decline and making further defiance almost inevitable.

In 1791, a new constitution promised the people of the Commonwealth good government, greater freedom and an end to the arbitrary powers of the crown and the aristocracy. Of course, it could not go well. Russia and Austria were both embroiled in war with the Ottomans, and Prussia had formed an alliance with the Commonwealth, so maybe the reformers felt safe. However, not only did Catherine regard it as a rebuke, and a challenge, but so too did King Frederick William II of Prussia. He dissolved his alliance with the Commonwealth, and the two autocrats found common cause with the Targowica Confederation of conservative Polish magnates to crush this pesky constitutional experiment. The Russians invaded in 1792 with an army of almost 98,000 men, against perhaps 50,000 defenders, but the war only lasted three months before Stanisław capitulated – a controversial decision at the time and since, given that his forces were still in decent shape – apparently hoping he could salvage a diplomatic solution. He was to be disappointed: not only was the new constitution annulled, but a Second Partition would see the Commonwealth lose another third of its territory to Russia and Prussia, and Russian garrisons stationed across what was left.

The sense that they had not been beaten but betrayed led to the third, final and fatal expression of resistance – the 1794 Polish Uprising. General Tadeusz Kościuszko, a veteran not just of the war with Russia but the American Revolutionary War, used the refusal of the 1st Greater Polish National Cavalry Brigade to be disbanded to satisfy Russian demands to raise the flag of rebellion. Supplementing his regular troops with the 'scythemen', peasant levies and volunteers bearing the implements of their profession, he fought a spirited but doomed fight against overwhelming odds, eventually put down by Russia's General Alexander Suvorov, who would become famous for never losing a battle in his long military career. The Third Partition which followed would see the Commonwealth disappear from the map, Austria, Prussia and Russia dividing what was left between them. Neither Poland nor Lithuania would re-emerge as states until after the First World War.

THE OTTOMAN FLANK: CAHUL, 1770

The irony was that Catherine was always more concerned with domestic politics than foreign wars, but circumstances did not allow her to avoid them. In particular, she saw the Ottoman Empire as at once a problem and an opportunity. There was much concern in the West that she was ambitious enough to try to take Istanbul, which as Tsargrad had been the lodestar of Rus' raiders and princes, and as Constantinople had been the cradle of Orthodox Christianity. Although later in her life, she would propose the ambitious but unrealistic 'Greek Project', which envisaged Russia and Austria partitioning the Ottoman Empire to re-establish an Eastern Roman Empire with its capital again in Constantinople, this came to nothing.

Nonetheless, she presided over a long-term campaign to roll back the Ottomans and make Russia dominant in south-eastern Europe, just as it was in the north-east. During the Bar Confederation rising, the French – who wanted the Ottomans distracted with a European war so that they could make their own moves on Egypt – encouraged an alliance with the rebels, persuading them to promise the Turks the Ukrainian regions of Volhynia and Podolia were they to win. Of course, they did not, but this encouraged the Sublime Porte, the Ottoman government, to ponder further intervention in the Polish–Lithuanian

Commonwealth. When a Cossack detachment crossed into Turkish territory when pursuing fleeing Polish rebels, the Turks chose to treat this as a serious offence and even imprisoned the Russian ambassador to the Sublime Porte.

Sultan Mustafa III was not wholly unaware that his army, while large – three times Russia's – was increasingly falling behind European standards. However, not only did he fail fully to appreciate just how far behind it was, but his efforts to modernize were impeded by conservatives, not least the Janissaries. Much like the *Streltsy*, they had degenerated from elite shock troops to self-indulgent Praetorians. His father, Ahmed III, had been deposed in a Janissary rising in 1730, and so Mustafa, while happy to hire European officers and take such steps as he could, never brought himself to push through the comprehensive reforms that were needed.

He was determined on war, even over the warnings of his advisers, reportedly saying, 'I will find some means of humbling those infidels.' Catherine was happy to oblige him, and in 1768 both sides mustered for war. In January 1769, the Crimeans began raiding Russian-controlled regions of what is now Ukraine at Mustafa's behest, but in April, Catherine's forces took the initiative, crossing the Dniester River into Moldavia and taking the fortress of Khotyn after an initial false start. They moved on to take the capital of Moldavia, Bucharest, while a smaller flying column largely made up of Don Cossack and Kalmyk cavalry struck back into Crimea.

In May 1769, the main Turkish force crossed the Danube, but thanks to supply problems, it moved slowly so the Russians were able to retain the initiative. Grand Vizier Mehmed Emin Pasha was at the head of a 100,000-strong army, with perhaps 50,000 more in two other armies moving along separate axes of advance, and perhaps 80,000 Tatars. However, he had no military experience and was unwilling to take chances and show a properly aggressive posture – much to the chagrin of Crimean Khan Devlet IV Giray – and allowed himself to be held up along the Dniester until a lack of food and mutiny in the ranks forced him to withdraw and regroup.

In 1770, though, the Sultan had had enough of Mehmed Emin Pasha's hesitancy: the Turks had a substantial lead in manpower, and needed to take advantage of that. By May, they had some 150,000 troops assembled, now under Ivazzade Halil Pasha, with 80,000

Crimean Tatars on call: a hammer he wanted swung at Field Marshal Pyotr Rumyantsev's army in Moldavia, which by then had been whittled down to around 38,000. This would be Russia's year, as they won a series of victories culminating in the Battle of Cahul in July. Some 17,000 Russian infantry and perhaps 5,000 cavalry faced a combined Turkish and Tatar army almost ten times its size – and won.

Having had his army ferried across the Danube, Ivazzade Halil Pasha rejected suggestions he await the Russians – perhaps remembering his predecessor's fate – and advanced to the village of Cahul. His force was made up of 80,000 light cavalry and 40,000 infantry, with another 80,000 Tatars some 12 miles away, ready to fall on the Russian rear. It was relatively weak in artillery, even if it could field some 40 of the massive guns beloved of the Turks, but Ivazzade Halil Pasha felt he had reason for confidence. Rumyantsev likewise knew that he was in a tough spot, and, true to his personal motto 'do not tolerate the presence of the enemy without attacking him', felt his best chance was to attack the Ottoman force before it could unite with the Tatars, and while his dwindling food supplies still lasted. He marched his force to just 7 miles from the Turkish camp. Ivazzade Halil Pasha, watching them make camp, decided to attack the next morning at 10, planning to sweep them into the Cahul River. This proved too leisurely a timetable (Russians joked after that 'the Turk cannot rouse himself from his bed before lunchtime'), and Rumyantsev beat him to the punch. An hour after midnight, 17,000 infantrymen, led by Grenadier regiments, silently filed out of the Russian camp, flanked by skirmishers. By dawn, they had formed into five squares, or rather flattened rectangles, their long sides facing the enemy, anchored by the typically tall and physically formidable grenadiers at each corner.

This is a close-order formation especially well suited to holding off cavalry, and the Turks obligingly launched a massive but disorderly charge. The well-drilled Russians briefly opened gaps in their squares through which light guns inside the formations blasted them with grapeshot, bringing down whole ranks of attackers, whose momentum was blunted by having to make their way through or over dead and dying horses and men. Nonetheless, by sheer weight of numbers, the Turks managed to surround two of the squares, so Rumyantsev sent his reserves to threaten their potential line of retreat, forcing them to withdraw.

By 8am, the Russians were advancing at a fast march towards the Turkish encampment. They were met by cannon fire and also a charge by the Turkish infantry. Fully 10,000 Janissaries stormed Lieutenant General Pyotr Plemyannikov's square, which was made up of four regular infantry regiments and a single Grenadier regiment, and crashed through it. The formation disintegrated, and fleeing soldiers, seeking sanctuary in General Pyotr Olits's adjacent square, risked breaking its cohesion, too, in what could have become a cascading collapse of the Russian line. Seeing the danger, Rumyantsev led his personal guard to the scene and famously managed to return some discipline to them with the simple command 'Rebyata, Stoi!' – 'Lads, Stop!' Fortunately, at this point the Russian artillery had found their range and began hammering the Janissaries, and the 1st Grenadier Regiment drove them to flight with a bayonet charge.

In the confusion, Prince Nikolai Repnin's square had managed to inch its way onto heights south of the Turkish camp, and opened up with musket and cannon fire from this vantage. This was enough to trigger a general flight, and by 9am – an hour before their planned attack – the Turks were routed. The Russian infantry were too exhausted to pursue, but Rumyantsev had kept a thousand Cossacks and hussars in reserve, whom he now unleashed to keep the Turks running. The next day, he sent a corps in their wake, who came upon the Turks as they were in the middle of trying to cross back over the Danube. They attacked, throwing the enemy into even greater disarray: the remnants of the army (which still outnumbered the Russians several-fold) scattered, many drowning as they tried to swim the wide, fast river. Meanwhile, the new Crimean khan, Qaplan II Giray, hearing garbled accounts of this unbeatable Russian army, turned for home.

It was a decisive victory. The Russians suffered just 364 dead or missing and another 557 wounded, compared with the Ottomans' tally of more than 20,000 killed, wounded or taken prisoner. Although the war would drag on for another four years, the Russians were finally demonstrating the combination of drill, formation and firepower that had so frequently defeated them in Europe. They systematically ground through Moldavia and Wallachia, south-west Ukraine and even, as a diversion, Georgia and the North Caucasus. Meanwhile, a Russian flotilla entered the Mediterranean for the first time in history, sparking a short-lived anti-Ottoman revolt in Greece, and bombarding Beirut.

In January 1774, Mustafa died, and his successor, Abdul Hamid I, quickly made peace overtures, leading to the Treaty of Küçük Kaynarca. Crimea technically became independent from the Ottomans but in practice simply saw its vassalage transferred from Constantinople to St Petersburg, being annexed outright in 1782. As well as substantial reparations, Russia gained the ports of Azov and Kerch, which, now that Crimea was also secured, meant its fleets had direct access to the Black Sea. It also pushed its borders forward to encompass south-western Ukraine, taking the lands between the Dnieper and Southern Bug Rivers, where it would found new cities, including Kherson, Odessa and Yekaterinoslav (literally 'the Glory of Catherine'). Finally, in a move that both underlined the weakening of the Sultan's authority and made further conflict almost inevitable, Russia became the official guarantor of the rights of Orthodox Christians living in the Ottoman Empire.

BACK FOR SECONDS: THE 1787–92 RUSSO-TURKISH WAR

As a protectorate, Crimea proved more of a problem, perennially subject to pogroms and bankruptcy, such that in 1783 Catherine simply annexed it, making a triumphant processional through this new province in 1787, accompanied by Habsburg Emperor Joseph II, much to the anger of the Turks. Egged on by Britain and France, they demanded that Russia surrender Crimea. In response, Catherine declared war, supported by the Austrians, catching the Turks somewhat by surprise. Nonetheless, they mustered their forces and launched an amphibious offensive on Kinburn to the west of Crimea, repulsed by troops under Suvorov. Meanwhile, Russia launched its own offensive in Moldavia, taking the cities of Chocim, Jassy and Ochakov. The news of this last defeat seems to have been the cause of the stroke that killed Sultan Abdul Hamid I in April 1789.

Another Greek revolt forced Constantinople to conclude a truce with Austria, but the Russians pushed on, winning victory after victory. Admiral Fyodor Ushakov, considered in many ways the navy's answer to Alexander Suvorov, demonstrated the capacities of the newly formed Black Sea Fleet by defeating a larger Turkish force at Tendra in September 1790. Not to be outdone, in December Suvorov himself took Izmail, at the mouth of the Danube, considered one of the Ottomans' most formidable bastions. With the threat that Suvorov would march on to

Constantinople, the new Sultan Selim III bowed to the inevitable. The eventual 1792 Treaty of Jassy recognized the annexation of Crimea, and saw Russia's border pushed to the Dniester River.

Catherine had never set out to be a warrior-empress, but nor did she shirk from conflict. In part, the problem was that Russia was taken just seriously enough by its neighbours to be seen as a threat, not quite seriously enough not to be provoked. Surrounded by powers in decline – Sweden, the Commonwealth, the Habsburgs, the Ottomans – Russia would find itself facing too many threats and opportunities not to be often at war. Catherine had seen herself as a force for civilization and culture, even if her successes in reforming the country beyond the confines of St Petersburg were limited. Nonetheless, when she died in 1796, her successors would face a very different kind of threat, and one which would emerge from distant France.

Want To Know More?

Robert Massie's *Catherine the Great* (Head of Zeus, 2012) is still the benchmark biography, although it is surprising there is no good English-language biography of Suvorov. The early chapters of Mungo Melvin's *Sevastopol's Wars: Crimea from Potemkin to Putin* (Osprey, 2017) give an interesting perspective on the Crimean dimension, while Quintin Barry's *War in the East: A Military History of the Russo-Turkish War 1877–78* (Helion, 2016) is a good study of this conflict, and David Nicolle's *The Janissaries* (Osprey, 1995) delves into this distinctive force. As for the Pugachev Rebellion, no less than the famous Russian poet Alexander Pushkin wrote the near-contemporaneous *The History of Pugachev* (Orion, 2001). On TV, the black comedy-drama *The Great* has, if you were wondering, only the most tenuous connection to the real history of Peter III and Catherine.

PART FOUR

Triumph and Decline

15

Russia versus the Antichrist

Borodino, 1812

1796	Death of Catherine; Paul I becomes tsar
1799	Russia joins the Second Coalition
1801	Murder of Paul; Alexander I becomes tsar
1806	Russia declares war on France
1806–12	Russo-Turkish War
1807–12	Anglo-Russian War
1808	Russia allies with France
1812	Napoleon invades Russia

It's quite common to demonize and denigrate one's enemy, but less so to regard – with every appearance of being serious – him as the Antichrist. Nonetheless, this is what Alexander I seems to have believed, after a Russian scholar had claimed to prove, through cabalistic numerology, that the letters in the phrase 'L'Empereur Napoléon' added up to 666, the 'Number of the Beast'. It was no accident that in 1806, when Russia (again) declared war on France, the Russian Orthodox Church dutifully issued a proclamation to be read from every pulpit that denounced Napoleon as 'a fierce enemy of the world... alienated from the Christian faith'.

As the century turned, so were European politics facing a different kind of tumult. The 18th century had been one of wars driven by imperial ambitions and shifting constellations of alliances. In the 19th, to these would be added the passions of revolution and the resurgence of efforts to unify the continent – something that ran very counter to Russia's long-standing interests. For Russia, it would mean at once one of its greatest triumphs – its struggle with Napoleon is known as the Patriotic War, second only to the Great Patriotic War against Hitler – and yet also one that flattered its power and position, giving rise to a complacency that would lead to crisis.

FROM PAUL TO ALEXANDER

Catherine's unloved and neglected son Paul was that most dangerous of combinations – energetic and foolish. He was a militarist, yet he feared wars of expansion. Like his father, Peter III, he confused pageant with power, and thought that introducing Prussian-style uniforms and Prussian-style drill would give him a Prussian-style army. The old campaigner Suvorov, who believed that the Russians had their own art of war and ways to victory – and of all people, he should have known – so infuriated the tsar by ignoring his guidance that he had him dismissed and banished to his estate, although he would quickly enough reinstate him when Revolutionary France began to burst its borders.

Paul I was an autocrat and a martinet, who would see the French Revolution, and especially the execution of King Louis XVI in 1793, as an affront against the natural order of things. As the new Jacobin regime harnessed the energy of revolution and France's large population (28 million, more than Russia's 25 million) to raise mass armies, they began winning victories against the plethora of nations committed to ending this political experiment, or at least confining it to its own frontiers. The Austrians, the Dutch, the Spanish, the Prussians – all would suffer serious defeats at the hands of the French. In 1796, a Corsican-born general by the name of Napoleon Bonaparte began to make his name, cutting through Austrian forces in Italy and even putting Vienna under threat. Nation after nation made peace with the French, joined them, or were invaded. The Austrian Netherlands, the Dutch Republic, Italy, Switzerland, country after country, region after region, fell to the French.

Napoleon's invasion of Egypt in 1798 revived attempts to contain this new threat, and this time Russia joined the Second Coalition, which also included Austria, Great Britain, Portugal and the Ottoman

Empire. The rehabilitated Suvorov was put in command of an Austro-Russian army and drove the French out of Italy, but hopes of then being able to invade France through Switzerland were dashed, and an Anglo-Russian expedition to Holland was also ultimately unsuccessful. Paul brooded over the defeats, and especially over the reports that his men were being blamed for them. Perhaps even more importantly, in 1799 Napoleon returned to Paris and installed himself as First Consul in what was in effect a coup. Paul withdrew from the coalition (which would soon unravel) and even began talking about an alliance with France against the Ottomans. After all, was France not an autocracy again, in fact if not in name? And were the arrogant British not siding with the Austrians and threatening the independent shipping of Russia's Baltic allies? On freeing Malta from French occupation, had they not refused to hand it back to the Order of the Knights Hospitaller, of which he was Grand Master? In a harbinger of the future 'Great Game', he even opened secret discussions about a Franco-Russian expedition towards British India.

IN AND OUT OF WAR WITH FRANCE

His own elites, already disenchanted, became increasingly worried. In 1801, after failing to persuade him to abdicate, a cabal of dismissed officers murdered him in his bed chamber. His eldest son, Alexander, may or may not have known about the plot – but he certainly never punished the plotters. Perhaps this ambiguity, neither organizing nor avenging his father's assassination, was fitting. After all, Alexander I was many things, often all at once: constancy was certainly not one of his characteristics. He believed in liberal reform, but was autocratic in manner and arbitrary in his rule. He spoke excellent English and was better educated about the outside world than his predecessors, but would go on to purge Russian schools of foreign teachers. He was by nature inconstant, and would change his policies towards France repeatedly. On his accession in 1801, he made peace with Britain and mended relations with both Austria and Prussia, while still briefly toying with a rapprochement with Paris. That soon passed, though, and he would join the anti-Napoleon coalition in 1805, denouncing him as 'the oppressor of Europe and the disturber of the world's peace' and 'the most famous tyrant the world has produced'.

However, the wars that followed were, for Alexander, largely defined by defeat after defeat: Mehrnbach (October 1805), Austerlitz (December 1805), Naples (spring 1806), Czarnowo, Pułtusk and Golymin (December 1806), Mohrungen (January 1807), Danzig (spring 1807), Friedland (June 1807), the tally was dispiriting, the cost in blood and treasure terrible. After Austerlitz, Alexander glumly concluded, 'we are babies in the hands of a giant', so it was perhaps inevitable that the inveterate flip-flopper would, in 1807, prove susceptible to the blandishments of this 'famous tyrant', when they met in Tilsit. Napoleon conjured a seductive image of Franco-Russian global co-dominion, which led to an alliance. In 1807, Alexander also declared war on Britain, following the Royal Navy's attack on Copenhagen (to prevent the neutral Danish fleet from being seized by the French) and joined the Continental System, Napoleon's economic blockade of Britain.

The degree to which neither side trusted the other became increasingly clear, though, and Alexander would do as little as possible to observe his side of the deal. The Russian fleet did nothing much to prosecute its war with Britain (rather, it was the Royal Navy that was more aggressive, notching up a series of local naval victories in the Baltic and Barents Seas), nor to enforce the Continental System. Quite the opposite: trade secretly continued, with Alexander's blessing. Likewise, although Russian forces took part in France's 1809 operations against Austria, they did so grudgingly and haltingly. In fairness, Napoleon was no more committed to what could increasingly be described as an alliance of inconvenience. Russia had been fighting an essentially and successfully defensive war with Turkey since 1806, and although Napoleon had promised to help, it became obvious that this was not forthcoming. In 1811, feeling the need to end this diversion of forces, Alexander turned to General Mikhail Kutuzov, who delivered enough of a blow to the Turks that they sued for peace, concluding the 1812 Treaty of Bucharest. Which, of course, was just in time.

PATRIOTIC WAR

Why did Napoleon invade Russia? The conventional answer is that it was in order to force them again to join the Continental System. France could not challenge the Royal Navy, so instead it would starve out this 'nation of shopkeepers' through economic blockade. It was likely more than that. Alexander had taxed Napoleon's patience with his vacillations. More than that, the demonic ambition that had driven Napoleon so far, likely could not let him stop. In 1811, he reportedly declared to his ambassador in Warsaw, 'in five years, I will be master of the whole world. There is only Russia left, I will crush it.' To this end, he mustered a *Grande Armée* of extraordinary proportions, half a million men drawn from 16 different nationalities: French, imperial vassals, mercenaries and Italian, Austrian and Prussian allies, from elite Imperial Guard to Piedmontese dragoons. Although Napoleon's armies were accustomed to living off the land, to support his behemoth, he still assembled 20 supply caravans and established magazines across Poland and East Prussia. Danzig became a particular hub, its warehouses holding enough supplies to feed 400,000 men and 50,000 horses for 50 days, while Vilnius, beyond rations for 100,000 men for 40 days, had 27,000 muskets and 30,000 pairs of shoes ready for resupply.

This was hardly a covert process, and in April 1812, Alexander I demanded French troops withdraw from Prussia and the Grand Duchy of Warsaw. Instead, on 24 June, the *Grande Armée* crossed into Russia, promising to 'terminate the fatal influence which Russia has exercised in Europe for the last fifty years'. One of Napoleon's great strengths had always been the speed he could get out of his armies, and he pushed them hard through western Russia. However, it soon began to be clear that, however careful the preparations, the emperor and his commanders had not fully grasped not just the sheer size of Russia, but the challenges of operating so far from the rich farmlands and dense road networks of Europe. Forced marches left men and horses alike overtaxed, and often meant that they outpaced supply wagons which struggled along dirt tracks. The Russians practised a savage policy of scorched earth, and hopes of foraging along the way often came to nothing. Typhus and dysentery soon became serious problems, along with simple hunger, straggling and desertion.

Nonetheless, this was not all that unusual in war at the time, and even though he lost perhaps half his fighting force in the first two months, Napoleon had the initiative and enough of an army to take on the 200,000 or so Russian troops under Princes Mikhail Barclay de Tolly and Pyotr Bagration, especially if he was able to keep their two contingents from connecting. The French army continued to outpace the Russian defence, until August, when Bagration and Barclay de Tolly could finally combine their forces at Smolensk, already halfway to Moscow. Napoleon was eager for a set-piece battle, hoping that a conclusive victory would force Alexander to come to terms. Barclay de Tolly was unwilling to offer him one, but his generals were insistent and his authority was under threat. Some 45,000 troops of the *Grande Armée* met 30,000 Russians, driving them out of Smolensk, which in the process was burnt almost to the ground. The casualties on both sides were pretty comparable, but nonetheless ultimately it was the Russians who withdrew.

Some of Napoleon's generals urged him to pause and winter there, but he was determined to press on and take Moscow: 'I have come once and for all to finish off these barbarians of the North. The sword is now drawn. They must be pushed back into their ice, so that for the next 25 years they no longer come to busy themselves with the affairs of civilized Europe.' He sent further missives to Alexander urging peace talks, but to no avail. Indeed, in one sense this proved the first of a number of Pyrrhic victories for Napoleon, as the tsar, dissatisfied with the conduct of the war, appointed General Mikhail Kutuzov as commander-in-chief. Barclay de Tolly and Bagration had thought that the way to defeat Napoleon was to challenge his advance, and they had failed. Kutuzov, instead, would harness the sheer scale of Russia, as well as her most formidable ally, 'General Winter'.

BORODINO, 1812

Kutuzov opted, like Barclay de Tolly, to take advantage of Russia's strategic depth, drawing the invaders further and further from their supply depots. He could not retreat forever, not least for the sake of his soldiers' morale, and so he chose to make a stand on defensible ground near the village of Borodino, less than a hundred miles from Moscow. Although he confidently boasted to his officers of driving the French back, he knew that his most reasonable goal was simply to bleed the *Grande Armée* further.

In order to give him time to fortify his positions, Kutuzov dispatched General Andrei Gorchakov to fight a delaying action near the village of Shevardino, where they hurriedly built a pentagonal redoubt. Napoleon's forces duly attacked, trying to encircle it. Three times they managed to break into the redoubt, and three times the Russians managed to drive them out, before Kutuzov ordered the ragged and battered defenders to withdraw. Meanwhile, the Russians had been digging, deploying and planning. Kutuzov arrayed his forces in a curve behind the Koloch and Kamenka Rivers. In the centre was the Rayevsky Redoubt, on which were mounted 19 12-pounder guns, and behind which Kutuzov placed four of his seven infantry corps and three cavalry corps. On the right flank, Barclay de Tolly's 1st Army comprised three infantry and three cavalry corps, behind the Koloch River. On the left, behind the Bagration Flèches – V-shaped earthworks – was his 2nd Army. With just two infantry corps, this was less numerous than the 1st, even after the addition of some pike-armed militia from Moscow, and the Flèches provided only partial protection. In total, the Russian forces amounted to some 120,000 men.

Seeing this, Napoleon opted to focus his efforts on the vulnerable left flank, while seizing the village of Borodino itself to distract Kutuzov. His plan was a classic rotation, breaking the left flank and pivoting the Russians round until they were trapped on the banks of the Koloch. With some 130,000 men at his disposal, he could afford also to assault the Rayevsky Redoubt at the centre, even while throwing forces at Bagration's positions.

At 5.30 on the morning of 7 September 1812, more than a hundred French guns started shelling the Bagration Flèches, while a division moved into Borodino under cover of the morning fog, dislodging the Life Guards Jaeger Regiment that had been holding it. By six, the first of what would be five infantry assaults on the Flèches began. Throughout the morning, control of one and then another of these positions would change sides, in bloody attack and counterattack, bayonet charge and grapeshot volley. By 11am, Napoleon had deployed some 45,000 troops supported by almost 400 guns for what would end up as the decisive assault. Around midday, the earthworks had been taken, and as Prince Bagration was carried, wounded, from the battlefield, his men began to retreat – but only to their next defensive line, along the small valley cut by the Semyonovsky River. There waited 300 Russian guns and fresh reserves including the Izmailovsky Life Guards Regiment. Napoleon's exhausted troops paused, although not for long, as cuirassiers and other cavalry were soon deployed to try to break through.

Meanwhile, Napoleon's forces had been hammering away at the Rayevsky Redoubt since about 9am. At first, the Russian guns exacted a terrible toll on the attackers, but even when supported by Kutuzov's artillery reserve, they could not hold them all at bay. The redoubt was briefly taken, but again furious bayonet work recaptured it. Of the 4,000 men of the first French regiment to break into the redoubt, only 300 would make it out alive. At this point, Kutuzov unleashed part of his cavalry reserve, Fyodor Uvarov's 1st Cavalry Corps, and eight regiments of Don Cossacks under Ataman Matvei Platov into the enemy's rear and flank. The result was confusion in the enemy camp, forcing the redeployment of forces that had been about to be fed into the attack on the redoubt, and perhaps a couple of hours' delay in the next phase of Napoleon's attack. It also may have discouraged him from deploying his Imperial Guard, lest the Russians launch another such nimble raid to his rear.

With his initial plan to force through the left flank now looking untenable, Napoleon chose to concentrate on the centre and the Rayevsky Redoubt. Fortunately for Kutuzov, the pause won by Uvarov and Platov allowed him to transfer reinforcements from the largely unchallenged right flank to the centre. By 3pm, Napoleon was ready to unleash the kind of hammerblow that had won him so many battles in the past. Behind a hellish storm of solid shot and case rounds from 150 guns came 34 cavalry regiments, and while the Russian guns in turn chewed through them – the redoubt earned itself the name 'the grave of the French cavalry' – it allowed the 4th Corps under Prince Eugene Beauharnais to storm the battery from the flank. By 4pm, the Rayevsky Redoubt had fallen, its packed earth walls thick with spent musket balls and shell fragments, splashed with blood.

The fighting began to subside. Characteristically, Napoleon would unleash his final reserve, his Imperial Guard, at the eleventh hour to clinch a victory. This time, he kept them back, and although this has been the subject of controversy and criticism since, it is likely that he simply did not believe they could make a difference, and he was not going to feed them into the meatgrinder for no reason. That night, Kutuzov withdrew his forces from the battlefield, and the exhausted *Grande Armée* let them go. The road to Moscow was open, but at terrible cost. This was the largest battle of the invasion of Russia and the bloodiest day of battle of the whole Napoleonic Wars. Napoleon had won, but at the cost of some 30,000 dead, wounded or captured. Kutuzov had lost perhaps 50,000, but already new units were being raised and trained across the length of this country. It was a terrible price, but one Russia could afford to pay.

THE RETREAT

On 14 September, Napoleon occupied Moscow without a fight. The city was largely empty, stripped of food, and soon would be in flames, although it is still unclear whether this was a deliberate tactic, taking 'scorched earth' to a new level, or accidental – either way, hundreds of Muscovites were later shot by the French as suspected arsonists. Napoleon's goal had never been a piecemeal destruction of the Russian army; instead, as had generally been the case in his European conquests, a set-piece victory or two and the seizure of a metropolis (while St Petersburg was the capital, Moscow was still the dominant city) would generally secure terms and capitulation. Yet these 'barbarians of the North' apparently didn't seem to know that they were beaten and ought to be suing for peace.

Through September, and into October, an increasingly exasperated Napoleon sent multiple communiqués to Alexander, expressing his hopes for peace, demanding only the surrender of Lithuania and the re-joining of the Continental System. He received no replies. He even toyed with marching on to St Petersburg, but his generals rightly objected, seeing no prospect in 'going towards winter, to the north', especially with Kutuzov's army still at large. Meanwhile, militias, bands of stragglers from the army, peasant guerrillas and flying columns of Cossacks attacked Napoleon's supply lines and harried any incautious and optimistic foraging parties. Stocks of food and fodder were shrinking at a worrying pace.

Moscow was not a trophy, but a trap. On 6 October, a successful Russian attack at Tarutino on a field force under Marshal Joachim Murat, who had been charged with monitoring Kutuzov's forces, marked the renewed confidence of the Russians. They had been mustering troops, even buying 50,000 muskets from Britain to make up for shortfalls in their own production. The next day, Napoleon began his retreat from Moscow. He still harboured dreams of returning after the winter, but his plans looked strikingly vague: 'Smolensk, Mogilev, Minsk and

Vitebsk... Moscow no longer represents a military position. I'm going to look for another position from where it will be more advantageous to launch a new campaign, the action of which will be directed towards St Petersburg or Kiev.'

As Kutuzov had anticipated, Napoleon led his remaining 110,000 troops along the Old Kaluga Road towards his base at Smolensk, avoiding territory already ravaged by war and picked clean of any supplies. Kutuzov arrayed his army across that road, forcing Napoleon to detour, and then engaged him at Maloyaroslavets. Although the French eventually took the town, Kutuzov's army was strong enough to force him instead to head to Smolensk back the way he had originally come, through barren lands. What was left of the *Grande Armée* was harried by Cossacks and disease alike. Kutuzov paralleled its stumbling march, herding it on its way. When it reached Smolensk, it found no great supplies of food, though, and after a week the French continued their retreat. When he spotted opportunities to deliver defeats in detail or cut off elements of Napoleon's army, Kutuzov would strike, but the key engagement would be at crossings over the Berezina River. Showing some of his old skill, Napoleon outmanoeuvred the defenders and built bridges across the river, but his army was caught by Admiral Pavel Chichagov's Danube Army on the right bank of the river, while Kutuzov engaged with his rearguard on the left. Napoleon ruthlessly sacrificed the latter, ordering the bridges burnt, and led an increasingly diminished force out of the battle. Of the half a million men who marched into Russia, only some 31,000 marched out (although maybe as many more eventually straggled their way home).

TO PARIS!

The war was not over, but momentum had swung against Napoleon. The 1812 Treaty of Örebro had already ended hostilities between Russia, Britain and Sweden and provided the basis for a new alliance. Seeing Napoleon's humiliation, Prussia joined the emerging Sixth Coalition, and Austria backed away from the French, first declaring neutrality, and then joining the coalition a year later. The German territories saw the brunt of the consequent battles, with major engagements in Lützen, Bautzen and Dresden. The October 1813 Battle of Leipzig involved more than half a million men, making it the largest battle in European history before the First World War. Meanwhile, the Duke of Wellington led his combined British, Spanish and Portuguese forces across the Pyrenees, as war came to France. Even Napoleon's brilliant last-ditch Six Days' Campaign, defeating multiple larger armies heading for Paris, could only delay the inevitable. On 31 May 1814, coalition armies marched into Paris – and it was Tsar Alexander who was at their head, clutching the ceremonial keys of the city. On 11 April, Napoleon abdicated, the war was over, and Russian officers who had seen Moscow burn were now strutting through Paris. (Indeed, the word 'bistro' comes from the command *bystro!*, 'quickly!', that they would imperiously shout at their waiters.)

The Russians had learned much from this war. Russia gained further territory, but above all the status as senior partner in the winning coalition. Alexander had abandoned his early liberal leanings and would form the Holy Alliance with Prussia and Austria to suppress revolutionary ideas and uphold divine right across Europe. He and his successor Nicholas would also take victory over Napoleon as apparent proof that, for all the talk of the need for modernization, Russia was still essentially safe and fine. Brushing aside the extent to which by 1812 Napoleon's forces were over-extended and his strategy against Russia was misconceived, this became a comforting mantra for conservatives looking for excuses not to grasp the nettle of reform.

Conversely, his generals learned valuable practical lessons in how mass warfare was revolutionizing their art. Whole populations would be mobilized to fight – in armies, in fields, in factories, in partisan bands – and the massive engagements this entailed, where armies could be measured in the hundreds of thousands, not tens of thousands, needed an equivalent economic mobilization. These armies could still move quickly, and Napoleon had rammed home again that war was often a matter of manoeuvre, but for that to work at these scales required proper staff – the charismatic 'great man' style of leadership needed to be underpinned by effective bureaucratic structures. The greater the mobility, though, the greater the logistical challenges, again requiring professionalism rather than mere élan. (The humble potato, which became a much more widely grown crop in 18th-century Europe, itself became important as a portable, easy to produce and easy to eat foodstuff, an early progenitor of the modern pre-packaged MREs – Meals Ready to Eat.)

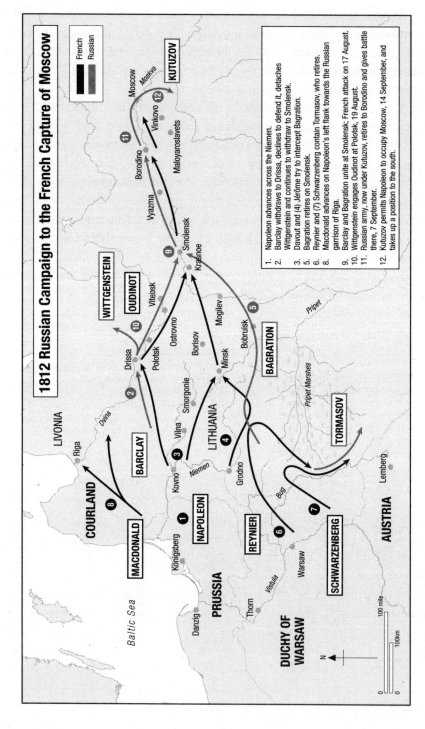

1812 Russian Campaign to the French Capture of Moscow

French
Russian

1. Napoleon advances across the Niemen.
2. Barclay withdraws to Drissa, declines to defend it, detaches Wittgenstein and continues to withdraw to Smolensk.
3. Davout and (4) Jérôme try to intercept Bagration.
4.
5. Bagration retires on Smolensk.
6. Reynier and (7) Schwarzenberg contain Tormasov, who retires.
7.
8. Macdonald advances on Napoleon's left flank towards the Russian garrison of Riga.
9. Barclay and Bagration unite at Smolensk; French attack on 17 August.
10. Wittgenstein engages Oudinot at Polotsk, 19 August.
11. Russian army, now under Kutuzov, retires to Borodino and gives battle there, 7 September.
12. Kutuzov permits Napoleon to occupy Moscow, 14 September, and takes up a position to the south.

Yet wars are also often engines of social and political change. This 'Patriotic War' was a people's war, and again, the militia and peasant guerrillas who harried the *Grande Armée* would generate a myth of shared endurance and victory that, ironically, contributed to rising discontent. Why should the people who had won that victory not gain from it? The early revolution in military affairs would elevate a new generation of educated professional soldier-specialists: the engineers and technicians, the mathematically trained artillerymen and the staff officers. In the process, new class divisions would begin to appear between the traditional aristocrats and the bourgeois 'new men'. Perhaps more dangerously, so many of the officers who fought their way across Europe would be exposed to radical ideas and a true awareness of the cultural gap between Russia and Europe. From this would emerge a political movement that posed a threat to the very institutions of tsarism and defined the conservative ideologies it would embrace for most of the next century.

Want To Know More?

Compared with many other conflicts, the challenge with the Napoleonic Wars is not a dearth but a plethora of books. Dominic Lieven's magisterial *Russia Against Napoleon* (Viking, 2009) is the single best account of the war from the Russian side and very highly recommended. Marie-Pierre Rey's *Alexander I: The Tsar Who Defeated Napoleon* (Northern Illinois University Press, 2016) is a good biography of this complex man, slightly let down by the translation. For a quick summary, Mike Rapport's *The Napoleonic Wars: A Very Short Introduction* (Oxford University Press, 2013) is exactly what it claims to be, and Philip Haythornthwaite's *Borodino 1812: Napoleon's great gamble* (Osprey, 2012) is a neat summary of the battle. Personally, I found Ridley Scott's film *Napoleon* (2023) to be so-so, and it certainly fails properly to portray the battles well – for that, Sergei Bondarchuk's *War and Peace, Part 1* (1966), with its cast of thousands of Soviet soldiers drafted in as extras, may lack the cinematic gloss of modern films but treats Borodino especially well.

16

Gendarme of Europe, Conqueror of the Margins

Dargo, 1845

1817–64	Caucasus War(s)
1825	Death of Alexander I; Nicholas I becomes tsar; Decembrist Revolt
1828–29	Russo-Turkish War
1830–31	November Uprising in Poland
1833	Bosporus expedition
1848	Year of revolutions
1849	Hungarian intervention

Soyuz Spaseniya (Union of Salvation) was one of the big cinematic releases of 2019, but also an oddly ambiguous one. It follows the young officers exposed to European culture and ideas during the Napoleonic Wars, members of the eponymous Union of Salvation. This secret society launched the abortive Decembrist Revolt of 1825 in the name of constitutionalism and the abolition of serfdom, which was bloodily and ruthlessly suppressed by the new Tsar Nicholas I, in a climactic (and brilliantly portrayed) showdown in St Petersburg's Senate Square. At a time of growing authoritarianism under Putin, who at one point had cited Nicholas as one of his inspirations, should this film be an ode to youthful dreams of reform, or a warning against the dangers of revolution? As is, it treads a fine line between both positions, but holds back from exploring the fundamental tragedy that it was this bid to secure reform that convinced Nicholas that revolutionary ideas not just in Russia but anywhere were a threat, such that his army became the reactionary 'Gendarme of Europe'. A trained soldier, Nicholas was keenly aware of the challenges of maintaining Russian military power. However personally brave in battle he would be, though, Nicholas proved too afraid of potential domestic unrest to embark on the kind of fundamental reform the empire would need to survive.

THE DECEMBRISTS

The Napoleonic Wars triggered a new period of revolutionary thought and agitation in Russia. The ideas of the French and American Revolutions appealed to some within the educated classes, and the sight of advanced and, as they saw it, 'civilized' West European cities and societies encouraged a kind of cultural inferiority complex among many who served and travelled there. It did not help that, since Catherine's reign, French language, literature and ideas had been considered the very peak of sophistication – the *beau idéal*, as it were – and this left the young aristocrats who formed the junior officer corps especially susceptible.

The sense among them was that the Russian monarchy needed to be brought within the limits of a constitution, and the feudal practice of serfdom abolished. Various secret or semi-secret societies emerged, especially within the junior Guard officers, such as the Order of Russian Knights, the Society of United Slavs, the Green Lamp and the Union of Salvation. This last became the most important for a while, although it was dissolved in 1817 following an internal schism over whether regicide during a *coup d'état* was an acceptable price of reform. Alexander I's early reformism had encouraged them, and his retreat into conservatism had thus been a particular disappointment. More societies emerged, united and reformed, but a conviction grew among their more radical members that the only answer was such a coup, and a conspiracy was formed to stage this in December 1825.

Travelling in southern Russia, though, Alexander caught typhus, and died in November. This created a momentary constitutional hiccup that encouraged the conspirators to go through with their plan regardless. Alexander had no legitimate heirs, so the crown ought to have passed to his elder brother Konstantin. However, he had surrendered his claim to the throne so that he could marry a Catholic Polish countess. Alexander had, however, chosen to keep this secret at the time, so although his younger brother Nikolai – Nicholas – was indeed the legitimate heir, many were confused or outright suspicious.

On Alexander's death, the royal guards swore allegiance in their ignorance to the absent Konstantin as his presumed successor. When Konstantin made his renunciation public, and Nicholas stepped forward to assume the throne, this provided a perfect opportunity for the conspirators, who encouraged St Petersburg's garrison not to swear allegiance to him. On 14 December, some 3,000 officers and men from the Moscow Life Guards Regiment, the Grenadier Life Guards Regiment and the Naval Equipage of the Guard, all elite units, mustered in Senate Square at the centre of the city, proclaiming instead their support for Konstantin. He was, frankly, something of a brute, and the writer and revolutionary Alexander Hertzen wondered 'why… the masses, for whom he did no good, and the soldiers, for whom he did only harm, loved him'. Nonetheless, he had been reinvented in the minds of the conspirators as a champion of constitutionalism. They anticipated mass defections to their side, but they were disappointed: some 9,000 loyalist troops stood against them.

After several hours' standoff, the 29-year-old Nicholas I entered the square, but when his representative, Count Mikhail Miloradovich, was fatally wounded by rebels, and fearing that if this dragged on into the night it would get out of control, he ordered first an abortive charge by Her Sovereign Majesty Empress Maria Theodorovna's Chevalier Guard Regiment and then turned to what France's Louis XIV had called the 'last argument of kings': artillery. Cannon on the other side of the square raked the rebels with grapeshot, and they soon broke and ran. Some tried to regroup on the frozen Neva River and seize Vasilyevsky Island, but Nicholas ordered the guns brought to the embankment and switched to solid shot. The cannon balls shattered the ice, and the remaining rebels again scattered, many falling into the icy waters.

What became known as the Decembrist Revolt was a terrible blow to the new monarch, not least because he thought of himself as soldier, not tsar. Given that Konstantin had been ahead of him in the line of succession, that is what he had prepared himself to be, and – as he was dutiful, energetic, forceful and unimaginative – this would probably have suited him well. Now, though, he had a crown drenched in Russian blood. This would colour his whole attitude during his 30 years in power. He was intelligent enough to realize that Russia needed reform, including addressing the serf question, but he regarded his primary duty as being to hold the line against anarchy and revolution. He looked at the empire with a soldier's eyes: he expected efficiency, discipline and loyalty. He was willing to work hard, had little appetitive for pomp, and was appalled by the corruption underpinning every aspect of the Russian state (once, he told his son Alexander, 'I believe you and I are the only people in Russia who don't steal.'). Sadly for Russia, and for much of Europe, given that he saw his mission as not something limited by borders, he would put much of this zeal and energy into a desperate attempt to hold back the clock.

THE GENDARME OF EUROPE

At home, Nicholas extended censorship, established the Third Section of His Imperial Majesty's Own Chancellery – in other words, the political police – and ducked the thorny issue of serfdom, however immoral and ultimately inefficient he knew it to be. He maintained a large military machine, which would grow to a million men, but it would be an increasingly outdated one. In part, this was because for Nicholas, just as for his father, Paul I, drill and discipline were too often mistaken for battlefield capability. However, it also reflected a deeper problem. Trained in engineering, Nicholas understood systems well enough to realize the connections between warfighting, technology, the economy and society. More modern methods and above all weapons would require Russia to develop its industries. This would accelerate urbanization and risk undermining the old social order, creating fertile soil for new revolutionary movements. It was again that classic dilemma: does the greater danger come from instability at home or potential vulnerability abroad? Buoyed by an unrealistic sense that victory over Napoleon had shown Russia's current strength, as well as how well his armies paraded, scarred by the Decembrist Revolt, Nicholas felt the former was then priority. At a time when the Industrial Revolution was taking off in Britain, Nicholas was putting limits on how many factories could be opened in Moscow.

At first, though, this would not seem to matter too much, as the main enemies would be revolutionary mobs, ragged hill people, and declining empires. Alexander's Holy Alliance was already looking pretty threadbare by the 1830s, but Nicholas nonetheless held to a sense that reaction had to be practised abroad as well as at home. In 1830, on hearing of a Belgian revolt against the Dutch, he made moves towards sending an army all the way across the continent just to put it down. In any case, he was busy dealing with trouble in Poland, at once part of the empire and yet also a distinct nation within it, possessing of its own rights and constitution, which were increasingly under pressure from the empire. The 1830 November Uprising was again spearheaded by discontented junior officers and cadets, but they were soon joined by people across Poland, Lithuania, Belarus and even Right-bank Ukraine (in other words, the northern and western regions which had long been subject to Polish influence and colonization). Nicholas's response was predictable, and in February 1831, a sizeable army deployed into Poland to crush the rebellion. The Poles fought bravely, but ultimately, in September, Warsaw, the last rebel stronghold, fell. Some 20,000 Poles preferred to march into Prussia and surrender there than give themselves up to the Russians. Next year, Nicholas's Organic Statute brought an end to Poland's special rights, making it just another province of the empire, and suppressed the Polish Catholic Church.

Indeed, one could argue that in the name of maintaining the status quo, Nicholas even saved age-old rival Turkey in 1833. The Orthodox Christian Greeks had again rebelled against the Sultan in 1821. Britain and France had supported them, but Alexander, true to his almost mystical belief in non-intervention, did not. Nicholas was more pragmatic, though, and in 1827, after talks with London and Paris, a joint British, French and Russian naval task force was dispatched to impose a peace settlement. At Navarino Bay, they were fired on by the Egyptian-Turkish fleet, which they proceeded to destroy, sinking fully 55 vessels. In response, Turkey closed the Bosporus to Russian shipping and declared war. In a brief conflict (1828–29), a Russian army crossed the Danube and began besieging Turkish fortresses in Rumelia (Bulgaria) and continued towards Constantinople. In September 1829, the Ottomans were forced into concessions which indirectly also led to Greek independence in 1830. That, in turn, encouraged Egyptian governor Mohammed Ali to rebel against the Sultan, and this war threatened the very survival of the Ottoman Empire. This time, Russia stood up for Istanbul, sending the Black Sea Fleet and 30,000 troops to the Bosporus, preventing the fall of Constantinople, and forcing Ali to come to terms.

However, it was in 1848 that the 'Gendarme of Europe' truly earned his title. Across Europe, a new middle class was chafing at aristocratic power, an emerging industrial working class was labouring under often terrible conditions, and peasants were being squeezed on the land, especially thanks to a poor harvest in 1846. Even many aristocrats were beginning to question absolutism, not least if they feared that a failure to reform today would mean a bloody revolution tomorrow. Liberalism was often connected to nationalism, as peoples in divided nations such as Italy or occupied ones such as Poland sought nationhood. In January, Sicilians rose against the Bourbon Kingdom of the Two Sicilies, and from then, a wave of revolution swept across Europe, from France to Hungary, Ireland to the Rhineland.

The Russian Empire itself was essentially untouched, but Nicholas was horrified and outraged by what he saw as an epidemic of ungodly anarchy. He urged his fellow monarchs to hold the line, especially King Frederick William IV of Prussia, who was being urged to accept a constitution. More directly, in 1849, at the request of Habsburg Emperor Franz Joseph, even though Russia was itself in the grip of famine and cholera, he sent 140,000 troops under Field Marshal Ivan Paskevich to help suppress the Hungarian rising. Although Paskevich was often far too cautious, unwilling to close for a decisive battle even though the combined Austrian and Russian forces had a clear advantage in numbers and firepower, by the beginning of September the rebellion was over and the Russians returned home.

THE HARDSCRABBLE MARGINS

Maintaining the status quo in Europe certainly did not mean holding back from imperial expansion elsewhere. The 19th century saw the Russians continuing their expansion in the North Caucasus and Central Asia, in often small-scale but both vicious and romantic struggles in what became Russia's equivalent of India's North-West Frontier for Britain, the tough borderlands where a generation of officers learned their trade. The Caucasus region is one where religious, ethnic, linguistic and tribal differences make for a human geography that was (and still is) as mixed and as dangerous as its physical contours, with Christian Georgia and

Muslim Azerbaijan straddling the plains between the Greater and Lesser Caucasus Mountains to north and south, Black and Caspian Seas to west and east. Russia to the north, Turkey to the south-west and Persia to the south-east all had their interests here.

Despite the ebb and flow of petty kingdoms annexed, allied or lost, the real Russian frontier here was the North Caucasus Line, a string of Russian forts and fortified Cossack *stanitsas* originally established along the northern edge of the Caucasus Mountains. Since the middle of the 18th century, it had slowly pushed west and south. However, this was often – as in the Far East – less about a deliberate policy of expansion as much as the confluence of three forces: political rivalries with the Ottoman and Persian Empires, the ambitions and enthusiasms of Russian generals and governors in the region, and the interests of local potentates, who might see in Russia a useful ally or protector.

A particular focus was Georgia, with whom Russia had had generally positive relations for centuries. In 1587, Russia had concluded an alliance with the Georgian Kingdom of Kakheti, and the 1783 Treaty of Georgievsk had made eastern Georgia a Russian protectorate. It hoped this would keep the Persians at bay, and that year, Russian engineers began improving the traditional path stretching to the eastern Georgian capital Tbilisi, such that troops and, more particularly, artillery could easily travel southwards. It was a symbol of Russian ambition that was not lost on Persia, which invaded in 1795. The Russians did nothing, though, as Tbilisi was burnt and 15,000 Georgians were taken as slaves. Only the next year did Catherine bestir herself to send a small army, which nonetheless had no problems marching down the Caspian coast, taking most of Persian-controlled Azerbaijan, and was poised to invade Persia itself. Then Catherine died, and Paul I ordered the army to withdraw, much to the annoyance of many within the military. In 1801, he annexed eastern Georgia, and through the century, the various western Georgian kingdoms would be incorporated, too, while the Georgian Military Highway was steadily developed as a first-rate road, and the artery of Russian power projection.

Yet in whose interests? For example, General Pavel Tsitsianov, who was appointed commander-in-chief of Georgia and Inspector of the North Caucasus Line in 1802, was descended of Georgian noble blood. He genuinely believed that Georgia's best chance of survival and success was under the wing of the empire, and did much to reconcile them to this future. However, he was also less willing than his more pragmatic predecessors to negotiate with the unruly Chechen hillfolk to the north-east, who often raided the Georgian lowlands. He launched a military campaign to burn their fields and take their livestock, which not only failed to cow the famously intransigent Chechens but led to more attacks, not just on Georgia but against settlements along the Line. In due course, this would lead inexorably to future wars in a classic pattern: the arrival of the imperial power destabilizes local politics and economies or puts it in the middle of long-established feuds. Seeing no other way to stabilize its frontier, it pushes forward to subdue this new threat, which may well be subdued – but leaves the empire now facing new potential challenges and challengers.

Likewise, one could argue that Tsitsianov's initiative also led to war with Persia. In 1803, he somewhat stretched his mandate of pacifying Georgia by threatening the Ganja Khanate to the south-east, a Persian vassal to which Tbilisi had some vague and debatable claims. When it refused to submit, Tsitsianov took it, triggering the 1804–13 Russo-Persian War. This was an essentially sporadic and small-scale conflict, as Persia and its vassals could field larger forces than the small armies the Russians could deploy given the war in Europe (sometimes with a five-to-one advantage), offset by the Russians' better training and technology. Napoleon's defeat in 1812 and peace between Constantinople and St Petersburg opened up the prospect of more Russian troops being sent. A clear Russian victory at Lankaran in January 1813 forced Persia to admit defeat. The 1813 Treaty of Gulistan saw much of both the North Caucasus and Transcaucasia ceded to Russia, something also confirmed by the 1829 Peace of Adrianople. The Persians and the Ottomans had abandoned most of their claims to the region (although it would not preclude future conflicts). All that was needed now was to make sure the locals got the message.

CARVING UP THE CAUCASUS: DARGO, 1845

The longest war in Russian history, at least as the Russians themselves count it, is its Caucasus War, regarded as running from 1817 to 1864. Many outsiders will never have heard of it, unless they have a passion for Leo Tolstoy, who wrote *Hadji Murat* (1912) set in this era, but in fairness that is not least because it is a stretch to call it a war. Rather, it was a whole array of expeditions, raids, incursions and shows of force associated with the annexation of the North Caucasus region, the struggle with the North Caucasian Imamate and the at best partial pacification of the region's myriad peoples, tribes and clans. For many of them, raiding was a way of life, an essential (and sometimes seasonal) way to gain livestock, blood young men, and even acquire wives and thus avoid inbreeding. What may be accepted give-and-take in its own terms was unacceptable to the encroaching imperial power. Taming these impudent bandits – as they saw them – living in the highlands between Russia and its new Transcaucasian possessions became a central plank of the empire's policies in the region, storing up problems and traditional enmities still smouldering today.

Indeed, General Alexei Yermolov, who commanded operations in the region from 1816 to 1827, actually made a virtue out of brutality, thinking he could cow the unruly *gortsy*, the 'highlanders'. He wrote to Tsar Alexander I that 'I desire that the terror of my name shall guard our frontiers more potently than chains or fortresses.' Sometimes, it worked. At one point, Chechens kidnapped a Russian colonel and demanded 18 carts of silver as a ransom. Instead of engaging in the traditional haggling over the ransom, Yermolov sent Cossacks to seize 18 respected village elders, threatening to hang them, if the officer was not released. He was. Nonetheless, although he did much to whip the Separate Caucasian Corps into shape and even built some of those fortresses, including Grozny – which means 'Terrifying' – he did more to stir up local anger. The 'peace' he imposed was a limited and conditional one, built out of bayonets.

It ensured that the Russians would face constant resistance, ranging from low-level guerrilla activity scarcely distinguishable from banditry, to the 30-year struggle against the North Caucasus Imamate, as much a religious as political movement, especially under the charismatic (and fortunate) Imam Shamil, who took control of it in 1834. In 1839, Shamil moved his base to the Chechen village of Dargo, in wooded uplands near the border between modern Chechnya and Dagestan. After a failed expedition to take Dargo in 1842, in 1844 Nicholas I appointed General Mikhail Vorontsov as governor of the Caucasus and commander of the Separate Caucasian Corps. Nicholas personally developed a plan to break Shamil's power in the region by taking Dargo and Shamil in a large-scale operation involving almost 10,000 Russian troops, Cossacks and local auxiliaries. Many generals experienced in the gritty Caucasus counter-insurgency had deep misgivings, sure that the highlanders would simply disappear into the mountains, sniping and ambushing as they went. Nonetheless, Vorontsov was initially eager – or at least expressed eagerness to the tsar who was promoting him – and considered this his first priority.

The idea was that three separate forces would be deployed. General Grigory Schwatz would lead local forces drawn from the Lezgin and Samur people in a feint, while Dargo itself was approached on two sides by a detachment from Chechnya under General Alexander Liders, a wily old veteran of pretty much every war since Austerlitz, and another from Dagestan under General Vasily Bebutov, who had already distinguished himself in the region. The preparations became more and more complex, with Vorontsov also bringing a sizeable personal retinue, but it was clear that Shamil's men, with eyes and ears in every town and village, knew what was going on. The operation was due to start on 31 May 1845, but even before then, General Schwartz was reporting ambushes being established along the Russians' planned routes of march. His 2,000 Lezgins helped clear the way, but it was a harbinger of the extent to which the Russians were operating very much on Shamil's turf. Shamil needed time to muster his forces – there were only around a thousand in and around Dargo normally – but he would have it, especially as even highlanders such as the Dagestani Avars, who did not necessarily support him and his tactics, were willing to take pot-shots at the Russians, block mountain passes and generally cause mischief on general principles. This slowed the attack long enough that he could assemble more than 4,000 fighters, mainly Chechens.

The two detachments met at the village of Gertma, while scouts managed to clear the Kyrk pass, through which they would have to march next. Russian losses were low, but the highlanders' even lower: their goal at this stage was to delay and weaken the attackers, not to engage in a stand-up fight with a larger and far better-armed force. As they marched to higher elevations, though, even the weather seemed against the Russians: unexpected rains turned into an unseasonal snowstorm. More than 400 soldiers fell victim to frostbite, as the Russian force became whittled down, little by little. By this point, they were penetrating into regions that had previously been considered inaccessible to Russian forces, but finding only empty and burning villages. Shamil could not retreat forever, though, and made a preliminary stand at the village of Andi.

This was duly stormed, but again, Shamil's men quietly withdrew before the Russians could encircle and close with them. By this time, to the problems of cold weather and dwindling rations was added the misery of occasional shelling from one or another of the rebels' captured cannon, manhandled into lofty firing positions and then spirited away.

By common consent, General Liders took operational command of the combined force, of 7,940 infantry, 1,218 cavalry and 342 guns, even while Vorontsov was still in overall charge of the expedition. Fortunately for the Russians, a resupply caravan was finally able to catch up with them, and on 6 July, they set out along the narrow, winding, 7-mile path to Dargo. The highlanders contested every step, having built successive barricades along the road from rubble and felled trees, from which they would snipe before retreating to the next. Nonetheless, the Russians forced their way to Dargo, which again they found abandoned and in flames, while they continued to be fired on from neighbouring vantages, which would have to be cleared one by one, involving tough climbs and tougher hand-to-hand fighting.

So the Russians had Dargo, but not Shamil. For a week, Vorontsov stayed there, as constant rain, hunger, disease and periodic fire from snipers whittled away at his force's numbers and morale. Another supply column was ambushed by at least 300 fighters, and while some got through to Dargo, about half the column was burnt or taken by Shamil's men, including three precious mountain guns. Vorontsov was in a bind; the operation had clearly failed, but he also had to consider the political context. If he simply retreated, it would raise Shamil's status yet further and encourage more to flock to his banner. So, to try to make a virtue out of a withdrawal, he opted instead to push forward and return to Russian-held territory via the rebel-held village of Gerzel-Aul. By this point, he was down to just 5,000 able men, and had almost 1,000 wounded to try to bring home. What was left of Dargo was again burned, as was any excess baggage – Vorontsov made an example of destroying all his property beyond a simple tent and camp bed, but many of his cronies were much less happy to be consigning fineries to the fire. Nonetheless, this seems to have done wonders for the ordinary soldiers' morale, and there are some suggestions that Liders had quietly suggested this to him for that very reason.

On 13 July, what was left of the army set out. It had to fight its way through a new string of fortified villages, subject to regular attacks that used the highlanders' knowledge of the terrain to cut deep into the Russian columns. At one point, General Liders found himself surrounded, and at another Vorontsov was nearly killed. By the time they had reached the village of Shovkhal-Berdy, the exhausted Russians could only take up defensive positions and await a relief column. For two days, they endured sniping and periodic attacks, until reinforcements arrived, shepherding them to Gerzel-Aul and then back to safety.

It was one of the most disastrous defeats of the Caucasus War, with the Russians losing some 5,000 men (including three generals) and, more to the point, a great deal of face. A chastened Nicholas would not try to dictate tactics to the Separate Caucasian Corps again. Shamil's men were understandably cock-a-hoop and, as one eyewitness account noted, thanks to the opportunities for plunder, 'the poor man, who previously did not have a donkey, acquired several horses.' Shamil himself would continue to fight against seemingly overwhelming odds until his capture in 1859, but his legend as an icon of highlander resistance would continue: after the 2022 invasion of Ukraine, Chechens opposed to Moscow formed the Iman Shamil Battalion to fight for Kyiv. Indeed, the roots of modern conflicts do not end there, for as his last war, Nicholas I would find himself fighting a coalition of Western nations for a strategic peninsula: Crimea.

Want To Know More?

W. Bruce Lincoln's biography *Nicholas I* (Northern Illinois University Press, 1989) is the best biography of the man and why he became the 'Gendarme of Europe'. Lesley Blanch's *The Sabres of Paradise: Conquest and Vengeance in the Caucasus* (John Murray, 1960) is a little dated but still a great study of the Caucasus conflicts. As well as Leo Tolstoy's *Hadji Murat* (1912: Knopf, 2012), Alexandre Dumas's *Adventures in the Caucasus* (1859) is a rollicking tale of travels through the region, if you can lay your hands on a second-hand copy (a translation is, alas, not in print, it seems). Tom Parfitt's *High Caucasus: A Mountain Quest in Russia's Haunted Hinterland* (Headline, 2024) is an account of a modern hike that nicely illustrates how history, kin and geography still matter in today's North Caucasus.

17

The Two Crimean Wars

Balaclava, 1854

1852	Church of the Nativity dispute
1853–56	Crimean War
1854	British and French arrive at Varna
	Anglo-French fleet deploys to Baltic
	Battle of Balaclava
1855	Death of Nicholas; Alexander II becomes tsar
1856	Treaty of Paris

I was living in Moscow in 2014 when, all of a sudden, everyone was an expert on Crimea. How it was the cradle of Russian Christianity, because it was in Chersonesos in the south-west of the peninsula where Grand Prince Vladimir – St Vladimir – was baptized. How Catherine the Great annexed it, to stop the Crimean Tatars from enslaving Russians. How Lenin should never have created a Ukrainian Soviet Socialist Republic within the USSR, because then there would have been no questions about its future. How it had been unfairly transferred from Russia to Ukraine in 1954 (when this was essentially a symbolic and administrative move, given that they were both part of the Soviet Union). Some of this was accurate, some not, but the enthusiasm for the annexation of Crimea on the part of Russians across the political spectrum, from ultra-nationalists to anti-Putin liberals, was genuine and palpable.

After all, the one aspect of its history that was often – for obvious reasons – not hyped and celebrated was what happened in the

1850s, when defeat did not simply demonstrate how technological backwardness was undermining Russian military power, even as the beginnings of industrialization were also challenging its political order. It is also not widely appreciated how far the Crimean War was really won in the Baltic, even while Russian and French and British troops brawled outside Sevastopol. As the world became more interconnected through commerce and communication, Russia itself would discover that this was a boon in peacetime, but often a vulnerability in war. The naval war in the Baltic and White Seas and the consequent blockade of Russian ports became an object lesson to Russia of the vulnerability of its economy, and the changing nature of war, which was waged in counting houses and marketplaces as much as muddy battlefields.

PRETTY BACKWARD

Nicholas may have wanted to hold back industrialization and everything that came with it, worried that this would include liberalism and revolution, but he was not foolish enough to believe this could be done without jeopardizing Russian security, nor powerful enough to prevent the spread of trade and capital, ideas and instability. By the end of his reign, industries were emerging, especially in textiles and metals. The first railways had been built, with a thousand miles of track already laid, and Russia could even build its own locomotives. Industrial productivity increased three-fold, and the share of the population living in cities more than doubled, from 4.5 per cent in 1825, to 9.2 per cent in 1858, even if more than two-thirds of all Russians were still serfs.

Potentially, this could have had a dramatic impact on Russian military capabilities, and yet the record was mixed, to put it at its most generous. The railway, for example, was definitely seen and promoted precisely as a military asset. In the 1830s, even though the Imperial army was essentially a standing force, mobilizing it fully would take up to six months. Although it would only be from the 1860s that real progress would be made in extending the railway beyond the initial line between Moscow and St Petersburg, there was a constant tussle between those interests who wanted lines to follow economic opportunity, and those who looked instead to security needs.

For too long, though, the fear that railways could spread revolutionary sentiment outweighed the logic that they also allowed the more rapid movement of men and materiel.

Meanwhile, Nicholas's own obsession with parade spectacle – after one, he wrote to his wife, 'I don't think there has ever been anything more splendid, perfect or overwhelming since soldiers first appeared on earth' – ensured that the army was kept pretty but backward. Future Minister of War Dmitry Milyutin complained:

> Even in military affairs, in which the emperor was engaged in with such passionate enthusiasm, the same concern for order and discipline prevailed; they were not hunting the fundamental improvement of the army, not adapting it to military purpose, just external harmony, a brilliant appearance at parades, the pedantic observance of countless petty formalities that dull human reason and kill the true military spirit.*

It was dominated by discipline and drill, often of the most brutal kind. 'Running the gauntlet' – having to pass through two lines of your fellow soldiers as they beat you, leaving your bare back a bloody ruin – remained a common administrative punishment, and it was considered an act of mercy when Nicholas I decreed that the victim would have to suffer no more than 3,000 blows! Soldiers spent much of the year forcibly billeted in peasants' huts, and their rations essentially comprised just various cereals, which would either be mixed with water to make an unappetizing porridge or double-baked as biscuits. Until 1849, the annual meat allowance for all soldiers – even the elite Guards – was just 37 pounds, the equivalent of 1.6 ounces per day. Even then, it was only increased to 84 pounds, while a typical British soldier's daily food allowance included one and three-quarters pounds of beef or other meat, or more than 17 times his Russian counterpart's. Some foreign observers were impressed by the efficiency and cheapness of this system, but it hardly made the army life any more appealing. Nor did it actually save as much money as they might have thought, as the age-old

---

*Quoted in 'Nikolai I i poteryannaya modernizatsiya', *Voennoe obozrenie*, 18 April 2024 at https://topwar.ru/240597-nikolaj-i-i-poterjannaja-modernizacija.html

Russian practice of *kormleniye*, 'feeding', while officially long-banned, was still widely practised, officers freely skimming from the funds at their disposal for their own ends, claiming to have more men in the ranks than really existed, selling supplies onto the civilian market (good horses, for example, might be traded for lame wrecks and a nice off-the-books payment) or even hiring out their men as cheap manual labour.

Relatively little effort was made to upgrade the basic weapons and equipment in use. The standard musket, the M1808 Tula Musket, was essentially a copy of a French flintlock design that originally appeared in 1717, even if in the 1840s many were converted into M1845s, using percussion caps instead of relying on sparking a pan of gunpowder to fire. These were still widely in use in the 1853–56 Crimean War, at a time when the British and French armies were increasingly issued with modern rifle-muskets. However, arguably the real difference was not so much in the technology as the training. On average a Russian soldier would only fire ten live rounds a year, which his British counterpart might expend in a single afternoon's training.

Of course, there were pockets of relative efficiency and even modernity. Officers and men who had served in the North Caucasus were, like their later Soviet counterparts who had fought in Afghanistan in 1979–89, not just battle-hardened in the numerous skirmishes and pocket wars of the imperial margin, but also replaced a degree of formalistic discipline with genuine unit cohesion. Some of the 'parquet officers', whose experience had been in the academies and ballrooms of St Petersburg, would express horror and amazement at the way junior officers from these units fraternized with their men. Likewise, the more specialist branches such as the artillery and engineering corps were the incubators of a new generation of educated technicians of war. It would emerge in the Crimean War, for example, that many junior officers in sapper units actually knew nothing about the practicalities of field fortification, because they had studied in the cadet corps rather than technical schools, so they had to depend on their non-commissioned officers, who would have gone to engineering school.

In 1853, the French observer Charles de Nercly wrote that the Russian soldiery were 'sober, impervious to fatigue, and in a word an admirable fighting machine, more intelligent than Europeans generally think, who would be a redoubtable instrument in the hands of a conqueror, a Russian Napoleon, should the winds blow in that direction one day in their icy regions."* One could question their sobriety at times, but it was certainly true that they were tough, resilient and often disciplined. However, they were soon about to clash with the foremost industrial and military powers of the time, and get a salutary warning that the almost-deliberate backwardness with which Nicholas had hoped to stave off domestic instability was weakening Russia's military strength at a time of accelerating change, and was leaving it less able to resist security challenges from abroad.

THE EASTERN QUESTION

The Crimean War was a long time brewing, and although its ostensible causes were rooted in the thorny question of managing the decay and decline of the Ottoman Empire, in practice it was – much like the later First World War – the product of the cross-cutting interests and suspicions of the powers of the age. French Emperor Napoleon III, who had seized power in a coup when he could not retain it constitutionally, was a British ally and eager for glorious opportunities to associate himself with his more famous uncle. The British were concerned about Russian expansionism, especially at the expense of an ailing Turkey, as they wanted to maintain a balance of power in Europe (and their free trade relationship with the Turks). The Ottomans were fighting for survival by this stage and saw their age-old enemy Russia as the most immediate external threat, given its claims to speak for the large population of Orthodox Christians under Turkish rule.

As for Nicholas, he had come to resent what he saw as European ingratitude and Russophobia, and believed (not without some reason) that London and Paris would relish the chance to see his shipping bottled up in the Black Sea, locked away from the Mediterranean. Perhaps just as importantly, he did not understand the complex politics of both Britain and France, the degree to which even an 'emperor' such as Napoleon III (who, after all, had been elected to power before he usurped it) had to manage the expectations of elites and

*Services Historiques de l'Armee de Terre, Vincennes, Memotres et Reconnaissances, vol. 1495, pp. 4–5, cited by John Keep, in the 1986 USAFA Harmon Memorial Lecture, 'Soldiering in Tsarist Russia'

electorates alike. As an autocrat, he felt he was dealing with similarly monolithic interlocutors and tended to see conspiracy and deceit behind the inconsistency and spin that is, alas, the stuff of politics.

Of all things, war was sparked by a dispute over respective faiths' rights over the Church of the Nativity in Ottoman-held Bethlehem. In 1852 Napoleon III, who had been backed by the Catholic Church, demanded they regain certain rights. Nicholas, whose inflexible notions of divine right meant that he considered Napoleon a usurper – he had already caused a furore in Paris by addressing him as *mon ami* ('my friend'), instead of the traditional *mon frère* ('my brother') – was outraged when the French demand was granted, over the claims of the Eastern Orthodox Church. Anticipating wrongly that he could count on Austrian and Prussian support, and that Britain would not side with France, Nicholas began to mobilize forces on the border with the Ottoman protectorates of Moldavia and Wallachia. Even his own chancellor and foreign minister, Karl Nesselrode, was convinced that this was unwise, writing in a letter to Filip Brunnov, ambassador to London, that Russia would find itself alone because no one had any interest in supporting it, and 'the combined fleets of Britain, France and Turkey will quickly finish the Russian fleet on the Black Sea.' He was right.

THE CRIMEAN WAR

In July 1853, Russian troops marched into the Danubian Principalities. Nicholas claimed to be standing up for the rights of Orthodox Christians within the Ottoman Empire, but in practice he wanted to extend his influence over the Balkans and, above all, establish control over the Black Sea Straits of the Bosporus and Dardanelles. He hoped that by a show of force, Sultan Abdulmejid I could be induced to come to terms, but once it was clear that he had British and French support, he rejected any compromise and declared war. The Turks fought hard, and were able to hold the advancing Russian troops at Silistra in what is now Bulgaria, but they were severely pressed, especially after a Russian squadron trounced a Turkish flotilla trying to relieve the besieged port city of Kars at Sinope in November 1853. The Russians were not only commanded by Admiral Pavel Nakhimov, one of the outstanding commanders of his age, but the battle also demonstrated the technological turn that was under way. The Russian ships were using new explosive shells, but both they and the Turks were in sailing ships, not the new paddle steamers that were replacing them, making this the last battle of the Age of Fighting Sail.

This brought Britain and France into the war. Their fleets, with embarked ground forces, entered the Black Sea in January 1854, landing at Varna. The question was, how could the allied powers, whose greatest strength in the theatre was their naval power, usefully contribute to the war, especially as by this stage the Russians were retreating as Austria had added its own ultimatum for them to withdraw? As they sat in Varna – Karl Marx caustically observing 'the French doing nothing and the British helping them as fast as possible' – pressure at home to act was mounting. In both France and Britain, propaganda about the 'Russian bear' and the so-called 'Massacre of Sinope' – Nakhimov's victory was implausibly recast as some kind of brutal act of mindless aggression – had created a climate of opinion in which it was deemed politically unacceptable simply to withdraw the expeditionary forces without some kind of major engagement and triumph to make it all seem worthwhile.

To this end, the decision was made to take the city of Sevastopol, home of the Russian Black Sea Fleet. In September 1854, a combined fleet of 360 ships sailed to Crimea. First they took the port of Yevpatoria, then made landing at Kalamita Bay, 28 miles north of Sevastopol. The Russians were caught flat-footed: they had known the fleet was on its way but had presumed it would land at Kacha, further south, and so the allied troops were able to disembark uncontested. It was a large army, but Sevastopol was well defended, especially from the north, so the plan was to march south, cutting Sevastopol off from reinforcement, and then lay siege to it from the south.

The Russians had had the time to rush forces to dig in on the Alma Heights, south of the Alma River, blocking the allies' planned line of march. On 20 September, the allies engaged. They had more troops – just under 60,000, to the Russians' 35,000 – but they had to fight across the river and storm high ground and fortified redoubts in the teeth of some 100 Russian guns. They carried the day, not least thanks to French attacks up cliffs that Russian commander Prince Alexander Menshikov had considered impassable, but with heavy losses. They lost 3,300 men to the Russians' 5,000, but their failure to pursue meant that an early chance to break the defenders was lost. Vice Admiral Alexander Kornilov, who was then trying to organize the defence of Sevastopol with just 7,000 soldiers, wrote that 'it is frightful to think what might have happened, had it not been for this cardinal error of the enemy's.' For days, Russian stragglers would stream back to Sevastopol to swell his garrison, which would grow to 18,000 thanks to them and the use of sailors as infantry. Part of the problem was that the respective allied commanders, Marshal Jacques Leroy de Saint-Arnaud and Lord Raglan, neither saw eye to eye nor ever accepted the authority of the other. Allied attacks were often poorly coordinated and relied on bloody-mindedness (and longer-ranged weapons, of which more below) as much as anything else.

The army marched on southwards again, to establish positions in and around the port of Balaclava, which was intended to be their supply base as they invested Sevastopol. The heat was terrible, clean water hard to find, and cholera, which had first decimated the allied soldiers at Varna, again began to spread, not least to Saint-Arnaud, who died, leaving command in the hands of General François Canrobert. Nonetheless, they made it to Balaclava and began from there to build siege lines around Sevastopol. Before that could be accomplished, though, Lieutenant General Pavel Liprandi hoped, with 16,000 men, to break the supply lines that made that siege possible.

BALACLAVA, 1854

The battle took place on 25 October in the heights and valleys north of Balaklava, bounded by the Fedyukhin Heights, the Sapun Mountain and the Black River, in the sector assigned to the British forces. They numbered some 20,000, including two cavalry brigades, the Heavy and the now famed Light, under the overall command of Lord Raglan. Against them, Liprandi fielded a mix of four cavalry regiments (two of hussars, two of Cossacks) and four infantry regiments (two of them jaegers, light infantry), as well as 64 guns, some 25,000 men in all.

Four large redoubts had been built on the Vorontsov Heights, overlooking the allied encampment. These were manned by Ottoman infantry and were the first target of Liprandi's army. Despite putting up tough resistance, a combination of artillery fire and bayonet charges drove them out, opening up the wide South Valley for Russian advance westwards towards the main allied force. Although two British divisions and some French forces began to march to reinforce them, at that moment only Lord Lucan's Cavalry Division, part of the 93rd Highlanders, and some remnants of artillery and Ottoman stragglers held the valley floor between the Russians and Balaclava.

At this point Liprandi dispatched Lieutenant General Ivan Ryzhov and his 3,000 cavalry – the Kiev and Ingermanland Regiments, supported by four squadrons of Cossacks – along the South Valley. He had believed he was sending them against the British artillery park, apparently having misidentified the tents of the British cavalry. Instead, they soon came upon the Heavy Brigade to his front, and the 93rd Sutherland Highlanders to the south, between him and Balaclava itself. Unable to ignore either potential threat, Ryzhov divided his force, sending the 1st Ural Cossack Regiment towards the Highlanders while the rest continued towards the British cavalry.

Sir Colin Campbell, commander of the Highland Brigade, had his men form a double line: this maximized their firepower, but left them dangerously exposed if the Russians were able to close, without the mutual protection of a bayonet-bristling infantry square. This part of the battle came to be known as the 'Thin Red Line' (*The Times* war correspondent William Russell originally wrote of the 'Thin Red Streak', but fortunately edited his own formulation), as the 93rd delivered two volleys from their new Minié rifles, breaking the Cossacks, who withdrew in disarray.

More extraordinary is what happened to Ryzhov's main force. It was taken aback when the Heavy Brigade – in total some 800 dragoons – came into sight, even though they outnumbered them about three to one and had the advantage of high ground, being up on the Causeway Heights between the North and South Valleys. General James Scarlett, on being made aware of the Russians' presence, had his force wheel (which would have left them at a severe disadvantage, had Ryzhov had the presence of mind to attack when they were re-forming) and then, counter to all the usual military precepts, charge this larger force, uphill. It was more of a trot than a charge in the circumstances, but nonetheless the smaller formation of largely heavier and better-trained British cavalry smashed into the Russians. After ten minutes of confused hack and slash, the larger Russian force withdrew, only to face a valedictory volley from the Royal Horse Artillery's C Troop.

Ryzhov's cavalry had lost fewer than a hundred dead in both engagements, and were able to withdraw thanks to another missed opportunity, this time the fault of the Earl of Cardigan's Light Brigade, which was close enough to have charged the retreating Russians in the flank while they were disordered, but instead simply looked on. The longer the small British forces held, the more time they gave reinforcements to interpose themselves between the battle and the port. This might have indicated a defensive strategy, but what would follow was the engagement that has come to define the battle: the glorious, foolish and now almost mythic Charge of the Light Brigade.

The cavalry advance had been blocked, but the bulk of Liprandi's forces were in control of the redoubts and the eastern end of the North Valley, where he had assembled his cavalry, before whom were arrayed eight guns of the 3rd Don Cossack Battery. Supporting them to the north, on the Fedyukhin Heights, he had eight battalions of infantry with 14 guns; to the south, on the Causeway Heights, 11 infantry battalions and 32 guns. Lord Raglan believed that the Russians – for whom he seemed to have a certain disdain – were so discomfited by their retreat from the South Valley that a show of force would be enough to send them scurrying from the Causeway Heights. Raglan had wanted Lucan to prevent the Russians from dragging captured British guns from the Causeway. However, ambiguous orders led Lucan to believe he was being told to launch an immediate attack on the guns at the end of the valley, over a mile down the very mouth of the entire Russian army. Which is what he proceeded to do, Light Brigade to the fore, to be followed by the Heavies (who were eventually ordered back once it became clear just how suicidal the charge was turning out to be). Hammered from the left, the right and the front, men and horses were cut down as canister rounds blasted through them. Nonetheless, they came on, charging the guns as their last vestiges of formation dissolved into a furious, frantic melee. As Russian lancers descended from the heights on each side to try to block any retreat, the survivors finally fled back to the British lines. Twenty minutes of bravery and idiocy had ravaged the Light Brigade: of its 697 men, 110 were dead, 129 wounded and another 32 taken prisoner. The Russians lost 33 dead or wounded.

Nonetheless, the Russians were shaken by this display of seeming lunacy – many could not believe that the British were not drunk when they launched their charge. Liprandi had won the day, on balance, but had lost the opportunity to take Balaclava, as by this point two British infantry divisions, as well as a French contingent, had moved to defend the port. On the other hand, the British could not deploy them to clear away his forces, lest they again leave Balaclava unprotected. The allies no longer had the same freedom as they closed their siege line around Sevastopol, but nor was the siege broken. Like so many engagements of the war, it was marked by considerable incompetence on both sides, not least as generals of a certain age found themselves ill-prepared for the new realities of war, from the longer ranges of modern rifles to the ever-increasing logistical demands.

Balaclava convinced both London and Paris to take the war more seriously – the only thing worse than fighting an unnecessary war to appease a jingoistic public is to lose one – and more troops were rushed to the peninsula. The original plan had been a quick, sharp raid: the destruction of the Russian fleet at Sevastopol and then a return to Turkey to winter, taking six weeks, maybe 12 at the outside. Instead, it was turning into a protracted siege that would roll over the winter of 1854–55 and require more men, as well as an expanded logistical effort to keep them armed and fed. The Italian Kingdom of Sardinia-Piedmont joined the war, sending 15,000 soldiers to support the allies, but divisions of both French and British troops also had to be sent to the Black Sea. Menshikov was also being reinforced, his army growing to some 107,000. However, his failure to relieve Sevastopol in November 1854 at the Battle of Inkerman, where 8,000 British troops managed to hold off a 37,000-strong Russian army long enough to be joined by French forces, essentially ended Menshikov's hopes of being able to break the allies in the field. He moved forces into Sevastopol to avoid their being encircled or defeated in detail, believing that the siege of Sevastopol would be decisive. Arguably, though, the war would be lost or won over a thousand miles away, in the frigid waters of the Baltic Sea.

THE OTHER CRIMEAN WAR

Even before the dispatch of the initial expeditionary force to Varna, British Foreign Secretary Lord Clarendon urged that 'in the event of war..., the Baltic must become a theatre of active operations.' There was a concern that Russian ships might slip through the Baltic and start raiding British and French shipping and coastlines. Yet this was an offensive more than defensive theatre for the British. Blockading Russian trade passing through the Baltic would have a serious impact on its economy. The presence of a strong Anglo-French fleet would also force Nicholas to keep a strong garrison in St Petersburg in case of direct attack. No wonder Clarendon concluded that 'one blow in the Baltic was worth two in the Black Sea.'

In March 1854, as the winter sea ice had begun to recede in the Baltic, allowing the passage of larger ships, a substantial British fleet was deployed: 18 ships led by the massive 131-gun first-rate ship-of-the-line HMS *Duke of Wellington*, brand new and powered both by sail and steam. This task force was then joined by a French squadron of 23 ships. Passing through the Danish Straits, they quickly bottled up the obsolete Russian Baltic Fleet (at the time comprising 26 ageing sailing battleships, nine steam frigates and nine sailing frigates), but also found themselves at something of a perverse disadvantage precisely because of their strength. Much of the Baltic is shallow and hard to navigate, especially close to the rocky coasts, and the allies needed more smaller and nimble craft rather than floating fortresses like the *Duke of Wellington*. The British fleet was structured to meet the Russians in battle on the open sea, which it would have done with aplomb and success – had the enemy proven suicidally obliging. Instead, the Russians largely hunkered down in their bases, protected by coastal artillery and, in a new development, large numbers of naval mines.

Maintaining a tight blockade was thus difficult, as smaller ships could hug the coast, and nor was it possible initially to strike directly at Kronstadt and directly threaten St Petersburg. Nonetheless, in August the allies took the unfinished fortress at Bomarsund on Åland, some 9,000 French soldiers and 900 British marines attacking overland, while the garrison was bombarded by sea. After the fortress's surrender, it was systematically dismantled. Later, the allies bombarded coastal forts and towns and the Russians themselves blew up their fortress at Hanko, the southernmost city in Finland, to keep it from capture, all 86 of its guns being sunk in the bay.

The allies could severely diminish Russian trade, though, and the share of Russian exports through its Baltic ports fell from 48 per cent before the war to just 2 per cent in 1855. A small squadron even ranged as far as the White Sea, shelling the port of Kola and raiding Russian trading ships. The fleet had to withdraw from the Baltic for the winter, but it would be replaced in 1855 by a larger one that was also much more directly geared for the needs of the campaign, with not just battleships to deter direct engagement, but also floating batteries and mortar ships for coastal bombardment, gunboats to patrol the coast, and even a repair ship and a floating hospital ship.

After an abortive attempt to lure the Baltic Fleet out of Kronstadt (in which four British ships were damaged by underwater mines), they again focused on blocking trade and systematically bombarding Russian bases and fortresses. Generally, the allied ships' guns had a greater range than the defenders', but heavily fortified positions were often impossible to destroy from afar. Unwilling to get involved in major amphibious operations, the allies were unable to level such key fortresses as Viapori (Sveaborg) outside Helsinki. Nonetheless, their ability to strike with impunity was a salutary lesson for the Russians, as to the possible threat to Kronstadt if a third expedition had been sent in 1856.

RETREAT TO REFORM

However, Nicholas I had died in March 1855 from the flu, being succeeded by his son, Alexander II, who had no illusions about the danger the war posed. In October, Sevastopol had finally fallen, after a concluding bombardment in which 307 guns fired more than 150,000 rounds on the beleaguered city and 60,000 troops had stormed the major redoubts protecting the southern approaches to the city. Meanwhile, Austria was threatening to join the allies now that they were looking safely victorious. At home, the costs of the war and the Baltic blockade (which cut total export trade by 80 per cent) led to a financial crisis, the printing of money and a devaluation of the ruble, whose silver content was cut from 45 per cent to 19 per cent. It would take until 1870 for the budget to be balanced again, and 1897 before the ruble could again be considered a stable international currency. Meanwhile, after the usual outburst of patriotism at the start of the war, discontent was growing. Leo Tolstoy, who served as a young artillery officer in the war, wrote a satirical poem about an engagement in which he fought, 'Song about the Battle on the Black River on 4 August 1855', a Russian defeat at the hands of a Franco-Italian force. A line became proverbial about the Russians' poor planning: 'It was smooth on paper, but they forgot about the ravines.'

Alexander II realized that the war was as dangerous as it was apparently unwinnable. Suing for peace, he found it easier to attain than he feared. After all, discontent at the war was growing in Britain, not least thanks to the excoriating dispatches in the *The Times* from William Russell, arguably the first real modern war correspondent, which detailed (and perhaps dramatized) the terrible losses and even more terrible conditions. Although new Prime Minister Lord Palmerstone was willing to continue the war with the aim of permanently degrading the capabilities of the Russian Empire, parliament was less eager, and in any case the French, who were contributing the lion's share of the expeditionary force, were happy to come to terms. The 1856 Treaty of Paris required the Russians to surrender Ottoman territory they had conquered in the war, demilitarized the Black Sea, and saw Moldavia and Wallachia effectively made into independent principalities, even if technically Turkish dependencies. It was a defeat for Russia, and for the moment certainly blocked any expansion to the south-west, but for Alexander this was no great hardship, as his focus would be to try to manage that most difficult of tasks: modernizing an authoritarian regime without losing control. He would fail.

Want To Know More?

There are many, many books on the Crimean War(s). John Sweetman's *The Crimean War 1854–1856* (Osprey, 2001) is a handy overview, while Andrew Lambert's *The Crimean War: British Grand Strategy against Russia, 1853–56* (Routledge, 2020) is densely written, but arguably the most important study contending that, in effect, the Crimean War is a misnomer for a conflict won in the Baltic. *Armies of the Crimean War, 1853–1856: History, Organization and Equipment of the British, French, Turkish, Piedmontese and Russian Forces* (Pen & Sword, 2023) by Gabriele Esposito is exactly what it claims to be. For light relief, George MacDonald Fraser's *Flashman at the Charge* (HarperCollins, 2006) takes his disgraceful anti-hero into Balaclava and then Russia: rip-roaring fiction, but well researched for all that.

18

Years of Decay

Tsushima, 1905

1861	Emancipation of the serfs
1877–78	Russo-Turkish War
1881	Assassination of Alexander II; Alexander III becomes tsar
1894	Death of Alexander III; Nicholas II becomes tsar
1900	Eight Nation Alliance intervenes in China
1900	Invasion of Manchuria
1904–05	Russo-Japanese War
1905	'1905 Revolution'

In 1996, I was temporarily seconded to the Foreign & Commonwealth Office's Research Analysts' section, largely working on Russian foreign and security policy, when an unusual request ended up on my desk, probably because no one else wanted to handle it. It was a query from the Russian Embassy: a delegation was heading to the port city of Hull in Yorkshire for some trade talks. Would they need increased security? The reason for this seemingly bizarre enquiry was that, by some accounts, the city is still technically at war with Russia, and has been ever since 1904.

On the night of 21–22 October 1904, the Russian Baltic Fleet was steaming through the waters of the Dogger Bank region, off the east coast of England, heading for the Far East via a long, circuitous route, to reinforce the desperately hard-pressed Pacific Fleet in its war with Japan, when they came across some trawlers from Hull, fishing for herring. The Russian captains already appeared to have been jumpy, even paranoid. They had carefully sailed round an imaginary minefield, and groundless rumours were circulating that somehow Japanese motor-torpedo boats had sailed all the way to European waters and were operating out of Danish waters. Then they spotted the trawlers in the fog, put two and two together, and made war.

They opened fire with everything they had, but the net result was just to sink one trawler and kill two fishermen. In the confusion and crossfire, two Russians were also killed and the cruisers *Aurora* and *Dmitri Donskoi* damaged by friendly fire. The supply ship *Kamchatka* lost the rest of the fleet in the fog and later claimed it had engaged three Japanese warships, which turned out to have been a Swedish merchantman, a French schooner and a German trawler. It fired 300 shells; none hit. This incident almost did mean war, as the Royal Navy's Home Fleet began to raise steam, but some hasty diplomacy and, in due course, the payment of reparations, managed to avert a crisis. Hull may not have forgotten this display of quite astonishingly inept seamanship (and, fortunately, gunnery), or at least that was what those diplomats seemed to presume. Fortunately, I was able to reassure them that they were likely to be fine. They were.

REFORM TO SURVIVE

In many ways, the Dogger Bank debacle had its roots in the failure properly to modernize the Russian military in the preceding decades, something that applied to training as well as technologies. It was not that they did not try. The Crimean War had been something of a watershed conflict, showcasing new technologies that were revolutionizing the science of war. Steamships and naval mines, longer-range rifles and rifled cannon, railways and telegraphs, all of these had made their mark, and if Russia did not keep up, it would be militarily vulnerable and diplomatically impotent in an age when might still largely made right. Alexander II also understood that economic reform was crucial to addressing that, and that this would start with the outdated and inefficient institution of serfdom. This would, he hoped, also forestall the dangers of rural revolution: it was, he said, 'better to abolish serfdom from above than to wait until it begins to abolish itself from below.'

The ensuing stream of reforms undoubtedly earned Alexander the epithet of 'Tsar-Liberator'. Alas, they would also kill him. Most importantly of all, his 1861 Emancipation Decree freed the serfs, but this proved a lethal half-measure, and rural unrest did not subside, it skyrocketed. The army – an army raised largely from the countryside – was increasingly being called out to put down riots and protests. Furthermore, the expansion of trade and industry meant more and more people were flocking to the cities. A new middle class was emerging, who had no real place in a society still polarized between nobility and peasantry, and a new working class, labouring in atrocious conditions. Urban terrorism also became a growing problem. At first Alexander felt he had no option but to crack down, but when heavy-handed repression proved only to worsen the problem, he swung in the other direction, deciding that his reforms had not gone far enough. Indeed, maybe it was also time for the Russian monarchy to constrain itself with a constitution?

Just at this moment, in March 1881, the *Narodnaya Volya* ('People's Will') terrorist group, having tried and failed to kill him seven times already, finally managed it on the eighth attempt. One man lobbed a bomb under his coach while he was being escorted through St Petersburg. It was bullet-proof, but when Alexander stepped from it, reassuring those around him 'thanks to God, I'm untouched', a second terrorist – reportedly but likely apocryphally shouting 'it's too early to thank God' – threw a second grenade, which mortally wounded him with both shrapnel and irony. Reform died with Alexander II, and his successors would seek, unsuccessfully, to combine economic modernization and political repression, an untenable policy that would lead to decline, disastrous wars, and the very revolution they so feared.

THE MILYUTIN REFORMS

One aspect of the late Alexander II's reforms that had made some progress was related to the military. In 1861, he had appointed Count Dmitri Milyutin, a former soldier turned military theorist, as Minister for War. His unenviable task was somehow to build an army able to compete with modern Western ones, while at the same time shrinking the unsustainably large defence budget. Rearmament would take time and money, but Milyutin quickly addressed the question of manpower. In the old system, the army was manned by peasants serving 25-year terms, who were selected by their landowners, most of whom used the opportunity to rid themselves of the unhealthy, the incompetent and the unruly. The prospect of their ever returning home was so small that they were bade farewell from the village with a funeral procession. The abolition of serfdom anyway made this no longer viable, so this was replaced in 1874 with universal conscription for six years in service and nine in the reserve (seven and three years, respectively, for the navy). At the same time, training was improved and some measures were made to make army life more bearable, improving rations and dramatically reducing the use of corporal punishment. Crucially, he introduced barracks: previously most ordinary soldiers had lived in shacks and dugouts or been billeted on peasant families. The idea was that this would encourage more soldiers to re-enlist after their first term, creating the basis for a cadre of long-term non-commissioned officers (NCOs). Army life was still unappealing and poorly rewarded, though: even by the early 20th century, the Russian army typically only had a single such NCO per company, while Germany averaged 12.

To save money, Milyutin devolved many responsibilities to what would eventually be 13 military districts, allowing him to prune the top-heavy and bureaucratic central ministry. More crucially, the size of the standing army would shrink – in line with practices of the time, the reserves would be mobilized in times of major war. Thanks to that and the expansion of the Russian economy, the share of the budget allocated to defence fell from nearly half in 1850, to 30 per cent in 1881, and 18 per cent by 1902.

Comprehensive rearmament was the goal, but would take time – and the longer it took, the more likely that yet newer advances would emerge. By the early 1860s, for example, about half the army had been issued new '6-line' (or .60-calibre) rifle-muskets, but then the 1866 Austro-Prussian War had demonstrated the advantages of the Prussian bolt-action Dreyse needle rifles, and so the Russians hurriedly first converted existing rifles to 'needle ignition' using a firing pin, and then began producing first the Krnka rifle and then the Berdan, designed by Colt and then built at Tula. Naval modernization would be harder, though, especially as the Russians tried to build their own steel-hulled warships both to save money and kick-start their own shipbuilding industry. Furthermore, there was too much of a focus on hulls and weapons, the physical stuff of maritime warfare, rather than on training, morale and esprit de corps. The same issues that contributed to the 1904 Dogger Bank incident also help explain why sailors, disenchanted, neglected and undervalued, were so prominent in the Bolshevik Revolution of 1917.

The new 'Milyutin army' would get its first field test in the next in the sequence of Russo-Turkish Wars. Sparked by international outrage at the treatment of anti-Ottoman rebellions in the Balkans and then a declaration of war against Turkey by Serbia and Montenegro, the war saw the Russians victorious. Serbia, Montenegro and part of Bulgaria became independent, and Russia – whose soldiers had been on the verge of marching on Constantinople until a British fleet came to warn them off – claimed more territory in the Caucasus. Nonetheless, while a victory, the test of war had also showed up continued weaknesses in everything from training at the company level to incompetence at the top. There was still a way to go.

THE REACTIONARY TURN

Alexander III was no liberal in waiting, and the murder of his father further confirmed his view that what Russia needed was not reform but discipline. He oversaw an era of oppression, especially of Russia's minorities, but also continued modernization, on the back of increased taxation of the peasantry. By the 1890s, the economy was growing at 5 per cent a year, and work began on the Trans-Siberian Railway, to stitch together this European and Asian empire. Much of this was done on the backs of over-worked and under-paid urban workers, who became increasingly restive. For now, tough policing and the scrutiny of the Okhrana ('Guard'), the secret police force established by Alexander in 1881, kept them just about under control – but not for long, it turned out.

Meanwhile, military modernization continued on its own momentum, with the navy gaining 114 new warships, including 17 battleships, making it third in the world behind Britain and France, even if rather less was still being done to address those perennial Russian intangible vulnerabilities of training, leadership and morale. These were, however, not to be tested: Russia fought no wars in his 13-year reign, earning him – perhaps rather generously – the nickname 'Peacemaker'.

He was worried about his heir, Nicholas, whom he considered too weak to be tsar. When Finance Minister Sergei Witte suggested making him chair of the committee managing the Trans-Siberian Railway, Alexander dismissed the idea: 'Don't tell me you never noticed the Grand Duke is... an absolute child. His opinions are utterly childish.' He may well have been right, but even so, when he died in 1894, Nicholas II duly ascended to the throne – the last of the Romanovs. He was weak enough to be dangerous for the regime, foolish enough not to understand the threats facing Russia, stubborn enough not to listen to those who did, and credulous enough to listen to people whom he really shouldn't have paid attention to. This includes those who assured him that a war with Japan would be a good thing, and that, as Interior Minister Vyacheslav Plehve airily put it, 'a nice, victorious little war' would unite and cheer the nation.

THE ROAD TO WAR IN THE FAR EAST

Where else could Russia assert its status as a great power? The Ottoman Empire was in decline, but it was clear that other European powers would not let Russia carve it up with impunity. The North Caucasus and Transcaucasia were now under Russian control, but pacification was a whole other matter. It was in the Far East that Russia's strategic planners thought to see the greatest opportunity, and certainly Nicholas II was willing to go along with them, especially when egged on by his cousin, Kaiser Wilhelm of a now-unified Germany, who may well have thought that pushing Russia towards Asia left Europe clear for his own ambitions.

China, after all, looked ripe for the plucking. It had just lost a disastrous war with Japan in 1894–95 over influence over Korea (in which more than a third of its troops had not even been issued firearms, just swords, spears and bows), and in 1897, a Russian fleet appeared off China's Liaotung Peninsula and, through a mix of negotiation and implied threat, secured a convention whereby Beijing leased it to Russia.

No time was wasted building up and fortifying Port Arthur, Russia's only warm-water port on the Pacific, which became the base for its Pacific Fleet. To support and supply it, they built the Chinese Eastern Railway through Manchuria, which was technically a Chinese–Russian joint venture but in practice was managed by the Russians, built to Russia's railway gauge, and guarded by Russian soldiers. Chinese Manchuria increasingly looked like a Russian protectorate.

In 1899, China then collapsed into the xenophobic Boxer Rebellion. Russia had been part of the Eight Nation Alliance, a 45,000-strong multinational force including Cossacks that had shouldered its way into Beijing to relieve the foreigners trapped in its Legation Quarter and force the Chinese government into a humiliating climbdown. St Petersburg also took advantage of the moment to invade Manchuria in a five-month operation in which 100,000 Russian troops smashed both Boxer rebels and Manchu bannermen (a kind of feudal military gentry). Although Russia had hoped to be able to secure a suitable deal granting it a degree of authority over the region, when China refused to negotiate, it was left in direct control over Manchuria.

The more Russia became active in the Far East, the more it would come into contact and conflict with a rising and ambitious Imperial Japan. As the latter became more dominant in Korea, for example, this worried the Russians. In 1901, Nicholas II had told Prince Henry of Prussia, 'I do not want to seize Korea but under no circumstances can I allow Japan to become firmly established there. That will be a *casus belli*.' Meanwhile, Japan was looking anxiously at the eastward creep of the Trans-Siberian Railway, seeing that, however limited, it brought with it Russian colonists, trade and troops. Disputes over Russia's occupation of Manchuria and timber concessions in Korea led to worsening relations, but Nicholas refused to compromise. He regarded Manchuria as crucial for securing Port Arthur, and Port Arthur as crucial for Russian access to the Pacific. He saw a war with Japan as ultimately inevitable, even desirable – and so too did the Japanese. That said, even though in December 1903 his own General Staff warned that Japan was ready to strike, very little was being done to prepare for this. There were multiple plans that had been drawn up, but none had been selected or acted upon.

The Japanese proposed a treaty which would, in effect, exchange acceptance of Russia's control of Manchuria for Japan's over Korea.

Nicholas, true to form, prevaricated, and in February 1904 – three hours before its formal declaration of war – Japan launched a surprise attack on Port Arthur. Although they were unable to close with the Russian fleet at harbour, protected as it was by heavy shore batteries, they damaged several Russian battleships and were able to bottle up the rest, while they landed troops in Korea unhindered. In April, the fleet made an abortive attempt to break out and reach Vladivostok, but at the Battle of the Yellow Sea – the first-ever major clash between fleets of steel-hulled battleships – it was turned back in a seven-hour gunnery duel. By then, the Japanese were also advancing by land through southern Manchuria.

In August, the Japanese attacked Liaoyang, the main Russian army base in southern Manchuria, and a hub on the railway line to Port Arthur. It was heavily fortified, and garrisoned by 50,000 men under General Alexei Kuropatkin, who until recently had been Minister for War (and so, arguably, deserved all that was coming to him). He had adopted an essentially defensive, attritional strategy, which gave the Japanese the initiative, but this engagement demonstrated the strengths and weaknesses of this approach. A roughly similarly sized Japanese force under Prince Iwao Oyama launched repeated attacks on Liaoyang, taking heavy losses, until Kuropatkin – who was convinced he was heavily outnumbered – opted to withdraw to Mukden to the south. This he could do in good order and unpursued because the Japanese were not only exhausted but, ironically enough, Oyama, fearing a Russian counterattack, had just decided to withdraw. Had Kuropatkin held his nerve for a few hours more, he would have held the city. As it was, the Japanese were able to cut the railway line to Port Arthur, which they had been besieging since April. By the end of the year Japanese ground troops had taken the Russian positions on Mount Vysokaya. From there, they could shell the fleet in harbour with near impunity. By January 1905, all the Russian Pacific Fleet's capital ships had been sunk or scuttled as a result, and Port Arthur surrendered.

THE FALL OF PORT ARTHUR

Nicholas had been openly contemptuous of these 'yellow monkeys' (it had not helped that, in 1891, he only barely escaped an assassination

FORGED IN WAR

attempt while travelling in Japan), but after the 1868 Meiji Restoration, the Japanese had been modernizing far more quickly and efficiently than the Russians. Their fleet had been modelled on the Royal Navy, and many of its capital ships had been bought from Britain. They were generally faster, more heavily armed and longer ranged, and their crews were disciplined and well trained. Its standing army of 268,000 men could quickly be expanded to 850,000 by mobilizing reserves and was conversely inspired by the German model, and proved aggressive and highly mobile in battle. They also had the key advantage of relative proximity: Russia may have been a larger power, but its main reserves were on the other side of the Urals, at the end of a partially built single-track ribbon of a railway: it took about six weeks to make the journey to Vladivostok, the eventual terminus of the line. The very fact that the Baltic Fleet had to be used to reinforce – or, as it turned out, replace – the Pacific Fleet illustrates the challenges of intercontinental warfare.

The war was a disaster for Russia. It started out with perhaps 95,000 troops across the whole Far East theatre, and reinforcement was often slow. Its troops frequently fought doggedly, but poor circumstances and even worse leadership kept them on the defensive. Barbed wire, machine guns and rapid-fire artillery made the assault bloody and dangerous, offering a harbinger of the killing fields of the First World War, but with speed, élan, and a willingness to take often frightful losses, the Japanese could still advance.

The fall of Port Arthur meant that the Japanese no longer had to fight on two fronts and could instead concentrate all their efforts on Manchuria. The Russians tried launching long-range cavalry raids to the Japanese rear to try to disrupt their supply lines, most notably in January 1905, when 7,000 men under General Pavel Mishchenko set out to cut railway lines, bring down bridges and destroy supplies. They had some success, especially in torching warehouses in Yingkou, but were forced to retreat lest they be encircled, and thereafter Oyama put greater effort into rear-area security, limiting the chances for a repeat, and the damage done to the rail lines was repaired within the day.

In February, as the bitter Manchurian winter began to recede, the two armies clashed at Mukden (now Shenyang), in what became the biggest land battle before the First World War. Both sides' forces had gathered: some 280,000 Russians and 270,000 Japanese. For once, Kuropatkin was planning to go onto the offensive, but the Japanese beat him to it, hammering the Russian centre with artillery, while outflanking them to the west. Eventually, the Russians were forced to withdraw. The Japanese had lost some 16,000 dead, twice the Russians' tally, but they had not only taken Mukden but all of southern Manchuria, and broken Russian morale. Although reinforcements would continue to stream in from European Russia, no further offensives were launched. All Russia's hopes now rested on the Baltic Fleet – now renamed the Second Pacific Squadron – which was at that point sitting off Cam Ranh Bay in French Indochina, taking on coal and supplies.

TSUSHIMA, 1905

Admiral Zinovy Rozhestvensky had originally been charged with breaking the blockade of Port Arthur, but those orders were long since moot. Instead, he was charged 'not to break through with some ships to Vladivostok, but to take possession of the Sea of Japan'. However, his fleet had just completed a seven-month odyssey that had put strain on crews and machinery alike, and so he opted precisely to try to get his fleet into Vladivostok undetected, both to gather up the ships remaining there and also prepare for combat operations. Strain on his ships' boilers and the fouling of their hulls meant that his squadron could not move faster than 9 knots, while under normal circumstances a ship like the newly built battleship *Borodino* could manage twice that.

This meant slipping through the Tsushima Strait between Korea and Japan, which he chose to do on the night of 26 May 1905, taking advantage of thick fog. However, while Rozhestvensky's warships were running dark, the hospital ship *Oryol*, in accordance with the rules of war, continued to burn its beacons. This was spotted by a Japanese ship, which used its new-fangled wireless telegraph to signal the location of the Russian fleet. Admiral Tōgō Heihachirō immediately began mustering the Japanese Combined Fleet for what would prove the conclusive engagement of the war. The Russian fleet had the advantage in battleships, 11 to Tōgō's five, but the Japanese had many more cruisers and destroyers, as well as numerous torpedo boats. More to the point, their ships were generally newer, in better condition and faster, which Tōgō would use to his advantage.

The first contact was at 8am, but the main Japanese fleet did not arrive until just after 1pm. Rozhestvensky, realizing that the Japanese would again have the initiative, had opted not to develop a battle plan but to respond to Tōgō's moves, which would prove to be a serious mistake when dealing with a more manoeuvrable enemy commanded by a capable and experienced admiral. Crucially, at an early stage the Japanese were able to perform the manoeuvre known as 'crossing the T', in other words, sailing across the front of the Russian line such that they could fire most of their guns broadside, while their enemies could only reply with their forward turrets, if they could get a line of sight at all. After the first volleys, the Japanese ships then turned parallel to the Russians, and what followed was a thundering exchange of fire, in which despite some early good shooting by the Russians, the Japanese advantages of accuracy and rate of fire soon began to count.

Battleships are powerful and resilient brutes, and although the Japanese flagship *Mikasa*, specially targeted by the Russians, was hit 15 times in just five minutes, nonetheless the first to be sunk was the Russian *Oslyabya*, fully 90 minutes into the battle. Then the magazines on the *Borodino* exploded, breaking the ship's back and sending it to the bottom. It was followed by the *Imperator Alexander III* and Rozhestvensky's flagship, the *Suvorov*. The admiral himself was knocked unconscious by a shell fragment but was taken off his burning ship onto the destroyer *Buyniy*. With his deputy, Rear Admiral Dmitry Volersam, already killed on the *Oslyabya*, the Russians lost any remaining coherence.

As night began to fall, the Russians had lost four battleships, and the Japanese none. In the dark, Tōgō unleashed his lighter ships to harry them, his destroyers and torpedo boats. They aggressively closed with the Russians, forcing them to disperse, and more of the ponderous pride of the Second Pacific Squadron began to be sunk or damaged. The battleships *Navarin* and *Sissoi Veliky* were torpedoed, the first sunk, the second so badly damaged that it was later scuttled, as were the cruisers *Admiral Nakhimov* and *Vladimir Monomakh*. The Japanese lost just three torpedo boats.

Rear Admiral Oskar Enkvist struck out with what was left of his cruiser squadron, eventually managing to make it to Manila where he was interned and his ships impounded. Rear Admiral Nikolai

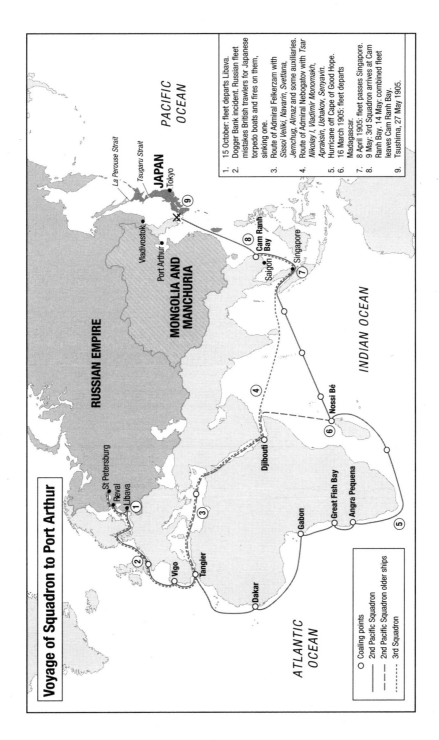

Voyage of Squadron to Port Arthur

PACIFIC OCEAN

La Perouse Strait
Tsugaru Strait
JAPAN
Tokyo

Vladivostok
Port Arthur
MONGOLIA AND MANCHURIA

RUSSIAN EMPIRE

St Petersburg
Reval
Libava

Cam Ranh Bay
Saigon
Singapore

INDIAN OCEAN

Nossi Bé

Djibouti

Great Fish Bay
Gabon
Angra Pequena

Tangier
Vigo
Dakar

ATLANTIC OCEAN

1. 15 October: fleet departs Libava.
2. Dogger Bank incident. Russian fleet mistakes British trawlers for Japanese torpedo boats and fires on them, sinking one.
3. Route of Admiral Felkerzam with *Sissoi Veliki, Navarin, Svetlana, Jemchug, Almaz* and some auxiliaries.
4. Route of Admiral Nebogatov with *Tsar Nikolay I, Vladimir Monomakh, Apraksin, Ushakov, Senyavin.*
5. Hurricane off Cape of Good Hope.
6. 16 March 1905: fleet departs Madagascar.
7. 8 April 1905: fleet passes Singapore.
8. 9 May: 3rd Squadron arrives at Cam Ranh Bay. 14 May: combined fleet leaves Cam Ranh Bay.
9. Tsushima, 27 May 1905.

○ Coaling points
—— 2nd Pacific Squadron
– – – 2nd Pacific Squadron older ships
······ 3rd Squadron

247

Nebogatov, who technically was the senior surviving commander, was unable to gain control of the fleet in the chaos and opted to try to lead his squadron out of the grip of the Japanese trap, but when he realized that he could neither evade nor outrun Tōgō's battleships, he surrendered. He knew he was likely to be court martialled and shot (in fact, this sentence was commuted to ten years in prison, and he was pardoned in 1909), but he told his men, 'You are young, and it is you who will one day retrieve the honour and glory of the Russian Navy. The lives of the two thousand four hundred men in these ships are more important than mine.'

Three ships – two destroyers and a cruiser – finally made it to Vladivostok, but the Second Pacific Squadron was destroyed, and with it Russia's last hopes. Twenty-one Russian ships had been sunk, including eight battleships, and five captured – all for the loss of three Japanese torpedo boats. As the Japanese moved on to take the Sakhalin Islands, and with riots and protests breaking out all across Russia, Nicholas had no option but to sue for peace. The Treaty of Portsmouth ceded Port Arthur and the southern half of Sakhalin to Japan and saw Russia forced to withdraw from Manchuria and accept that Korea was in Japan's sphere of influence. This 'nice, victorious little war' had turned out not to be nice, victorious or little.

THE GREAT DRESS REHEARSAL

A public which had originally embraced the war was angered by tales of bloody defeat, which crystallized their general discontent. When a peaceful crowd seeking to present a petition to the tsar in January 1905 was instead met with volleys of gunfire, this became fury. After this Bloody Sunday massacre, the country erupted into all kinds of violent protests, strikes and mutinies. There was no real coherence to it, no motivating ideology or controlling force, as much as a widespread sense that enough was enough: minorities angry at how a deliberate policy of Russification was marginalizing them and their traditions, factory workers tired of poor conditions and pay, former serfs struggling with the debts they were saddled with during Emancipation, soldiers demobilized into a struggling economy, the list went on. Landowners' mansions were looted and burned, factories went silent, and over 400 mutinies left the military chain of command near breakage.

However, there was no clear demand, and no one truly able to weld this mood of dissent into a coherent political movement, and a combination of political concessions and repressions was able to restore some kind of order by the end of 1907.

Bolshevik leader Lenin would later call the 1905 Revolution the 'Great Dress Rehearsal' for the one-two revolutionary punch in 1917 that would first topple tsarism and then see his Communists take power. However, this was a dress rehearsal in so many other ways, too. The Milyutin Reforms had been at best a partial remedy for the problems facing Russia in an age of war and insurrection; they would have been a valuable beginning, but as has so often been the case in Russia's history, reform ended up unfinished. In Manchuria, the Russians had technology that was broadly the equal, if not superior to that of their enemies, and the advantage of the defence, but numerically equivalent Japanese armies had beaten them again and again for this very reason. Russian soldiers could and did fight with determination and individual skill, but too often their officers did not even try to understand them, their orders were incomplete or poorly considered, their training inadequate, and the simple but crucial processes behind ensuring they had protection from the elements and a hot meal sorely neglected. As observed by an embittered veteran of the North Caucasus wars – whose lessons on the importance of the basics of soldiering had been so deliberately forgotten – 'the Russian army went into the Far East thinking all it had to do was wave a flag and fire a machine gun, and victory would follow.'

Too much of the same naivety would be evident when Russia joined the First World War: incompetence, backwardness and over-confidence would prove a lethal combination. There were, of course, many who appreciated the scale of the problem, but between 1905 and 1914, there was no appetite for hard choices and realistic assessments. It was a time when a surly and unpopular army would be involved time and again in suppressing local protests, even while often being expected to feed and fend for itself (in 1907, for example, one in eight enlisted men was still engaged full-time in tailoring, to run up uniforms for his unit). It was also a time when new powers were rising – Japan, Germany, the United States – and the old multi-ethnic land empires were in crisis: first it was the Ottomans, then the Austro-Hungarians, and now Russia.

Want To Know More?

Richard Connaughton's *Rising Sun and Tumbling Bear: Russia's War with Japan* (W&N, 2004) is a good summary of the war, as is the more compact *The Russo-Japanese War 1904–05* by Alexei Ivanov and Philip Jowett (Osprey, 2004). Mark Lardas's *Tsushima 1905: Death of a Russian Fleet* (Osprey, 2018) covers this particular engagement, while *The Tsar's Last Armada: The Epic Journey to the Battle of Tsushima* by Constantine Pleshakov (Basic, 2003) is an evocative look at the Russian perspective. *The Tide at Sunrise: The Russo-Japanese War, 1904–1905* (Multi-Man, 2010) is probably the best wargame detailing this conflict so far.

19

Apocalypse of an Empire

Tannenberg, 1914

1905   1905 Revolution
1911   Assassination of Stolypin
1914   Russian entry into the First World War
1916   Brusilov Offensive
       Central Asian rebellion
1917   February Revolution and the downfall of tsarism
       'Great October Revolution'

Modern Russia has seen something of an explosion of military re-enactment, and while at public events and festivals one can come across everyone from Roman legionaries to samurai, there is a particular passion for cosplaying tsarist soldiers of the final years, the doomed officers and men who in 1914 would march into a war their leaders did not understand, their economy could not sustain, and their society ultimately would no longer accept. I once asked one such enthusiast, bedecked in the brass-buttoned black uniform of the 1st Life Grenadier Ekaterinoslav Regiment, quite what the appeal was of a unit that would be ground away through the First World War and by the end of 1915 only retained a quarter of the men with whom it had entered the conflict. He talked about unit traditions (including being an early and enthusiastic adoptee of 'English boxing'), but above all, it was that sense precisely of taking a stand before the Apocalypse, of the tragic grandeur of a time when it was possible to see the end of everything you were meant to protect – but to do your best regardless. It seemed to me to be a sobering and depressive kind of hobby, but clearly he and his friends, who were nodding away, were of one mind.

The Tsarist Empire was already moribund, but the systemic crisis that was the First World War, the first truly industrial war, made this obvious. A 19th-century army was fed into the meatgrinder of a 20th-century war, and found wanting. The result was two revolutions: first the downfall of tsarism, and then the Bolshevik coup, a three-century dynasty destroyed by a war it had misguidedly embraced.

A SYSTEM IN CRISIS

The tragic irony is that there were many in Russia clear-eyed enough to have understood the lessons of the past hundred years of conflict. Napoleon had been defeated, but only after he had overreached, and still managed to impose his rule on most of the continent. Nonetheless, his victories were only partly thanks to his generalship; they were to a great degree the product of a whole new way of thinking about and organizing for conquest, of the mobilization of total national effort and the creation of a machine able to combine farms and factories, levies and taxes, aristocratic élan and popular nationalism into warfighting capacity. Napoleon may have famously disparaged the British as a nation of shopkeepers, but his empire was built on clerks, farriers, sutlers, engineers, accountants and census-takers as much as cuirassiers and cannon.

The Caucasus Wars had produced a generation of hard-fighting soldiers and officers, but many of their experiences were too specialized for the mass wars to come, and in any case they were often marginalized and ignored. The real test was Crimea, and this was one Russia failed, not because of the spirit of its soldiers, but the degree to which they were no more able ultimately to answer the challenge of superior technology on the battlefield than that the national economy could withstand blockade in the Baltic. Tsushima represented a stark example of both how a rival nation could modernize effectively, but also just how far poverty and the debilitating effects of fear of revolution, which ensured any reforms would only be partial, was holding Russia back.

The 1905 Revolution opened a very brief window of opportunity. Initial promises of constitutional reform were soon rowed back, and new Prime Minister Pyotr Stolypin embarked on a campaign of vigorous repression (such that the hangman's noose became known as a 'Stolypin necktie'). The armed forces found themselves on both sides of the barricades. When Moscow was gripped by general strike and the Kremlin besieged by revolutionaries including deserters from the city garrison, the Semyonovsky Guards Regiment under the notorious Colonel Georgy Min was dispatched from St Petersburg. The revolutionary neighbourhoods were shelled into submission, as Min himself warned his troops 'act without mercy. There will be no arrests.' When the artillerymen of Sveaborg on the Finnish coast mutinied in 1906, it was the navy that bombarded them until loyalist troops could disarm them. The result would be a legacy of bitterness and mistrust that would poison relations between officers and men, Cossacks and regular troops, Russian and non-Russian soldiers.

Stolypin realized that martial law, repression and the Okhrana secret police were only a temporary answer, and that for the monarchy and the system to survive, Russia needed to be transformed – and that, in turn, meant finally resolving the rural question. He embarked on an ambitious effort to encourage a new class of rural entrepreneur, the kind of prosperous yeoman farmers who were the backbone of German conservatism. In the short term, he was successful. Agricultural productivity increased by almost 15 per cent, and tax revenues grew with it. He was even able to curb the court, and the infamous Rasputin, a faith-healing monk of scandalous repute whose proximity to the royal family was becoming a problem, fled to Jerusalem when it became clear that Stolypin was contemplating having him arrested.

He understood that this was a matter of survival. When a monument to Stolypin was erected in central Moscow in 2012, it was engraved with one of his famous lines: 'We must all unite in the defence of Russia, coordinate our efforts, our duties and our rights in order to maintain one of Russia's great historic rights – to be strong.' He saw this first of all in economic and political terms – military strength would naturally follow. As ever, though, reform threatened many established interests and created losers as well as winners, and his enemies whispered into poor, weak Tsar Nicholas's ear that his prime minister was becoming too arrogant and too powerful. Empress Alexandra, who had fallen under Rasputin's spell and believed the mystic could cure their son Alexei's haemophilia, whispered poison into the other. In 1911, at a performance at the Kiev Opera also attended by the tsar, Stolypin was fatally wounded by a revolutionary, in what some suspected was an operation sanctioned by Nicholas.

Arguably, Stolypin's death was also the death of the last hope to reform tsarism – and thus also the death of the system. Certainly Lenin thought so, regarding it as proof that the 'last, the last conceivable, road for tsarism' had been closed. Given the war that was looming, it is questionable whether he could have done much to save the system. He had hoped he could have had 'twenty years of peace' to complete his grand design. Nonetheless, it was clear that with him gone, so too was the last real impetus for change. Reform was stymied, Rasputin moved back to St Petersburg, and tsarism was dead, too, even if it did not yet know it.

THE SLIDE INTO WAR

The Great War was arguably at once unwanted and unavoidable. Tensions in Europe had been building steadily: the old land empires of the Habsburgs, the Ottomans and, truth to tell, the Romanovs were in decline, the scope for rivalries to be sublimated into imperial expansion was diminishing, and an ambitious and self-confident Germany, unified by Prussia in 1871 in the teeth of French resistance – broken in the 1870–71 Franco-Prussian War – was seeking its 'place in the sun' as eventual Reich Chancellor Bernhard von Bülow would put it. The irony was, of course, that Russia was not yet thinking of itself as another of the potential declining powers. On the eve of war, Nicholas II even approved a plan that envisaged taking advantage of a European war finally to take Constantinople, the Bosporus and the Dardanelles.

By then, after all, the so-called Great Powers of Europe were already assembled into two mutually suspicious blocs: the Entente, including Russia, France and Britain; and the Triple Alliance of Germany, Austria-Hungary and Italy. It was an age of fear. France, still smarting at its defeat in 1871, feared Germany's rise; Germany feared the implicit threat of a war on two flanks because of the Franco-Russian alliance; Britain feared Germany as a new rival at sea; Austria-Hungary feared the dissolution of its empire, and Russian ambition; Russia feared war, but feared being caught unawares even more.

Together, those six countries alone could amass more than 16 million men under arms when mobilized, while a naval arms race had been raging between Great Britain and Germany. The spark that ignited this volatile situation, though, came from the Balkans, where the retreat of Habsburg and Ottoman power had left unstable and precarious new nations still in the shadow of the old empires. When Bosnian Serb terrorist Gavrilo Princip assassinated Archduke Franz Ferdinand, heir to the Habsburg throne, during a visit to the Bosnian capital Sarajevo in June 1914, Austria-Hungary chose to blame independent Serbia, whose ambitions to form a Slavic union in south-eastern Europe posed a threat to its own possessions. On 23 July, after assuring itself of German support, Austria-Hungary made a humiliating series of demands to Serbia that it knew it could not accept. The Germans had wanted to keep any conflict limited, and had encouraged their allies to strike quickly, but the ultimatum process dragged out the crisis and made it public.

Russia saw this as a challenge to its own credibility, especially given its past sparring with both the Ottomans and the Habsburgs over the fate of the Orthodox Slavs of south-eastern Europe. The Russians had no desire to be embroiled in a war, but they were also well aware just how much slower their forces were to mobilize than their Western neighbours'. Two days after Austria-Hungary declared war on Serbia on 28 July, Nicholas ordered a partial mobilization. At this stage, there was still a belief – or at least hope – that Vienna was involved in heavy-handed posturing more than anything else, and that this would be enough to prevent hostilities. Indeed, the day beforehand, Nicholas sent a telegram to his cousin 'Willy', more formally known as Germany's Kaiser Wilhelm II:

I foresee that very soon I shall be overwhelmed by the pressure forced upon me and be forced to take extreme measures which will lead to war. To try and avoid such a calamity as a European war I beg you in the name of our old friendship to do what you can to stop your allies from going too far. Nicky.

Yet strategic necessity took second place to familial bonds. Germany's nightmare was precisely being caught between the French hammer and the Russian anvil. 'Nicky' may be making peaceable noises, but what if, his spine stiffened by promises of French support, he plans war? If Berlin waits to see what happens when the lumbering bear has finally mobilized the more than 5 million men at its disposal, then it may well be too late. To address this scenario, since 1905 Berlin had had ready the Schlieffen Plan, which envisaged a lightning pre-emptive offensive to knock France out of the war before it was really in it, so that its forces could then be pivoted back to the Eastern Front by the time the Russians were ready to move.

It was a cunning plan. Unfortunately, like so many cunning plans, it had such a range of moving parts that it was almost certain it would go wrong. As it was, a planned strike into France through Belgium met more resistance than expected, giving the French more time to prepare. Meanwhile, Italy was hesitant to get involved in a war in which its own interests did not seem directly at stake. The Germans had counted on the Italians attacking France, to divert some of its army, and that its fleet – which included fully six dreadnoughts – would challenge the Royal Navy in the Mediterranean. As it was, Rome, which neither Vienna nor Berlin had bothered consulting in the march to war, opted first to sit the war out and then in 1915 actually to join the other side. Finally, the Russians managed to mobilize part of their army quicker than anticipated and were able to make an early move into East Prussia, forcing the Germans to transfer forces to the East instead. There was no quick victory for anyone, and a war had started in Europe that would spread around the world and devour more than 18 million lives – and ultimately destroy all three of those land empires in the balance.

TANNENBERG, 1914

On 17 August, as Russian forces were advancing into East Prussia, four infantry divisions found themselves tangling with a German one at Stallupönen (now Nesterov, in Russia's Kaliningrad region). This first battle on the Eastern Front ironically saw the Germans commanded by Hermann von François, of Luxembourger stock, while the Russian general, Paul von Rennenkampf, was a Baltic German. The Germans were outnumbered almost three to one, but the Russians were outmarched and out of touch with each other, and suffered serious losses, even as von François withdrew to join up with the rest of General Maximilian von Prittwitz's 8th Army at Gumbinnen (now Gusev). On 20 August, von Prittwitz, egged on by the aggressive von François, attacked the Russians in the hope of being able to execute almost his own Schlieffen Plan, breaking von Rennenkampf's 1st Army before it could meet with Alexander Samsonov's 2nd Army, and then focusing on the latter. The Germans acquitted themselves well, but as on the Western Front, not quite quickly or well enough. Both sides took heavy losses, but the 1st Army held, and von Prittwitz even began advocating a withdrawal, abandoning East Prussia and taking up defensive positions west of the Vistula River. However, in his own dispatches to the General Staff, von François slammed him for timidity, and they agreed, recalling him and replacing him with Field Marshal Paul von Hindenburg, who would promptly deliver two telling defeats on the Russians, at Tannenberg and the Masurian Lakes, which would act as forewarnings of the senseless slaughter ahead.

Within a day of arriving at the front, Hindenburg and his new chief of staff, General Erich Ludendorff, had decided on an ambitious and aggressive operation that would essentially flip the Gumbinnen attack, leaving August Mackensen's 17th Corps and some cavalry units to fix Rennenkampf's army, while concentrating on Samsonov's 2nd Army. If the two Russian armies could combine, then the Germans would be in trouble. However, in what was just the first of a series of blunders, the Russians had seen signs of an initial withdrawal to the Vistula while Prittwitz was still in command and presumed a general retreat was under way and that East Prussia was in the bag. Besides, General Yakov Zhilinsky, the overall commander of the North-Western Front, was a man in a hurry, having foolhardily pledged simultaneous offensives against the Germans and the Austrians. He wanted to believe that he could quickly snap up East Prussia, so Rennenkampf was ordered to shift his line of advance towards the Baltic coast, to cut off Königsberg, while Samsonov was instructed to intercept these notionally retreating forces. In practice what that meant was that the two armies were actually moving not closer, but further apart: by the time Hindenburg struck, they were divided by some 80 miles and the chain of the Masurian Lakes.

The Germans had the advantage of mobility thanks to their railways – the Russian trains were of a different, wider gauge; so, past their own border, they could only use whatever rolling stock they could capture, and their enemies made a point of destroying what they could not use. Thanks to this 'scorched rail' strategy, Russian supplies were having to be brought from the railheads by horse-drawn cart. Samsonov's men had been marching for nine days even before they crossed the German border, and were already running low on those staples of the Russian soldier's diet: tea and bread. Nor was there much scope for foraging. Samsonov warned Zhilinsky that 'the country is devastated, the horses have long been without oats, and there is no bread', but his superior was unmoved.

Even more fortuitously, the Germans had crucial intelligence about their enemies' plans. They were getting reports from locals as the invaders advanced, but also an unexpected intelligence windfall which allowed them to know not only where they had been, but where they were going. The Russians, like all the combatants, were beginning to use wireless telegraphy to transmit orders at the corps and army level, but as they had not given Samsonov an up-to-date code book, were not encrypting them. On 25 August, Hindenburg was gifted with the complete set of Rennenkampf's movement orders for his 4th Corps, which in effect told him that he did not have to worry about the 1st Army and could safely turn against the 2nd. Another such intercepted message would give him the 2nd Army's composition and movement orders. He was in the rare and fortunate position of knowing far more about his enemies' forces and intentions than they could possibly realize, and Hindenburg chose to strike fast, to encircle and destroy Samsonov's army before the situation could change.

Fought across a week, this was less a single battle as a series of interconnected ones, in which some 150,000 German troops took on some 190,000 Russians. Samsonov had been pushing his troops hard, not least because he in turn was being pushed by Zhilinsky, still entertaining fantasies of trapping a demoralized German army retreating towards the Vistula. His men were tired, hungry and strung out along the line of march. Now that he knew Rennenkampf was otherwise occupied, and seeing that Samsonov's flanks and centre were separated, Hindenburg could use the opportunity to strike at both Russian flanks. He withdrew Mackensen's corps from the north, leaving just a cavalry screen to warn him if the 1st Army stopped heading towards Königsberg, and while they were on the march, unleashed François onto Samsonov's left flank.

On 25 August, François began his attack, his advance guard making early progress and taking the town of Seeben. Thanks to those invaluable railways, the rest of his corps and more ammunition could quickly follow. The next day, Mackensen engaged Alexander Blagoveschensky's

Russian 6th Corps. It was hard fighting, but the Germans were able to split the Russian right flank, albeit not without losses, but when Blagoveschensky fled to the rear, the day was clearly lost for the Russians. Still, Hindenburg needed a quick win, to avoid the risk of being caught between Samsonov and Rennenkampf, and by all accounts the evening of the 26th was a tense one for the German commanders.

Next morning, though, when François opened with a heavy bombardment of the Russians near Usdau, what was intended just as a preliminary to an infantry assault actually sent the Russians into flight. Samsonov's left flank began to unravel, and François was soon in a position to swing eastwards and block any further Russian retreat. The Russians had been continuing to grind away at the German 20th Corps, which was planted across their front, but when they belatedly realized that they were being encircled, their morale quickly collapsed. Attempts to break through François's line and escape the trap meant crossing open fields, the perfect killing ground for German artillery and machine guns, criss-crossed by the beams of searchlights at night. More and more Russians began to surrender, such that it became a problem managing the columns of prisoners. Perhaps had Samsonov hesitated less and concentrated his forces on a single point, the encirclement might have been broken, but by then there was scarcely any pretence of an overall Russian plan. On 30 August, Samsonov himself, unable to regain control of what had become a panicked mob, walked into the forest and shot himself rather than face capture and dishonour.

It was a catastrophic defeat for the Russians. Samsonov's 2nd Army was essentially no more. It is a sign of the scale of the defeat that the estimates for the number of killed or wounded vary so wildly, from 30,000 to 80,000, with the truth likely somewhere near the higher end of the range. Over 90,000 were captured, including 13 generals, and only 10,000 got away. There were only 12,000 German casualties, by contrast. Hindenburg had set himself the task of 'not merely to win a victory over Samsonov. We had to annihilate him.' This he undoubtedly accomplished. In the Battle of the Masurian Lakes (2–16 September) that followed, the Russians would be driven out of East Prussia at the cost of another 100,000 dead, wounded or captured.

The Russians often fought hard, and well, but Tannenberg – the name was a political choice, deliberately connecting to and redeeming the defeat of the Teutonic Knights there in 1410 – highlighted crucial issues which were going to dog them throughout the war. Russia's generals had not adapted to a modern style of war that, on the Eastern Front, would not be the trench war stalemate of the Western one, but shaped by mobility, the capacity to use roads and railways to concentrate forces and firepower to establish local superiority. What would later be called C3I – Command, Control, Communications and Intelligence – was crucial, in the first major war which would see not only radio interception but also the use of aircraft to spot for artillery and track enemy advances, radio and field telephony. Even when the Russians had field telephones and signalmen, for example, they were often short of the wire to connect them. This is another example of the usual issue of failed logistics, something becoming all the more important, reflecting the increasingly voracious needs of modern war. This was not just an issue of railway gauges but also proper planning – mobilization had been done at such speed that Samsonov's army lacked field bakeries, for example – and industrial capacity. At the time, Russia's factories were producing just 13,000 bullets a day, which a single machine-gun company with eight Maxim M1910 guns could get through in perhaps five minutes of sustained fire.

Nonetheless, while the Germans had won back East Prussia, to do so they had had to divert forces from the Western Front, which was quickly becoming a bloody stalemate. The Russians had gambled on a quick push to Berlin to end the war; the Germans on knocking out France to avoid a war on two fronts. Both were disappointed.

FIGHTING, FAILING, FLOUNDERING

One step forward was often followed by one or two bloody steps back. They had failed in the initial offensive against the Germans, but the Russians had more success against the Austro-Hungarians. At first, a pre-emptive Austro-Hungarian offensive into Poland looked as if it might disrupt Russian operations, but after the Battle of Gnila Lipa at the end of August, they were on the back foot, losing Lemberg (Lviv) as their line began to collapse. The Russians were able to take Eastern Galicia and in September began to besiege the fortress-town of Przemyśl in what is now Poland. It would eventually surrender in March 1915, after the longest siege in Europe during the war. By the end of the extended struggle for Galicia, the Austro-Hungarians had lost perhaps

325,000 dead, wounded or captured to the Russians' 225,000. Thus, by the end of 1914, despite Tannenberg, the Russians could tell themselves the honours of battle were even.

That would not last, and 1915 saw the Russians increasingly in retreat, not least as the Germans, bogged down on the Western Front, decided to focus on the East. The result was a series of battles of epic scale, with the Russians usually coming out the worse. The May–July Gorlice-Tarnów offensive, for example, saw around 1.5 million German and Austro-Hungarian troops engaging almost as many Russians, throwing them out of Galicia in confusion, with total losses of more than a million dead, wounded or captured. Russian forces were often simply unable to respond to the changing battlefield in time, and for all that they preached a doctrine of concentrated strike, combining all forces into coordinated offensive operations, they were simply unable to bring together the intelligence and reconnaissance needed to know how and where to act in time. Beyond that, despite shipments from the allies, there were shortages of all-important artillery ammunition, and even if now there were enough rifle cartridges, there were simply not enough rifles: 100,000 were needed each month, but the country's factories could only manufacture 42,000. So they lacked some 300,000 still, and some units went into battle with the rear ranks unarmed, expected simply to pick up the guns of the front-rankers when they fell in the battle.

In what would prove another momentous blunder, Tsar Nicholas dismissed his popular cousin, Grand Duke Nikolai Nikolayevich, from his role as commander-in-chief and assumed that position himself. In part, it was because he thought it was his duty; in part, it was to reap the rewards of what he believed would be an ultimately victorious war. His own ministers beseeched him not to, warning that 'your adoption of such a decision threatens, in our extreme understanding, Russia, you and your dynasty with grave consequences.' Nicholas, resolute at all the wrong moments, would not be persuaded, and it did indeed help ensure his eventual downfall and death. Both to support his British and French allies by pulling troops away from the killing fields to the west, and also because he seems genuinely to have believed Russia had the chance of success if it were able to take the initiative, he demanded an offensive spirit from his generals, something that simply cost Russia more lives.

To the south, the Russians were able to make gains against the Ottomans, especially, ironically enough, once Grand Duke Nikolai Nikolayevich had been demoted to the position of Viceroy and Commander in the Caucasus. Britain needed Russia to distract the Turks, who were pressing them hard in Mesopotamia (Iraq), so he launched a winter offensive that took Trabzon, on the south-eastern Black Sea coast. Against the Germans and Austro-Hungarians, though, the year would be much more mixed. The Brusilov Offensive – named for its mastermind, General Alexei Brusilov, commander of Russia's South-Western Front – was a triumph, even if in hindsight a Pyrrhic one. Launched in June 1916, this three-month operation saw more than 1.7 million troops thrown primarily at the Austro-Hungarians, with the goal of relieving pressure on both the Western Front and Italy. There was also the hope that this could knock the Austro-Hungarians out of the way – both sides kept succumbing to such dreams of a decisive single blow, not fully understanding how, in an age of modern, total war, this is so much easier said than done.

Having come to realize that the next best thing to having good intelligence on your enemy is to worsen theirs on you, preparations for the offensive were obscured by allowing the Germans to intercept misleading radio messages and similar countermeasures. Then, after the customary massive preliminary bombardment meant to blast breaches in the enemy defences and shatter their cohesion and morale, the Russians attacked from positions dug as close as possible to the Austro-Hungarian lines. Considerable progress was made at first, but as usual, a well-organized initial attack degenerated into a disjoined series of follow-up operations of wildly varying competence. By August, German forces had been rushed east to reinforce the hard-pressed Austro-Hungarians, rains were making the roads impassable and thus severely hindering resupply, and the momentum of the offensive was petering out.

It was the high point of Russian offensive operations, but both sides lost around 1.5 million men, and although it did encourage Romania to join the Entente allies, the sheer scale of the losses in men and materiel would place a crippling burden on the Russians. The German offensives had put the more industrially developed parts of the Russian Empire – Poland, Belarus and the Baltic States – at risk. Efforts to relocate industries to the east largely proved too little, too late, and also very disruptive of production. When Warsaw fell in July, for example, most of the city's defence industries were still present, intact and ready for the Germans to use. The same was true when Riga fell in September, denying Russia its most important port on the Baltic, after Petrograd – as St Petersburg had been renamed to lose its 'Germanic' overtones.

A GATHERING STORM

Meanwhile, the factories at home were restive. Enough food was still being produced in the country, but the distribution system was in chaos, not least as crucial railway stock was being run without adequate maintenance, so that by mid-1916 almost a third was out of service. Supplies were disrupted, prices rising and shops empty. By the end of that year, prices for food and other basics had quadrupled. The need to feed the voracious war effort meant that conscription was increasingly becoming little more than press ganging, and was stripping the farms of much-needed workers. When the decision was made in mid-1916 to impress Central Asian men between the ages of 19 and 43 into labour battalions, it sparked a rebellion in Russian Kazakhstan and Kyrgyzstan that was brutally suppressed at the cost of anything up to a quarter of a million deaths. The country was under martial law, censorship increasingly heavy-handed, and political repression escalating, but still, strikes were growing. In Petrograd alone, there were some 300 in 1915 and more than 680 the following year. More worrying for the authorities was that economic strikes were increasingly explicitly political – and spreading in defence-critical industries such as metalworks.

With the tsar involved with the war, day-to-day governance was increasingly in the hands of German-born Tsarina Alexandra, which was bad enough, especially as she was heavily influenced by the infamous Rasputin (until his murder by Russian aristocrats – possibly assisted by a British MI6 officer – at the end of 1916). It became increasingly easy for revolutionaries and dissidents to present reverses in the war as being a direct result of there being 'a German on the Russian throne, alien to the country and its people', in the words of nationalist parliamentarian Vladimir Purishkevich. Even within the aristocracy, there was a feeling, as one put it, that 'unless the tsar falls, tsarism will fall.'

A perfect political storm was brewing. The next year would see the balance of the conflict tip towards the Entente powers, as the United States joined the war. However, it was too late for tsarist Russia.

Want To Know More?

Dominic Lieven's *Towards the Flame: Empire, War and the End of Tsarist Russia* (Allen Lane, 2015) is a brilliant modern study of this war from the Russian perspective, both scholarly and readable. *Tannenberg 1914: Destruction of the Russian Second Army* (Osprey, 2022) by Michael McNally is a good summary of this pivotal battle, but Prit Buttar is the real doyen of modern writers looking at the Eastern Front, and his *Collision of Empires: The War on the Eastern Front in 1914* (Osprey, 2016) and *The Splintered Empires: The Eastern Front 1917–21* (Osprey, 2018) are especially noteworthy for those looking for detailed military analyses of the war. A different perspective of the war is offered by the film *Battalion* (2015), which follows the formation of the First Battalion of Death, an all-woman Russian unit raised in the desperation of the last years of the war.

PART FIVE

Red Star Rise and Fall

20

Red Victory

Tsaritsyn, 1918–19

1917	February Revolution and the downfall of tsarism
	July Days
	October Revolution and the Bolshevik coup
1918	Treaty of Brest-Litovsk
1918–22	Russian Civil War
1922	Formal creation of the Union of Soviet Socialist Republics

My grandfather, having served through the First World War as a machine-gunner in the 7th Battalion Royal Berkshire Regiment, found that the Armistice did not offer him a quick mobilization and trip home but instead an attachment to the Rifle Brigade's 4th Battalion and the long journey to Tiflis (Tbilisi) in Georgia, part of one of Britain's several deployments to the fragmenting territories of the Russian Empire, as much about controlling vital resources as combating the dreaded scourge of Bolshevism. Fortunately for him, he did not see action – he had already seen enough – but he returned after a year, with a sketch pad full of exotic images of the places and people he had seen.

This was, after all, just one of the many unexpected side effects of two revolutions that took place in 1917. Seizing power in the cities would prove unexpectedly easy for Lenin and his Bolsheviks; holding it and extending it across the country would prove the real challenge.

The messy and vicious Russian Civil War (1917–22) and the longer struggle against *basmachestvo* rebellions in Central Asia were what really defined the new Soviet state, and arguably created the conditions that led to the rise of Stalin.

THE ACCIDENTAL REVOLUTION

As of the start of 1917, Russia still seemed a formidable power. Its army had swollen to 6.9 million, backed by another 2.2 million reserves. However, it had been forced onto the defensive, its morale was at breaking point, and revolutionary and anti-war agitation in the ranks was spreading. Even basic supplies were running low, and front-line soldiers' bread rations had been cut by a third – while bread lines in the cities were sometimes hundreds long. Some 34,000 soldiers were deserting every month, not least as officers and men in the rear, seeing the carnage that would await them when they rotated into the front line, increasingly resisted such orders. Even Cossacks, for so long the stormtroopers of the tsarist order, began to refuse orders to put down mutinies.

Nicholas simply would not believe there was a serious threat to the state, though. Major General Alexander Spiridovich, head of the Palace Police, wrote about the public mood: 'A catastrophe is approaching... Everyone is waiting for some kind of revolution. Who will do it, where, how, when – no one knows anything. But everyone is talking and everyone is waiting... They hate the Empress, they don't want the Tsar anymore.'[*] Meanwhile, fearful politicians, ministers and even generals began quietly to discuss how to respond if the situation hit crisis point. That point was reached in February 1917. Workers at the Putilov Factory, the largest industrial plant in Petrograd and a cradle of revolutionary sentiment, went on strike. Their protest quickly grew, and within a few days a quarter of a million men and women were crowding the streets, demanding an end to the war, to rationing – and, increasingly, to the tsar. The capital was paralysed, and Nicholas ordered Petrograd military commandant Lieutenant General Sergei Khabalov to suppress

---

[*]Alexander Spiridovich, *Velikaya Voina i Fevralskaya Rovolutsiya, vol. 3* (1961), available online at http://militera.lib.ru/memo/russian/spiridovich_ai/03.html

the protests by force. He was reluctant to take extreme measures, but as the protests became a general strike, the failure or inability of the authorities to act emboldened the rioters.

It is certainly not that there were not enough troops. There were some 160,000 soldiers present, but most were simply being temporarily quartered there in cramped and miserable conditions, all too well aware that their next stop would be the front. Had Khabalov moved quickly and decisively, perhaps he might have been able to disperse the protests – this time. He could just as easily have triggered a bloodbath. As it was, though, mutinies began within the army units, too. First, a battalion of the Volyn Jaeger Life Guards Regiment, then elements of the other notionally elite Imperial Guards regiments: the Moscow, Preobrazhensky, Semyonovsky and Grenadier Regiments. A trickle of desertions became a flood.

Even as Nicholas detached Adjutant General Nikolai Ivanov to muster troops to retake his capital, parliamentarians established the Provisional Committee of the State Duma as an interim government, committed not to the tsar's removal as much as the creation of a constitutional monarchy. Nicholas headed back to Petrograd in outrage, but strikers and revolutionaries had closed the railway lines to the capital, forcing him to head back to Pskov. There, he was met by General Nikolai Ruzsky, commander of the Northern Front, and a delegation of Duma deputies, demanding he abdicate for the good of the nation. By all accounts, when he balked, Ruzsky forced a pen into his hand and put a prepared statement in front of him, barking 'sign, sign! Don't you see that there is nothing else left for you? If you don't sign, I can't be responsible for your life.' Nicholas tried to abdicate in favour of his brother, Grand Duke Mikhail Alexandrovich, but he recognized a poisoned chalice when one was put to his lips, and said he would only accept the crown if it were offered to him by representatives of the public. So, Nicholas and his family were placed under protective custody by the Provisional Government, and a dynasty that had emerged as the answer to a time of war and chaos in the 17th century was toppled almost exactly 300 years later in response to another.

Although this took place in March 1917, it is known as the February Revolution, because that was the month according to the Julian calendar that Russia still used rather than the more widely employed Gregorian one. Arguably, it was not only not in February, but it was not really a revolution either. Certainly the Duma, the Provisional Government, even Ruzsky, had not set out to end the monarchy. The Romanovs no longer ruled, but the Provisional Government essentially tried to maintain its state apparatus, even its war, in its absence. It was almost as if they could not conceive of a Russia without a tsar. Meanwhile, the bourgeois forces that dominated it were contending with new sources of power in the streets, especially the soviets – councils – which were emerging among the strikers and revolutionaries. The question was whether the Provisional Government could actually assert itself and win the authority genuinely to control this huge and fractious country. The answer turned out to be that it could not.

ENTER THE BOLSHEVIKS

The next few months are often called the time of Dual Power, as the Provisional Government dominated by the Kadets (Constitutional Democrats) and the Petrograd Soviet vied for authority. Ultimately, though, neither had real power, and both could essentially neutralize the other. A particular problem for the Provincial Government was that they remained committed to the war, both so as not to alienate Russia's allies and also out of a pragmatic understanding that to sue for peace from a position of weakness would be to invite punitive terms. With the hope of being able either to hasten the end of the war, or at least gain a more favourable negotiating position, at the end of July the Kerensky offensive – named after Minister for War Alexander Kerensky – was launched to try to knock Austria-Hungary out of the war. Some 900,000 Russians took on just over 250,000 Austro-Hungarian and German troops – and lost. The subsequent counterattack saw them surrender almost all the gains in Austria-Hungary they had made in the war, take 60,000 casualties, and essentially doomed the government.

A range of revolutionary forces were waiting in the wings, not least of which was Vladimir Ilyich Ulyanov, better known as Lenin, and his Bolsheviks. The word *bolshinstvo* means 'majority', but in practice the Bolsheviks were a minority faction within the wider Social Democrat movement which – again, names can deceive – was socialist and revolutionary. However, while the bulk of them favoured incremental change while building up a mass political movement, Lenin believed in the power of a small, dedicated revolutionary vanguard.

Seeing him as a potentially useful source of instability, in April the Germans had helped him get back to Russia from exile in Switzerland. Arriving in Petrograd to a tumultuous welcome from his supporters, he immediately declared himself opposed not just to the Provisional Government, but anyone who believed in half-measures: 'The people need peace; the people need bread; the people need land. And they give you war, hunger, and no bread.'

Soon, Petrograd would be rocked by the July Days, an inchoate series of violent protests and riots triggered by the arrival of mutineers from the front. Lenin was uncharacteristically uncertain, suspecting it was too soon to try to seize power, but the government nonetheless took the opportunity to try to arrest the Bolshevik leaders, forcing Lenin briefly to flee to Finland. Without coordination or a clear goal, as the Petrograd Soviet was still unable to assert its authority over the streets, the unrest was suppressed, but the government, now led by Kerensky, was looking weaker than ever. The propertied classes were left convinced that it could not survive, let alone guarantee their security. The hungry and angry masses were hungrier and angrier than ever, and could see no hope in the existing regime. Crime was rife, as armed deserters and rural bandits alike took what they wanted, depriving the rest of what they needed. The very bonds holding the multi-ethnic empire together seemed to be fraying. Western Ukraine, after a brief period of Russian success in 1914, was back under Austro-Hungarian control. Through the 19th century a sense of Ukrainian identity had been growing, though, and in March 1917, nationalists in Russian-held Kiev created a council, the Central Rada, demanding greater autonomy. The Provisional Government bowed to necessity and recognized it – much to the chagrin of many stalwarts of the old order – and opened negotiations, potentially encouraging other minorities within the empire.

Meanwhile, the Germans were continuing to advance, and Supreme Commander General Lavr Kornilov was reaching his breaking point. Originally, he had supported the Provisional Government, and even been the man who took the tsar and his family into custody. Under his command, the 8th Army had delivered near enough the only victory during the Kerensky Offensive. Kornilov had been infuriated by the disruptive actions of the Petrograd Soviet, and especially its Order Number One, which had told soldiers to form soviets in their own units and obey its orders above those of the Provisional Government. Angry at what he saw as Kerensky's weakness, he began preparing to march on Petrograd to restore order, sending Lieutenant General Alexander Krymov and the so-called 'Wild Division' – the Caucasian Native Cavalry Division – ahead.

Kerensky tried dismissing Kornilov, but to no avail. In desperation, he had to turn to the Petrograd Soviet and the Bolsheviks for survival. Revolutionaries working on the railways halted the trains bringing Kornilov's men to the capital. Bolshevik leaders such as Leon Trotsky were let out of prison to muster some 25,000 of their supporters into Red Guard detachments to protect Petrograd, armed from the government's own arsenals. The 'Wild Division' was likely chosen on the assumption that soldiers from the North Caucasus would have fewer compunctions about firing on Russians, but a delegation from the revolutionary Union of North Caucasian Peoples persuaded them to stand down, and they arrested their officers and hoisted red flags. Kornilov's attempted putsch dissolved in chaos and mutiny; he was arrested (though soon to escape), and Krymov shot himself in disgrace.

RED REVOLUTION

However, the Provisional Government had been humiliated, the power of the Soviet demonstrated – and the Bolsheviks were now armed, with no intention of handing back their guns. Even so, many of the revolutionaries were still uncertain, thinking their best bet was a coalition government with the Kadets. Lenin scorned such half-measures: returning to Petrograd, he harangued and cajoled his Central Committee into an armed uprising. By this time, they dominated the Petrograd Soviet, and through that, its Military Revolutionary Committee, prepared to seize power. When Kerensky incautiously shut down the Bolshevik newspaper *Pravda* (Truth), this provided the pretext to act, and on 25 October by their old calendar (now 7 November), they struck.

At the signal of a blank shell fired from the cruiser *Aurora*, Red Guards and revolutionary sailors from the Baltic Fleet stormed the Winter Palace and arrested the Provisional Government. Almost without a shot, the city's railway stations, telephone exchanges, arsenals and power stations were also taken. For all the mythology about a popular rising, this was a coup – and a successful one, at that. That was the easy bit. Lenin issued a series of decrees that seemed to offer peace, bread and land: an armistice, bread supplies for the cities, and the transfer of land to the peasants. Meanwhile, elections would be held to a Constituent Assembly to shape this new state, while a new Council of People's Commissars, chaired by Lenin himself, ran the government for the moment. Making good on those promises, though, would be difficult. In the elections to the Constituent Assembly, the Bolsheviks got only 24 per cent of the vote (although twice that among soldiers), with the rival Socialist Revolutionaries (SRs) getting about half. Lenin had not staged a revolution only to hand it to anyone else: the Assembly sat for a single day in January 1918, electing senior Socialist Revolutionary Party member Viktor Chernov as its president, before Red Guards dissolved it at bayonet point.

Meanwhile, delivering on peace was proving difficult, too. Initially, the Bolsheviks assumed that, following their example, the exhausted proletarians of Europe would rise up and sweep away their wicked old imperialist regimes. Newly appointed Commissar for Foreign Affairs Trotsky said of his position, 'I shall issue a few revolutionary proclamations to the peoples and then close up shop.' The idea was to string out peace talks long enough for these revolutions to erupt. However, as the Germans continued to advance and even toughened their demands, Lenin convinced his peers that peace had to be bought, whatever the price. The result was the swingeing Treaty of Brest-Litovsk, where an armistice was agreed on 15 December 1917, even though it would take until 3 March 1918 for the actual treaty to be hammered out. The new government ceded the Baltic States to Germany and Kars in the South Caucasus to Turkey. It recognized the independence of the new Ukrainian People's Republic (UNR) and agreed to pay 6 billion German gold marks in reparations.

Not only did the harsh terms of the treaty dismay even many Bolsheviks, but it led inexorably to civil war. It freed up army units which had been locked into the front line, and while many simply disintegrated as conscripts seized the opportunity to head home, others became the core of a series of so-called White or counter-revolutionary factions, led by figures such as Kornilov, Admiral Alexander Kolchak and General Anton Denikin. It triggered small-scale Allied interventions intended either to support the Whites in the hope they could, as

Winston Churchill would put it, 'strangle the infant Bolshevism in its cradle', or prevent the Germans from seizing crucial assets. The initial deployment of British troops in Murmansk in 1918, for example, was actually welcomed by the Bolsheviks, as they – and the French, Italians and Canadians who soon joined them – were tasked with preventing German incursions to take the northern ports. The Treaty did not stop the Germans, who showed that their support for the UNR was just a pretence, making Ukraine a protectorate under Field Marshal Hermann von Eichhorn, disbanding the Central Rada and installing General Pavlo Skoropadsky as hetman. Finally, the treaty was also the last straw for those SRs who had still been willing to work with the Bolsheviks. In July 1918, they staged an abortive rising against the new government, which in March had moved its capital back to Moscow, and most of their leaders were arrested.

In order to retain power, the Reds, the new Bolshevik regime, would have to fight a brutal civil war against all comers. They would ultimately be successful, but it would be a darkly formative process, in which the last vestiges of idealism and democracy present within the movement would be lost in the desperate fight for survival. From it would emerge a new Soviet state, one that was ruthless, centralized, militarized and oppressive.

THE RUSSIAN CIVIL WAR

There is no clear start or end date for the Russian Civil War, nor a neat sense of its trajectory or even participants. While often characterized as a struggle of Reds versus Whites, not only were the counter-revolutionary forces numerous and often implicitly competing with each other, but there were also rival socialist movements such as Komuch, the Committee of the Constituent Assembly, a Socialist Revolutionary Party-dominated army active around Samara and Kazan in the south. Then there were nationalist armies hoping to use the opportunity to wrench themselves free of the empire, and fully 13 different foreign intervention forces, from the American North Russia Expeditionary Force, better known as the Polar Bear Expedition, deployed to Arkhangelsk, to the 2,000 Chinese troops who briefly occupied Vladivostok – and my granddad. Then there were wild cards such as Nestor Makhno's anarchist Revolutionary Insurgent Army of Ukraine, to the Czechoslovak Legion which ended up fighting its way all across the country along the Trans-Siberian Railway, to be evacuated from Vladivostok, or even 'Bloody Baron' Roman von Ungern-Sternberg, an unstable and bloodthirsty renegade White general who eventually set himself up as a warlord in Mongolia with the dream of reviving the Mongol Empire.

Even as the Treaty of Brest-Litovsk was being finalized, German troops were pushing Russian forces out of Finland, and with the support of not just the Germans but also Poles, nationalists in Belarus declared an independent state. That said, like Ukraine, 'independent' Belarus was really just a German protectorate. Likewise, as German forces pushed into the Don region in May, they threw their weight behind General Pyotr Krasnov's Cossacks of the All-Great Don Army, which at the start of 1919 would unite with the Volunteer Army, first established by General Kornilov and then after his death in April 1918 led by the rabidly nationalist and anti-Semitic Denikin, forming the Armed Forces of the South of Russia. When his forces were eventually pushed back to Crimea in 1920, he would be succeeded by 'Black Baron' Pyotr Vrangel, who led the evacuation of almost 150,000 men, women and children by sea as Bolshevik forces closed in on them.

Off to the east, in Omsk, an unstable alliance of leftist and rightist anti-Bolshevik forces known as the Directory, or the Provisional All-Russian Government, was broken by a White coup in November 1918, which elevated Admiral Kolchak as military dictator with the grandiose title of Supreme Ruler of Russia. Meanwhile, there were also White forces in the Baltic States and Finland, who in 1919 declared their own Government of the North-West Region under General Nikolai Yudenich. He was backed by London, which forced him to acknowledge Estonian independence, and launched two attacks on Petrograd in spring and summer 1919, with 17,000 troops supported by six tanks supplied with crews by Britain. When the Bolsheviks recognized the independence of the Baltic States and signed a peace treaty with Estonia, though, his army was stood down and a third would end up in Russian prisons.

Down in the Caucasus, Georgia, Armenia and Azerbaijan together established the Transcaucasian Democratic Federative Republic in April 1918, a body which lasted a whole month before falling apart, the three nations becoming independent states, until they were reconquered in

1920–21. These were only a few of a multitude of short-lived and self-declared states that would largely be brought back into Moscow's fold – by force, subversion or negotiation – through the Civil War. Some could have been perfectly viable, others were positively ephemeral, such as the Soviet Republic of Soldiers and Fortress-Builders of Naissaar. Declared in December 1917 by some 90 sailors at a naval base on an Estonian island, for two months they claimed independence and taxed the local population, before being chased out by the Germans.

The new Soviet government would seem outmatched and was certainly outnumbered, but it did have some crucial advantages. It held the main cities, the nodes of the communications network and the home of industry. Its enemies were divided, often rivals. It was able to draw on substantial numbers of soldiers and sailors, and was pragmatic enough also to recruit tsarist officers as 'military specialists'. It had a powerful propaganda message that, once foreign powers began supporting some White factions, could be turbocharged with nationalism. When that did not work, it also demonstrated its capacity to use astonishingly brutal methods. This was an ugly conflict by any standards, marked by anti-Jewish pogroms (especially by Denikin's men), reprisals against civilians and the murder of suspected enemy agents and collaborators, as well as forced conscription and the requisitioning of food from starving peasants. However, the truth of the matter is that, in the main, the 'Red Terror' was more effective, organized and brutal than its White counterpart, especially through the operations of its new political police, the Cheka, the All-Russian Extraordinary Commission for Combating Counter-Revolution, Profiteering and Corruption.

Broadly speaking, after a perilous 1918, in which the Bolsheviks were pushed back to Central European Russia and parts of Central Asia (and Nicholas and his family were murdered, out of fear they might be rescued and become a focus for counter-revolution), 1919 saw the Red Army weather a series of White offensives. They lacked coordination, coming from the east in March, the south in July, and the west in October, which meant that the Reds could use their control of the railways to move forces from one front to another to check each in turn. The end of the First World War in November 1918 and subsequent dissolution of the Habsburg Empire and disarmament of Germany also took away the pressure from the west. By the end of that year, the Reds were on the offensive. In 1920, they began to throttle the Whites, and could also begin to turn to forcing secessionist elements back under their control. Most foreign forces withdrew that year (although Japanese troops lingered in the Russian Far East until 1925). By 1921, the divided Ukrainians had largely been subdued, and although the 1919–21 Polish–Soviet War was a defeat, the 1921 Peace of Riga that followed did fix the borders of Soviet Ukraine and Belarus.

THE SIEGES OF TSARITSYN, 1918–19

Trying to chart the ebbs and flows of this multi-vector conflict in a single chapter would be impossible, but the successive sieges of the Tsaritsyn help illustrate some of its trends and complexities. A Volga River port and factory city in south-west Russia and Bolshevik stronghold thanks to its large industrial workforce, it would have a torrid half century, given that Tsaritsyn, now Volgograd, was known as Stalingrad between 1925 and 1961. Three times, Krasnov's All-Great Don Army would besiege it: in July–September 1918, September–October 1918 and January–February 1919. Later that year, in May–June 1919, the Volunteer Army would manage to seize Tsaritsyn, only for it to be retaken by the Red Army in January 1920. It was an episode of the wider war that would see key figures such as future dictator Joseph Stalin and Commissar for War Trotsky in contention, foreshadowing their later, dramatic break. Where Cossack cavalry (on both sides), armoured trains, workers' militias and British tanks would all play a role.

Krasnov's first assault on Tsaritsyn saw him assemble 45,000 men and 150 guns in an attempt to sweep the Reds from the northern reaches of the Don and take Tsaritsyn to prevent it from being used as a base for operations against his flank. They slightly outnumbered the defenders, with an apparent advantage in artillery, so Krasnov sent two armies directly against the city, and a third, smaller force to block any potential reinforcements. The challenge of command in a state defined by a political movement quickly emerged for the Reds. Trotsky, as Commissar for War, had appointed Lieutenant General Andrei Snesarev as commander of the North Caucasus Military District, which included Tsaritsyn. He proved able and energetic, but soon clashed with the newly arrived representative of the Council of People's Commissars, Joseph Stalin. His duties were strictly to ensure the flow of grain to the centre, but he began interfering with military affairs. He had a deep-rooted suspicion of the 'military specialists' who had crossed over from the tsarist officer corps and furthermore considered Snesarev one of his rival Trotsky's men. He had him arrested and replaced with one of his own cronies, the deeply mediocre Kliment Voroshilov. In order to avoid an open split in the Bolshevik Party leadership, Moscow exonerated Snesarev but left Stalin and Voroshilov in effective command.

Stalin used the Cheka to continue purging the local military commanders, while complaining to Lenin that 'the situation in the south is not easy. The Military Council inherited a completely disrupted situation, partly thanks to the inertia of the former military commander, partly conspiracy'. It very much sounded as if he were getting his excuses for defeat in first. However, fortunately for the Reds, the Whites were unable properly to coordinate their operations and thus failed to prevent the reinforcement of the city, especially thanks to the presence of several armoured trains, which gave the Reds longer-ranged artillery than anything the Whites possessed, as well as river boats of the Volga flotilla. Although 12,000 troops under General Konstantin Mamantov did make it into the city's suburbs, they were then confronted by trench lines which had been hastily built by dragooned local citizens, forced to labour by the Cheka. Mamantov's men lacked the artillery to make much headway and were forced to withdraw when their flank was exposed to a Red counterattack. The city held, but at terrible cost, losing 60,000 soldiers and civilians to the Whites' 12,000.

A second attack by Mamantov in September was better prepared with a slightly smaller force of 38,000 men, but supported by eight armoured trains of their own and heavier artillery. However, Tsaritsyn had also been reinforced, and was guarded by 40,000 men and 13 armoured trains. Nonetheless, the Whites this time had a clearer plan of attack. Pushing back the Red 10th Army, they had reached the outskirts of the city by early October, while flying columns of Cossacks managed to cut its railway links. (Meanwhile, Stalin again sent a telegram to Lenin demanding that Trotsky be investigated for allegedly undermining Tsaritsyn's position; Stalin was recalled to Moscow instead.) As the Whites ground forward, the 1st and 2nd Peasant Regiments – essentially, levies press-ganged from the countryside – defected to the Whites, opening up a substantial gap in the Reds' defensive line. In a desperate move, a column of armoured trains was moved to bombard the attackers, backed by regular artillery. Their combined fire was devastating, but was not enough to prevent advance White forces slipping closer and closer to the centre of the city.

The tide was turned by unexpected reinforcements in the form of the 1st 'Steel' Rifle Division. Its commander, Dmitry Zhloba, had quarrelled with the commander-in-chief of the North Caucasus Front and so had decided unilaterally to support Tsaritsyn. His men made a 500-mile forced march and on 15 October fell on the flank of the attackers, routing the Astrakhan Regiment and forcing the Whites again to retreat lest they face encirclement.

A third attack, launched on 1 January 1919, was less of a serious threat, not least because weather conditions made resupply and cavalry movements difficult, but in May, Denikin ordered Vrangel to take Tsaritsyn, to which end he assembled three corps from his Caucasus Army. With the defence of the city now back in the hands of an experienced officer, Leonid Klyuyev, it was much more seriously defended, with two rings of barbed wire, earthworks and trenches. However, the needs of other fronts meant that the garrison had been scaled down to 16,000 infantry and 5,000 cavalry, and this would also be a larger and more carefully planned attack than the first three.

A first assault, on three axes, was eventually pushed back after three days of bitter fighting. However, this time there was no 'Steel' Division waiting in the wings, and the Whites not only guarded their flanks well, but they also quickly repaired the railway bridge across the nearby Sal River, allowing them to bring heavier equipment into play, including both armoured trains and 17 tanks supplied by the British: nine machine-gun-armed Medium Mark A Whippets, one of which was crewed by British soldiers, and eight heavy Mark Is with cannon. The tanks ploughed through the city's defences, shrugging off machine-gun and rifle fire and driving horrified Reds – who had never before seen them in action – to flight. The Whites exploited these breaches to storm the city, and after two days' hard fighting, the city was taken. Not, admittedly, for long, as from late August the Reds began to counterattack, first launching raids along the Volga, taking advantage of their riverine superiority, then launching an on-and-off siege that saw it retaken on 3 January 1920.

The back-and-forth flow of territorial control; the equally fluid chain of command that saw Bolshevik politics trump military realism and a division commander opt to relieve Tsaritsyn on his own authority; the use of terror and conscripted labour – all of these were characteristic of the Russian Civil War. Ultimately, the Reds would win, but only at the cost of becoming a militarized authoritarianism, and at terrible cost: all told, anything up to 12 million died, mostly civilians, and many from famine and disease. In 1922, this new state (technically several, albeit all under Bolshevik control: the Russian and Transcaucasian Soviet Federative Socialist Republics and the Ukrainian and Belorussian Soviet Socialist Republics) was formally renamed the Union of Soviet Socialist Republics, but even as Lenin looked to potential means of rebuilding the economy through partial liberalism, he suffered the first of a series of strokes that would lead to his death in 1924 and the rise of Stalin.

Want To Know More?

Evan Mawdsley's *The Russian Civil War* (Birlinn, 2001) and W. Bruce Lincoln's *Red Victory* (Simon & Schuster, 1990) are classic overviews of this conflict, while David Bullock's *The Russian Civil War 1918–22* (Osprey, 2008) is a shorter overview. *A Nasty Little War: The West's Fight to Reverse the Russian Revolution* (John Murray, 2024) by Anna Reid is a very readable account of the Allied interventions. For a change of pace, *Triumph of Chaos* (Clash of Arms, 2019) is a lovingly, almost obsessively detailed wargame of the Russian Civil War, not for the faint-hearted, for whom the quick but surprisingly engaging solitaire game *Soviet Dawn* (Worthington, 2021) may be a better bet.

21

The Great Patriotic War

Stalingrad, 1942–43

1917–26	Basmachestvo
1918–20	Russo-Polish War
1918–22	Russian Civil War
1924	Death of Lenin
	Attempted putsch in Estonia
1936–38	Great Terror
1936–39	Spanish Civil War
1938–39	Clashes with Japan
1939	Molotov-Ribbentrop Pact
1939–40	Winter War with Finland
1941–45	Great Patriotic War

Nothing, nothing at all, seems to have anything like the same historical resonance in Russia today as the Great Patriotic War, the genuinely epic and truly existential struggle against Nazi Germany. From my own experience talking to Russian students, though, what is striking is just how long and deep a shadow it casts. Young men and women who could provide chapter and verse on how 8,000 tanks brawled at the Battle of Kursk, or why Marshal Konev was actually a better commander than the more famous Zhukov, often also have an at best vague sense of the extravagant brutality of Stalin's rule in the preceding decades, shaped by the Gulag labour camps, all-embracing terror, and a succession of crises and wars, civil, foreign, declared and undeclared. This may be the result of a new propaganda that seeks to downplay Stalin's crimes, but perhaps also simply that there is a limit to how much inhumanity most people want to internalize.

After all, the end of the Civil War hardly brought peace and tranquillity to the Soviets. The country was in ruins, the economy in chaos, and in March 1921, even the sailors and Naval Infantry (marines) of Kronstadt naval base, once at the very vanguard of the revolution, rose against the Soviet government, believing it to have become too dictatorial. In perhaps a vindication of their beliefs, they were crushed, their leaders tried in secret and hundreds shot. In Central Asia, the *Basmachi* – a term derived from the Uzbek word for bandits – would continue their sporadic rebellion, especially in the Fergana Valley stretching from Uzbekistan into Kyrgyzstan and Tajikistan, into the 1930s, although generally it was considered effectively suppressed by 1926. Indeed, in 1929–30, in a harbinger of future disaster, it even tempted the Soviets into cross-border incursions into Afghanistan. The fraternal state, for all its protestations of peaceful intent, would spend an inordinate amount of time fighting, at home and abroad.

SOCIALISM IN ONE COUNTRY
(AND SUBVERSION EVERYWHERE ELSE)

Trotsky had advocated permanent and aggressive support of revolution abroad, but Stalin was much more conservative, at least at first. Less concerned with Marxist-Leninist ideology, more interested in consolidating his own grip on power, his policy was 'Socialism in One Country' – essentially, sacrificing dreams of world revolution in the name of securing the USSR. Nonetheless, the Bolshevik Party, now the Communist Party, was an intensely political and theoretical movement, which genuinely saw itself as the vanguard of a global movement. A combination of this outlook and a keen awareness that the capitalist world was at once more powerful and also implacably hostile, meant that the Soviet government was from the first committed to campaigns of subversion abroad, the kind of multi-vector propaganda, disinformation and disruption operations now called 'hybrid' or 'grey zone' warfare. The Communist International (Comintern) movement, for example, was committed to supporting wider Soviet interests, through disruption and subversion. It stirred up strikes behind the lines during the 1918–20 Soviet-Polish War, for example, and provided the pretext for the reconquest of Azerbaijan and Armenia in 1920 by staging Communist coups, so that the new governments could invite the Red Army in (local sympathizers were not as numerous in Georgia, though, so it had simply to be invaded the next year).

In 1924, Comintern was used to coordinate with the Estonian Communist Party in a plot to use a general strike as the pretext for a coup by domestic revolutionaries, supported by Soviet agents, so as to invite the 'fraternal assistance' of the Red Army. The venture fizzled out when the security forces and general public responded swiftly and forcefully, and the Soviets opted not to go ahead with the planned intervention. Nonetheless, this was in many ways an early example of what would become a staple of the Cold War and then Vladimir Putin's political war with the West.

This balance between hostility and caution would be the watchword of Stalin's early policies. He was perfectly willing to sacrifice foreign sympathizers and Communists if there was advantage to be gained, as his real focus was at home. Stalin was, after all, from the first aware of the need to defend the socialist Motherland before everything else and that this meant modernization: as he would warn so memorably in 1931, in the past, Russia had been 'beaten' by all kinds of enemies 'because of her backwardness'. Successive tsars had been aware of the need for thoroughgoing agrarian reform to drive industrialization, but had been unable or unwilling to act with the kind of ruthlessness and focus this would demand. Stalin, who quickly purged the Party of any actual or potential rivals and established himself as unquestioned autocrat, would have no such constraints.

In 1928, he launched his first Five-Year Plan for economic development, envisaging a 'Great Leap Forward' in heavy industry. This would have to be on the back of an agrarian revolution, and the next year he launched a campaign to collectivize the countryside, essentially forcing peasants to become employees of the state – in many ways a 20th-century spin on serfdom – in massive new collective and state farms. Many resisted, especially in richer regions such as the black-earth lands of Ukraine, and Stalin responded with extravagant brutality. At least a million were deported to the Gulag labour camps, and famine largely resulting from the forced requisition of grain killed at least 6 million, especially in Ukraine. In its own murderous way, though, collectivization worked, shattering the old social order of the countryside and giving the state unprecedented control, which it used to extract a greater share of production. This it spent on funding industrialization, not least by selling grain to the capitalist West in return for technology and expertise. An essentially agrarian nation was reshaped as an industrial powerhouse – and a warfighting one, at that.

THE RED ARMY

The resulting development of the Workers' and Peasants' Red Army, though, would prove a difficult process. The same features of Stalinism that would arm and equip the Soviet military would also come close to shattering its ability to fight. In 1936–38, the USSR was stalked by the Great Terror, in which Stalin systematically purged the Party of anyone he considered a rival, a potential threat, or simply insufficiently loyal. In the process, he gutted the Red Army's officer corps. In just 18 months, three out of five marshals, eight of nine admirals, 13 of 15 army commanders, and some 55,000 officers overall were dismissed, killed or sent to the Gulags. Stalin finally had his revenge on those 'military specialists', and in the process also managed to waste some of his best commanders and theoreticians. Marshal Mikhail Tukhachevsky, for example, whose thinking about the 'deep battle' is still relevant today – and who led the suppression of the Kronstadt mutiny – was shot after a show trial for his alleged membership of a mythical 'Trotskyist Anti-Soviet Military Organization', which revolved around his signed confession. Notionally freely given, it later proved to be spattered with his own blood.

Until the Second World War the Red Army (technically then still known as the RKKA, the Workers' and Peasants' Red Army) would suffer from what were often the mutually opposed dictates of politics and professionalism. The Bolsheviks originally held to naïve and utopian notions of a popular militia formed from volunteers under local soviets, their commanders elected by their men, their orders subject to discussion within the unit. Indeed, they immediately abolished formal ranks, replacing them simply with positions, such as 'company commander'. These notions quickly broke down in face of the need to fight sustained and large-scale operations, and so while there were indeed volunteer 'shock' units raised from dedicated Bolsheviks, increasingly a more conventional kind of army emerged, not least thanks to the introduction of the *voyenspetsy*, the 'military specialists' drawn from the tsarist officer corps. By the end of the Civil War, they would account for more than 80 per cent of regimental, divisional and corps commanders – albeit under the steely gaze of military commissars, political officers granted wide powers to overrule line officers giving the 'wrong' orders and monitor the zeal and ideological purity of the unit as a whole. By spring 1918, conscription had been reintroduced, and by the end of the year, the Red Army was already almost half a million strong. Next year, a standard uniform was introduced, with the iconic red star.

Trotsky was very much at the forefront of this recreation of a more conventional army. In 1918, he had written, 'we need a real armed force, constructed on the basis of military science.' In this, he faced considerable opposition from the more idealistic Bolsheviks. The pragmatic Lenin backed him, while the experience of the Civil War demonstrated the value of a strong chain of command. By the end of 1920, the Red Army had swollen to 5.5 million men, substantially larger than all the White forces put together, and a testament to the Bolsheviks' organizational capabilities. Nonetheless, as the war came to a close, this needed to be reduced, both to satisfy an exhausted populace and also to free up labour for the fields and factories.

By 1924, it had shrunk to half a million, again. As Trotsky lost authority and Stalin rose, for a while the Red Army was turned into a force largely based on territorial units maintained as skeleton units, which would be bulked up by reservists and conscripts in case of war. This was a model geared more for national defence than offence, and reflected the state's lack of resources at the time. As the state began to get a tighter grip on grain production and also gained more confidence, in 1935 it rolled back the territorial initiative and began rebuilding a Red Army fit for a dangerous new era. Expansion began, and by 1939, the age of conscription was lowered from 21 to 19. By the time of war with Nazi Germany, it had grown back up to 5.4 million men. Furthermore, the fruits of industrialization were beginning to close the technology gap with the USSR's potential antagonists. Through the 1930s, the number of artillery pieces increased seven-fold, and the number of tanks ten-fold, for example.

REVOLUTIONARY WARFARE

What was striking was that although the Red Army would never have all the resources it would want or need – its backbone was the simple infantryman with a Mosin–Nagant 91/30 rifle dating back to the 1890s, marching to battle on foot – it would also prove a hotbed of innovation, in theory if not always in practice. In part, this was because of their own experiences: unlike the blood-soaked stalemates of the Western Front, the Eastern Front and the Civil War had been characterized by fluid manoeuvre operations which not only left the Soviets still committed to retaining cavalry forces (despite Trotsky's sense that they were 'a very aristocratic kind of troops, commanded by princes, barons, and counts') but early devotees of fast-moving mechanized warfare. Furthermore, Stalin's industrialization brought within it a modernist, futurist cultural turn in Soviet culture, fascinated with the dynamism, speed and power of industry, which left the government open to new ideas capitalizing on emerging technologies.

Tukhachevsky, for example, was an outspoken and – until his fall from grace – persuasive advocate for the mechanization of the Red Army. This encouraged Soviet designers to work on their own tank designs, initially largely based on the British Vickers E, imported in 1930. By 1935, the Soviets could field more tanks than the rest of the world combined. Many were light, but the T-35, a 50-ton 'land battleship' with five gun turrets and ten crew, although cramped and unreliable, demonstrated that they could also build on a different scale. Nor were the Soviets blind to new possibilities in the air. Although it remained a prototype, they even rebuilt a mammoth Tupolev TB-3 bomber as a flying aircraft carrier, bearing up to five fighters. Likewise, the Soviets were early adopters of parachute-dropped airborne forces, establishing their first dedicated unit in 1930, but even before then made the first-ever combat drop. In 1929, soldiers were dropped to break the siege of the town of Gharm in Tajikistan by *Basmachi* rebels.

Meanwhile, military thinkers such as Alexander Svechin and Georgy Isserson were also arguably ahead of their time in how they addressed questions of war in the 20th century. The former, for example, explored the notion that there was an intermediary, operational stage of warfare between the tactical (winning the battle) and the strategic (winning the war), and is very much associated with an 'attritional' approach to warfare, wearing the enemy down through defensive operations. Isserson, by contrast, along with Vladimir Triandafillov, advocated an 'annihilation' approach, winning by 'deep battle', aggressively driving fast-moving forces into the enemy's rear to disrupt their capacity to fight.

To a considerable extent, though, this period of imaginative and innovative thinking was brought to an end by Stalin's purge of the officer corps. Triandafillov died in an air crash in 1931, which was possibly a mercy given that Tukhachevsky, Svechin and so many more of the creative military thinkers ended up killed by Stalin's executioners, and their ideas became heresies. Many of the large mechanized units developed for deep battle, for example, were disbanded, their tanks parcelled out in penny packets as infantry support. One of the reasons why Soviet tank and air forces did not acquit themselves well in the Second World War was precisely that, having been early adopters in doctrinal as well as technological terms, they fell behind in both in the mid to late 1930s, only belatedly realizing their mistake when they found themselves again tested in real battle: intervening in the Spanish Civil War (1936–39), fighting a small, undeclared war with Japan (1939) and invading Finland (1939–40).

While Fascist Italy and Nazi Germany supported the Nationalists in Spain with tens of thousands of combat troops, Stalin's support for the Republicans was largely confined to equipment and military advisers. Watching the German Condor Legion try out new equipment and tactics in Spain, as well as blood a new generation of pilots and commanders, was a chastening experience for the more realistic among the Soviet observers deployed there. However, this was quickly eclipsed by more direct tests of their capabilities in 1939. After Japan occupied Manchuria in 1931–32 and set up a puppet regime there, it had begun to cast its eyes to Mongolia – then allied to Moscow – and dislodging the Soviets from their positions in the Far East. There had been repeated low-level clashes between Japanese and Soviet troops and border forces, culminating in a two-week series of battles in July–August 1938, when Marshal Vasily Blyukher – who, frankly, had been promoted beyond his capabilities – had his men take the disputed Changkufeng Heights. A smaller Japanese force managed to take and hold the Heights, but eventually withdrew as part of a diplomatic settlement. Nonetheless, the precise border between Japan's Manchurian puppet state, Manchukuo, and Mongolia was still under question, with Tokyo claiming the border was 10 miles further west than Moscow and Ulaanbaatar, who instead placed it along the Khalkhin Gol River. Blyukher was withdrawn and replaced by General Georgy Zhukov, who would be one of the great commanders of the Second World War, with the mandate to end Japanese 'provocations' by giving them a bloody nose and end this distraction from Europe, where a much more terrible war was looming. Meanwhile, the Japanese Kwantung Army, based in Manchukuo, was restive and known for its poor discipline, especially among its units of Manchu Chinese auxiliaries. Many of its officers were spoiling for a fight.

When, in May 1939, some Mongolian cavalrymen crossed into disputed territories in search of grazing for their mounts, they were attacked by Manchu troops. This led to an escalating series of clashes that soon involved Japanese and Soviet regulars, as companies gave way to battalions, and battalions to regiments. By the end, 60,000 Soviet and Mongolian troops were squaring off against 75,000 Japanese, while the eventual commitment of over 1,000 aircraft was also unprecedented for a conflict of this scale. By September, the Soviets had ultimately won this undeclared war, but again, despite Zhukov's evident strengths as a commander, many of the lessons learned were unwelcome. Their junior and middle-ranking officers were often amateurish or rigid. Their pilots were consistently outflown by the Japanese. While they had more airpower and heavy armour at their disposal than the Kwantung Army, these were often already dated. Every Japanese aeroplane had its own radio, for example, allowing greater coordination. Although Soviet bombers had them, fighters relied on visual cues, such as the laying down of white fabric arrows on the ground pointing pilots towards the enemy. In the earlier 1930s, the Soviets had dreamed up complex and sophisticated notions of highly mobile warfare in which tanks, mechanized infantry, paratroopers, artillery and airpower would all be combined seamlessly to punch through enemy lines and break their forces from the rear. It seemed increasingly as if the Red Army simply lacked the commanders, communications and training to turn this into reality.

THE SLIDE TO WAR

Even more sobering would be the experience of the Winter War with Finland. Stalin had had no real doubts that war was inevitable with a Nazi Germany that regarded Slavs as subhuman and the rolling plans of

Russia as suitable *Lebensraum*, 'living space' for future Aryan colonists. He had tried to explore the prospects for an alliance with Britain and France, but they were still suspicious of the Soviet state and did not show any great enthusiasm. Stalin's suspicions that, ideally, they would have seen Nazi and Soviet totalitarianisms rip each other apart, and then deal with the battered victor, were not wholly unfounded. Early in 1939, negotiations on a tripartite alliance with Paris and London were under way but only slowly. When it emerged that the head of the British delegation to the all-important military component of the talks, retired admiral Sir Reginald Drax, was not actually authorized to make any promises, and had been instructed to drag the negotiations out as long as possible, the Soviets effectively gave up on the idea. One of the key problems was, after all, that after the purges and the indifferent performance in both Spain and Mongolia, there was what turned out to be an exaggerated sense of Soviet weakness. British Prime Minister Neville Chamberlain not only openly mistrusted the Soviets, but openly described as 'pathetic' those who 'believe that Russia is the key to our salvation'.

With Britain and France apparently unreceptive, Stalin, ever the ruthless pragmatist, turned to making a deal with Germany. The two pariah nations had a past record of economic and even military cooperation, but after May 1939, when Stalin replaced as People's Commissar for Foreign Affairs Maxim Litvinov – a Jew, who had supported the tripartite talks – with the pliable Vyacheslav Molotov, the USSR began to sound out the scope for secret negotiations with Germany. On 23 August 1939, Nazi Germany and Soviet Russia announced a ten-year non-aggression pact. A secret, supplementary protocol to this Molotov-Ribbentrop Pact defined their respective spheres of interest, giving Moscow free rein in the Baltic States, Finland and parts of Romania, while the two countries agreed to partition Poland between them, with the Germans getting the lion's share.

Neither Hitler nor Stalin had any intention of being bound by this piece of paper. However, Hitler – who had fought in the First World War and was acutely aware of just how difficult Germany had found fighting on both the Western and Eastern Fronts – wanted the USSR neutralized while he snapped up the rest of the continent. Likewise Stalin, aware of the relative backwardness of his forces, wanted time to arm. Crucially, and very nearly catastrophically, he was convinced he had won himself at least until spring 1942, and his armament plans were drawn up to match.

In any case, on 1 September 1939, German troops crashed into Poland, and within a week were on the outskirts of Warsaw. On 17 September, the Soviets attacked from the east, and despite valiant resistance, by mid-October Poland was under enemy occupation – and the Second World War had begun. While Hitler focused on his western flank, preparing for an attack on France the coming spring, Stalin looked to his western flank, too, out of a combination of opportunistic imperialism and defensive preparation. The Baltic States were threatened into allowing forward basing of Soviet troops and Finland was faced with similar demands, as well as the redrawing of their border to provide greater security for Leningrad, the city that had been St Petersburg. The Finns refused.

In November 1939, then, the Soviets threw 21 divisions, almost 450,000 men, into an invasion of Finland intended to bring the whole country under Moscow's control. The Finns were outnumbered but tenacious, inventive and, just as important, better prepared for temperatures that could go down to as low as -43 degrees centigrade. The Soviets, by contrast, had a detailed plan of attack, but one which failed properly to account for the geography and conditions, and even when they had clear strengths, often misused them. They initially, for example, threw their tanks at the enemy in frontal charges as if they were medieval knights, allowing the Finns to block them with improvised obstacles and then burn them out with the firebombs that, ironically enough, came to be known as Molotov cocktails. Likewise, in the Battle of Raate Road in January 1940, in what would be an eerie harbinger of the mismanaged attack on Kyiv in 2022, some 14,000 troops from the Soviet 44th and 163rd Rifle Divisions were retreating along the road from Suomussalmi, when they were ambushed. With its way forward and back blocked, the column was destroyed piecemeal by a force less than half its size, which only ended up taking 400 casualties to the Soviets' 8,000. Amidst the spoils later gathered by the Finns were not only much-needed ammunition and tanks, but even the instruments of a military band that the overconfident Soviets had included, so sure were they of impending victory.

Although the initial commander, Kirill Meretskov, had bullishly claimed that the whole country would be occupied in a couple of weeks, at most, it would take more than three months before the Soviets, heavily reinforced and with their goals substantially scaled back, were able to impose a deal on the Finns. They concentrated 14 divisions into an assault on just a 10-mile stretch of the defensive Mannerheim Line, and once they had broken through into the Karelian Isthmus, then even the stubborn Finns had to concede. Finland remained independent – but at the cost of 11 per cent of its territory, ceded to Moscow as a security buffer. It was a victory for the USSR, but a Pyrrhic one. It had cost a third of a million casualties (more than half to frostbite and illness), and the lacklustre performance of the Red Army had confirmed to Hitler and the Western Allies alike that the Soviet Union was a paper tiger (or bear?). It would also ensure that Finland would join Germany in its invasion of the USSR, in its so-called Continuation War.

As for Meretskov, he was arguably lucky. In early 1941, Stalin publicly upbraided him, calling him 'courageous, capable, but without principles, spineless'. Things could have gone very badly for him had the Red Army not needed all the experienced officers it could find. (Even so, he was arrested by the NKVD political police, but released after two gruelling months of beatings and torture.) After all, for all that Stalin was convinced he had until 1942 before he had to fight the Germans, the storm that was Operation *Barbarossa*, the largest offensive in history, was about to break, and the USSR would be fighting for its life.

OPERATION *BARBAROSSA*

On the morning of Sunday, 22 June 1941, 7,000 German artillery pieces blasted the Soviet lines, along with more than 2,500 combat aircraft. Behind them came some 3 million German and allied troops, including 19 *panzer* (tank) divisions and fully 30 divisions of Finnish and Romanian troops, eager to be in on the presumed kill. In any authoritarian regime, the most dangerous potential point of failure is the top, and this certainly proved the case here. The Soviets had considerable forewarning, from agents and intercepts, to deserters coming over the line the night before, warning that they had orders to attack. Yet Stalin was convinced that he had won more time, and that this was a cynical plot by the British to try to provoke him into starting a war, so until it was too late he ordered his troops to refrain from taking up combat positions.

Hitler had declared that 'we have only to kick in the door and the whole rotten structure will come crashing down', and this was one almighty kick. In the first day alone, Soviet forces along the almost 1,000-mile border had been pushed back, enveloped or shattered, and almost 1,500 aircraft were destroyed on the ground. The 'rotten structure', though, would prove a great deal more resilient than Hitler had anticipated, and a combination of ruthless tyranny, obdurate patriotism, industrial production and foreign assistance would see the Soviets through the initial crisis. As with Napoleon before him, eventually Hitler would be forced into a painful, hard-fought retreat as defence became counterattack and eventual victory.

The German equivalent to 'deep battle', the *Blitzkrieg*, or 'Lightning War', likewise relied on taking fullest advantage of the new capabilities of mechanization and airpower. Armoured formations would punch breaches in the enemy line, fragmenting it so that the individual remnants could be enveloped and destroyed by the follow-on infantry, while air attacks – including the notorious Ju 87 *Stuka* dive bombers – disrupted their attempts to reform, as well as their lines of supply and communications. Tactics that had worked in Poland and France would in some ways prove of Pyrrhic value in the rolling plains of the USSR. The Germans made dramatic gains, and at first, it even looked possible that Hitler's expectations of rolling all the way to the Urals in three months might be achieved. In the process, though, they began to strain their supply lines, especially as the Soviets practised the time-honoured tactics of scorched earth. Besides, while at first – especially in Ukraine, given the recent famine – the Germans were often welcomed as liberators, their racial ideology and heavy-handed practices quickly alienated the civilian population, generating a partisan movement that would be a constant threat and drain on resources.

The Soviets also had unexpected strengths. They had fielded some 150 divisions, but whereas the Germans thought they could muster no more than an extra 50, in fact they could quickly mobilize an extra 200. They had also presumed from the first that they would need to reconstitute their forces several times over in the event of a major war, and not only had the industrial base to match but were able to relocate much to the east to prevent the Axis powers from capturing or destroying it. It is an interesting question whether the Soviets would have been as able to carry out this logistical feat had they not had so much practice moving huge numbers of people around, as they had filled the Gulags.

Theirs was a war fuelled by patriotism, tyranny, terror and – however little today's Russians may like to admit it – extensive assistance from their allies, ranging from 3,300 British- and Canadian-built Valentine tanks to food and industrial supplies from the United States. The Soviets proved able to put up with extraordinary hardship, but one has to admit that this is a little easier when the alternative is a vicious fascist regime offering your people at best life as illiterate slaves – or a bullet in the back of a head from the NKVD. Even the Gulag camps were pressed into service, thousands of *zeks*, prisoners, recruited as cannon fodder in penal battalions, while scientists and technicians who had fallen foul of Stalin's state worked in the *sharashkas*, special research centres inside the Gulags, such as the famous aviation designer Andrei Tupolev and Sergei Korolyov, father of the Soviet space programme.

The trajectory of the war on the Eastern Front is as simple in outline as it was complex in detail. The initial offensive saw three army groups spear into the USSR: Army Group North headed for Leningrad, Army Group Centre struck for Moscow, and Army Group South first aimed for Kiev, then planned to wheel towards the oil-rich Caucasus. Early advances, despite the stubborn resistance of individual units, meant that by September, the Germans had surrounded Leningrad, taken western and central Ukraine, and were just 200 miles from Moscow. A new drive towards Moscow was launched in October, but the weather worsened, resistance stiffened, and the Germans troops were tired. This was meant to have been a quick operation, and most of the Germans were not equipped with clothing fit for the Russian climate, especially in what proved the coldest winter of the century, and their tanks and trucks likewise were found to be unsuited to the conditions. Since 1966, huge tank traps at Khimki, almost 14 miles north-west from central Moscow, mark what is meant to have been the closest German troops got to the capital. Nonetheless, they found it impossible to take it that winter, however much of a scare they gave the Soviet government. The embalmed body of Lenin was spirited from his mausoleum and secreted in Tyumen in Siberia, and much of the government was quietly relocated, too.

The war so far had gone terribly for the Soviets, who had lost 4.5 million dead or wounded, and another 3 million had been taken prisoner

Invasion of the Soviet Union

— Pre-invasion Soviet border
Ɒ Front line on 1 September 1941 (start of Operation *Typhoon*)
∎ ∎ ∎ Front line on 30 September 1941
← Direction of German advance
•••••• Farthest German advance

FINLAND

Lake Ladoga

RUSSIA

Leningrad

Tallinn
ESTONIA

LATVIA

Volga

Kalinin

Moscow

LITHUANIA

Dvina

Smolensk

Kaluga

Minsk

Bryansk

BELORUSSIA

Pripet

Pripet Marshes

POLAND

Korosten

Kiev

Lokhvitsa

Kharkov

Don

Dnieper

UKRAINE

Dnepropetrovsk

Stalingrad

Dniester

HUNGARY

Odessa

Sea of Azov

N

ROMANIA

Danube

Black Sea

0   250 miles
0   250km

(of whom 2 million died, largely from overwork and underfeeding), but the Axis forces had lost some 730,000 men, too, and were running low on fuel, food and spares. Siberian divisions, accustomed to the temperature, were rushed to Moscow, and troops would march through Red Square at the 7 November parade in commemoration of the 1917 Revolution and straight on to battle. By December 1941, the Soviets at last had more troops than the Axis forces, but even so, the myth that it was always a contest between their quantity and German quality is just that. It is true that the force ratio would continue to shift in Moscow's favour, from 1.2:1 at the end of 1941 to something like 2:1 by early 1943, but from 1943 onwards it was not so much that the Soviets were continuing to grow in numbers as that the Germans were unable to make up their losses. Besides, on a local level, the Soviets often did not have any or much of an advantage in numbers: to focus on manpower is to underplay the importance of determination and generalship. In any case, on 6 December, General Zhukov launched a counter-offensive with these fresh troops that began to push back the exhausted Germans, but Hitler forbade any general withdrawal. In the process, he increased the casualties the Germans took, but forestalled any potential rout. By the end of winter, many of his divisions were at no more than a third to half their original strength, but they still held much of European Russia, Belarus and Ukraine.

On the principle that one's enemy's enemy is, if not a friend, at least a useful ally, Britain and the USSR had started cooperating, with British Prime Minister Winston Churchill signing an Anglo-Soviet Agreement in July 1941. The UK's senior military commanders had been sure the Soviets would collapse in a few weeks or months, but Churchill, that obdurate critic of Communism, was more optimistic: 'I will bet you a monkey to a mousetrap that the Russians are still fighting, and fighting victoriously, two years from now.' A monkey was slang for £500, a mousetrap just £1, and Churchill was right. Then, when the Japanese struck at Pearl Harbor on 7 December 1941, and Germany and Fascist Italy incautiously joined with Japan and declared war on the United States, Stalin could afford to scale down further his troops in the Far East, sending them westward, and count on even greater lend-lease aid, such as the Willys Jeeps, which were so ubiquitous that every similar small utility vehicle was called a *villis* long after the war.

STALINGRAD, 1942–43

Hitler's goal was to starve the USSR of its resources – but also to gain them for himself. Germany was critically short of oil, so in summer 1942, the Germans focused on the south, planning to take both the industrial city of Stalingrad (formerly Tsaritsyn) and the Caucasus. The oil city of Maikop fell, but as Stalingrad became the blood-soaked proving ground of Soviet and Axis will and capability, more and more forces were diverted there, blunting the German advance towards the oil fields.

Stalingrad, a sprawling mess of factories and apartment blocks stretching 30 miles along the Volga River, was not simply a strategic objective for its tank and tractor plants, its Volga River port and shipyards, but also its very name. To both Hitler and Stalin, there was a symbolic power to control of the city that bore the Soviet leader's name, which goes some way to help explain the escalation on both sides that made this battle so pivotal. The advancing German forces of the 6th Army under General Friedrich Paulus first engaged the defenders of the Stalingrad Front on 17 July: 18 divisions against the defenders' 16, with a strong advantage in both tanks and airpower. They pushed steadily towards the city, as on 28 July, Stalin issued his Order No. 227, demanding 'the strictest order and iron discipline', and concluding, 'it is time to finish retreating. Not one step back!'

By the end of July, the Germans were already looking to reinforce the 6th Army, with General Hermann Hoth's 4th Tank Army diverted from the Caucasus attack, and in August Stalingrad itself was under attack. Bombing raids by the Luftwaffe's 4th Air Fleet strewed the city with high-explosive and incendiary munitions, 1,000 tons of them just on its first massive day of sorties, 23 August, turning it into a rubble-choked ruin that, ironically, would block German mechanized advances and helped turn the fight into a house-to-house close-quarters battle of sniper, booby-trap, ambush and bayonet.

By 13 September, the last efforts to keep the Germans out of the city had failed. Red Army regulars, local militias, NKVD security troops, even technical students crewing vehicles they had salvaged and repaired were all thrown into the battle. Locations such as the grain elevator, Stalingrad Tractor Factory and Red October Steel Factory became strongholds which were fought over time and again, as Soviet troops would reinfiltrate by night ground they had had to abandon by day. Nonetheless, the Germans were slowly able to push their way across the city towards the Volga, across which the Soviets were sending whatever reinforcements they could funnel into the battle. The Soviet forces were left clinging desperately to its west bank.

While the Germans were focusing on this savage battle, though, and sending more and more of their best troops into the meatgrinder, the Soviets were preparing a counterattack: Operation *Uranus*. On 19 November, in a massive pincer movement, over a million Soviet troops smashed into the poorer-quality Romanian troops on the German flanks, cutting the 6th Army's supply lines and then trapping a quarter of a million German troops inside Stalingrad. Hitler was as inflexible as Stalin and refused to allow Paulus to try to break out of this trap. Instead, futile efforts were made to break the encirclement from without, and supplies dropped by air. None of this was enough, though. Hitler even promoted Paulus to field marshal, reminding him that no German officer of that rank had ever been captured. In effect, he was asking him to fight to the death. Instead, on 31 January 1943, he surrendered, and within a couple of days the surviving 91,000 men of his command (including 24 generals) would follow suit.

One could make the case for other battles being more pivotal on the Eastern Front, such as the defence of Moscow in 1941, the 872-day-long siege of Leningrad, or the July–August 1943 Battle of Kursk (the single largest battle ever to date, involving more than 2.5 million soldiers). However, Stalingrad marks almost the end of major German offensive operations; it saw the Soviets beginning to outpoint even the masters of *Blitzkrieg* in manoeuvre warfare, and Hitler abandoned his attempts to take the Caucasus. By the end of February 1943, the Germans had ceded all the territory they had taken in their 1942 offensive, and although they tried to regain this initiative with Operation *Citadel*, a massive attack at Kursk, they would discover that they were fighting a very different Red Army from the one that they had torn through in 1941. Stalin had been forced to elevate professionalism over political reliability, reducing the role of the commissars and even reinstating generals who had been languishing in Gulag camps. The officer corps was becoming more confident, and as more and more units were raised, the fundamental advantage of the USSR's larger population was coming into play.

NA BERLIN!

It was hardly the case that the war was won; there would be much further bloodshed and jeopardy, and the combination of Western Allied support and operations in North Africa, and then the invasions through Italy and France, would be crucial in the eventual victory. Nonetheless, momentum was now swinging the Soviets' way. By late 1943, German strategy was essentially defensive, aimed at trying to make any further roll-back of its conquests across Europe impossible, or at least prohibitively expensive. Yet the strength of the German military had been its capacity to attack, to keep its enemies off balance, to leverage its speed and ability to concentrate in battlefields of its choosing. Trying to defend a long border against a more numerous enemy was always going to be difficult: by the end of 1943, 3 million German troops were facing 5.5 million Soviets, and Kiev was back in their hands.

Ultimately, Hitler seems not to have been able to overcome his deep-rooted prejudices and take fully seriously the threat from the 'subhuman' Soviets. Even as Stalin was giving considerable autonomy to some highly able officers – not just Zhukov, but also Generals Ivan Konev, Konstantin Rokossovsky, Vasily Chuikov, Nikolai Vatutin and more – Hitler was micromanaging ever the more and proving increasingly intolerant of any officers who questioned his strategic vision. In 1944, he seemed willing to write off some forces and territory in the East – including Army Group Centre, destroyed in the Soviet 1944 summer offensive – on the assumption that losses could always be made up. As a result, he actually transferred forces, including some of his best units, west to face the Allied threat, especially after the June 1944 Normandy landings. The Soviets took fullest advantage. Minsk was retaken in July 1944, and by the end of the month Soviet advance columns were even at the outskirts of Warsaw. The Polish underground rose and briefly took back the city, but Stalin, with characteristic ruthlessness, let the Germans bloodily crush them before his troops moved in. Just as in 1940, when the NKVD had massacred nearly 22,000 Polish officers and intellectuals at Katyn, he was doing what he could to eliminate those who might be a threat to a future Soviet take-over. He was no longer thinking of survival, but empire.

On rolled the Red Army. Finland capitulated, and the Baltic States fell. A new government in Romania hurriedly switched sides and joined the Allies in the face of this juggernaut. The Germans hastily pulled their troops out of Greece lest they be cut off, as the Soviets moved across Bulgaria and into Yugoslavia. By January 1945, Budapest was surrounded, most of Poland had fallen, and the Soviets were at the Oder River, marking Germany's eastern border. More and more, one would see among the unofficial slogans painted on the sides of Soviet tanks, *Na Berlin!* – To Berlin!

In January 1945, Konev, Zhukov and Rokossovsky launched a three-pronged attack against the German front in Poland: Warsaw fell, then Kraków and Łódź, plentiful stocks of American trucks allowing an army that for so long had marched on foot to become increasingly motorized. With the advance guard of Konev's 1st Ukrainian Front reaching the German border, Hitler finally appreciated the danger of his position, but even so wasted time and one of the last of his battleworthy units, the 6th Panzer Army, in a bid to relieve Budapest. Meanwhile, a desperate bid to scrape together new forces saw schoolchildren pressed into service and *Reichsarbeitsdienst* (Reich Labour Service) militias issued weapons.

By the end of January, Zhukov's 1st Belorussian Front had reached but was blocked at Küstrin, on the Oder River just 40 miles east of Berlin. Meanwhile, Rokossovsky's 2nd Belorussian Front swept northwards to cut off Army Group Centre in East Prussia: 25 more German divisions lost to the Führer. Together, the Oder and Neisse Rivers formed the last real defensive line between the Red Army and Berlin: 200 contested miles from the Baltic coast to the Bohemian frontier, even as the Western Allies were battling their way over the Rhine. Joined by Rokossovsky, Konev and Zhukov used the subsequent pause to build up their forces, until by April some 187 divisions, 2.5 million Red Army troops in all, were facing 767,000 defenders, many by this stage simply hoping that they would have a chance to surrender to the British and Americans rather than the Soviets. On 16 April, after a barrage of a million artillery rounds, Zhukov and Konev launched a pincer movement aimed at Berlin, while Rokossovsky cut through German formations north of the city. The two commanders had a sometimes fraught and competitive relationship, and both wanted the honour of taking the city. As it was, Konev's men were first into Berlin, from the south, but he was then diverted south-west to meet up with advancing US troops, while to Zhukov went the glory of storming the centre and seeing the red flag hoisted over the Reichstag (in a moment that was later carefully re-staged for the right propaganda photo). On 30 April, Hitler took his own life in the ruins of the Chancellery rather than be captured by the advancing Soviet troops. His successor, Grand Admiral Karl Dönitz, sought to allow as many German soldiers and civilians to flee west into the US- and British-held areas as possible. Nonetheless, on 7 May, he unconditionally surrendered and the war in Europe was over.

The Second World War wasn't quite concluded. At the February 1945 Yalta Conference with Churchill and then-US President Franklin D. Roosevelt, Stalin had committed to join the war against Japan 90 days after Germany's surrender. On 9 August, 1.5 million Soviet troops duly marched into Manchuria, on the same day that the Americans dropped a second atom bomb on Nagasaki. It was a huge and ambitious undertaking carried out across an area the size of Western Europe, but the lessons the Soviet officer corps had learned about coordinating massive operations stood them in good stead. Although paratroopers had largely only been used as elite infantry in Europe, in the Manchurian operation and the subsequent invasion of South Sakhalin island, they were accelerating Soviet advances by seizing airfields and strategic locations to clear the way for ground advances and resupply from the air. However traumatic the atomic bombings had been, the rapid Soviet advance helped tip the scales in Tokyo towards surrender, as a strategy designed entirely around defending Japan from an Allied invasion from the south could not also defeat a simultaneous Soviet move from the north. On 15 August 1945, Japan surrendered and the war was finally over.

SUPERPOWER

This had been the ultimate test of Stalin's USSR, one which not only challenged every aspect of the system, but also transformed it. The cost had been extraordinary. The country had lost anything up to 27 million military and civilian dead, a bite taken out of the demographic pyramid that would leave it with a skewed male-to-female ratio, disproportionately affecting Belarusians and Ukrainians as the locus of so much of the fighting. A generation had been brutalized, whether through the hardships of the home front or the savagery of the war (which also led to a serious problem of abuse and rape in occupied territories), a trauma layered onto those left by the Great

Terror, collectivization and Civil War. Indeed, a quarter of a million Soviets who had been taken prisoner by the Germans were then sent to the Gulag, suspected either of cowardice for surrendering or dangerous exposure to Western values and lifestyles. Even the physical landscape was altered: many cities bear the scars of war to this day, and mines, unexploded shells and the bones of the fallen are still being discovered.

Yet it had also left the USSR a superpower, and one now brought together by a common myth of suffering and victory. Much of Stalin's planning in the endgame of the war had been directed towards strengthening the Soviet Union's position after the peace. He fundamentally mistrusted the West (indeed, he fundamentally mistrusted almost everyone and everything) and presumed that just as he was trying to project his forces as far and as fast as possible to secure territory and resources, so too were they. He had also feared that the British and Americans might make a separate peace with the Germans and then combine with them to take on the Soviets. After all, this was not just what some American and German generals and politicians were advocating, but the new US president, Harry S. Truman, had said back in 1941 that he thought the Nazis and Soviets should be left to kill each other off. In this he was doing the Western Allies a disservice, but for Stalin, precautionary paranoia was a way of life. Either way, the leader of the country treated as a militarily negligible pariah before the war ended it as one of the 'Big Three' world leaders, his troops in control of a broad swathe of Eastern and Central Europe (from which he would largely not see them withdrawn). Just as loot from Western Europe began to appear across the USSR, from the German grand pianos that became a feature in Party elite apartments to the wristwatches that, once a rarity, almost became an accepted sign of a soldier who had fought in Europe, so too the Soviets would take whatever they could for the reconstruction effort, whole factories being dismantled and sent back to the USSR.

Stalin would also emerge at once legitimated as national leader as never before, but also boxed in by elites who had themselves cohered in war, as he had had to tone down his old tactics of divide and rule and constant rotation of officials to prevent them from building up alliances and power bases. He would then seek to cut them back down to size. Zhukov, for example, was exalted as the 'Marshal of Victory' – but then would later fall foul of Stalin's jealousy and be demoted to command of backwater military districts. Overall, though, the experience of shared suffering and triumph on the Great Patriotic War would unite the country, creating a heroic national legend of once again saving the world from barbarism. Stalin, the 'Great Helmsman', was elevated to mythic status, despite his earlier and almost fatal blunders. The war had shattered the Soviet Union, yet also made it, just in time for a whole new war, a Cold one.

Want To Know More?

There is a bewildering array of books on the Great Patriotic War, including *When Titans Clashed: How the Red Army Stopped Hitler* by David Glantz and Jonathan House (University of Kansas Press, 2015), Jonathan Dimbleby's *Barbarossa: How Hitler Lost the War* (Penguin, 2022), Alexander Hill's *The Red Army and the Second World War* (Cambridge University Press, 2017) and Catherine Merridale's *Ivan's War: Life and Death in the Red Army, 1939–1945* (Picador, 2007). For more specific aspects, see David Murphy's *The Finnish-Soviet Winter War 1939–40: Stalin's Hollow Victory* (Osprey, 2021), Anna Reid's *Leningrad: Tragedy of a City under Siege, 1941–44* (Bloomsbury, 2012), Anthony Beevor's *Stalingrad* (Penguin, 2007) and *Fortress Dark and Stern: The Soviet Home Front during World War II* by Wendy Goldman and Donald Filtzer (Oxford University Press USA, 2021). For a sense of how the narrative in state-supported film has changed over time, you could compare the harrowing *Come and See* (1985), set during the occupation of Belarus, with *Panfilov's 28 Men* (2016), following the heroics of Soviet soldiers holding back the German advance – purportedly based on a real story but probably a piece of suitably stirring propaganda.

22

Cold War

Kabul, 1979

1948–49	Berlin Blockade
1949	Explosion of first Soviet atom bomb
1953	Death of Stalin
1955	Warsaw Pact formed
1956	Suppression of Hungarian rising
1961	Sino-Soviet split
1962	Cuban Missile Crisis
1968	Suppression of Prague Spring
1978–88	Soviet-Afghan War
1985	Gorbachev becomes General Secretary
1987	Intermediate Nuclear Forces (INF) Treaty
1989	Revolutions across Warsaw Pact nations
1991	August Coup
	Collapse of the USSR

It was summer 1991, the Soviet Union only had five months to live, and I was sitting with a veteran of the invasion of Afghanistan in his tiny, damp kitchen. Nonetheless, he was perversely cheerful. He and some of his fellow veterans, known as *afgantsy*, had just been taking part in one of the anti-government protests that were becoming an increasing feature of Soviet life, a response to the food rationing, medical shortages and broken promises that had become such a feature of those final years of the USSR. The reason he was so upbeat was that they had just managed to persuade the neighbourhood council to allow them to set up a memorial – if they could raise the funds themselves – to the 'soldier-internationalists' who had fought in all kinds of unacknowledged foreign wars since 1945. 'We may be going hungry,' he admitted, 'but at least before we starve we can let people know that we have been fighting and dying not just in Afghanistan, but in all kinds of foreign wars for decades, and all for those' – there followed a string of truly inventive invective – 'commies in the Kremlin.'

The Cold War was an era of triumph and tragedy. The Second World War had left the USSR as a superpower, with its forces ensconced in Central Europe, a position Stalin had no intention of relinquishing. Bit by bit, Soviet control was imposed on the countries of the future Warsaw Pact, while a desperate drive was launched to develop the atom bomb and establish the basis for the balance of terror: it had its first successful test in 1949. As Moscow and Washington adapted to the new reality of life in the nuclear age, conflicts largely became proxy wars outside the rival power blocs of NATO and the Warsaw Pact. However, it would slowly become clear that the USSR simply could not keep up with the arms race. The invasion of Afghanistan in 1979, which brought the costs of the Kremlin's imperialism into every Soviet household, would mark the slide into imperial collapse.

BUILDING AN EMPIRE

What Stalin had taken, he was reluctant to give up. Following its 1945 defeat, Germany was divided into British, French, US and Soviet sectors, with Berlin – deep within the Soviet sector – similarly partitioned. Stalin quickly moved to set up a puppet regime in the Soviet-held east of the country, and when attempts to find some common settlement broke down in 1948, the Soviets began to blockade the other sectors of Berlin. In response, the Allies supplied their sectors with an extraordinary, 323-day airlift. Eventually, Stalin backed down, and Germany ended up divided into a democratic Federal Republic in the west and a Soviet-dominated Democratic Republic in the east.

Nonetheless, this was classic Stalin, pushing as far as he could, and only retreating when he absolutely had to. The Marshall Plan, a

US project to spend $17 billion helping European countries rebuild, albeit as liberal democracies, was in particular seen (not wholly without reason: 5 per cent of these funds went to the CIA) as a serious challenge, and Stalin both refused to participate and forced countries in what he saw as the USSR's sphere of influence to follow suit. Moscow's grip closed on East and Central Europe. The Baltic States had been annexed outright. Communists had staged a coup in Bulgaria in 1944, backed by the Red Army. The pro-Soviet Democratic Bloc took over in rigged elections in 1947. The Romanian Workers' Party and the Communist Party of Czechoslovakia seized power in coups in 1947–48 and 1948, respectively. By means of what became known as 'salami slice' tactics, little by little the Hungarian Socialist Workers' Party took over other parties until it was in sole control by 1949. Only really in the Balkans did Stalin's ambitions sour. Under Communist partisan leader Josip Broz Tito, Yugoslavia initially aligned itself with Moscow, but Tito split with Stalin in 1948 and instead adopted a position of neutrality, and while Albania's Stalinist leader Enver Hoxha would join the Warsaw Pact, the Soviet-led security alliance formed in 1955 as a response to NATO, it would always remain quirkily and repressively independent.

Ultimately, this was an empire being built in the shadow of the Red Army, and maintained by secret police forces modelled on – and largely controlled by – their Soviet 'big brother', which by 1954 was known as the KGB, the Committee for State Security. These satellite states were very much intended to serve Stalin's USSR, providing a security buffer in Europe, extra military forces in case of war, and resources to help rebuild the Motherland. Yet like many other imperial powers, the Soviet Union came to learn that empires also come at a price. Increasingly, they actually had to be subsidized, with cheap Soviet gas or oil, and from time to time, imperial authority would need to be reasserted, whether crushing the protests by hungry and disillusioned East Germans in 1953 or indeed being set on protesters in the southern Russian city of Novocherkassk, at least 26 of whom were killed in food riots in 1962.

The death of Stalin in 1953 triggered a flurry of behind-the-scenes political intrigue from which Nikita Khrushchev would emerge as the new General Secretary of the Communist Party. More for political than moral reasons, in 1956, he launched a campaign of selective 'de-Stalinization' that placed the blame for past abuses on Stalin alone, even though Khrushchev had been one of the dictator's right-hand men. After years of Stalin's personality cult, this rocked the foundations of the puppet regimes across East-Central Europe, and in Hungary, student protests quickly escalated, until tens of thousands of anti-communist protesters were clashing with government forces. Ernő Gerő, Secretary of the Hungarian Workers' Party, desperately appealed for assistance, and Georgy Zhukov, then Soviet defence minister, launched an intervention on 24 October 1956 that became an invasion when more and more elements of the Hungarian military also turned against the regime – and the Red Army forces deployed to protect it. Marshal Konev led a second, larger intervention, Operation *Whirlwind*, with 17 divisions, and they ground their way into Budapest and imposed a new loyalist regime, which launched a vicious campaign of purges and arrests. Nonetheless, Hungary would henceforth be kept on a looser leash, allowed to adopt some limited capitalist measures to try to pacify the population.

In 1968, when newly elected Czechoslovak First Secretary Alexander Dubček launched an idealistic liberalization campaign known as the Prague Spring, Soviet General Secretary Leonid Brezhnev (who had ousted Khrushchev in 1964) was alarmed at what he saw as a dangerous precedent that risked undermining the rest of the Soviet bloc. After attempts to persuade Dubček to abandon his dream of 'socialism with a human face' failed, on 20 August Brezhnev launched Operation *Danube*. *Spetsnaz* special forces in plain clothes touched down at Prague's Ruzyně Airport in a passenger plane claiming to need to make an emergency landing because of engine trouble. They quickly seized the airport, so that paratroopers from the 7th Airborne Division could be brought in to seize the city. Meanwhile, 170,000 Soviet troops (18 divisions), supported by 55,000 from Bulgaria, Hungary and Poland, crossed the border from the north, east and south, their tanks painted with broad white 'invasion stripes' to distinguish them from the identical ones of the Czechoslovak army. (Some 15,000 East Germans were also to take part, but at the last minute it was decided to keep them on the border, to avoid raising unwelcome parallels with the Nazi invasion of 1939.) Soon, the force would swell to half a million, as Brezhnev trusted in overkill and the flimsy pretence that this was a multinational act of 'support'. Faced with such overwhelming odds and with orders from Defence Minister General Martin Dzur to stay in their barracks, the Czechoslovak military put up no serious resistance. Despite some violent protests, the Prague Spring was soon extinguished and a repressive new regime was imposed.

The risk of a similar intervention in Poland – which would have had the potential to be very bloody indeed – was one of the factors behind the declaration of martial law in 1981. A long and deep economic recession had led to the emergence in 1980 of an anti-government trade union, *Solidarność* (Solidarity), at the Lenin Shipyard in Gdańsk. It rapidly grew, not least thanks to the patronage of the Catholic Church, until it began to worry Brezhnev. Moscow put pressure on Warsaw to crack down, sending unannounced almost two extra divisions' worth of tanks to Borne Sulinowo, the base of the Soviet 90th Guards Tank Division in north-western Poland. According to some, Polish leader General Wojciech Jaruzelski quietly requested Soviet support if things got out of hand, while according to others, he feared that if he did not act, Moscow might. Indeed, Brezhnev had come close to doing so in December 1980, with plans drawn up for a joint operation with Czech and East German troops under the cover of the Soyuz-80 (Union-80) military exercises. What Jaruzelski may not have realized is that, by 1981, the Kremlin had decided intervention would be unsafe and unwise. According to secret meeting transcripts later released after the Soviet collapse, Yuri Andropov, the long-serving KGB chief who would soon succeed Brezhnev, was clear: 'We can't risk such a step. We do not intend to introduce troops into Poland. That is the proper position, and we must adhere to it until the end. I don't know how things will turn out in Poland, but even if Poland falls under the control of Solidarity, that's the way it will be.'

Either way, in December 1981, Jaruzelski announced the creation of the Military Council of National Salvation (WRON) – essentially a junta – and the imposition of martial law. There followed a brutal period of repression that never managed to break *Solidarność*, which would eventually lead the first post-communist government in 1989. Although the Soviets did not intervene to try to shore up this part of their crumbling empire, it was clear that for the Poles, this was a constant fear.

LOSING THE COLD WAR,
ONE MICROCHIP AT A TIME

The Soviet alliance with the Western Allies had always been a pragmatic one, and the only surprise was quite how quickly it soured once the war was over. In response to Stalin's creeping take-overs, in 1946 Churchill was already warning that:

> From Stettin in the Baltic to Trieste in the Adriatic, an iron curtain has descended across the Continent. Behind that line lie all the capitals of the ancient states of Central and Eastern Europe. Warsaw, Berlin, Prague, Vienna, Budapest, Belgrade, Bucharest and Sofia; all these famous cities and the populations around them lie in what I must call the Soviet sphere.

This iron curtain would eventually take physical form in barbed wire, concrete barriers, minefields and dog runs as the Soviet bloc states struggled to keep their populations from fleeing, but it was as much as anything else a geopolitical concept. The Cold War – a description that seems to have emerged from the writings of George Orwell – was kept chilled precisely by the new potential for Armageddon. In nine closed cities, so-called 'atomgrads', to which entry was tightly controlled and which were scrubbed from the maps (Sarov, home of the euphemistically named All-Union Scientific Research Institute of Experimental Physics, for example, was known simply by the codename Arzamas-16), Soviet scientists hurriedly sought to catch up with the Americans. Which they managed to do: by the 1950s, they were building up a stock of atomic bombs, and in 1960, the first intercontinental ballistic missile (ICBM), the R-7/R-7A, was operational in Soviet service. Thanks to this, the Soviets were also able to steal a march on the Americans, using a modified R-7 to launch *Sputnik*, the first artificial satellite, in 1957. This, in particular, caused great consternation in the United States, only magnified when Yuri Gagarin became the first human in orbit in 1961.

It certainly seemed, in the early years of the Cold War, that the Soviet Union had momentum on its side. A reflection of this was in 1956, when Khrushchev incautiously told Western ambassadors that 'we will bury you.' His bullishness may have seemed understandable.

The Soviet economy had recovered unexpectedly well after the devastating war, not least thanks to the looting of occupied Eastern Europe, worth possibly as much as the whole Marshall Plan. The Soviet Union was safe thanks to its new nuclear arsenal, and while the colonial powers of the West were wrestling with the retreat from empire – France was at war in Indochina, Britain granted India independence in 1947, and was divesting itself of its African colonies, one by one – Communist China was still a 'younger brother' to the Soviets, even though its leader, Mao Zedong, would split with Moscow in 1961.

Nonetheless, for all the Soviet Union's early assumptions that it could win the Cold War against the *Glavny Vrag* – Main Enemy – the United States, in practice the burden of this struggle would become increasingly self-destructive. The Stalinist planned economy had, in its own bloody way, proven extremely effective at bootstrapping the USSR out of an agrarian era and into the industrial age. It could not really adapt to the post-war era of rapid change, where heavy industry gave way to high technology. A paranoid security state finds it hard to nurture the kind of innovation and inter-disciplinary thinking that would become so important. Having lagged as a result of an odd ideological decision to regard cybernetics as a Western 'pseudo-science' designed to undermine the rights of the workers, for example, Soviet mathematics and theoretical studies of computing were often every bit as good as the West's. However, they proved unable to produce the actual machines, to scale and with the necessary quality control, and so by the 1970s were essentially resorting to stealing or copying Western models. This helps explain the almost hysterical fear among Soviet leaders when US President Ronald Reagan announced his Strategic Defence Initiative – 'Star Wars' – in 1983, which envisaged breaking the nuclear stalemate by capitalizing on American technological advantage with an anti-ballistic missile defensive network of early warning satellites, lasers and interceptors. It proved impossibly overambitious – indeed, it may have been intended primarily to spook the Soviets into compromise or overreaction – but was taken at face value by a Kremlin which was painfully aware it was falling behind in the technology race, and perhaps as a result exaggerated Western capabilities. A Soviet anti-regime joke common in technical circles in many ways said it all, in an era of miniaturization: '*Pravda* has just announced a new breakthrough! The Soviet Union has built the largest microchip in the world.'

Crucially, the economy simply was not up to the task of funding both empire and arms race, especially given its dependence on oil and gas exports, which would leave it at the mercy of fluctuating global prices. It is not coincidence that the later swing towards reform and renewed détente under Mikhail Gorbachev coincided with a collapse in global oil prices, from $53 per barrel in 1983 to $10 in 1985. Meanwhile, the price of empire was growing. Originally possessions to be plundered for reconstruction resources, the Warsaw Pact countries would become burdens, needing to be subsidized and garrisoned. As the USSR began to seek allies and clients abroad, it would again find that they expected aid, weapons supplies, even direct assistance. Egyptian leader Gamal Abdel Nasser, for example, proved adroit at playing Moscow off against Washington. Eventually, the Soviets had to, in effect, outbid the Americans to win his friendship, in 1956 offering him a loan of $1.12 billion at a well-below-market interest rate of 2 per cent to build the Aswan High Dam. Likewise, after the Cuban Revolution of 1959 brought to power the Marxist regime of Fidel Castro, the USSR ended up subsidizing its economy through paying over the odds for its sugar.

THE POTEMKIN ARMY

Defence spending would become an even more crippling burden, and arguably bring down the USSR. It certainly produced, on the face of it, a formidable military machine, over and above its nuclear forces. From its end-of-war peak of 11.3 million, it had fallen to 3.6 million by 1960, a level at which it remained until the later 1980s, with just under 200 manoeuvre divisions. To this, though, should be added the KGB's Border Troops and the Interior Ministry's own forces, many of whom were motorized or mechanized infantry, even *Spetsnaz*, and who together amounted to another half a million. The Ground Forces were tank- and artillery-heavy, configured for aggressive offensive operations on the plains of Europe (or northern China), largely manned by conscripts serving two-year terms (from 1967; before then it had been three), but even this huge army was envisaged as just a skeleton awaiting mobilization. The experience of the Great Patriotic War ensured that

Soviet military planners thought in terms of a mass war, with a military designed to handle the mobilization of another 9 million reservists who had served within the past five years – and a total potential mobilization base of fully 50 million. The Warsaw Pact could contribute up to another 3 million troops.

Nonetheless, however impressive these forces may have looked rolling through Red Square, there were serious shortcomings. In many ways, the Soviet leaders were as seduced by pageantry and parade as Tsars Paul or Nicholas. Training was often cursory, with too few live rounds used to hone marksmanship, and military exercises more like carefully choreographed combat theatre, meant to impress the Party leadership and foreign observers alike, rather than genuinely to test and build the skills of officers and men. A brutal hazing culture, known as *dedovshchina* ('grandfatherism') saw the longer-serving conscripts bully their juniors, seriously undermining unit cohesion. Practical command skills hard-won in the Great Patriotic War fossilized into unthinking discipline and an unwillingness to take the initiative. Corruption often trumped competence in promotions, and although the power of the political commissars was scaled down dramatically, politics nonetheless still often shaped doctrine and practice.

On the face of it, the technology at their disposal was impressive, often even cutting edge, from assault hovercraft to land marines on beaches, to their own vertical take-off 'jump jet', the Yak-38. To take that as an example, though, unlike the rival British-designed Harrier, the Yak-38 was so underpowered that even with limited ordnance it had a short range, and it had an unfortunate tendency to flip over if one of its two lift jets died. The Soviets aspired to a 'blue water navy' able to contest the world ocean, but in practice they had to content themselves with trying to deny neighbouring seas to an enemy, with submarines and missile-firing surface ships. In general, it would be wrong to disparage the Soviet military too much: it could fight well, and many of its systems, if not the most advanced, were certainly good enough. But it was never as formidable as it seemed, and as it devoured something like 15 per cent of GDP according to the CIA (around double the share spent by Russia in 2024, in the midst of the Ukraine war), one could certainly argue that Moscow was not getting a good return on its investment.

WORLD (PROXY) WAR I

Besides, the post-war Soviet Union was not simply content to defend the Motherland, but out of a combination of ideology, hubris and a sense that this defence needed to be on a global scale, it was also engaged in a proxy war across the globe. The advent of nuclear weapons and the doctrine of Mutually Assured Destruction meant that the direct threat to either the USSR or USA (or, indeed, NATO and the Warsaw Pact) was dramatically reduced. However, the mutual suspicions and rivalries had to be vented somewhere, and that turned out to be everywhere from sporting competitions to proxy conflicts around the world, and especially in the Global South, where new nations were rising and old empires falling.

Korea was apportioned between Soviet and US occupation zones in 1945, although in many ways it was China that took on the main role of supporting the Marxist north in the subsequent war (1950–53) that left it divided. Moscow supported North Vietnam and the Viet Cong rebels in the 1955–75 conflict and the Arab nations in their several wars against Israel. It sent supplies, aid and advisers to encourage like-minded revolutionary and anti-colonial movements across the world, and this even brought the world close to nuclear war over Cuba, after the ousting of the US-backed Batista regime at the start of 1959. Considering how close Cuba was to a hostile United States – which had embarked on a campaign of sabotage and backed the abortive 1961 Bay of Pigs invasion by Cuban exiles – it was eager to lock in Soviet support. Meanwhile, the Soviets were angered by a US decision to place Jupiter nuclear missiles in Italy and Turkey, which they regarded as an escalation, especially as Turkey was on their border. As a result, the Kremlin agreed to base missiles in Cuba, just 90 miles from the US mainland, as a response and to make up for their relative weakness in long-range ICBMs. To the Americans, it was this that was an escalation. US President John F. Kennedy rejected plans for a full-scale invasion and opted instead for a blockade to prevent the arrival of the missiles. In October 1962, even though Khrushchev had told his son Sergei that the Americans 'would make a fuss, make more of a fuss, and then agree', he was forced to back down and accept a deal, not sending missiles to Cuba secretly in return for the withdrawal of the Jupiters. He could hardly do otherwise: for all his posturing, the Soviet

Union was in no state to challenge NATO (it still only had 20 ICBMs able to hit the US mainland, even if they all worked), and his generals had made that clear to him. Although he did not know it at the time, it was the beginning of the end for Khrushchev: there had been too many blunders, too much erratic decision-making, and by bringing the USSR close to a nuclear war it could not win, he convinced many within the elite that he had become too dangerous. In 1964, he would be toppled in a political coup and replaced by Leonid Brezhnev. Still, Brezhnev was also committed to the notion of a global struggle with the West, which would play out in other battlefields, from Africa to Afghanistan.

Indeed, one proxy war could fuel another. In 1975, for example, US spy satellites spotted an unexpected new phenomenon in Angola, which had just secured independence from Portugal: baseball diamonds. Angolans didn't really play much baseball – but Cubans did. Increasingly, the Soviets would seek to use their clients in these struggles, from the Cuban military advisers used to support regimes in Angola, Ethiopia, Congo and Nicaragua, to the East German Stasi secret police helping to train up their counterparts in countries including Mozambique, South Yemen and Syria. Nonetheless, this determination to play a global role, and challenge the USA and the West generally at every point – driven by a zero-sum world view which saw any Soviet gains as a loss to the 'Main Enemy' and, more to the point, vice versa – continued to push Moscow into expensive and counter-productive adventures.

KABUL, 1979

A particular example of both the strengths and the weaknesses of the late Soviet military and leadership alike was the invasion of the Democratic Republic of Afghanistan (DRA) in December 1979. The year before, the Marxist People's Democratic Party of Afghanistan (PDPA) had seized power in this impoverished Central Asian nation, but from the first it was riven by bitter rivalries that turned bloody when one faction's leader, Hafizullah Amin, had his counterpart, Nur Mohammed Taraki, murdered. Amin was a man in a hurry and his heavy-handed efforts to force change on a country still largely dominated by the village, traditional leaders and Islam, quickly generated a powerful backlash. Amin unleashed his secret police, but the tortures and disappearances only worsened matters. Moscow had little enthusiasm for the PDPA and even less for Amin himself, but the Shah had just been toppled in the Iranian Revolution and there was a fear that militant Islam was on the march: if Afghanistan fell to jihad, might it spread to the culturally Muslim Soviet Central Asian republics? Just as bad, there were suggestions that the American-educated Amin was in secret negotiations with Washington: if Moscow did not step in to resolve the situation, might it 'lose' Afghanistan to its rivals?

Amin was begging for military assistance against the rebels, and the ageing Soviet leadership was unsure what to do, but a consensus soon emerged that Amin had to go. The plan was to replace him with a more pragmatic figure able to reunite the PDPA and to make a show of force sufficient to overawe the rebels. The Soviet leaders confidently imagined it would take no more than six months to stabilize the country, pacify the rebels and maintain their influence. They were, to put it mildly, wrong, but in fairness Defence Minister Dmitry Ustinov, an old crony of Brezhnev's, did not dare relay to the ruling Politburo, or Party cabinet, the concerns of his generals. Brezhnev himself had suffered at least one stroke and heart attack and was very much in decline. Foreign Minister Andrei Gromyko saw everything in terms of the East-West conflict, and KGB chief Yuri Andropov may have known better but was manoeuvring to replace Brezhnev and didn't want to rock the boat.

A team of *Spetsnaz* commandos were covertly brought into the Afghan capital, Kabul. Officially the 154th Independent Special Designation Detachment of the 15th Independent Special Designation Brigade, but generally known as the Muslim Battalion, they were largely ethnically Central Asian, so they could blend in with the Afghans. The plan was to run two operations concurrently: *Storm-333* and *Baikal-79*. The first was a surgical strike to eliminate Amin, along with sabotage attacks across Kabul to paralyse Afghan government forces. The second was the invasion of Afghanistan itself, involving the airlift of the 103rd Air Assault Division directly into Kabul, while some 65,000 ground forces crossed the border at Kushka to the north-west and Termez to the north-east. They would swing round the main ring road connecting the country's principal cities, taking them on the way, while the newly imposed PDPA leader, Barbak Karmal, exhorted DRA forces not to oppose their Soviet 'brothers'. After all, Moscow wanted to keep them as intact as possible, so they could take the war to the *mujahideen* rebels, while the Soviets garrisoned the cities.

On Christmas Day, troops of the Soviet 40th Army began to cross the border on the pretext of coming to help the regime and conduct training exercises. Then, on the night of 27–28 December, *Storm-333* was launched. Despite some of the blunders (including one particular friendly fire incident that killed KGB Colonel Grigory Boyarinov), perhaps inevitable with any such operation, *Storm-333* was strikingly successful. The Muslim Battalion, along with two units of KGB special forces operators, *Zenit* (Zenith), drawn from its covert operations school, and *Grom* (Thunder), from its *Alfa* counter-terrorism unit, along with a company of the 345th Guards Independent Air Assault Regiment, stormed the Tajbeg Palace, Amin's residence. He was found and killed, officially by grenade fragments but probably a deliberate execution. Overall, fewer than 500 Soviet special forces took on almost five times their number of relatively elite DRA troops, and suffered just nine deaths, to the Afghans' 200. Meanwhile, raids on a variety of strategic targets across the city, from the General Staff and secret police headquarters to the TV centre and the notorious Pul-i-Charkhi Prison, ensured chaos within the DRA ranks and an essentially unopposed invasion.

Likewise, *Baikal-79* had been meticulously planned, from whether Soviet vehicles could negotiate road tunnels on the way, to calculating the necessary supplies of buckwheat porridge, and largely went without a hitch. There was no real resistance, and by the morning of the 28th, Soviet military police were already directing traffic in Kabul and the new government was being installed. However, it would very quickly become painfully evident how mistaken were the Kremlin's complacent assumptions that the Afghan people, especially in the conservative, religious and independent-minded countryside, would accept foreign invasion. Nor would the DRA army be willing and able to lead the way in counter-insurgency while the Soviets watched their backs. If anything, the opposite was true, and the mutiny in Baghlan province of the DRA's 4th Artillery Regiment in January 1980 would be an early warning of just how unreliable they would be.

On the one hand, this showed what the Soviets could do, when everything went to plan. Despite the last-minute improvisations during *Storm-333*, the actual invasion was a textbook operation. The Soviets used their classic *maskirovka* – strategic deception and camouflage – to conceal their plans from Amin and the West alike, and struck during the holiday period, when the latter was distracted. The deployment of troops was well organized and worked as seamlessly as any of the major military exercises they conducted. However, the fundamental premises were flawed. The old men in the Kremlin misunderstood the situation on the ground and would or could not listen to those who had a better sense of the challenges ahead. Convinced that they were in a desperate zero-sum struggle for global supremacy – even though in practice Washington had very little real influence in Kabul, and even less interest – they felt they had no choice but to invade. What was envisaged as a short, sharp demonstration of Soviet will and power, much like the suppression of the Prague Spring in 1968 (indeed, the near-senile Brezhnev several times actually referred to Afghanistan as Czechoslovakia), instead became an open-ended war of occupation and pacification that would last ten years before the Soviets withdrew, not so much beaten as exhausted, at a cost of 15,000 lives.

If the political leadership was flawed, so too was the military execution, as soon as things no longer continued going to plan. The Soviet Army, built for mass operations on the plain, was unprepared in terms of training, equipment and doctrine for a scrappy counter-insurgency in Afghanistan's mountains and scrubland. They had an overwhelming advantage in firepower, but time and again did not know how to direct it, and ended up relying on brutal scorched-earth tactics. Junior officers had little idea how to use their own initiative, senior officers little idea how to encourage it, without breaking the very principles of discipline and top-down command that were meant to be their greatest strength. Crime, drug-taking, looting and indiscipline became endemic. This was not a war the General Staff had expected to fight, and it took considerable time to adapt. In fairness, the Soviets did learn lessons, and the 40th Army became something of a test bed for new ideas. However, they were never really applied more broadly, in part because the General Staff felt it would distract from their core mission, preparing for a potential war with NATO, and in part because the military was facing the unexpected threat of downsizing following the election of a new General Secretary in 1985: Mikhail Gorbachev.

ENTER GORBACHEV, EXIT THE USSR

In 1989, PepsiCo, the company behind the fizzy drink, very briefly found itself the sixth-largest naval power in the world, thanks to Gorbachev. In fairness, this was no fighting force, but a collection of 20 vessels – a cruiser, a destroyer, a frigate and 17 submarines – destined for Norwegian scrap yards, swapped in return for expanded production and sales in the Soviet Union. After all, as far back as 1972, PepsiCo had begun exchanging soft drink for hard: Pepsi for Stolichnaya and Sovetskaya vodka, reflecting how challenging business could be at a time when the ruble was not traded on international markets, generally pegged at a wholly artificial value of one to the US dollar. However, the soda-for-subs deal was also a mark of Gorbachev's desire to scale down the USSR's massive arsenals and trade military power for economic survival.

He came to power still believing in Marxism-Leninism, convinced a system mired in corruption, inefficiency, backwardness and cynicism simply needed a little reform to be fixed. During his six years in office, he would become increasingly radicalized and desperate, as he came to realize just how intractable these problems were. The first Soviet leader not to have had active experience in the Great Patriotic War, he was not so consumed with the kind of paranoias about the West that in 1983 had led the Kremlin briefly to believe that NATO's ABLE ARCHER wargames, instead of being exercises simulating a potential response to Soviet invasion, were actually preparations for a genuine nuclear first strike. He also had very practical reasons to improve relations with the West. He needed foreign technology and investment, but also to scale down that onerous defence budget. With only a wafer-thin majority in the Party's Central Committee, though, he could not afford to alienate the hardliners by unilateral cuts, so he assiduously courted US President Ronald Reagan both to secure mutual arms control deals, and to establish the kind of framework that would allow him to withdraw Soviet troops from Afghanistan.

The Intermediate-Range Nuclear Forces Treaty was signed between the USSR and the United States in 1987, paving the way for the withdrawal from service of a whole class of missiles. In 1988, Soviet forces withdrew from Afghanistan, and Gorbachev announced a plan to cut the defence budget initially by 14 per cent, reducing the armed forces by 500,000 men. He also bowed to the inevitable and accepted that Moscow's dominance over East-Central Europe was all but over, if it were not going to be maintained by force. Most of the regimes fell to popular protest and elite division in 1989, and although the Warsaw Pact was only formally dissolved in 1991, by then it was already dead. The Treaty on Conventional Armed Forces in Europe, signed in 1990, even set ceilings for all kinds of conventional military equipment in Europe, from the Atlantic to the Urals.

Hence deals like the PepsiCo one, and also the growing anger of the High Command and more conservative elements within the Party and the security apparatus. As nationalist pressures rose, and the army found itself deployed either to try to keep the peace between rival peoples or, more often, suppress secessionist protests (such as in Tbilisi, Georgia, in 1988, Baku, Azerbaijan, in 1990, and the Baltic States in 1991), many of the generals increasingly came to feel they had to act or see the Soviet Union torn apart. This led to their staging a coup in August 1991, trying to forestall Gorbachev's most ambitious move yet: a new Union Treaty that would reconstruct the USSR not as an empire in all but name, but a genuine confederation of nations, each able to secede and with greater control over their own affairs. No one had any doubts that the defence budget would be further cut. The coup fizzled out within three days, to a large degree because although many Soviets were willing to protest against it, most of the military was not willing to use force to support it. When even one of the eight plotters behind the coup, Defence Minister Dmitri Yazov, was persuaded by his subordinates to stand down, it was doomed. Yet the balance of power had shifted when the August Coup failed, and local, republican presidents such as Russia's Boris Yeltsin now had the whip hand. Yeltsin had a grudge with Gorbachev – who had first promoted him, then sidelined him when he stepped on too many toes – and the chance now to indulge it. He refused to sign the new Union Treaty, ending Gorbachev's hopes of being able to reshape the USSR. Instead, as his last act as Soviet president, on Christmas Day 1991, he signed the Soviet Union out of existence.

Want To Know More?

Odd Arne Westad's *The Cold War: A World History* (Penguin, 2018) is a classic, although Sergei Radchenko's excellent *To Run the World: The Kremlin's Cold War Bid for Global Power* (Cambridge University Press, 2024) looks specifically at Moscow's perspective. Roger Reese's *The Soviet Military Experience: A History of the Soviet Army, 1917–1991* (Routledge, 1999) is a good, scholarly overview, while David Glantz's *The Military Strategy of the Soviet Union: A History* (Routledge, 2001) adopts a very top-level perspective. On Afghanistan, Roderic Braithwaite's *Afgantsy* (Profile, 2011) is a very good general history, and I have written a number of titles including *Storm-333* (Osprey, 2021) and *The Panjshir Valley 1980–86* (Osprey, 2021). For the geopolitical strategists out there, *Twilight Struggle* (GMT, 2005) is an interesting and immersive game of the Cold War, while *9th Company* (2005) is a well-made and visceral Russian film about the Afghan War, not to be watched before a flight.

PART SIX

Back to the Future

23

Bringing Russia 'Off Its Knees'

Tskhinvali, 2008

1991	Warsaw Pact disbanded
	USSR dissolved
1993	Yeltsin shells parliament
1994–96	First Chechen War
1999–2009	Second Chechen War
1999	Vladimir Putin becomes acting president
	(elected, 2000)
2007	Munich speech
2008	Invasion of Georgia
	'New Look' military reforms announced

It was 1993, and my first trip to this new-old country, the Russian Federation. The shops were empty, the mood on the streets was bleak, but Sasha was unexpectedly upbeat. He had a hut.

The Warsaw Pact had been formally disbanded on 25 February 1991, leaving half a million Soviet troops (and 150,000 dependents) still left in countries technically no longer under their control and eager to see them gone. Hundreds of thousands returned to a homeland that had no homes or use for them. There were whole officers' families forced to live in a single bedroom, and companies bunking down in unheated tank sheds. This was the fate of the 11th Guards Tank Division's 44th Guards Berdichevsky Red Banner Tank Regiment, which had just been hurriedly withdrawn from Königsbrück in East Germany and relocated to Vladimir, 120 miles east of Moscow. There was talk that the new unified Germany was paying to have new barracks built, but for now most of the regiment was occupying a half-built school complex, missing windows taped up with plastic sheeting, bedrolls on concrete floors for beds. But Sasha, whom I met while he was visiting his parents in Moscow, was something of a wheeler-dealer. He had managed to get an ageing UAZ-452 van that needed an engine tune-up written off as scrap, and then swapped it with a local in exchange for a small hut on the outskirts of town. It had no electricity, but it did have a wood-burning stove. Above all, it was not shared with a dozen snoring, grumbling, smoking, unwashed platoonmates. Technically, it was against regulations for Sasha to live off base, but considering the overcrowding, his officers – most of whom, he said, 'were skiving off themselves, when they weren't dead drunk' – were happy to turn a blind eye. Sasha was happy.

Very few others were, though. The 1990s was a decade of chaos at home, humiliation abroad. Russia was in effect defeated in the First Chechen War, when it tried to bring an unruly subject nation to heel, and sidelined in international relations. The armed forces slid into corruption and confusion. With Russian military power at an apparent nadir, the scene was set for a man who promised to 'raise Russia off its knees': Vladimir Vladimirovich Putin. At first, he would seem to be succeeding, but to a large degree by picking fights with weaker enemies (Chechnya 1999, Georgia 2008) and striking at opportune moments (Crimea 2014, Syria 2015). Nonetheless, for a while there seemed a new mood of martial triumphalism in Russia. Tragically, it would go to Putin's head and embolden him to invade Ukraine in 2022, embroiling Russia in a bloody war that would devour so many of the economic, political and even military gains of the two preceding decades.

BANKRUPT ARMY

When the USSR was disassembled, to a large extent military forces and assets passed to whichever of the newly created republics in which they found themselves. There were exceptions, with nuclear forces all being passed to Russian control (not least because Moscow retained the launch codes, rendering them unusable), and Russia still retaining the right to base its Black Sea Fleet in the Ukrainian peninsula of Crimea. At first the new Russian Federation said that it would retain just a minimalist National Guard of 100,000 men, but in 1992 President Boris Yeltsin instead announced the creation of the Armed Forces of the Russian Federation under General Pavel Grachyov, former commander of the Airborne Forces.

There were all kinds of radical ideas for reforming the Russian military, which as of 1993 had an establishment strength of 2.8 million men, but these came to nothing but shrinkage. The Russian state was in a crisis both economic and political – indeed, in October that year, Yeltsin would shell his own parliament into submission and rewrite the constitution. The Russian generals – who until very recently had been Soviet generals – tried to maintain the old ways of war, and a mass army to match. In practice, the armed forces shrank dramatically as officers resigned in droves and young men ignored their draft notices, such that by 1996, it was down to 1.6 million, but this was not accompanied by any real rethinking of its composition or how it would fight. In effect, the Russian army was a smaller and poorer Soviet one. Nor was Grachyov the man to turn things round. An able paratrooper, he had been picked for his loyalty, and it quickly became clear that he was out of his depth as minister. Instead, like so many before and after him, he focused on enriching himself and his friends: he even acquired the nickname 'Pasha Mercedes' for his alleged embezzlement of luxury cars with funds meant to cover the withdrawal of forces from Germany.

When, in 1995, a defence ministry spokesman warned that 'if no radical decision is made shortly, the Russian army may well find itself on the verge of starvation', he was not exaggerating. There were tales of soldiers being given animal feed in Siberia, pet food in the Urals. Some unit commanders were in effect renting their soldiers out as labourers just to make sure they could be paid something, and theft and embezzlement became rife. There were even persistent claims that *Spetsnaz* commandos were not only moonlighting as mafia hitmen, but actually running training courses for gangsters. Meanwhile, the naval transports that plied the routes between St Petersburg and the exclave of Kaliningrad, sandwiched between Poland and Lithuania, returned packed with cars stolen in Europe for resale back home, just as supply flights from the 201st Division, still based in Tajikistan, flew home full of Afghan opium, taking advantage of the fact that the civilian police and customs had no right to stop and search them.

TWO CHECHEN WARS

The Russian army found itself involved in a range of local clashes, largely generated by the haphazard way the new successor states had not so much been created as just happened, and were often poor and unstable, even compared with Russia. In the 1990–92 Transnistria War, the remnants of the 14th Guards Army (by then actually scarcely more than divisional strength) informally supported the ethnic Russian secessionists of the Transnistrian breakaway state on the left bank of the Dniester against the Moldovan government. In the 1992–97 Tajik Civil War, the 201st Division (later renamed the 201st Base) was deployed in support of government forces.

However, it was the disastrous First Chechen War of 1994–96 that truly revealed just how far the Russian army had sunk. The Chechens had long chafed under Russian rule, and took advantage of the crisis in the state – and Yeltsin's incautious call for regions to 'take as much autonomy as you can swallow' – to declare themselves independent. Yeltsin was not about actually to let them go and create a dangerous precedent, so first he launched his own Bay of Pigs, sending a force of loyalist Chechens to seize power, but this proved as ignominious a failure as the American plot against Cuba. With Grachyov airily assuring him that a single paratrooper regiment could take the capital Grozny in two hours, in December 1984 Russia invaded. A mix of special forces, regular troops and paramilitary Interior Troops, almost 24,000 altogether, rolled into Chechnya apparently unaware of the locals' will and capacity to fight. They eventually took Grozny, after two months, not two hours, and massive air and artillery bombardments that killed up to 35,000 civilians as well as hurried reinforcements that more than doubled the size of the Russian force. Even so, the Chechens fought back, demonstrating their skill as guerrillas, and even managed to recapture Grozny in August 1996, with just 1,500 fighters. Meanwhile, the Chechens were also turning to terrorist attacks to take the war to the Russians, with a mass hostage-taking in June 1995 at Budyonnovsk in southern Russia, to which it took Prime Minister Viktor Chernomyrdin personally to negotiate a peaceful resolution, by conceding most of the Chechens' demands. The war became massively unpopular at home, and in August 1996, the Khasavyurt Accords ended the war. It was a mutually unsatisfactory compromise: Chechnya dropped its claims to independence but gained near-autonomy in practice. It was a humiliation: the Russian Federation, a nation of 148 million people and spanning two continents, had been humbled by a pseudo-state with a population of perhaps 1.3 million, less than a tenth of Moscow's alone.

It was a telling symbol of Russian decline. Grachyov was finally sacked, but nonetheless all the inefficiencies, clumsiness, brutality and corruption of the armed forces had been put on public display. This helps explain why redeeming this national embarrassment would be such a priority for a grey KGB officer turned politician who would make a meteoric rise to the presidency. From the very genesis of the new Russia, there had always been a complex ambiguity towards the West. There was a desperate desire to match its quality of life, to gain access to its consumer goods and services, and there was also a desire by many to emulate its democratic practices. However, there was also growing disillusion, fuelled by a sense that the West actually wanted a Russia that was weak and knew its place, from the way prominent Western economists had encouraged the crash privatizations that saw a handful of oligarchs become vastly rich, while ordinary people lost out, to support for Yeltsin's deeply dubious 1996 election win over the Communists. This suspicion was evident in a toughening of Russia's international position, culminating in the infamous 'Pristina Dash' during multinational peacekeeping operations in the Balkans. Russia had played a role within UNPROFOR, the UN Protection Force which sought to keep the peace after the former Yugoslavia had exploded into civil war. Later, when the Albanian Kosovans tried to break away from Serbia in 1998–99, the Russians insisted on being part of the Kosovo peacekeeping force (KFOR), even though they were closely aligned with Serbia. In June 1999, Russian paratroopers rushed to secure Pristina International Airport ahead of NATO, leading to a tense standoff that could have escalated had KFOR's commander, British Lieutenant General Mike Jackson, not ignored the orders he was getting from NATO supreme commander General Wesley Clark, reportedly saying, 'I'm not going to start the Third World War for you', and opened direct negotiations with the Russians.

Eventually, both sides stood down, but in Russia this was seen as evidence that a more bullish approach could win dividends.

This was certainly the lesson taken by the newly appointed prime minister, Vladimir Putin, who was about to be installed as president by Yeltsin's unexpected retirement at the end of 1999 and a hasty and carefully managed election. He was determined to, as he saw it, save a Russian Federation that was on the verge of collapse, and had already put in motion a renewed war against the Chechens, both to cauterize this bleeding wound and also to demonstrate his own tough-guy credentials.

While still prime minister, Putin had overseen a massive build-up of troops and supplies ready for another invasion. The Russian population demonstrated no particular enthusiasm for tangling with the fearsome Chechens again, though, so he needed a pretext for war. This was dropped into his lap when jihadist extremists, whose power had been growing steadily in Chechnya, launched an incursion into neighbouring Dagestan in August 1999. Combined with a series of mysterious terrorist bombings inside Russia (which most analyses conclude was an inside job, carried out precisely to generate the kind of anger and fear needed both to justify war and convince people they needed a security-oriented president such as Putin), this gave him the excuse he needed.

In October 1999, Russia re-invaded. This was an altogether more serious venture, with a force more than three times the size of its predecessor: 50,000 soldiers and another 40,000 Interior Troops under Colonel General Viktor Kazantsev, commander of the North Caucasus Military District. They slowly ground their way down the country, the army leading the way, the Interior Troops mopping up behind. Reaching Grozny, they pounded it with airpower, artillery and rockets until it was in ruins before moving in, forcing the rebels to be destroyed in their positions or flee the city. By February 2000, the city was theirs – even if only 21,000 civilians remained, scratching out some kind of life in the rubble.

The southern highlands still provided shelter for many rebels, but here Putin relied on a growing number of Chechen fighters, often former rebels, disillusioned by the way their nation had been hijacked by Islamic extremists or simply eager to join the winning side. They knew the rebels' ways and their hideouts, and could take the war to them much more effectively than any but the best of the *Spetsnaz* 'hunters' also deployed in the vicious skirmishes that marked the closing phases of the war. In practice, by the beginning of 2001, the war was all but won, even if the so-called 'counter-terrorism operation' was only formally lifted in 2009. It was a pitiless war: perhaps 50,000 civilians dead or missing (including many who seem to have met their ends during the 'filtration' process, as the security forces hunted rebel sympathizers), 9,000 actual insurgents, and at least as many Russians. Putin didn't mind, though: he had wanted a decisive and symbolic triumph to establish his credentials as a ruthless and relentless champion of the Russian state. He did not even balk at installing a dynasty of Chechen quislings in Grozny: first Akhmat Kadyrov, a former rebel commander, then after his assassination in 2004 and a necessary regency while he reached the minimum legal age for the post, his son Ramzan. Moscow even ended up having to pay through the nose for its victory, with upwards of 80 per cent of the Chechen regional budget paid by the federal government, much of which ended up spent on the Kadyrovs' lavish lifestyles and vanity projects. That was still worth it for the new president.

PUTIN TURNS

After all, he could afford it. Until the 2008 financial crisis, Russia was on the rebound, and Putin could afford to think ambitiously. From the very beginning of his presidency, he was spending money on rebuilding Russia's ramshackle military. One focus was trying to increase the proportion of volunteer *kontraktniki* compared with conscripts, whose term of service was reduced from 24 to 18 months, and then 12 months in 2008. The generals complained that this meant that conscripts were properly trained and able to be used for only around three months of their service, but the point was that, especially in the early years, Putin really envisaged fighting only relatively small wars, which would generally be fought just by the professional soldiers.

There was no question but that he was becoming increasingly angry at a West that, he felt, was treating Russia unfairly, marginalizing and undermining it, and trying to deny it a rightful place as a great power, which in his mind was its birthright. At a pivotal speech in Munich in 2007, he accused the West – and he really meant the USA – of seeking to impose on the world a 'unipolar' model, in which it was the dominant power, through 'an almost uncontained hyper use of force – military force – in international relations, force that is plunging the world into an abyss of permanent conflicts'. He may have already begun suppressing political opposition at home and fought a brutal counter-insurgency in Chechnya, but in his mind he had been offering an honest deal with the West: observe Russia's legitimate (to him) interests at home and in its strategic neighbourhood, and we will observe yours, whether going along with the US invasion of Afghanistan in 2001 (even allowing its forces to be resupplied through Russia) or swallowing its concerns over the 2003 invasion of Iraq and initial expansion of NATO into Central Europe. As one foreign ministry insider put it to me at the time, 'as far as he is concerned, Russia has made all the concessions, the West has made all the gains.'

Still, the generals, Soviet veterans to a man, resisted meaningful reform, wanting to keep a Soviet-style mass army (not least as that meant a continued need for lots of generals). The real turning point came with the invasion of Georgia in 2008. Although he seems soon to have accepted that the Baltic States were lost to Moscow, Putin clearly regarded the other post-Soviet states as part of Russia's sphere of influence, necessary buffer and satellite states. In 2004, the American-educated Mikheil Saakashvili was elected president of Georgia and led a determined attempt to detach his country from Russia and move closer to NATO and the European Union. To Putin, this was an open challenge that demanded an unambiguous response, not simply to retain hegemony over Georgia, but as an object lesson for other successor states which might harbour similar aspirations. This was exacerbated when, at a summit in Bucharest in April 2008, NATO blandly affirmed that Ukraine and Georgia 'will become members of NATO' without giving any clear sense of an actual route to joining the alliance.

It was a crass compromise. The truth was that there was no consensus within NATO about letting these countries join, but no one wanted openly to admit this. The woolly statement, though, was enough to give West-leaning forces in both countries false encouragement – and alarm Moscow, which saw this as an encroachment on what it felt was its legitimate 'zone of privileged interest', in the words of Dmitry Medvedev, then technically president but essentially a figurehead for Putin. He had officially stepped down to the position of prime minister for 2008–12, to keep to the letter, if not the spirit, of term-limit laws, even while still very much in charge.

TSKHINVALI, 2008

So the Russians began encouraging two rebellious regions of Georgia which had already established de facto independence, Abkhazia and South Ossetia, to start needling Saakashvili. Again, Putin wanted a pretext, to give him the appearance of responding to another's aggression. Georgian villages were shelled, police ambushed, and the hot-headed Saakashvili took the bait. In August 2008, 12,000 Georgian troops and 4,000 Interior Ministry paramilitaries moved into South Ossetia, bombarding its capital, Tskhinvali, and in the process killing two Russian peacekeepers based there. Putin had his excuse.

Although sock-puppet president Medvedev reportedly balked at the last minute, a quick phone call from Putin – who at the time was in Beijing – brought him back into line, and Russia's contingency plans were activated. Elements of the 42nd and 19th Motor Rifle Divisions, as well as the 10th and 22nd *Spetsnaz* Brigades were stood up, and even as the Georgian troops were already on the outskirts of Tskhinvali, Moscow's forces were making their way to the Roki Tunnel connecting South Ossetia with the neighbouring Russian Federation Republic of North Ossetia. The Georgians were able quickly to encircle the city, but they had failed to anticipate the level of resistance from the locals. The decision had been made to deploy Interior Ministry paramilitaries for the initial move into Tskhinvali, because they had assumed they would face protest rather than gunfire and Molotov cocktails. Besides, although the Russians were besieged in their base, there was a separate North Ossetian peacekeeping battalion that was now openly fighting alongside the militias. The Interior Ministry troops were largely lightly armed and driving thin-skinned Turkish-made Cobra personnel carriers that proved vulnerable to the defenders' weapons. As the battle for Tskhinvali became a confused urban brawl, the Georgians decided to deploy two regular light infantry battalions that they had been holding in reserve.

They began to make progress, and by early afternoon of the first day of the war, the Georgians controlled more than a third of the city. Nonetheless, at this point an attack by two Russian Su-25 ground attack aircraft killed more than 20 Georgian soldiers of the 42nd Light Infantry Battalion. The Georgians were shocked: they had been told that they would be in control of the city before the Russians could rouse themselves. As rumours spread of Russian regiments on the outskirts of the city – they were actually hours away – the 42nd withdrew from the city, spooking the rest of the Georgian force. Panic proved contagious, and despite the best efforts of field commander Brigadier General Mamuka Kurashvili, by mid-afternoon they had essentially abandoned Tskhinvali altogether.

By the evening, order had been restored and the last available reserves, the 2nd Brigade and the 53rd Light Infantry Battalion, committed to a renewed push to take the city. It had all taken too long, though. By then, more than 3,000 Russian troops were already in South Ossetia, belated combat air patrols were keeping Tbilisi's planes out of the sky, bombers were hitting targets in Georgia itself, and the positions around Tskhinvali were just in artillery range of the advancing task force. An abortive Georgian push on the city from the south saw them get no further than the outer suburb of Gujabauri, just as the advance reconnaissance company of the Russian 135th Motor Rifle Regiment had reached the northern city limits.

The Georgians pulled back, regrouping at Gori, less than 20 miles to the south. All was not necessarily lost: with the exception of its admittedly elite 1st Brigade, which had been deployed to Iraq as part of the multinational occupation force, Tbilisi had near enough its entire army on or inside the South Ossetian border. There might still be time to take the politically symbolic capital before their enemy could consolidate. After all, the initial Russian deployment was no larger than a single Georgian brigade, so all was not lost, Saakashvili persuaded himself.

The next morning, Kurashvili launched a renewed attack, led by elements of the 2nd Brigade. In the early afternoon, they began to move back into Tskhinvali from the south under cover of an artillery bombardment, just as two companies from the 135th Regiment, accompanied by overall Russian field commander Lieutenant General Anatoly Khrulyov, were entering from the west. The Russians and the 2nd Brigade's reconnaissance company blundered into each other, and Khrulyov was wounded in the ensuing exchange of fire. At first, the Georgians had the advantage as the rest of the Georgian brigade joined the fray, but Russian reinforcements including *Spetsnaz* soon arrived, and crucially were able to spot for artillery and Su-25 fire support. Ultimately, the Georgians were forced to retreat, as more and more Russian forces arrived – even as yet more were spilling through the Roki Tunnel.

Saakashvili's gamble had failed. Tskhinvali was held, while Russian Naval Infantry were landing in Abkhazia, and a missile boat from the Black Sea Fleet was forcing Georgia's miniscule navy to stay in port, sinking one patrol boat in the process. Russian forces drove halfway to Tbilisi before stopping, not – as Western diplomats might like to claim – because of urgent negotiations, but because the point had been made: had Moscow wanted, it could have done much more, but instead contented itself with humbling the Georgian upstarts and making Abkhazia and South Ossetia its fully fledged protectorates.

This was a win, but not quite as effortless as the Kremlin might have anticipated. It had been preparing for war for some time and was hardly pitted against a peer: Georgia's total population was only one-twentieth of Russia's. The initial advance was less organized than it should have been (one veteran of Georgia and Afghanistan I spoke to drew very unfavourable comparisons with the 1979 invasion), and the Russians frequently failed properly to coordinate their forces. Of the six aircraft they lost, three were to friendly fire, and more of their vehicles were lost to breakdowns and accidents than enemy action. This was not an indictment of Georgian troops, who often fought with dash and determination, but a Russian military that simply was not mastering the basics of modern war. Tanks were destroyed because reactive armour canisters (meant to explode pre-emptively to disrupt incoming missiles) were empty, the use of old maps meant that long-abandoned airfields were bombed, and a failure of the communications network forced Khrulyov to borrow a journalist's satellite phone to give orders. Nor was the chaos just in the field. Back in Moscow, the General Staff's Main Operations Directorate was caught in the middle of an office move, the ZAS secure-traffic telephones in their old offices cut off, and their new ones not yet connected. Furthermore, early Georgian airstrikes had been able to happen because the micromanaging Chief of the General Staff Nikolai Makarov, a Ground Forces officer through and through, initially forgot to activate the Air Forces.

Had there not been such a huge discrepancy between the two nations. Had there not been field commanders such as Khrulyov who were both competent and aggressive to act on their own initiative. Had the Georgians taken more serious steps to close the Roki Tunnel. Had all kinds of contingencies not worked in Moscow's favour, things could have gone very differently – and the Kremlin and the generals alike knew this. They won more than anything through luck and brute force. For the recently appointed defence minister, Anatoly Serdyukov, who had been looking for opportunities to break through the habitual conservatism of his generals and institute what became known as the 'New Look' military reforms, it was a perfect opportunity.

Want To Know More?

Modesty be damned, I explore this era in a great deal more detail in my *Putin's Wars: From Chechnya to Ukraine* (Osprey, 2022), as well as my smaller and more detailed *Russia's Wars in Chechnya 1994–2009* (Osprey, 2024) and *Russia's Five-Day War: The Invasion of Georgia, August 2008* (Osprey, 2023). Dodge Billingsley's *Fangs of the Lone Wolf: Chechen Tactics in the Russian-Chechen Wars, 1994–2009* (Helion, 2022) is an excellent study of how the Chechens could hold off the Russians so well and long, while *The Guns of August 2008: Russia's War in Georgia* by Svante Cornell and S. Frederick Starr (Routledge, 2009) is a classic on this conflict. Arkady Babchenko's *One Soldier's War* (Grove, 2009) is a harrowing autobiographical account of being swept up in the horrific maelstrom of Chechnya. *Prisoner of the Mountains* (1996) is a Russian film based on Tolstoy's 1872 short story 'The Prisoner in the Caucasus', transposed into the First Chechen War, and is an interesting micro-scale study of relations between Russians and Chechens.

24

Putin's Hubris

Kyiv, 2022

2008	Invasion of Georgia
	'New Look' military reforms announced
2014	Annexation of Crimea
	Start of undeclared war in the Donbas
	MH17 shoot-down
2015–	Intervention into Syria
2022–	War with Ukraine
2024	Putin begins his fifth term as president

It's always worrying when people start to parrot government talking points. I'd known Viktor for years, never really a friend so much as an academic acquaintance working in a similar field. He was younger, a product of the 1990s rather than Soviet times, which had left him with an easy cynicism, an assumption that anything anyone in power said was self-serving nonsense. In some ways it was no surprise that he very definitely cut all ties when, in 2022, the Russian government barred me indefinitely for my supposed Russophobic views (which I would very fiercely contest – personally, I think Putin is the biggest enemy of the Russian people, but that's a whole other story). The last time I spoke to him, in 2021, gone was his 'a plague on both your houses' scepticism. In its place was a fiery conviction that Vladimir Putin – a man he had previously mocked for everything from his style of speaking to his policies – was indeed, in a phrase commonly found in official statements, the man who had 'lifted Russia off its knees'.

I don't know what happened, especially as at the same time most Russians were actually getting tired of the ageing grey dictator and his increasingly implausible tough-guy schtick. Nonetheless, he was a very different man, and as he had risen through the academic system, he was increasingly echoing this kind of nationalist triumphalism back at the Kremlin, in reports commissioned to order by the Presidential Administration, and sharp-toothed TV sound bites. One of the great unknowns, after all, is how far the Kremlin got trapped in a loop, commissioning reports and encouraging pundits to say the things it wanted to hear, only to be convinced by these comforting lies. The tragedy is that this mood, along with Putin's own complacency thanks to previous successes and likely a growing desperation to make his mark as one of Russia's great state-building heroes, led to the disastrous decision to invade Ukraine in 2022, in the process all but destroying the very military he had spent two decades building, just like Ivan the Terrible devouring his own emerging state.

THE NEW LOOK MILITARY

Anatoly Serdyukov, who had been appointed defence minister in 2007, had previously been the minister for taxes, but it was his time in the 1990s as chief executive of a homewares company that ensured he would be widely and dismissively known among his generals as the 'furniture salesman'. After all, he was trying to rein in some of their unofficial perks (like using soldiers to build their holiday homes or chauffeur their wives and mistresses) and, more to the point, enforce unpopular reforms on them. For a time, they could constructively ignore him, but he had the backing of the Kremlin, was able to appoint the like-minded and forceful General Nikolai Makarov as his Chief of the General Staff, and then was given the perfect opportunity with the five-day war in Georgia.

He quickly announced a sweeping programme of military reform, framing it as the most radical change since the Great Patriotic War. The goal was to create a 'New Look' military that was smaller, but much more capable and flexible, optimized for the kind of limited interventions in what Moscow called the 'Near Abroad' – the post-Soviet states – rather than the kind of mass war that seemed increasingly unlikely. The plan was to cut the armed forces by 130,000 to a million by 2012, with a continued increase in the proportion of volunteers; the establishment strength would fall to 220,000 officers, 425,000 professional *kontraktniki*, and just 300,000 national servicemen. In the process, there would be severe cuts to the bloated officer corps, with a 22 per cent reduction in the number of generals and even greater cuts to colonels and majors. After all, at the time there were twice as many majors as lieutenants, and painfully few professional NCOs, a traditional weakness of the Russian military.

Previously, the basic building block of the Ground Forces had been the division, typically 10,000–12,000 strong, but it was replaced with the smaller, more flexible brigade, of some 3,000–4,000 men. Its firepower, though, would be enhanced by more modern weapons and communications and targeting systems: the aim was that by 2020, 70 per cent of all weapons systems in use would be of the latest generation, and the rest at least modernized. From 2012, each would be able to generate a self-contained Battalion Tactical Group (BTG) from its *kontraktniki*, a small expeditionary force with its own artillery, air defence and other capabilities.

This was an ambitious plan, and although much progress was indeed made by Serdyukov and his successor, Sergei Shoigu, it would later become clear that reorganization was easier than a genuine cultural revolution. Despite efforts to foster initiative in the junior officer corps and combat the brutal *dedovshchina* hazing culture, in a crisis, old habits would quickly reassert themselves. Nonetheless, the new armed forces certainly looked the part. Thanks to continued high spending and political priority, much seemed to change. New Western-looking uniforms, with body armour and night-vision systems, began to be issued (even if there would never be enough of the latter); a range of new vehicles and aircraft began to be developed (even if they were destined not ever to be produced in large numbers); new ships began to be laid down (even if some would not be completed because war with Ukraine would deny them the naval engines they needed). In effect, Russia would actually acquire two armed forces: one that was relatively modern, professional and advanced, and a larger rump that was still behind the times, and in effect being cannibalized by the reform process. After all, as one captain asked me, 'which ambitious and able officer would ever settle for being stuck in one of the "country brigades",' referring to those still much less 'New Looking' than others, 'when you can pull strings?' As he admitted, having served six months in a 'country brigade' before paying his commander to get him a transfer to a more prestigious unit, 'if nothing else, you get stuck with the dregs.' Arguably, this did not matter as long as the Kremlin was confining itself to smaller-scale operations, which only needed a cherry-picked small proportion of the overall force. However, it would prove the success of these better units that would give Putin a mistaken sense of his armed forces as a whole, and lead him into a disastrous miscalculation.

CRIMEA, 2014

At first, though, he clearly felt he had reason for confidence, not least in his military's response to the Revolution of Dignity (also known as the Euromaidan) in neighbouring Ukraine. Since 1991, Kyiv had been involved in a protracted and halting nation-building project, with nationalist and liberalizing forces often stymied by corrupt leaders, many of whom were happy to make deals with Moscow. In 2013, President Viktor Yanukovych first agreed to sign a free trade and association agreement with the European Union, then reversed his position under Kremlin pressure once it realized that this would effectively lock Ukraine out of the Eurasian Economic Union, Moscow's instrument to keep regional economies dependent on Russia. This triggered widespread protests that snowballed into a much wider campaign against the corruption, human rights violations and Russian influence behind Yanukovych's government. A protest camp was established in Kyiv's Independence Square, and police efforts to clear the camp and suppress the demonstrations proved heavy-handed enough to anger, but not organized or resolute enough to suppress. On 22 February 2014, Yanukovych fled the country and a new interim government took power before early presidential elections could be held in May.

This deeply alarmed Putin, who not only regarded Ukraine as rightfully a Russian vassal, but specifically because of the threat to the

Black Sea Fleet's bases in Crimea. Besides, he seems genuinely to have believed the protests were stirred up, even directed, by the West. Crimea, which had been transferred from Russia to Ukraine in 1954, has a strategically crucial position in the Black Sea, and while the lease on the Russian naval facilities had been agreed through to 2042, there was a not-wholly unjustified fear that the new government might rescind it. The General Staff had had contingency plans for taking Crimea dating back to the 1990s, although there is no evidence this reflected any serious intent. Indeed, apparently, the cases containing this outline plan were almost lost when the Main Operations Directorate moved offices in 2008: the index codes were confused, so it was for a while misfiled as a contingency for an attack on Iran. Nonetheless, on their basis, Putin approved an operation on 23 February, with *Vremya Cha* – zero hour – set for 4am on 27 February.

Although there were almost 20,000 Russian military personnel on the peninsula, most were sailors, technicians and logistical personnel, with fewer than 2,500 combat troops (albeit from the relative elite Naval Infantry and *Spetsnaz*). There were more Ukrainian personnel present and although again most were not front-line combatants, there were still more than 6,000 marines and 2,500 security troops. The Russians would thus have to rely on speed, deception and subversion if they were to avoid a full-scale conflict. Which they did in a textbook operation, a near-bloodless take-over in which local sympathizers and proxies staged protests, under the cover of which Russian special forces seized the key locations, closed the access points from the mainland, and blockaded Ukrainian units in their barracks. Much was made that these 'little green men' (the Russians call them 'polite people') were not wearing insignia, which left Kyiv and the West temporarily uncertain whether they were mercenaries, Black Sea Fleet personnel acting on their own initiative, or what they seemed to be: invaders. However, this was only part of the efforts to generate as much confusion and uncertainty as possible. Russian agents in the Ukrainian military intercepted commands or distributed false reports. Military intelligence hackers crashed systems and jammed communications. Local gangsters, Afghan war veterans, Cossacks and even biker gangs were recruited to give the Russian operation the appearance of being a local rising. As soon as the peninsula was locked down, though, heavier forces were rushed there, not least to secure it before Kyiv was quite aware of just how few Russian soldiers they were actually facing.

Within a week, Crimea was essentially in Russian hands, although some Ukrainian garrisons held out longer before changing sides or agreeing to withdraw to the mainland. On 16 March, a referendum on joining Russia was held, and Moscow's proxies unsurprisingly reported a 97 per cent vote in favour. On 21 March, Putin signed a law making Crimea part of the Russian Federation. Of course, this was wholly in contravention of Ukrainian and international law, but possession has proven nine-tenths of the law. Most Russians regarded Crimea as rightfully theirs anyway, and Putin's personal approval ratings shot up to over 80 per cent, even though this would in hindsight be a dangerous misstep.

FROM THE DONBAS TO ALEPPO

The ease with which Crimea was taken and the extent to which the Ukrainian military failed to put up a fight – or outright defected – created its own momentum and encouraged some to start thinking more ambitiously. There were those in the south-eastern Donbas region of Ukraine, heavily populated by Russian-speaking Ukrainians, who had largely voted for Yanukovych, who feared the new government in Kyiv. Most did not want to join Russia as much as protect their rights and maybe gain more autonomy within Ukraine, but there were also radicals, who were supported and encouraged by Russian nationalists, both adventurers on the ground and schemers in the Kremlin. Initially, Putin was willing to wait and see, to allow the activists freedom to act in this new 'grey zone' conflict, in case it proved useful. In due course, Russia began encouraging more nationalists to go and fight, and supplying them weapons. The shooting down in July 2014 of the civilian airliner MH17 with a Russian-supplied missile, though, forced Moscow to come off the fence. As government forces seemed on the verge of suppressing the insurgency, Russian troops were sent in to protect the self-proclaimed rebel 'people's republics'. Putin had never wanted the Donbas, just leverage with Kyiv, but Russia found itself stuck in a small-scale undeclared war with Ukraine that not only proved expensive but also steadily worsened its relations with the West.

The United States in particular responded with both limited economic sanctions and a concerted campaign to isolate Russia politically, infuriating Putin. Meanwhile, one of Russia's few remaining client-allies, Syrian dictator Bashar al-Assad, was looking perilously close to losing his civil war against an array of different rebel forces, including some with US backing. As much to demonstrate that attempts to isolate Russia would fail as to save Assad, in 2015 the Russians intervened to prevent the regime falling. In September, combat aircraft began deploying to the airbase at Hmeymim, north of Damascus, which became the base for a contingent which would provide crucial assistance to the regime. The Russian public was lukewarm about this particular adventure and so, as it became clear that airpower was not enough, and ground troops would be needed, Moscow turned to the Wagner private military company. Established in 2013 under Yevgeny Prigozhin, a businessman whose whole commercial empire was built around doing whatever the Kremlin needed doing, it had seen limited and covert action in the Donbas, but in Syria it would provide much-needed muscle for ground operations at a time when the Syrian army was in a very poor state. Crucially, by relying on a mercenary army – even if in practice it was established and paid for by Moscow – the Russian government could continue to reassure its own public that their boys were not at risk.

It was an indiscriminate and merciless war, in which cities such as Aleppo and Palmyra would be hammered by everything from cruise missiles to crudely improvised 'barrel bombs' heaved out of helicopters, and turned to corpse-strewn rubble just like Grozny. The Russian way of war was not necessarily to use brutality for its own sake, but certainly would not shy from it if it was considered necessary. By 2020, the war had not been won, but had at least stabilized to Damascus's advantage. The government, which in 2015 had not even been able to secure its capital, was in control of most of the cities of the populated coast and about two-thirds of the country overall. Nonetheless, about half the pre-war population were refugees, with 5.5 million having fled the country. For the Russian Air Force, it was a great training opportunity, and an opportunity to test out everything from drones to *Kalibr* cruise missiles. As for Wagner, in a pattern that would prove familiar, having served its purpose, it was then all but discarded, and when its funding was cut, Prigozhin was forced to cut a side-deal with Damascus that led it incautiously to take part in a joint attack on oil and gas fields at Deir ez-Zor that triggered a devastating US response – after the Russian commanders at Hmeymim had denied all responsibility for them. Prigozhin was forced to withdraw his troops, beginning a feud with Defence Minister Shoigu that would later flare into full-blown mutiny in 2023.

POLITICAL WAR AGAINST UKRAINE

For the moment, though, Putin felt confident. His shiny new army had taken Crimea, sustained a small-scale deniable war in the Donbas, and turned the tide in Syria. What he seems not to have appreciated is how far Crimea and Syria were both very specific conflicts with limited goals, able to be fought on a relatively small scale, and thus only with the best of the units at his disposal. He was left with an unrealistic sense of Russian military capabilities (and, perhaps, of his own strategic genius). Having created a system in which everyone around him knew better than to challenge him (as a former Russian spy told me in 2015, they had learned that 'you don't bring bad news to the tsar's table'), who was going to disabuse him?

Meanwhile, Ukraine remained defiant, for all Moscow's blandishments, bullying and browbeating. As a result, in spring 2021, while maintaining a campaign of subversion and disruption, the Russians also began building up forces along the border under the flimsy pretence of training exercises. It is still unclear whether Putin planned an invasion from the start, or – as is more likely – he was characteristically hedging his bets, seeing what a little performative intimidation might shake out. Under the shadow of potential Russian invasion, investors began to pull out of Ukraine and the economy slumped. Given time, this campaign might have secured the sort of concessions from Ukrainian President Volodymyr Zelensky (who was coming under pressure from some Western leaders to avoid invasion at any cost) that Putin could have considered a win, including a firm commitment not to join NATO. Yet Putin was also convinced that, as he had told a surprised US President George W. Bush in 2008, 'Ukraine is not even a country', because, as he later claimed in his 2014 speech marking the annexation of Crimea, Russians and Ukrainians 'are one people. Kiev is the mother of Russian cities. Ancient Rus' is our common source, and we cannot live without each other.' Needless to say, most Ukrainians begged to differ. Ukraine's past had indeed been as part of the Rus' lands, but also as part of Lithuania, Poland, the 'Wild Fields', imperial Russia and the Soviet Union, often several at once – but history is not destiny, and in 1991, 92 per cent voted for independence from the USSR and, by extension, Moscow.

Yet Putin seems to have convinced himself, with the active connivance of his closest cronies, that Ukraine was ripe for the picking, so why wait? Without even informing his own generals until the last minute, he decided on a short, sharp military operation to oust (or kill) Zelensky in the name of a wholly fictional 'de-Nazification' (doubly ironic considering his Jewish heritage) and instal a puppet government that would accept Ukraine's rightful place within Russia's orbit. The Ukrainian people, he assumed, would largely accept their fate, with no more than protests and localized insurgent violence in response, which was why a large proportion of the invasion force was actually made up of National Guard riot police rather than soldiers.

As it was, there seems to have been little proper planning, which was done by a small, secretive circle around Putin instead of the full General Staff apparatus. Combined with the conviction that this would not be a real war – the models were presumably Czechoslovakia 1968 and Crimea 2014, even if in many ways Afghanistan 1979 was more apposite – this meant that the eventual invasion, launched on 24 February 2022, broke pretty much every precept of Russian military doctrine and the carefully developed notions of how such a major war against a country of more than 40 million people would be fought. Most of the commanders involved had no more than a week's notice, and there were only fuel, ammunition and other consumables stocked up for two weeks of war. Rather than a devastating preliminary Massed Missile-Aviation Strike (MRAU), there was a rather limited series of attacks, presumably because there seemed little reason to destroy assets that would soon be in Russian hands. Instead of a combined-arms ground offensive along a limited number of axes under a single overall commander, there were separate attacks, each essentially independent, all around the Russian and indeed Belarusian border with Ukraine – along with a lightning strike to take Kyiv.

KYIV 2022

At 8am on the 24th, helicopters lifted a battalion from the 11th Guards Air Assault Brigade, escorted by Ka-52 gunships, in a bid to seize the Antonov Airport at Hostomel, north-west of Kyiv, so that it could be used to bring in reinforcements and heavier equipment for a direct strike against the Ukrainian capital. At the same time, Russian special forces and assets in Kyiv launched an attempt to kill Zelensky, while the word went out to a network of agents across the country to begin a campaign of disruption. From the first, things did not go quite as planned. Determined resistance meant that Antonov Airport only fell the next day, and then counterattacks by local militias followed by the 3rd Special Purpose Regiment and the 4th Rapid Reaction Brigade made any large-scale use of the airport untenable. Eventually, it would take troops advancing overland to secure it, but by then it was too damaged to be used.

Zelensky was kept safe, and according to the Ukrainians, some 60 Russian saboteurs were 'neutralized'. The Americans offered to evacuate him, but according to a senior US intelligence official, his reply was the instantly memeable, 'The fight is here; I need ammunition, not a ride.' His transformation from a comedian-turned-politician with declining public support to an icon of national resistance was just one of the unexpected developments of this war, and contributed not only to Ukrainian morale and unity, but also the level of foreign support, as he proved willing and able to inspire, cajole and guilt-trip Western leaders as the need arose. Meanwhile, most of the notional agents turned out to have been more willing to take Moscow's money than actually turn quisling when push came to shove. Many were arrested, others disappeared or simply ignored their orders, while the country united in resistance, assembling Molotov cocktails in Kyiv and lining up to be issued AK-47 rifles: 18,000 in the first day alone.

The Russians escalated air and missile attacks, but a quick seizure of the city (Putin had reportedly thought three days would be enough) was no longer viable. Instead, ground forces began pushing forward in an attempt to reach and encircle Kyiv, with forces from the Eastern Military District (the 29th, 35th and 36th Combined Arms Armies) attacking south from allied Belarus via the Chernobyl nuclear disaster site, while the Central Military District's 2nd Guards and 41st Combined Arms

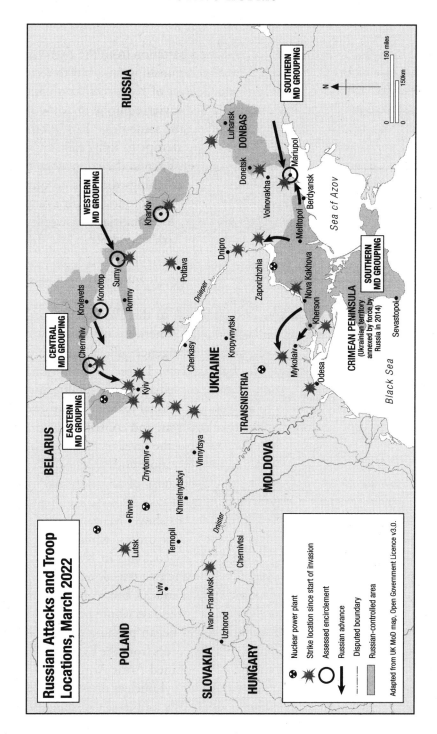

Russian Attacks and Troop Locations, March 2022

Army attacked from the north-east, via the town of Brovary. By the 28th, a massive Russian mechanized column was snaking its way south from allied Belarus towards Kyiv, via Prybirsk and Ivankiv. Stretching some 40 miles, it comprised around 10,000 troops from at least ten battalion tactical groups, with almost 1,000 tanks, 2,400 personnel carriers, self-propelled guns and supply trucks, all marked with white Vs and Zs to distinguish them from their Ukrainian counterparts. What might have seemed like a formidable task force quickly became a well-armed traffic jam, stymied by breakdowns, Ukrainian ambushes and simple incompetence. Many units had only enough fuel for the three days this initial phase of the operation was expected to take, and ended up abandoning vehicles when supplies dried up. Embezzlement meant that there were trucks fitted with cheap Chinese duplicates instead of heavy-duty, all-weather tyres, which quickly became shredded in tough conditions or bogged down in the mud. The state of the ground is one explanation why, like some Napoleonic-era army, it stuck to advancing in a vulnerable column along a road. It was bad enough that a lack of planning led to congestion and confusion, but this was dramatically exacerbated by Ukrainian attacks using anti-tank weapons (including Western-supplied Javelin and NLAW systems), drones and even improvised explosives to destroy vehicles at the heads of columns to force them to stop and push the wreck out of the way – only for the new leader to become a target.

In theory, it should have taken just two days to reach the outskirts of Kyiv, but by the beginning of March, the Russian column was still more than 15 miles away and apparently stalled. This was no longer an advance, but a narrow, vulnerable salient jutting into hostile territory. By 22 March, the Ukrainians had mustered the forces to launch a counterattack across the Kyiv region, and on the 29th, Moscow bowed to the inevitable and announced that it was pulling back from Kyiv. Instead, it focused its efforts on the south and east, locked into a brutal war that, as of writing, shows no sign of ending.

It was a bizarrely ill-conceived operation. In all fairness, many Westerners who before the war anticipated an easy Russian triumph quickly over-corrected and took to painting them as irredeemably incompetent, corrupt and thuggishly clumsy. Neither extreme perspective is accurate. As it was, had the Russians been luckier at Hostomel, or more willing to take losses in the early stages of the attack and pushed forward regardless, they might well have reached Kyiv, even if taking it would have been another matter. Nonetheless, it was a costly failure, which left the Russian advance routes littered with abandoned and wrecked vehicles. Why?

The first was the degree to which the military professionals were either only informed of the invasion at the last minute or, even if they knew better, were ignored by Putin. He imposed his prejudices and built a whole plan of attack round them, such that some of his soldiers were even issued parade dress, ready for a victory march down Khreshchatyk, Kyiv's main street. Second, this mass war necessarily drew not just on the best of the Russian military, but pretty much all the deployable Ground Forces, bar conscripts, at least. This helps explain the wild variation in the morale and quality across the force. Some displayed a flexibility and initiative almost on a par with the well-motivated Ukrainians, but most were still almost Soviet in their inability to deal with circumstances that deviated from their orders. Third, as Putin was so confident, and did not want to risk the political fallout from sending 18-year-old conscripts into battle, a peacetime Russian army was deployed against a mobilized Ukraine. In those early days, the Russians fielded 136 BTGs, but most shared a critical shortage of the most basic military element of all: the infantryman. Infantry fighting vehicles, meant to transport a squad of troops, were in some cases trundling into battle empty, while without ground support, tanks proved all too vulnerable to ambushes.

This was, in short, a triumph of autocracy over technocracy. Putin had been building a potentially powerful military, but not only was it ironically being reoriented towards smaller interventions rather than a major war with a serious rival (tellingly, the division has since been revived as a larger unit better suited to such a conflict), this was still very much a work in progress. The Russian military is being reconstituted, even as it fights its vicious war, but as a much more ramshackle structure, a product of expediency, not design. In 2024, for example, it produced 1,500 tanks to replace its battlefield losses, but fewer than 200 were actually new, the rest being refurbished from stocks of mothballed 1970s and 1980s vintage. Elite units such as the *Spetsnaz* have been decimated by being thrown into battle as glorified infantry, and will take years to re-form. All told, Putin took an advantageous position and sacrificed it on the altar of his hubris.

Want To Know More?

Colby Howard and Ruslan Pukhov's edited collection *Brothers Armed: Military Aspects of the Crisis in Ukraine, 2nd edition* (EastView, 2015) is especially interesting for the Russian perspective it gives on Crimea and subsequent developments. Mungo Melvin's *Sevastopol's Wars: Crimea from Potemkin to Putin* (Osprey, 2017) is a more conventional history of the peninsula's military history, while Anna Arutunyan's *Hybrid Warriors: Proxies, Freelancers and Moscow's Struggle for Ukraine* (Hurst, 2023) draws on unique in-country research to untangle the complex genesis of the Donbas war. It is still too early to tell the history of the full-scale war, although Serhii Plokhy's *The Russo-Ukrainian War* (Allen Lane, 2024) is the best we have so far. Among the many excellent reports freely available from the UK's Royal United Services Institute, *Preliminary Lessons in Conventional Warfighting from Russia's Invasion of Ukraine: February–July 2022*, by Mykhaylo Zabrodskyi, Jack Watling, Oleksandr Danylyuk and Nick Reynolds (RUSI, 2022), is especially worth noting. My *Putin's Wars: From Chechnya to Ukraine* (Osprey, 2022) also covers the lead-up to the invasion and very early thoughts, while *Putin Takes Crimea 2014* (Osprey, 2023) digs into that particular operation. Never one to pass up on a venture that could both make money and build a legend, Prigozhin bankrolled a series of films casting his Wagner mercenaries in the best possible light. *Tourist* (2021), for example, is set in the Central African Republic and is a competent-enough action film, if you're interested to see how Wagner pitches itself.

25

Conclusions

The Insecurity State

Russia is a country with a history that spans more than a thousand years and has practically always used the privilege to carry out an independent foreign policy.

VLADIMIR PUTIN, MUNICH SPEECH, 2007

Vladimir Putin clearly fancies himself something of a historian – even if, as a professional historian, I feel much of his 'work' would struggle to get a passing grade, laden as it is with factual inaccuracies and the careful cherry-picking of evidence to fit his argument. His 2021 essay *On the Historical Unity of Russians and Ukrainians*, with its closing affirmation that 'the true sovereignty of Ukraine is possible only in partnership with Russia… For we are one people' was little more than a manifesto for invasion, justified through his interpretation of the historical relationship of the two nations. More recently, interviewed by US media commentator Tucker Carlson in February 2024, he treated his bemused interlocutor to a rambling half-hour lecture on the history of Russo-Ukrainian relations from the ninth century, having promised to 'take only 30 seconds or a minute'.*

---

*'Exclusive: Tucker Carlson Interviews Vladimir Putin', *YouTube*, 8 February 2024 at https://www.youtube.com/watch?v=fOCWBhuDdDo

However willing he is to trawl through Russia's real and mythologized past for justifications and grievances, though, Putin – like most of his predecessors, Soviet, tsarist or Rus' – appears still trapped by past assumptions that arguably largely no longer apply. Time and again, Russia's history has by definition been a military one not simply because of its environment and the threats and incursions of its neighbours but also its own assumptions about the world and the limited options it believes are at its disposal. Karl Marx once said that 'history repeats itself, first as a tragedy, second as a farce' – but what can we call it when it is a fifth or a five-hundredth repetition, other than a tragedy?

As Russian bombs rain down on Ukrainian cities, as Russian mercenaries buttress authoritarian regimes around the world, and as Russian intelligence officers hack systems and organize assassinations across the West, it is perhaps understandably unfashionable to suggest that insecurity, real and perceived, has been at the heart of so much of this country's history. It sounds too glib, too much like an excuse. Yet it is not. The tragedy in question – for Russia's neighbours, of course, but also for the Russians themselves – is how far this pervasive sense of insecurity has bred a strategic culture that sees the world primarily in terms of threats and presents attack as the best means of defence. Only a strong, ruthless and demanding state can maintain the capacity for such 'offensive defensiveness' on the part of what is often a relatively impoverished, unmanageable and backward nation. Russia's fault and failure is not to appreciate that changing times and military-political realities mean that it is possible to get out of this vicious circle of insecurity and aggression. As the nature of war, the character of the challenges facing not just Russia but all nations, and the usefulness of military force changes in the 21st century, there are some reasons to believe neither geography nor history needs to be destiny.

DEFINED BY CONQUEST

Lucky is the nation that has not experienced invasion, even conquest. Italy was once the heart of an empire that bestrode most of the known world, only to be sacked by barbarians, broken into feuding city-states and principalities, fought over by the greater powers of Europe, and only unified through conquest. Just as Piedmont essentially brought the rest of Italy together by bayonet and shot, so too did Bismarck's Prussia form a new Germany in the teeth of French resistance and war. France, in the form of the Normans, conquered England, and in later centuries the English would periodically return the favour. Many countries may celebrate their victories, even some of their glorious defeats, but what is so special about the Russians that they have made a cult of their vulnerability, even as they built an empire that spanned Eurasia?

In part the answer, as discussed in chapter 1, is simple geography, and the degree to which this has made Russia fair game for would-be conquerors from so many points of the compass. (A Russian thinktanker once joked to me that 'at least the Polar Bears haven't mobilized against us yet, so the north is safe.') To the west were the more advanced European threats, while to the east there always seemed another marauding steppe people, as the Pechenegs gave way to the Polovtsians, and the Polovtsians to the Mongols. For that matter, many Russians fear that the Chinese will follow this same path of conquest in the 21st century.

However, there is also the fear that invasion means not just conquest, but the destruction of something greater. That could be the extermination of a people, as promised by the Nazis (and, to a degree, by the Teutonic crusaders of the 13th century), although it was also symbolized by the piles of skulls heaped around Mongol-sacked Kiev. More often it risked the extinction of some greater ideal or cause. Ever since the fall of Constantinople in 1453, after all, the patriarchs had presented the survival of Russia, haven of the Third Rome and the true Christian creed, as a religious duty with no less fervour than the commissars had exhorted Soviet citizens to defend what, in line with Stalin's doctrine of 'Socialism in One Country', was the essential wellspring of Marxism-Leninism.

One can, of course, question how accurate such apocalyptic fears may have been, but that is irrelevant, so long as they are believed. They certainly contributed powerfully to the country's emerging strategic culture, its collective notions about what constitutes a threat, how best to respond and when and how wars ought to be fought. Strategic cultures do change over time, but they are like geography: a river may burst its banks, wander and cut a new valley, but typically over a period of years, just as plate tectonics will take centuries and millennia to warp a plain into a mountain range. Prince Vladimir the Great of Kiev, Vladimir Lenin and Vladimir Putin may share more of a strategic culture than they might be willing to admit.

But do the same precepts apply in the nuclear age? With its arsenal, buried in distant, hardened silos, ready to be launched from aircraft, and nestling in the bellies of stealthy, deep-cruising submarines, can Russia seriously fear extinction any more, other than in some thermonuclear mutual suicide pact? The atomic bomb does not guarantee absolute security: it did not stop the Chinese from initiating border clashes in 1969 any more than it overawed the Chechens in 1994, but that was because it was not credible that Moscow would use such a weapon in such conflicts. But were some new Napoleon to muster the forces of NATO (or China) in the name of conquest, however unlikely this would be, then Russia has its ultimate deterrent. Arguably, this is why Reagan's 'Star Wars' initiative was so alarming, frightening the old men of the Kremlin into fearing that they would lose this 'last argument of commissars' – but it came to little, and for the foreseeable future, the prospect of a reliable and total defence against an arsenal of the size and variety as Russia's remains a pipe dream.

FEAR OF THE OTHER, FEAR OF THE SELF

So the existential fears that equated invasion with unutterable catastrophe may no longer truly apply. They may even be receding from the collective unconscious of the Russian people. Certainly, Putin's efforts to recast his imperial war in Ukraine as a response to a comparable threat to Russia from a 'Russophobic' NATO using Kyiv as a proxy to try to dismember the nation are having only limited traction. Nikolai Patrushev, until 2024 Putin's hawkish Security Council secretary and de facto national security adviser, claimed back in 2015 that the United States 'would really like for Russia not to exist at all. As a country.' Yet even as Western-supplied weapons were being used to repel Russian attacks in Ukraine after 2022, polling suggested no more than a quarter or a third of the population truly supported the war and, by extension, saw Russia as under that kind of threat. A survey of young Russians carried out by the Chicago Council on Global Affairs and the Levada Centre in February 2024, in the midst of the Ukraine war, found twice as many regarding terrorism as the greater threat than the United States and NATO, and almost three-quarters believed Russia needed to improve its relations with the West.

In Putin's increasingly black-and-white rhetoric, though, there is no middle ground any more: if Russians are not 'patriots' (as he defines it), they are 'traitors'. The fact that a substantial cohort of Russians do not accept his vision of their country as a beleaguered fortress will present new challenges to the Kremlin in the future, especially when political opposition re-emerges, or the North Caucasus again explodes into violence. Another of the staples of Russian security is, after all, the regular pendulum swings between fear of external threat and fear of internal unrest. Sometimes, the greater challenge seemed to come from without, which typically demanded modernization and reform, whether emancipating the serfs after the Crimean War or Stolypin's agrarian reforms after defeat in the Russo-Japanese War. Yet change is hard to manage, and tends to destabilize the existing order. Tsar-Liberator Alexander II and Stolypin were both assassinated, after all. So the pendulum swings back to domestic security, reforms are left incomplete, and the regime becomes conservative, hoping simply to preserve the status quo. Which it may do, for a while – until some new shock from outside its borders again focuses the mind on how its backwardness leaves it vulnerable to foreign threats.

This has arguably always been an artificial binary, though. For the Varyag Prince of Kiev, was raiding 'Emperor-City' Constantinople simply a foreign adventure? It was also about domestic security, gaining the glory and loot that could keep a usurper in power. The reason why this dilemma was so intractable was, ironically, precisely because Russia's vulnerabilities seem to dictate such a demanding and ruthless state. It needs buffer territories to provide it with greater strategic depth, inclining it to wars of expansion and influence: Stalin's incursion into Finland was really just a 20th-century reprise of Peter the Great's efforts to secure his capital, St Petersburg, by expansion along the Baltic coast. To wage these wars and defend its open and lengthy borders, it also needs armed forces that are larger than it can reasonably afford, just as it must spend over the odds to catch up with more advanced neighbours. To be able to do this in light of the country's essential poverty, it *must* be authoritarian and autocratic. It must tax its own people all the harder: 'let us starve, but let us export,' said Finance Minister Vyshnegradsky in 1891, even if it was Stalin who truly brought this policy to its logical extreme. It must also be performatively ruthless. Maintaining control of such a sprawling nation, even in the modern age, entails empowering potentially wilful agents, whether the Don Cossacks who took Azov, the governors who pushed forward Russia's frontiers in Transcaucasia and the Far East, or Ramzan Kadyrov, the wilful tyrant of Chechnya (as of writing, he is reportedly ill). The state then needs must respond with overkill when they go rogue, in the desperate hope that this deters the next such incident. After all, Russia's violent history is not just one of wars, but of rebellions, from the 1327 Tver rising against the Golden Horde that Moscow had to suppress, through the great Cossack rebellions such as Pugachev's against Catherine the Great, to the Wagner mutiny of 2023, which saw a couple of thousand mercenaries get to within a couple of hundred miles of Moscow.

The very ruthlessness and rapacity Russia's rulers have felt their situation demanded has thus proven not to be the answer to their vulnerabilities but often their cause. It is not that they had to prioritize either foreign or domestic threats; it is that by addressing one, they exacerbated the other. The *Streltsy* mutinied against Peter the Great because they were corrupt and arrogant, but also because they feared there would be no room for them in his modernized military (and they were right). Likewise, the Wagner mutiny was triggered by their founder Yevgeny Prigozhin's defeat in a power struggle, which would mean they were in effect going to be taken over by a defence ministry that saw unity of command as essential in the war with Ukraine. Ivan the Terrible created his *Oprichnina* to protect himself from the boyars, but in the process left his country all the more vulnerable to the Crimean Tatars. Even in the 16th century, security was holistic.

This certainly should have been clear by the 19th century. The Crimean War was a harbinger of a world in which these neat divisions between foreign and domestic threats meant less and less. Russia lost not only because of backward technology and social organization, but also because the Baltic blockade was undermining its economy and threatening unrest at home. Discontent resulting from military defeat, hardship, taxation or conscription was one thing, but increasingly it could be generated directly and deliberately by enemy action. In the modern age of cyberattacks, information operations, sanctions and lawfare (the use of legal systems to damage or deter the enemy), this is ever more the case: a leveraged buyout of a strategic industry might be a greater threat than a border intrusion, and internet trolls pumping out seductively disruptive disinformation might do more real harm to national integrity than any commando raid. Some may write about this so-called 'hybrid war' as if it were a modern invention, but really it is an age-old way of conflict, massively magnified by the interconnectivities of the modern age. Certainly it is the view of the Kremlin that this is how the West fights its wars, that, in the words of Chief of the General Staff Valery Gerasimov in 2012, 'the role of nonmilitary means of achieving political and strategic goals has grown, and, in many cases, they have exceeded the power of force of weapons in their effectiveness', such that 'a perfectly thriving state can, in a matter of months and even days, be transformed into an arena of fierce armed conflict, become a victim of foreign intervention, and sink into a web of chaos, humanitarian catastrophe, and civil war.'

THE BEST DEFENCE IS A GOOD OFFENCE

So what? Well, this also puts into question one of the central elements of Russian strategic culture, in many ways best summed up by that lesson Putin says he learned running with street gangs in post-war Leningrad: that if a threat is looming, it is best to strike first. After all, when to wait for an attack so often means cities burned by the enemy, and the earth scorched at your own hand, it seems to make sense. When Vladimir Monomakh wanted to deliver a blow to the Polovtsians, he struck first at their pasture lands. Once it was clear that Mamai had no intention of settling matters peacefully, Dmitri Donskoi was already on his way to Kulikovo. Ivan the Terrible did not wait for Kazan to give him a new pretext to attack. Peter the Great had no qualms picking a fight with Sweden when he saw an opportunity, even though in hindsight triggering the Great Northern War hardly helped Russia's position in the long run. Of course, often this was impossible or politically unwise or – just ask Stalin – an opportunity missed, but it remains the ideal.

There is a thought experiment called the Prisoner's Dilemma which posits that two individuals are given the choice to compete or cooperate. If they both cooperate, they both win; if they both compete, they lose small; however, if one chooses to compete and the other to cooperate, the former will win big, and the latter lose proportionately badly. A moral or optimistic response might be to cooperate, in the hope the other player does the same – but the ruthlessly rational one is to compete. In many ways, this encapsulates the perverse and self-destructive logic of Russian strategic culture. If your bias is to strike first, it also predisposes you to presume hostile intent, because you do not want to be caught out (and genuine cases of being caught out such as Port Arthur 1904 and *Barbarossa* 1941 are mobilized to rationalize this bias). Thus, Russia is more likely to assume a threat and respond to that assumption, as the Soviet leadership may have come close to presuming catastrophically over ABLE ARCHER in 1983. Yet Russia's potential antagonists know this, and thus may feel that *they* need to strike, before Russia does. This was, after all, why 'Willy' did not feel he could rely on 'Nicky's' protestation of peaceful intent in 1914 and activated the Schlieffen Plan.

It is not just that war has become so expensive these days. Although it has: a Second World War T-34 tank took anything from 3,000–9,000 man-hours to produce, but the latest T-14 Armata, a high-tech design Russia arguably cannot afford, is estimated to require at least 100,000. It is also that, in an age when everything from trade and information to politics and migration can be weaponized (in 2023, Finland closed its borders with Russia because Moscow was deliberately channelling asylum seekers largely from Yemen, Somalia and Syria there), it is often hard to know when you are under attack, let alone the best way to respond. One can hardly re-run Olga's harrowing of the Drevlians just because an unidentified hacker has crashed your national air traffic control, or a foreign company has snapped up the African supplier of a rare earth your industries require.

NOT FOREVER WARS – BUT FOREVER FEARS

So, one could argue that Russia's strategic culture is not simply out of date; it is now actually bad for Russia. Of course, this is easy to say, especially for an outsider, but hard to address because this is not like a military doctrine or government policy: it is about deep-rooted and often unconscious assumptions and geopolitical reflexes. How can Russia change strategic culture? Sometimes, it takes a particular leader, who is able to channel deeper political processes. Arguably Gorbachev made a first move on this, making a deliberate decision to assume that the United States could actually be a good faith partner, not the 'Main Enemy', and that Soviet security could best be guaranteed through disarmament and agreement, not threat and an arms race. He was drawing on the exhaustion of the country, spent in every sense of the word, from the Cold War. Like Pyotr Stolypin, with his promise, 'give me 20 years of peace and you will not know Russia', he did not have the time his task required.

Sometimes, it takes a shock. Perhaps defeat – or Pyrrhic victory – in Ukraine will be Russia's equivalent of the 1956 Suez Crisis for Britain, or France's 1962 defeat in the Algerian War: the moment when a former imperial great power is forced to begin to come to terms with its new, diminished status and the degree to which its old policies and attitudes are self-harming. The Russian Federation, a country built on the bones of empire and which regards great power status as being its birthright, has not yet had to address its demons. Someday, it will have to, and from that rather more healthy attitudes may emerge.

Or they may not. There are all sorts of positive signs, from the courageous protesters who stand against the Ukraine war, to the degree to which it is the promise of fat salaries, not patriotic fervour, which is currently getting Russians to enlist. Indeed the growing stridency of official propaganda is in effect an admission of failure to cut through. In the words of a former Russian TV producer, 'they need to shout because they know people aren't listening.' Yet it will take a great deal to wean Russia off its martial fantasies, habitual sense of vulnerability and grievance, and deep-seated belief that war is what defines it. Vladlen Tatarsky, the Ukrainian-born bank robber and insurgent turned fiercely nationalist Russian war blogger quoted at the start of this book, was invited to a ceremony in the Kremlin in 2022, celebrating the annexation of four Russian-occupied regions of Ukraine. 'We'll triumph over everyone, kill everyone, loot everything we want,' the exhilarated 'turbo-patriot' gushed into a camera. 'Everything will be the way we like it. Let's go, and God bless.'

It is a tired cliché to describe a country as being at a crossroads: in some way or another, every country is at a crossroads every day. Yet the early 21st century is a time of realignment, which offers a particular opportunity for re-invention. Russia is by no means a negligible power, but nor is it any more one of the poles of the world. Just as Cossack muskets trumped Siberian tribespeople's bows, dreadnoughts made most older battleships obsolete, and the atom bomb changed warfare, the fundamentals of warfare are being questioned by equally fundamental economic evolutions, as artificial intelligence, quantum computing and additive manufacturing – 3D printing – will create unpredictable new markets, opportunities and synergies. A rising China, a (temporarily?) stumbling West, the emergence of new powers in the Global South – these all throw into question old strategic assumptions. Vladimir Putin himself, a septuagenarian shaped by the experiences and assumptions of the decaying USSR, will likely prove a transitional figure – but a transition to where? Russia may remain trapped in the dangers of the past – or how it chooses to interpret them as guides to the present day – but it also has a chance, an option to break out and appreciate that a nation forged in war need not be defined by it forever.

Want To Know More?

Gregory Carleton's *Russia: The Story of War* (Harvard University Press, 2017) and David Stone's *A Military History of Russia: From Ivan the Terrible to the War in Chechnya* (Praeger, 2006) are the best attempts to distil the martial story and culture of this country into a single volume. Graeme Herd's *Understanding Russian Strategic Behaviour* (Routledge, 2022) is a dense but conceptually rich study of how past assumptions play out in the present. My own *The Weaponisation of Everything* (Yale University Press, 2022) looks at the wider picture of how conflict is changing in the 21st century.

Index

References to maps are in **bold**.